Information Systems
for Accounting and Management

Information Systems
for Accounting and Management
Concepts, Applications, and Technology

Joseph W. Wilkinson

Dan C. Kneer

Arizona State University

Prentice-Hall, Inc., Englewood Cliffs, New Jersey 07632

Library of Congress Cataloging-in-Publication Data

Wilkinson, Joseph W.
    Information systems for accounting and management.

    Includes bibliographies.
    1.   Management information systems.
2.   Accounting—Data processing.   I. Kneer,
Dan C., (date).   II. Title.
T58.W56 1987   658.4'038'0285   86-30644
ISBN 0-13-464405-0

Editorial/production supervision
    and interior design: **Cheryl Lynn Smith**
Cover design: **Ben Santora**
Manufacturing buyer: **Ray Keating**

Printed in the United States of America

10   9   8   7   6   5   4   3   2   1

ISBN 0-13-464405-0   01

Prentice-Hall International (UK) Limited, *London*
Prentice-Hall of Australia Pty. Limited, *Sydney*
Prentice-Hall Canada Inc., *Toronto*
Prentice-Hall Hispanoamericana, S.A., *Mexico*
Prentice-Hall of India Private Limited, *New Delhi*
Prentice-Hall of Japan, Inc., *Tokyo*
Prentice-Hall of Southeast Asia Pte. Ltd., *Singapore*
Editora Prentice-Hall do Brasil, Ltda., *Rio de Janeiro*

To Tiffany and Tuffy

Contents

Topic Four: Networking, Telecommunications, and Distributed Data Processing   164

Topic Five: Data Bases and Data Base Management Systems   194

Topic Six: Decision Support Systems   230

Topic Seven: Computer Control and Audit Concepts and Techniques   257

Topic Eight: Emerging Technology   297

Preface

This book of readings is intended for use as the primary text in a graduate management information systems course, or as a supplementary text in an undergraduate information systems design course. It provides a spectrum of articles on management information systems (MIS) that range from the introductory to the technically advanced.

The theme of the book is reflected in the title: *Information Systems for Accounting and Management: Concepts, Applications, and Technology.* The book presents *concepts* concerning a variety of topics, in order to provide the reader with a solid systems foundation and to provoke stimulating discussions of enduring and emerging ideas and issues. In addition, it includes real-world *applications* in certain key topic areas to assist the reader in bridging the gap between theory and practice. Moreover, the last several topic areas contain articles concerning advanced *technology.* These articles have been included not only to expand the reader's technical knowledge, but also to encourage the reader to consider the impact of information processing developments upon the MIS.

We believe that this book is distinctive in several respects. First, as noted earlier, it includes a variety of articles on current and emerging technology. These articles focus on topics like the following: data base systems, distributed data processing systems, decision support systems, including financial planning models, computer-based (EDP) auditing techniques, microcomputers, office automation, and expert systems. Second, the book emphasizes critical but often neglected concerns related to computer security and control. Third, each topic area is introduced by a "bridge" that provides a foundation for that topic and that synthesizes the selected readings. Fourth, each article is followed by approximately eight questions, in order to highlight the major points and provoke thought. Finally, the selection of articles represents, we believe, a sound balance of the available literature in the systems field. We have attempted to locate those articles that present the most important concepts and issues, as well as the most interesting applications, in a clear and readable manner. The up-to-dateness of the selected articles, while important, was a secondary factor.

The following survey of topic areas attests to the comprehensive and balanced coverage of this book of readings: *Topic Area One* introduces the characteristics of a MIS, the planning necessary to achieve an effective MIS, and related behavioral concerns. *Topic Areas Two* and *Three* address the traditional MIS development life cycle and related economic, organizational, and management concerns. *Topic Areas Four, Five,* and *Six* examine technological developments in both hardware (i.e., distributed data processing and teleprocessing equipment) and software (i.e., data base management systems and decision support system software), and consider their impacts upon the MIS. *Topic Areas Seven* and *Eight* explore current developments in computer auditing, the impacts of microcomputers upon MIS, and several emerging technologies (i.e., expert systems, and office automation).

We wish to express our gratitude to the authors and publishers who have kindly granted permission for the reprinting of articles. As is customary, we assume responsibility for any errors or omissions in the book.

J. W. Wilkinson

D. C. Kneer

Information Systems
for Accounting and Management

TOPIC ONE

Planning of Management Information Systems

Management information systems (MIS) have come of age. They are proving their value in organizations of all types — ranging from long-established large business corporations and government agencies to newly-established small business ventures. Moreover, they are capable of becoming significantly more valuable with the incorporation of newly emerging techniques and technologies.

This first topic area reviews a variety of key MIS concepts. In addition to presenting basic definitions, it contrasts the differences between the modern-day MIS and the traditional accounting information system. It also examines the systems development life cycle, probing the nontechnical as well as technical considerations that affect the success of systems development. Finally, this opening topic area explores systems planning processes and procedures.

INFORMATION SYSTEM DEFINITIONS

Broadly speaking, an *information system* is intended to provide information to specific users. In an organization such as a business firm, the users of the information system are the firm's managers, employees, customers, suppliers, and owners, as well as government agencies and perhaps the investing public.

Information is derived from *data,* i.e., raw facts or kernels. An example of a kernel of data is "four pounds." Data become information when processed or analyzed so as to improve the user's understanding of a situation. Thus the above example of a data kernel becomes information when expressed in this analysis: "Four pounds represents the amount of the unfavorable materials variance incurred on production line 26 this week."

Information generated by the business firm's information system may be classified according to its three major uses:

1. Mandatory information is used to conduct day-to-day operations.
2. Statutory information is used to satisfy legal obligations.
3. Discretionary information is used to support decision making.

While all three of these information uses are important, it can be argued that the third is the most crucial to business success. Prospective owners need discretionary information to aid in deciding whether or not to invest in the firm's equities. Managers need discretionary information as the basis for

1

deciding upon future plans. They also need discretionary information to indicate when corrective actions with respect to current operations are necessary. If adequate information is not available for such decisions, the firm's objectives are not likely to be met. In fact, the firm's longevity might be severely curtailed.

A management information system (MIS) is a business information system whose primary purpose is to provide managers with the information they need to make decisions. In other words, it is a decision-oriented information system for users who have especially demanding sets of information needs. Not only must a typical MIS provide information of widely varying content, but the information provided must accord with such properties as timeliness, conciseness, and accuracy.

EVOLUTION OF THE MIS FROM THE TRADITIONAL ACCOUNTING SYSTEM

At one time in the not-so-distant past the information system of the typical organization consisted of a traditional accounting system with manual processing. That is, it employed clerks, source documents, card files, accounting books, manual procedures, processing machines or devices, and controls to produce financial statements and operational reports. (In numerous small business firms the same condition prevails today.) This traditional accounting system was designed and managed by the firm's accountants.

During the past three decades, however, the information system has significantly changed in many organizations. While the basic features of the accounting system have remained intact, entirely new systems have been designed and installed. These new

information systems are often functional in scope, and thus have been given such titles as *marketing information systems* or *production information systems.* Increasingly, though, the newly developed information systems are called *management information systems* or *decision support systems.*

Regardless of the labels by which they are known, newly developed information systems in most organizations generally exhibit improvements over the traditional manual accounting systems. Certain of these improvements are a result of computer technology, while others are due to decision-oriented design approaches. In most organizations these improvements have been planned and managed by persons other than the firm's accountants.

System Improvements Due to Computer Technology. Computer hardware and software have moved through four generations since the first commercial computers were put into use around 1950. Present-day computers are dramatically improved over the early computers in several respects:

1. Equivalent computing power in much smaller frames
2. Much faster computing and transfer speeds
3. Much larger storage capacity
4. Much greater reliability

Present-day computers also provide a variety of features, such as multiprogramming, overlapping, and virtual storage. In addition, they allow designers a variety of options. For instance, options available with respect to input/output devices include terminals, voice input and response devices, and laser printers; options available with respect to file media include magnetic hard disks, floppy disks, and magnetic tapes. Recent years have seen the emergence of other options, such as microcomputers and data communications networks.

Most information systems incorporate a portion of the aforementioned computer developments, while some reflect the full panoply of state-of-the-art computer technology. Every information system thus touched by computer technology is the beneficiary of tangible improvements. On the other hand, these improvements are sometimes acquired at a high cost in dollars and added problems.

Because computer technology is exerting an increasing influence upon the design and management of information systems, several topic areas in the second half of this book are devoted to recent technology-oriented developments.

Decision-Oriented System Design.   The orientation of the traditional accounting system is toward *transaction processing.* In designing such a system the focus is upon the efficient processing of each type of transaction. Thus, the system primarily serves the clerks who are involved in the processing. As a result, the system consists of relatively unintegrated data-processing applications, with a set of files devoted to each application. Each department exhibits a proprietary attitude with respect to the data files maintained in its area. The financial statements and reports which are generated at the end of each accounting period are essentially by-products of the transaction-processing activity.

A *decision orientation,* accompanied by a firm-wide perspective, is the hallmark of a true MIS. In order to understand an MIS we must fully grasp this primary characteristic. The first article in this topic area helps us to do so.

The article by Lin and Harper begins by illustrating the several transformations performed by the traditional accounting system. Then it reviews the five steps in the decision process, together with the three types of decision processes employed by managers. The article argues that current information systems should not be limited by the traditional financial accounting and transaction-oriented approaches. Instead, a modern accounting information system is most useful when it is primarily decision-oriented — i.e., when it serves as an MIS. The article concludes by discussing what must be determined when designing a decision-oriented information system.

Team Approach to System Development. The roles of accountants have been altered during this movement toward computer-based MIS. They no longer are solely responsible for the design and management of their firms' information systems. Instead, systems development is now viewed as the joint responsibility of systems professionals and systems users. Included among the key users are accountants as well as managers, engineers, and others.

All the remaining articles in this topic area stress the importance of such joint efforts. They note that systems projects are ideally planned and conducted by teams composed of both trained MIS analyst-designers and informed users.

SYSTEMS DEVELOPMENT LIFE CYCLE

Every information system undergoes one or more life cycles. A life cycle begins with a systems planning phase. Then it moves through systems analysis, systems design, systems implementation, and systems operation-evaluation phases. Each developmental phase is critical to the successful functioning of the information system. These phases are viewed as being sufficiently important to warrant extensive attention during the first half of this book.

The second and third articles in this introductory topic area focus on matters that are of great concern during the systems development phases. In effect, they provide panoramic views that are explored more intensely within the following two topic areas.

The article by Hax illustrates the planning, analysis, design, and implementation of a comprehensive MIS for a hypothetical distributing and manufacturing firm. The emphasis of the article is upon specific *information needs* to be satisfied by the MIS. It is particularly enlightening with respect to procedures for assigning priorities to the individual systems projects. The article also introduces such design approaches as top-down planning, modular construction, systems integration through common files, and evolutionary development.

The article by Carroll emphasizes that behavioral aspects of systems development are just as crucial as the technical aspects. If they are ignored, the success of a systems development is placed in jeopardy. Among the behavorial aspects that should be treated are the relationships between systems designers and systems users, the leadership of the project team, and the dynamics of the change process.

Carroll's article also considers the implications of behavior upon the system design. He points out that the designer of a decision-oriented MIS must take into account the individual differences of the various users, both with respect to (1) the nature of the information to be provided, and (2) the mode by which the users are to acquire the information. For instance, many managers may want information to be presented in a graphical format; on the other hand, many managers do not want to acquire information via direct interaction with microcomputer keyboards.

THE SYSTEMS PLANNING PROCESS

Planning consists of defining future objectives and specifying how the objectives are to be achieved. The planning process is quite complex in the typical organization, since it involves all of the managers and is conducted on several levels.

Levels of Planning. Many organizations conduct planning on three levels: strategic, tactical, and operational. These planning levels exhibit different characteristics. For instance, they each entail different time horizons and require different types of information.

Strategic Planning. Strategic planning is conducted at the highest level and over the longest time horizon. It consists of deciding upon the collective actions and resources needed to achieve an organization's overall set of objectives. Strategic planning leads to the development of a master plan for the organization that may extend five or more years into the future.

Determining the organization's overall objectives or goals is the first order of business in strategic planning. These objectives represent the standards against which progress is to be measured. They also provide guidance in establishing the organization's strategies (i.e., policies) and in making important strategic decisions. To provide effective guidance, the objectives must be clearly stated, compatible with each other (to the greatest extent possible), and broad in scope. They should also be stated in quantitative terms and be applied to definite time horizons. For instance, an objective might specify that the market share for the organization's primary product is expected to reach 30 percent within five years.

With the objectives established, the top managers of an organization can then focus upon developing a strategic-level master plan. This plan, which should be developed and revised on an ongoing basis, reflects the actions and allocations of resources needed to meet the challenges and take advantage of the opportunities offered by the organization's environment. One key portion of the plan, for instance, is a capital budget that shows expected expenditures for approved projects.

Developing the master plan requires that a number of decisions be made. In order to make these decisions, the managers need a variety of information. Information needed for strategic planning should generally reflect the characteristics of the strategic level. That is, it should be drawn largely from the environment, be broad in scope, and pertain to the long-term future. While the managers will desire as much information as possible to be expressed in dollar terms, certain of the relevant information will only be available in qualitative terms. Thus, in the case of a new product decision, the managers will need not only the expected unit costs and profit margins, but also the expected trends in consumer tastes.

Strategic Systems Planning.   An effective MIS can provide the needed information for strategic planning. In turn, the principles of strategic planning can aid managers in establishing the nature and sequential development of the MIS.

The article by Head clearly delineates the need for and advantages of strategic systems planning. It also distinguishes strategic systems planning from systems planning at lower levels. However, its main contributions are (1) to discuss the principles of sound strategic systems planning, and (2) to illustrate the content of a thorough strategic systems plan.

Tactical and Operational Planning. Below the strategic level are the tactical and operational levels. Tactical planning consists of translating the strategic plan into narrower, shorter-term plans or programs. An instance of tactical planning occurs when the long-term marketing plan is translated into a specific advertising program for the following year or 18 months. Operational planning consists of translating the tactical plans or programs into very narrow and short-term programs, schedules, or actions. An instance of operational planning occurs when the plant maintenance program for this year is translated into a maintenance schedule for next month. (However, it should be noted that the terms *tactical planning* and *operational planning* are used interchangeably by some authors.)

Integration of Multilevel Systems Planning.   Systems planning thus includes the translation of the strategic systems plan into lower level plans. In the context of information systems planning, the tactical and operational plans generally relate to specific application systems projects. Effective systems planning requires that the plans for these application systems projects be smoothly integrated with the strategic systems plan.

Various approaches for achieving this integration have been described in recent articles. One successful approach has been devised by Weyerhaeuser.[1] As detailed in the article, Weyerhaeuser's systems planning process results in plans of action for the current year, for the next calendar year, and for five years into the future. The planners first establish a company-wide view of what information systems are needed. Then they employ the critical success-factors methodology and information flow diagrams to identify key information needs of each application system. Next they evaluate the existing systems against the requirements, assess the costs versus the benefits, prepare schedules, and finally develop the proposed plans of action.

SYSTEMS PLANNING QUESTIONS

Systems planning is fraught with difficulties. Five of these difficulties are expressed in the following questions:

1. How may an information system development be effectively aligned to meet the strategic objectives of the organization?
2. Which systems projects should be established within the strategic systems plan, and which should be scheduled for completion first; i.e., what priorities should be assigned to the newly defined systems projects?
3. What is the best information system architecture, i.e., structure, to employ for a particular organization?
4. How should systems resources be allocated among competing systems projects and organizational units?
5. Which systems development methodologies and approaches should be selected during the systems planning process?

SYSTEMS PLANNING METHODOLOGIES

A recent article by Bowman, Davis, and Wetherbe (not included) develops a model within which possible answers to the aforementioned questions may be framed.[2] This model of systems planning consists of three stages: strategic planning, organizational information requirements analysis, and resource allocation. Useful methodologies that can provide answers to each of the questions are offered in this article and others.

The first question, which arises during the strategic planning stage, can be attacked by the strategy set transformation methodology. Answers can also be formulated through the use of models that portray the information resources, entities, and functions via structured planning methodologies[3] and through the use of the stages-of-growth methodology.[4]

The second question, concerning the defining and prioritizing of systems projects, deals with the transition from the strategic plan to operational level plans, i.e., the interface between the first and second stages in the three-stage model. This question can also be answered with assistance from structured systems planning methodologies. Thus, after function-centered and data-centered models are developed at the strategic level, they are exploded into more detail by means of various hierarchical diagrams and flow charts. The resulting operational-level models show data linkages, the frequencies of system activities, and the sequences of functional activities. By reference to such models, systems planners can more easily identify feasible systems projects and establish logical priorities. Another methodology that aids in the prioritizing of projects is known as business systems planning.

The third question, which is the subject of the information requirements analysis stage, can be addressed by such methodologies as business systems planning, critical success factors, business information analysis and integration, and ends/means analysis.

The fourth question, concerning resource allocation, is obviously the subject of the resource allocation stage. It can be addressed by such methodologies as return on investment, charge-out, and zero-based budgeting.

The fifth question concerns the evaluation of the respective methodologies. While this question cannot be fully explored within the limited space allotted to this topic area, an article concerning methodologies appears in the following topic area entitled Systems Analysis and Design.

NOTES

1. See Pran N. Wahi, Kenneth A. Popp, and Susan M. Stier, ''Applications Systems Planning at Weyerhaeuser,'' *Journal of Systems Management,* March 1983, pp. 13–21.

2. Brent Bowman, Gordon Davis, and James Wetherbe, ''Three-Stage Model of MIS Planning,'' *Information & Management,* No. 6, 1983, pp. 11–25.

3. Jim Highsmith, ''Structured Systems Planning,'' *MIS Quarterly,* September 1981, pp. 35–54.

4. As proposed by C. F. Gibson and R. L. Nolan, ''Managing the Four Stages of EDP Growth,'' *Harvard Business Review,* January-February 1974, pp. 76–88.

A Decision-Oriented Management Accounting Information System*

Management accounting should be concerned with the application of appropriate accounting and management concepts and techniques to provide useful financial information for management in planning, controlling and making economic resource allocation decisions.

Following an examination of the traditional management accounting information system, this paper considers the relationship between management accounting and the decision process. Management planning and control systems are then briefly reviewed. Finally, a decision-oriented management accounting information system is recommended.

TRADITIONAL MANAGEMENT ACCOUNTING INFORMATION SYSTEM

A traditional management accounting information system is based on a financial accounting information system as shown in Figure 1.

Data Collection. The purpose of this step is to collect economic data which can be represented by dollar amounts. The economic events are called transactions. All the data are collected in terms of source documents.

Transformation 1: A recording function is performed in this step. Each event affects two accounts, i.e., debit and credit sides. In computerized accounting systems the journals or books of original entry may have disappeared, but the journalizing function is still retained.

Transformation 2: A classification function is performed in this step. Each item of data is recorded in the ledger accounts. And data are aggregated in these accounts before the next transformation step.

Transformation 3: A summarizing function is performed in this step. All account balances are computed and presented in a trial balance. The sum of all debit balances should be equal to the sum of all credit balances.

Transformation 4: Storing, classifying, summarizing and analyzing functions are performed in this step in order to prepare various management reports.

Report 1: These reports are called financial statements. They include balance sheet, income statement, and statement of changes in financial position.

*By W. Thomas Lin and William K. Harper. Reprinted from an article appearing in *Cost and Management* by W. Thomas Lin and William K. Harper, Nov.-Dec. 1981, by permission of The Society of Management Accountants of Canada.

Figure 1.   The Traditional Accounting Information System

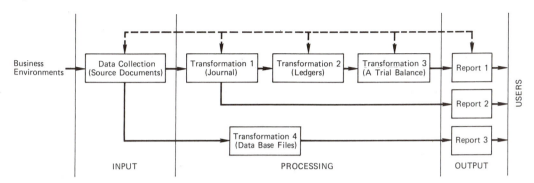

Report 2: These reports are generated from specialized journals and subsidiary ledgers, e.g., a summary of cash receipts and disbursements, accounts receivable balance or sales classified by customers, etc.

Report 3: These are various management reports such as exception reports, comparative reports, and interpretative reports.

Control: The control function is performed at each step, e.g., the controls in data collection are internal controls such as hierarchy of approval, separation of duties, and the use of pre-numbered vouchers; the controls in transformation 1 and 2 are generally accepted accounting principles, charts of accounts, debit-credit rules and internal control; the control in transformation 3 is the trial balance; the controls for reports are internal and external audit procedures and generally accepted accounting principles.

Traditional accounting information is not primarily decision-oriented. It overlooks the interface with other systems and the provision of more relevant information for higher-level purposes. Under the existing framework, accounting data are used largely for control rather than for planning and decision making. The new management accounting information system should be decision-oriented.

MANAGEMENT ACCOUNTING AND THE DECISION PROCESS

The usefulness of accounting information is measured entirely by its actual or potential contribution to the decision-making process. Accounting for decision making involves a particular way of viewing the decision-making process in business. Murdick and Ross[1] break down the decision activity into five steps as shown in Figure 2.

What relevance does this decision-making process have to accounting? The tie between

Figure 2.   Decision-Making Process

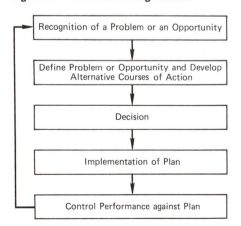

the accounting process and the decision-making process is basically one of information. Accounting is a data-providing function which is required at each step of the decision-making process.

The first step, recognition of a problem or an opportunity, is a search activity. Information is necessary for identifying the important problem variables. Decision-makers need environmental, competitive, and internal information about the problems and opportunities. For example, management accountants use a favorable or unfavorable variance generated by a standard cost system to tell management that it has a problem, or a decision to make.

The second step, define the problem or opportunity and develop alternative courses of action, generates alternative activities. A standard cost system does not define the alternatives nor does it tell which alternative is best. But the newer breed of management accountant has used opportunity or incremental cost concepts to provide alternatives, say make or buy a machine, for a special decision.

Accounting information is used in the third step, decision, to predict levels of uncontrollable variables or results for alternative courses of action. For example, the choice of investment alternatives may be judged against a rate-of-return criterion, and information about the alternative must be provided in rate-of-return form.

Accounting information is used in the fourth step, implementation of plan, to communicate details of objectives, plans and control standards.

The fifth step, control performance against plan, needs accounting information on results and performance. Compare the results against the plan and this feedback information may lead to a revision of decision rules.

Traditional accounting information is designed primarily for control purposes. The data generated are past data and monetary data. What is needed to provide more effective aid to the decision process is both monetary and nonmonetary data, and all future, present, and past data.

MANAGEMENT PLANNING AND CONTROL SYSTEMS

In *Planning and Control Systems: A Framework for Analysis,* Robert Anthony develops a taxonomy for managerial activities consisting of three categories: strategic planning, management control, and operational control.[2]

> *Strategic planning is defined as:*
> "The process of deciding on objectives of the organization, on changes in these objectives, on the resources used to attain these objectives, and on the policies that are to govern the acquisition, use, and disposition of these resources." (p. 16)
>
> *Management control is:*
> "The process by which managers assure that resources are obtained and used effectively and efficiently in the accomplishment of the organization's objectives." (p. 17)
>
> *Operational control is:*
> "The process of assuring that specific tasks are carried out effectively and efficiently." (p. 18)

Planning and control systems are used to facilitate decision making. The emphasis in this paper is on the information requirements of management. Though Anthony's three categories are not perfectly satisfactory, they do provide a basis for a consideration of these needs.

Some examples of strategic planning activities are choosing company objectives, planning the organization, setting policies and acquiring a new division. Management control activities include formulating budgets and advertising programs, planning working capital, measuring, appraising, and improving management performance, etc. Operational control activities include controlling hiring and inventory, scheduling production, measuring, appraising, and improving workers' efficiency, etc. (Anthony, p. 19)

To fit Anthony's framework, we have endeavored to set the characteristics of information needs for strategic planning, management control, and operational control as shown in Exhibit 1.

Anthony's classification of business activities is helpful to managers since the distinction between planning and control is significant to top management. This framework is also helpful to accountants since every classification has different information characteristics.

Within this framework, management accounting systems should provide the following information:

Strategic planning
— long-range planning as well as information for mergers and acquisitions with the emphasis on evaluating the financial impact of the alternatives upon the economic performance of the company.

Management control
— budget preparation, cash flows, pro forma operating statements, breakeven analysis, and responsibility accounting variance analysis information.

Operational control
— income statement generation, short-term cash management, production and inventory control information, labor distribution and efficiency reports.

The management accountant should help other information system designers to pro-

Exhibit 1. **Information Needs for Strategic Planning, Management Control, and Operational Control**

INFORMATION CHARACTERISTICS	STRATEGIC PLANNING	MANAGEMENT CONTROL	OPERATIONAL CONTROL
1. Sources of information	Primary, external, some internal	Primary internal, some external	Internal
2. Measurability	Quantitative and qualitative factors	Quantitative, some qualitative factors	Quantitative factors
3. Level of aggregation	Aggregate	Aggregate at higher managerial levels and detailed at lower levels	Very detailed
4. Timeliness	Highly variable, old data; irregular planning	Current and historical data; regular planning and control	Very current, real-time data; regular control
5. Time horizon	Long-range future	Short-range future or recent past	Present time or very recent past
6. Accuracy	Low, uncertainty	Accurate	Highly accurate
7. Frequency of use	Irregular	Periodic	Frequent
8. Types of information systems	Special one-time type of reports; inquiring system	Many regular reports	Deterministic, fixed reporting procedure

vide effective information for those decisions within the framework. He should understand the characteristics of information needs before providing information for management planning and control.

A DECISION-ORIENTED MANAGEMENT ACCOUNTING INFORMATION SYSTEM

The recommended management accounting information system is decision-oriented. The following crucial questions should be considered before designing a new system:

1. What are the various information output requirements which must be served? The decisions will include determining information needs for different users, and their requirements for speed, accuracy, volume, and cost.
2. What data should be collected or generated and transformed into information to serve reporting and decision model requirements?
3. How should the data be collected, interpreted, transmitted, etc.? The decisions will include how to collect data, to code and classify it, to measure it, to transmit and communicate it, to analyze it, to store the necessary item in the memory system for future retrieval, and to report and display required information.
4. How frequently should data be collected, interpreted, and stored? How often should the resultant information be retrieved and displayed?

The recommended management accounting information system is different from the traditional "transaction-oriented" accounting system. In the traditional system, management accounting is a part of or a derivative of the system. In a decision-oriented system, financial reporting is part of the new system.

A proposed management accounting information system is set out in Figure 3.

The new management accounting information's components and their functions are discussed as follows:

1. Data collection. This system starts from decision makers. Either collect data directly according to decision makers' needs or, from their state of arts, formulate decision models which determine information requirements. A data collection component performs sensing, classifying, and recording functions.

2. Data transmission. Based on Shannon and Weaver's three levels of communication problems,[3] the following questions can be asked in a data transmission component:

Level A — The technical problem
(A) How accurately and relevantly does the management accountant record the selected data?
(B) How accurately are the data being processed and transmitted?

Level B — The semantic problem
(A) How precisely does the output of the management accounting information system convey the desired meaning?
(B) How accurately and effectively does the decision-maker interpret the received output?

Level C — The effectiveness problem
(A) How effectively does the decision maker use the received output?
(B) How well will the decision maker's ultimate behavior correspond to the predefined objectives?

3. Data processing. This component performs data compression, analysis, update, and delete functions. The traditional transformation functions such as journalizing, posting, footing, trial balancing are included in this component.

4. Reports. This component considers the report format, timing, and data display

Figure 3.   A Decision-Oriented Management Accounting Information System

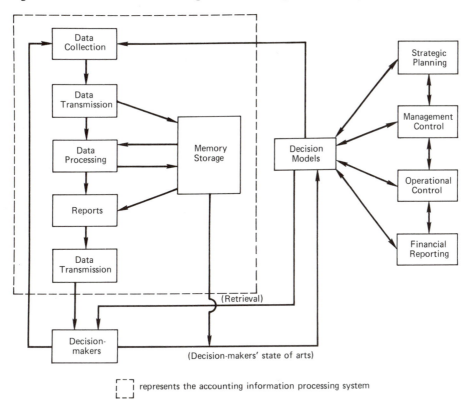

$\begin{bmatrix} - - \\ - - \end{bmatrix}$ represents the accounting information processing system

methods. The reports include financial statements and various management reports.

5. Memory storage. This component performs the following functions:

(A) Organization of data base. To facilitate retrieval of information, the data base must be structured in a way that shows important relationships among the data elements.

(B) Use of keys, labels, directory, indexing for ease in identifying stored data and facilitating retrieval.

6. Decision models. An effective management accounting information system, in addition to providing continuous data-

gathering and processing, must be integrated with the planning and control systems. Formal and informal decision models are representations of various decision problems or problem-solving procedures. The management accounting information system should provide relevant information for the decision models' inputs. An effective management accounting information system should consider different information characteristics of strategic planning, management control, operational control, and financial reporting.

7. Decision makers. Management accountants have to examine the decision

makers' environment, taking into consideration the behavioral aspects of the decision makers and all relevant people.

CONCLUSION

The major goal of a management accounting information system is to provide information that is useful to management in making decisions. Accordingly, the management accountant should know how management makes decisions. In order to provide information for effective planning and control, a management accountant should set up the taxonomy of information characteristics, information generating methods for managers' various strategic planning, management control and operational control activities.

The future of the management accounting information system should not be embedded in the traditional financial accounting system. It should be decision-oriented; it should emphasize data base management and consider both technical and behavioral factors.

NOTES

1. Robert G. Murdick and Joel E. Ross, *Information Systems for Modern Management* (Englewood Cliffs, N.J.: Prentice-Hall, Inc., 1971).

2. Robert N. Anthony, *Planning and Control Systems: A Framework for Analysis* (Boston: Graduate School of Business Administration, Harvard University, 1965).

3. Claude E. Shannon and Warren Weaver, *The Mathematical Theory of Communication* (Urbana: University of Illinois Press, 1949).

QUESTIONS

1. In what ways does a modern accounting information system differ from the traditional financial accounting information system?

2. How does any accounting information system differ from a "true" management information system?

3. What features of an information system become critically important when decision support is the primary purpose?

4. Discuss the relation of a decision model to the data and information handled by an information system.

5. How might a decision model for a strategic planning decision differ from a decision model for an operational control decision? From a decision model for a management control decision?

6. Information has been defined as data made meaningful through processing. Discuss how such information properties as relevance, accuracy, timeliness, and conciseness may modify this definition. Especially consider cases where these properties are negatively represented in an item of information (e.g., where an item is inaccurate).

7. How do the information needs of external users differ from the information needs of managers?

8. Contrast the properties of information needed to make the following pairs of decisions:
   a. A decision where to locate a new plant versus a decision concerning which employee to assign to a specific job tomorrow
   b. A decision concerning the elimination of a department versus a decision concerning the possible reassignment of a manager having cost responsibilities

9. Can a formal information system be expected to provide all information

needed for making the typical strategic planning decision?

10. Discuss the considerations that pertain to the design of information systems to aid in each of the following decisions:

a. How to expand plant capacity
b. How to reduce operations costs
c. Whether to introduce new products
d. Whether to replace a delivery truck

Planning a Management Information System for a Distributing and Manufacturing Company*

INTRODUCTION

This paper describes the design and implementation of a comprehensive management information system for a distributing and manufacturing company. The objectives of the information system are to support management's routine operational activities, to allow for adequate planning, and to control effectively the execution of those plans by using timely and accurate information.

In order to permit specific comments regarding the content of a management information system (MIS) plan, the discussions are based on a hypothetical firm, American Imports, Inc. (AII). The elements of the plan represent activities required in planning a management information system for most distributing and manufacturing companies. AII is predominantly an importing and distributing organization, although it does manufacture about 15 percent of its products. The firm has decided to expand its manufacturing activities in the future, which will affect the manufacturing and physical distribution control system. The product line of AII is complex and highly technical; in addition, the products carry a two-year service guarantee which forces AII to operate and train a group of professionals responsible for the maintenance of AII products.

American Imports uses fairly informal and rudimentary procedures to collect and process information; most procedures are designed to serve the accounting department. Plans are underway to computerize these accounting activities, since the growing volume of data results in serious difficulties for timely and accurate delivery of information.

Management information system development at AII is typical in that accounting is the first activity to be recognized as an information system element, and the first procedure to be computerized. Although helpful to managers, the current accounting system only provides an historical evaluation of company performance from a financial viewpoint. American Imports seeks to

*By Arnoldo C. Hax. The ideas presented in this paper primarily are the result of the author's professional experience as a consultant for the Management Science Division of Arthur D. Little, Incorporated. In particular, the author would like to acknowledge Dr. Harlan C. Meal, Head of the Business Logistics Group at Arthur D. Little, for his contribution to the present study. Reprinted from "Planning a Management Information System for a Distributing and Manufacturing Company," by Arnoldo C. Hax, *Sloan Management Review*, Vol. XV, pp. 85–98, by permission of the publisher. Copyright © 1973 by the Sloan Management Review Association. All rights reserved.

expand the information system to cover a wide range of management functions such as marketing, production, purchasing, personnel, and engineering.

In planning this expansion, it is important that All avoid isolating the various project teams working at the functional level; isolation often results in duplication, and obstructs the ultimate coordination of information at the higher levels of the organization. Decision processes within the firm are complex, and it is artificial to divide them into components on the basis of management functions in divisions or departments. Consequently, top management must coordinate individual decisions to ensure that goals of the entire organization are attained, inconsistencies among departmental decisions are avoided, and suboptimization is prevented.

While individual team efforts must be closely coordinated, a tightly linked, integrated system is not advocated because a change in a minor part disrupts the whole system. A better way to approach MIS planning is through a modular design which allows great flexibility in designing, implementing, and updating each system module. Nonetheless, there must be some commonness in input and output specifications as well as file design so that exchanges among the system modules are easily accomplished, and overall management needs fulfilled.

The Planning Study.   All should undertake the planning study before domestic manufacturing activities become large-scale. The goal is to present a practical approach for MIS design which can unify and direct the MIS project. Design, development, and installation of a management information system are more expensive and time-consuming if not completed before activity increases. To develop this plan, three basic tasks require completion:

1. Analysis of primary and secondary information requirements by those responsible for each managerial area
2. Development of a preliminary information system design to satisfy these information needs
3. Development of a time scale for activities and an estimate of requirements

In the following sections of this paper, results of these three tasks are presented. In the final section, the cost-benefit implications of a management information system are examined.[1]

INFORMATION REQUIREMENTS

The design of a comprehensive management information system is a lengthy project which requires constant updating and maintenance. Moreover, the MIS scope is enormous, encompassing many kinds of information requirements. Some information is essential for proper management of the enterprise; some is useful, but secondary for decision making. Priorities must be assigned for various types of information, from which a schedule for system design and implementation is developed.

In allocating priorities it is important to classify types of information by the decisions they support. Several frameworks for decision making have been suggested which have significant implications for MIS design, such as Anthony's taxonomy of operational control, management control, and strategic planning, or Simon's programmed and unprogrammed decision making.[2] These classifications consider only the managerial activity for which information is supplied. It is useful in practice to add other dimensions to the information taxonomy in order to assign priorities for MIS design. These dimensions for information classification — functional, departmental, and product type — will now be discussed.

Functional Requirements. Distinctions must be made among information needed to *conduct* daily operations, to *control* current performance, and to *plan* strategically for future performance. Of these functional requirements, first priority is assigned to operations, second priority to control, and third priority to planning information. Defining this set of priorities does not imply postponement of the planning and control information systems until the operational system is fully implemented. To do this would be to deny managers any immediate, significant assistance; planning and control systems are those which serve most to improve the capability of profitable management. Nevertheless, minimal functioning of the operational information system is imperative before initiating the planning and control information systems.

Operations   The basic operational information requirements of AII can be divided into four areas: accounting, order processing, goods procurement, and manufacturing. The accounting system prepares and maintains the journals and general ledger, including accounts receivable, accounts payable, and payroll. Because the large volume of accounting data already impinges on the timely and accurate delivery of information, the accounting system should be computerized early.

Order processing involves editing customer orders, acknowledging orders, providing documentation for shipments, preparing invoices, and providing information to the accounting system for billing. The smooth operation of such a system is essential for maintaining continual customer satisfaction. To improve management operations and ensure a smooth processing of orders, computerization of this system is of high priority. Presently, the bulk of order processing at AII is done manually, with a high error rate

and generally unsatisfactory performance. It is both convenient and economical to computerize the system *while* improving it, rather than first improving it on a manual basis and then converting to computerized procedures.

Merchandise procured from Europe is the major source of products sold by American Imports. To maintain adequate cognizance and control of procurement activities, formal systems are required. Computerizing these systems beyond the current state, however, is not a high priority even though more comprehensive control of detailed procurement is available with computerized systems.

Manufacturing is a minor, yet growing, part of AII's activities. In the future, formal systems and procedures will be necessary to maintain operational control of manufacturing processes; but implementation of these systems now is not a high priority.

Control and Planning   AII is similar to many firms in that control and planning functions are accomplished in an informal fashion with little assistance from routine information systems or planning procedures. As AII becomes more complex, the development of formalized control and planning procedures and their eventual computerization will be necessary. Therefore, in planning the management information system, these future information requirements must be recognized.

Departmental Requirements. Complex information needs exist in each department of American Imports. These needs vary among departments, and different supporting systems are demanded. The primary requirements of departmental information closely parallel those of the operational information systems. The second priority requirements are for improvements in information available to control current performance

(performance *vs.* plan and cost *vs.* budget) within each department.

The departments of materials management, marketing, and finance have the highest priority information requirements. Lower priorities can be assigned to manufacturing, technical and engineering, and personnel department requirements.

The informational needs of materials management are listed in Table 1. Most of the variables are standard for a distributing company. Two special items, however, arise from the nature of imported merchandise. First, in the inventory control category, a long range procurement plan is required; procurement lead times from Europe are much longer than domestic manufacturing lead times, and result from the need to supply manufacturing planning information to Europe. The second item, in the warehousing category, is the cost of custom clearance and packaging, especially returnable packaging.

The information requirements for marketing are listed in Table 2. None of the major categories of information listed is currently available for use by marketing managers. Items such as sales *vs.* plan, and sales expense *vs.* plan are essential tools for dealing with marketing problems.

The basic financial information system needs for American Imports are similar to those for any manufacturing and distributing firm. These needs can be grouped into three categories: basic operational systems, basic control information, and special control information. Basic operational systems include general ledgers, special accounts, and journals. These operational systems allow the preparation of operating statements (profit and loss), balance sheets, and cash flow analyses. Basic control information enables

Table 1.   Information Requirements for Materials Management

INVENTORY CONTROL	PRODUCTION PLANNING
Inventory status	Production requirements
Ordering (or setup) cost	Regular production cost
Inventory carrying cost	Hiring and firing cost
Purchasing quantity discounts	Capacity availability
Desired service levels	Production rates
Forecast requirements	Production smoothing inventory
Procurement lead times	Capacity planning
Imported product procurement plan	Overtime production cost

TRAFFIC	PURCHASING
Bill of lading	Vendor information
Carrier characteristics	Vendor performance
Rate and routings	Product specification
	Open orders

WAREHOUSING
Operating expense *vs.* plan
Operating performance
Finished product status
Custom clearance and packing costs

Table 2.   Information Requirements for Marketing

SALES	ORDER ADMINISTRATION
Sales *vs.* plan	Order processing
Sales expense *vs.* plan	Customer service data
Market expense plans (by product type and geographical area, in dollars and in units)	**SERVICE**
MARKET PLANNING	Spare parts inventory (centrally and at branches)
	Historical product structure
Forecast	Service personnel and training data
Territorial trends	
Competitive product data	Service performance and cost

two comparisons to be made; performance is compared with plan and cost is compared with budget. This information is provided for each major operating element and for the entire corporation. The most important item in the special control category is the inventory investment reports, since a wide variety of such investments exists at both headquarters and branches. Second in importance are reports on accounts receivable and aging of receivables, which allow detection of bad debts and decrease the payment time of receivables. The financial information requirements are summarized in Table 3.

Manufacturing activities at All are relatively simple to manage at present and do not require substantial additional support from management information systems. As manufacturing activity broadens, more support will be needed.[3]

Table 3.   Information Requirements for Finance

FINANCIAL STATEMENTS	BUDGET CONTROL
Operating statement (profit and loss)	Departmental performance *vs.* plan
Balance sheet	Inventory investment, by class
Cash flow	Receivables aging

Engineering activities will parallel manufacturing activities in growth. The primary requirement for management information in engineering is project control information. This information now is provided reasonably well, but as activities increase more comprehensive and detailed systems will be needed.

A lower priority can be attached to management information systems for technical activities, since they deal primarily with new product development and do not use formal or computerized information systems extensively. Personnel follows the same pattern. Quality control and quality assurance primarily are concerned with product importation problems; early attention to computerized systems is not required.

Product Requirements. New products, revisions of existing products, and old, well-established products each generate different information requirements. *Current products* are those for which production or procurement orders are re-releases of designs previously manufactured or purchased. *Revisions* are modifications of previously issued designs, and *new products* are brand new designs. Functionally, the treatment of revisions and new products in the information system is the same. *Special products* are production items designed to be made only once.

Since the largest percentage of sales comes from current products, development of information systems for these products has the highest priority. A computerized system to deal with revisions and new products as well as their entry into the current category has secondary priority. Finally, it is not likely that any substantial computerization will be required for handling special products.

Summary of Information Priorities.   The priorities for information system development are summarized in Table 4.

BASIC INFORMATION SYSTEM

Component Systems.   In order to meet the information requirements just described, five major information systems are necessary: logistics, marketing, accounting and financial, service, and engineering and technical (each of which has many subsystems). The component systems listed are not completely independent since there are connections among all of them for input and output purposes.

Logistics is the major operational information system for the firm. It provides data for physical supply and distribution in such areas as procurement of imported products and raw materials, control of manufacturing, control of inventories, and control of the distribution activity. A skeleton diagram is shown in Figure 1. The system utilizes a large

number of files, several of which are also used by other component systems.

Marketing is much simpler than the logistics system, since it summarizes accounting and sales information developed in the accounting and logistics systems. Basic marketing reports can be obtained by processing files which are maintained by other major systems.

Accounting and financial is a general system which maintains the operating information requirements and produces efficient financial controls.

Service is a special information system needed because of the importance of service activities at American Imports. This system maintains status and performance information of the service activity (e.g., maintenance, repair, and spare parts records) at All headquarters and in the branch offices.

Engineering and technical is a special purpose system for use in new product development and engineering data control.

System Design Principles.   There are several general principles to be followed in the development of all these systems. First, systems are integrated through the use of common sets of files: for example, there should be only one file of each type of information, and each function requiring the information should refer to that file. Economy and accuracy in file maintenance would be preserved since duplication is not necessary.

The second major requirement in system design is that each component system be

Table 4.   Priorities for Information System Development

FUNCTIONAL	DEPARTMENTAL	PRODUCT
1 Operational	1 Marketing, finance, materials	1 Current products
2 Control	2 Manufacturing, engineering	2 Revisions and
3 Planning	3 Technical, personnel, quality	new products
	control and quality assurance	3 Special products

Figure 1. Logistics Information System

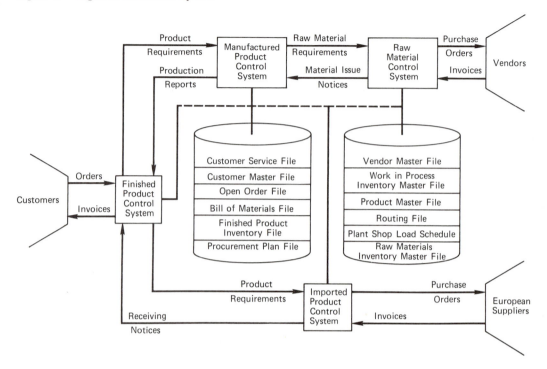

modularized, allowing any major subfunction to be removed without significant modification in other subfunctions. For example, the logistics information system includes both inventory record keeping and inventory control systems, but it should be possible to modify the inventory control modules without significant modification in the inventory record-keeping modules.

Another reason for modular construction is that the system can be designed, developed, and implemented in manageable segments. Implementing the entire logistics system as a single package is not feasible. Even the order processing system, which is a large module in the logistics system, can be further subdivided for the purpose of design, development, and implementation. One of the most important aspects of overall system

planning is that of isolating modules in a way that provides the most improvement at the earliest date, while keeping the modules small enough to be easily implemented.

The final design requirement is that the system be developed in an evolutionary fashion. The simplest modules that require the fewest master files should be assembled first, followed by more complicated modules that use the existing files. As the system evolves, early modules may be redesigned to reflect more refinement or sophistication.

SYSTEM PLAN

Three aspects must be considered in planning the management information system: a schedule for developing system modules and their subsystems, the organizational requirements of the project, and manpower and monetary resource requirements.

Development Schedule. The five component information systems — logistics, marketing, accounting and finance, service, and engineering and technical — each can be broken down into many modules. The schedule of the design, development, and implementation of modules follows directly from the information priorities developed earlier.

In the logistics system, the order processing and finished product inventory status modules demand the earliest attention. Since sales analysis is closely associated with order processing and inventory accounting is related directly with finished products inventory, these systems also require early attention. Second priority modules in the logistics system are inventory control, finished products forecasting, and procurement planning.

In the accounting and financial area, the first priority modules are the general ledger, accounts payable, and accounts receivable systems. The early implementation of the general ledger system is a departure from usual practice in computerizing accounting activities. Often computerization is deferred because of difficulty in transforming a comprehensive general ledger system from a manual to a computerized basis. At American Imports no manual general ledger system exists; thus, it will be convenient to implement a computerized general ledger system, rather than first develop a manual one and then computerize it. Budgeting control modules, which generate expense *vs.* budget statements, profit and loss statements, and cash flow analyses, have second priority.

Product structure information modules require the earliest attention since they support both the marketing and the engineering and technical systems.

The current service information system will be continued on a manual basis; however, further service cost information and a refinement of the spare parts inventory accounting system are needed additions to the current system.

Organizational Requirements. Development of a computerized information system demands integration of many user needs and requires resolution of technical issues. Effective handling of these tasks can be accomplished only with the participation of both users and technical personnel. Users must identify information needs and define the frequency and content of reports generated by the system. Systems analysts and information system specialists are responsible for the efficient handling of technical issues such as computer programming, input/output processing, and information storage and retrieval.

A common way to secure effective participation of both groups is to organize a project team, whose members are devoted exclusively to MIS design and development, and a steering committee composed of the executive officer and the heads of all user departments. AII's steering committee includes the General Manager, the Director of Operations, the Marketing Manager, the Materials Manager, the Controller, and the Electronic Data Processing (EDP) Systems Director. These employees manage the operating elements involved in the initial system design. When manufacturing information systems become more important, the Manufacturing Manager also should join the steering committee.

The steering committee specifies broad system objectives; it meets regularly both to assist in setting targets and deadlines, and to review the progress of the project team in achieving its objectives. The committee specifies the types of reports to be provided rather than relying on the project team's suggestions for useful reports. Steering committee members must recognize that monitoring of plans and progress cannot be delegated to any subordinate.

The project team is managed by a single project manager responsible directly to the General Manager of All. This team includes systems analysts and programmers charged with the design and programming of major systems, and a systems technical design group which establishes programming standards, deals with questions of hardware and software selection, establishes file design characteristics, and provides the general context within which the system is developed. Because the technical design group functions in this coordinating role, it can efficiently delegate subsystem design responsibility to sub-project teams as the need arises.

It often is desirable to augment internal resources used in the MIS project with assistance from professional service firms. One category of assistance is contract programming: by contracting out some of the work, peak programming loads are absorbed without increasing the size of the internal programming staff. Other roles of outside assistance are those of general counsel to project management and reviewer of systems design. By acting as counselors and reviewers, consulting firms help assure establishment of realistic deadlines and maintenance of system relevance.

Resource Requirements. The resources required to design, develop and install an information system for American Imports cannot be known precisely until detailed planning and programming specifications

have been completed. Nevertheless, upper and lower bounds can be estimated. The three main component costs are project management time, task force (internal and external) time, and computer time. The time required of steering committee members is not a relevant cost since the management guidance they provide is part of their normal job functions.

Project management requirements vary with the size of the project team. One full-time project manager is needed at the start. As the scope of the project increases, two to four sub-project managers may be added over the next two years. The amount of systems analysis and programming time required also increases during the project life. In the first year, 10–15 man-years may be needed. Depending on the extensiveness of the MIS project, this estimate may increase to 10–20 man-years during the second year. High levels of task force commitment will continue during the third year if the MIS effort is ambitious; otherwise, they should drop to zero by the end of the third year.

Computer estimates are highly uncertain and depend on the scope of the project. In general, program testing and machine checkout requirements will increase as the project nears completion. During the first year, cost estimates should range from $10–20,000 while during the third year they may reach as high as $25–125,000.

Project resource requirements are summarized in Table 5. An estimate of $15,000 per man-year is used to convert time estimates to yearly dollar costs. It should be noted that the estimated project cost does not represent the total incremental cost of developing a computerized management information system. Since better management information is of utmost importance to American Imports, the alternative costs of

Table 5. Bounds on Resource Requirements

	YEAR 1	YEAR 2	YEAR 3
Steering committee	nominal	nominal	nominal
Project management	1½–2 man-years	2–3 man-years	2–4 man-years
Task force internal/external	10–15 man-years	10–20 man-years	6–20 man-years
Computer time	$10–20,000	$15–50,000	$25–125,000
TOTAL COST	$160–245,000	$165–350,000	$115–425,000

developing manual systems to produce the needed information must be considered in order to assess the incremental cost.

INFORMATION SYSTEM BENEFITS

The benefits that accrue from an improved management information system must be weighed against the costs of developing and maintaining it. Although benefits such as "providing timely and accurate information to support management decision making at all levels" and "decreasing the involvement of talented management in routine activities" are easily recognized, they are difficult to quantify. Nevertheless, a systematic attempt must be made to identify and assess the benefits of the MIS in terms of the specific impacts it will have on the firm. An attempt will be made here to identify areas within American Imports where substantial savings can be achieved.

In the logistics area, the most important savings are from reduced inventory investments, since inventories are a significant percentage of AI's working capital. It is not uncommon to reduce inventory investments drastically through the use of more elaborate control procedures which can be incorporated into the inventory control module. These savings are evaluated easily by simulating the application of control rules to a sample of the total stocked items.[4] The procurement planning module also contributes to the reduction of inventory; safety stocks, which may be inflated by poor forecasts, are eliminated; transportation costs are decreased; and seasonal fluctuations in demand are anticipated. These savings also can be estimated. The inventory control and procurement planning modules improve customer service as well, by helping to reduce back orders and delivery lead times.

The most significant potential benefits in the financial area accrue from the accounts receivable and budgeting modules. The aged receivables schedule generated by the accounts receivable system can help reduce the percentage of bad debts and decrease the mean age of receivables. The budgeting module can aid detection of unnecessary expenditure and provide a financial control mechanism for each responsibility center. Again, these benefits are relatively easy to quantify.

The sales analyses reports generated by the marketing information system give decision making support to the assignment of sales quotas, allocation of advertising efforts, and selection of distribution channels. This type of information has not been available previously. Although more difficult to assess than those of the financial and logistics areas, the potential savings in the marketing area are very significant.

Operational and control data provided by the manufacturing information system should help increase the utilization of equipment and manpower and decrease the work-in-process inventory.

Table 6. Dollar Benefits of the New System

MODULE	CUMULATIVE THREE-YEAR SAVINGS
Logistics and service	$400–650,000
Financial	$300–450,000
Marketing	$100–200,000
Manufacturing	$50–150,000

It has been argued that the computerization of many clerical jobs will result in substantial savings for the firm. These benefits, in practice, are usually illusory since low paid clerical personnel are replaced by expensive computer specialists.

Table 6 provides estimated cumulative savings for the three years of MIS development at American Imports. The ranges correspond to the levels of sophistication available in the final MIS design.

SUMMARY COMMENTS

The main objective of a management information system is to provide managers at all levels with supporting information to help plan operations and measure actual results against those plans. In this paper, an attempt is made to provide a framework for MIS planning in a manufacturing and distributing organization. Emphasis is placed on classifying and ranking information needs. A modular, evolutionary design schedule then is proposed for the basic information systems. The most important part of the planning study, however, is an evaluation of the cost and benefits of an improved MIS. A special attempt is made to quantify specific benefits so that the impact of the management information system can be evaluated.

NOTES

1. This paper emphasizes the planning of an MIS in a manufacturing and distributing company; for technical issues associated with the design and development of an MIS, see Becker and Hayes [2], Blumenthal [3], Brandon [4], Brown [5], Gorry and Scott-Morton [8], Kriebel *et al.* [9], and Magee and Boodman [10].

2. See Anthony [1], Simon [13], and Gorry and Scott-Morton [8].

3. The manufacturing information requirements are: production scheduling, routing, job control, work-in-process inventory, manufacturing cost, and bill of materials.

4. See Brown [5], and Magee and Boodman [10].

REFERENCES

1. ANTHONY, R. N. *Planning and Control Systems: A Framework for Analysis.* Boston, Harvard University Graduate School of Business Administration, 1965.

2. BECKER, S., and HAYES, R. *Information Storage and Retrieval: Tools, Elements, Theories.* New York, John Wiley and Sons, 1963.

3. BLUMENTHAL, S. C. *Management Information Systems: A Framework for Planning and Development.* Englewood Cliffs, N.J., Prentice-Hall, 1969.

4. BRANDON, D. *Management Planning for Data Processing.* Princeton, Brandon/Systems Press, 1970.

5. BROWN, R. G. *Decision Rules for Inventory Management.* New York, Holt, Rinehart, and Winston, 1967.

6. EMERY, J. C. *Organizational Planning and Control Systems.* New York, Macmillan, 1970.

7. FORRESTER, J. W. *Industrial Dynamics.* Cambridge, Mass., MIT Press, 1961.

8. GORRY, G. A., and SCOTT-MORTON, M. S. "A Framework for Management Information Systems," *Sloan Management Review,* Vol. 13 (Fall 1971), pp. 55–70.

9. KRIEBEL, C. H., VAN HORN, R. L., and HEAMES, J. T. (eds.). *Management Information Systems: Progress and Perspectives.* Pittsburgh, Carnegie-Mellon University Graduate School of Industrial Administration, 1971.

10. MAGEE, J. F., and BOODMAN, D. M. *Production Planning and Inventory Control,* New York, McGraw-Hill, 1967.

11. MURDICK, R. G., and ROSS, J. E. *Information Systems for Modern Management,* Englewood Cliffs, N.J., Prentice-Hall, 1971.

12. ORLICKY, J. *The Successful Computer System.* New York, McGraw-Hill, 1969.

13. SIMON, H. A. *The New Science of Management Decision,* New York, Harper and Row, 1960.

14. STOKES, P. M. *A Total Systems Approach to Management Control.* New York, American Management Association, 1968.

15. ZANI, W. M. "Blueprint for MIS," *Harvard Business Review,* November-December 1970, pp. 95–100.

QUESTIONS

1. What are the major phases in the development of an MIS?

2. What are the conditions for a successful development of an MIS?

3. Discuss the use of each of the following approaches in the article: modular, top-down, bottom-up, evolutionary, sequential, decision-oriented.

4. Why must priorities be established for the long-range development of the overall MIS?

5. What were the priorities that were established for AII?

6. On what bases were the priorities established?

7. How have the operational information requirements been subdivided at AII? (Discuss the subdivisions from the highest to the lowest levels.)

8. How have the functional departments been organized at AII?

9. Discuss the information needs for each of these departments.

10. Why do the component information systems differ in certain respects from these organized departments?

11. Contrast the responsibilities of the steering committee with those of a project team.

12. Why are both a steering committee and a project team needed?

13. Discuss the component costs that can be estimated.

14. What are the potential benefits to be gained from the newly developed information system?

15. What activities should follow the complete implementation of the newly designed information system?

16. Is systems development at AII ever likely to be completed?

Behavioral Aspects of Developing Computer-Based Information Systems*

Much has been written in recent years about computer-based information systems and their development within organizations. This is a vital topic, for information systems are increasingly being found to be essential for organizational success. And with the advent of the microprocessor revolution and the pervasiveness of minicomputers, it is difficult for managers to escape getting involved in a computer selection and installation or a systems development within their organizations.

After a computer system has been acquired, systems developments are necessary to create or enhance applications and the information systems. So often, however, the issue of systems development is viewed simply as a series of steps that must be accomplished. To be sure, there are a number of steps required to complete the systems development: an investigation of need, a feasibility study, systems analysis, systems design, programming and testing, and implementation and evaluation.

It is especially important, however, that this series of steps take place within a behavioral climate in which success or failure can be dictated by the manner in which the people in the organization are treated and dealt with as the systems development takes place. It has been seen time and again that intimate knowledge of the behavioral facets of the systems development is just as crucial as a knowledge of the technical aspects of the system when change is being introduced.

This point can be made most vividly by considering an actual experience. A large bank was in the process of computerizing one of its major departments. Little consideration was given to the impact this change would have on the department's staff. Many of the employees feared the uncertainty created by the impending computerization. Rumors began to spread about the computer replacing staff members. Some key employees, whose jobs were not actually in jeopardy, left the bank and sought positions elsewhere. In sum, the bank lost a group of key employees because little attention had been given to the human factor and other behavioral implications.[1]

What we would like to do here, therefore, is to consider what some of these behavioral aspects are and see what knowledge is important in efforts to improve systems development. We will discuss the systems development team, characteristics of users and specialists, the nature of team leadership, the change process, and other factors involved in improving systems development.

THE SYSTEMS DEVELOPMENT TEAM

To begin with, it is useful to stress that a system development is typically performed by teams of people.[2] Depending on the project, the systems development team may involve a variety of kinds of people, but each project team typically includes a group of users, or managers, for whom the system is being designed. The team also includes a group of systems analysts, systems de-

signers, programmers, and other specialists who represent the data processing staff of the organization. The users and specialists are directed by a project manager who is responsible for coordinating the efforts of the two groups as they move toward the team's objective. The project team, then, could be pictorially represented by the diagram shown as Figure 1, where the team has received input from the organization's steering committee or top management group.

As we attempt to portray some of the behavioral aspects of systems development, our focus of attention will tend to be on these two groups, the nature of the leadership re-

Figure 1.   The Systems Development Team

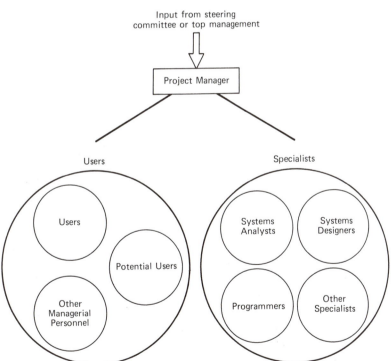

Source: Hugh J. Watson and Archie B. Carroll, *Computers for Business: A Managerial Emphasis,* rev. ed. (Dallas, Texas: Business Publications, Inc., 1980): 355. Copyright 1980 by Business Publications, Inc. Used with permission.

quired for successful development efforts, and the change process through which the project team and organization must evolve. Other research that has been shown to be important in improving systems development will also be discussed.

USERS AND SPECIALISTS

Since the users (or potential users) of new systems and the specialists who will carry out the technical analysis and design are the key parties to a successful systems development team effort, it is important to understand their personal and professional characteristics. Because the basic personality and professional differences between these two groups often result in conflict and possible systems development failures, more effective systems development efforts can be achieved if you are aware of these fundamental differences. Indeed, it might be said that the understanding of these two classes of individuals is vital to effective development efforts.

The differences between computer users and specialists are so profound that several writers have alluded to C. P. Snow's *Two Cultures and the Scientific Revolution* to describe them. The book focuses on the gulf that separates the scientist from the rest of society. Snow asserts that the attitudes, behavior, and language of the nonscientist and the scientist are so different that they define separate cultures between which there is a dangerous gulf of mutual incomprehension.[3] Such is the case with computer users and computer specialists. These differences, which have been documented time and again, can be seen quite clearly in the four categories identified by Paul Lawrence and Jay Lorsch. The categories include: (1) goal orientation, (2) time orientation, (3) interpersonal orientation, and (4) formality of

organizational structure.[4] *Goal orientation* refers to the different kinds of goals users and specialists have. *Time orientation* refers to the fact that they are concerned with problems in a different time frame — short run versus long run. *Interpersonal orientation* refers to people-orientation (users) versus problem-orientation (specialists). And, *formality of organizational structure* refers to the degree of precision and formality in their reporting relationships, control systems, and performance criteria. Figure 2 summarizes a comparison of computer specialists with computer users along the four dimensions.

When we look at the differences between computer users and computer specialists, we begin to understand the orientation of each group as it approaches the systems development task. One observation should be made clear: the differences between these two groups are normal and are the result of the demands of their respective jobs. Their differences are much like the basic differences that exist between production and sales people in most organizations. Knowing what these differences are, however, is an important bit of behavioral knowledge that is helpful to all those involved in systems development.

NATURE OF TEAM LEADERSHIP

Given the differing nature of the two major groups involved in systems development, it is apparent that it takes a special kind of individual to lead the group effectively. The work of Lawrence and Lorsch suggests that an effective leader in a highly differentiated group such as this would be the one who could span the two worlds of the groups involved. In other words, the time, goal, and interpersonal orientations of the project manager should be situated midway between those of the users and the specialists.

Figure 2.   **A Comparison of Computer Specialists With Computer Users***

ORIENTATION	COMPUTER SPECIALISTS	COMPUTER USERS
1. Goal Orientation	Member of a profession with transferable skills. Applying latest computer technology. Solving problems in elegant ways. An agent of change.	Focus on present employer. Getting job done without interruption. Cheapest, simplest, most workable solution. Resists change.
2. Time Orientation	Long-term projects. No need for immediate feedback.	Dependable results now, not later.
3. Interpersonal Orientation	Problem oriented. A systems thinker.	People oriented. Get things done through people.
4. Formality of Organizational Structure	More freedom of action. Fewer formal rules and hierarchy. Project oriented, not hierarchy. Works directly with people, bypasses chain of command.	Works through the formal, established organizational channels. High premium placed on hierarchy.

*Much of this is summarized from Kintisch and Weisbord: 7-8. Refer to Note 3 on page 40.

Source: Hugh J. Watson and Archie B. Carroll, *Computers for Business: A Managerial Emphasis,* rev. ed. (Dallas, Texas: Business Publications, Inc., 1980): 356. Copyright 1980 by Business Publications, Inc. Used with permission.

Project managers are often assigned without management's giving due consideration to the special talent needed to effectively bridge the natural gap between users and specialists. The above research suggests, however, that higher effectiveness can be achieved if an individual is identified who occupies this middle ground of orientations. The project manager must understand the methods of thinking, methods of operating, and points of view of the two groups if effective communication, coordination, and integration is to be achieved. The good leader, therefore, will be one who is perceived by the team members as independent of any particular point of view or goal except the project's success.[5] Thus, management must give very careful attention to the selection of the project manager, for this selection on its own can determine the success or failure of the project.

In addition to selecting the leader carefully and ascertaining the different characteristics of users and specialists, knowledge of the change process involved in the systems development is vital. Knowledge of the change process suggests additional ways in which the systems development can be managed from a behavioral point of view.

THE CHANGE PROCESS

Though we mentioned earlier that there are steps or interrelated states that a systems development must go through, behavioral theory suggests that effective analysis, design, and implementation must be explicitly viewed as a dynamic process. Of the entire implementation situation, the most important single aspect over which we can exert the most direct influence and control is that of our own behavior, both as users and specialists.[6] The process approach thus permits us to examine these behaviors, to identify patterns that are especially effective or ineffective, and to translate this knowledge into approaches which can be used to increase the success and effectiveness of our efforts. The focus becomes, therefore, one of managing the change process.

The principal approach that has been suggested as a model for systems development is known as the planned change approach.[7] This approach is based on the Lewin/Schein view which conceptualizes any change as entailing three distinct phases: unfreezing, moving (or changing), and refreezing. Unfreezing, the first stage, requires a "felt need" for change of existing, stable behavior patterns. Moving, the second stage, is the "action" phase which requires learning new attitudes and behaviors that are integral parts of the change. Refreezing, the third phase, involves the stabilization of the change and the integration of new behaviors and attitudes into existing patterns and relationships. This sequence is an iterative process and will likely be repeated several times in any sizeable change effort.[8]

The main advantage of this process-oriented view is that it leads to consideration of the entire implementation process — from initial planning and feasibility testing through installation and evaluation — rather than just the "action stage," which has typically been the focus in systems development.[9]

Two recent process-oriented research studies provide interesting and useful insights into the systems development process. One study showed that activity *conducive* to the changes required at each of the three stages (unfreezing, moving, refreezing) was associated with greater overall project success. Conversely, activities which discouraged the changes needed at these stages were associated with project failure.[10] The study also showed (1) a tendency for poor performance at one stage to be followed by poor performance at later stages, and (2) a strong association between the quality of activity at the refreezing stage and overall project success.[11]

A second study found that successful systems development projects tended to conform more closely to the prescriptions of the process model than did unsuccessful projects. As in the previous study, it was also found here that the refreezing stage was most strongly associated with project success.[12] It was concluded that organizationally complex projects seemed especially sensitive to the quality of the unfreezing stage whereas projects that required less organizational change seemed more sensitive to technical and procedural aspects of the moving stage.[13]

Other aspects of the change process that are important here include a concern for resistance to change, the degree or magnitude of change, whether those implementing the systems development are viewed as technicians or change agents, and other suggestions that fall in the realm of effective management of change.

Resistance to Change. Resistance to change such as that created by a systems development typically occurs in some of the following ways: the withholding of data and information, the provision of inaccurate information for purposes of sabotage, distrust of computer output, and the demonstration of lowered morale. Lowered morale may show up as a lack of cooperation, sullen hostility, sloppy effort, or indifference.[14]

Employees resist changes such as those represented by systems development for economic, personal, and social reasons. One employee of a large manufacturer worried about economic security: "I fear I'll lose my job. I can't afford that! At a minimum my hours may be reduced." Another employee talked about personal considerations: "I dislike the new computer because it makes my job more boring. Furthermore, I think my self-esteem and reputation have been reduced." An insurance supervisor had social reasons: "The new system that was installed resulted in my department being divided and long-time friends of mine moved to a new area in the building."

As we saw in an earlier example, change has repercussions that produce multiple effects. A systems development that might have an intensity of $3\times$ may affect others and eventually result in an intensity of $85\times$. This is known in the behavioral sciences as the chain-reaction phenomenon. Beyond this, the resistance to change manifested may further aggravate the problem.

To address some of the problems created by resistance to change and change's many effects, consideration needs to be given to the degree of change, how specialists will view their roles, and some suggested guidelines for introducing systems changes.

Degree of Change.   Since systems developments vary in the amount of change they imply, they also vary in amount of demand placed on the implementation process. For a small scale systems development, attention to the technical dimension may be adequate. On the other hand, for a large-scale change, other dimensions, such as the cognitive, interpersonal, and political, become important.[15]

Technicians or Change Agents.   Closely related to the issue of how much change is being introduced by the systems development is the question of whether the specialists involved are going to view themselves primarily as technicians or as *change agents.* The technician's approach is to accept management's definition of the problem, build a system to solve that problem, and turn the system over to the users. This approach may work well on small projects but not necessarily on larger ones. Large projects usually require the specialist to be a change agent who really understands the users, keeps the users involved throughout, and makes sure the users understand what is happening and why.[16]

The role of change agent is, indeed, a difficult one and may require that the systems analyst or specialist assume a variety of roles at different times throughout the systems development process. For example, it has been suggested that the systems analyst may need to assume the posture of persuader, catalyst, confronter, or even imposer in the change agent role. Figure 3 illustrates in flow chart form what some of these roles might be, and Figure 4 illustrates how these roles might alter as the change involved moves from least severe to most severe.

The success and future of a systems analyst may just well depend on his ability to assume the right behavioral role with the right people at the right time.[17]

Managing Change.   One expert observed that people do not resist change so much as they resent the way it is introduced. Introducing and managing change successfully can circumvent some resistance. The introduction of a systems development can be improved if certain useful guidelines are followed when introducing change. Part of the solution entails the manager asking the right

Figure 3. Activities and Roles of the Systems Analyst

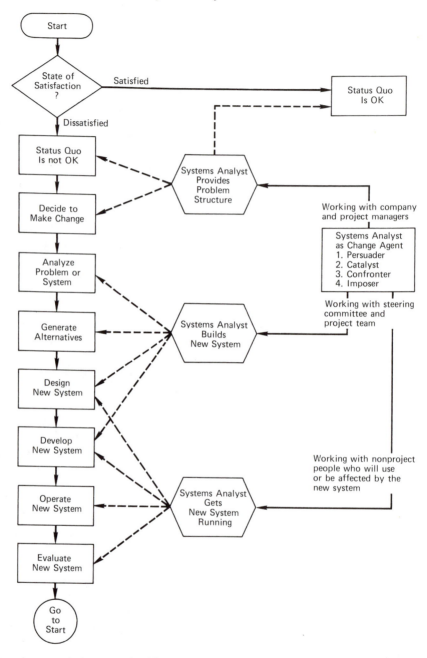

The systems analyst may work with many people at various stages in the development of a system, including managers, programmers, operators, and users. He or she may have to play a different kind of role—persuader, catalyst, confronter, or imposer—at each stage.

Source: William Feeney and Frea Sladek, "The Systems Analyst as a Change Agent," *Datamation*, November 1977: 86. Reprinted with permission of *Datamation* ® magazine, copyright by Technical Publishing Company, a Dun & Bradstreet Company, 1977. All rights reserved.

Figure 4.   Role Selection Strategy for the Systems Analyst

Least Severe Change	IN THE ANALYST'S JUDGEMENT	ROLES
	Change proposed by management will work ⟶	Persuader role used to bring dissidents into line.
	Management has difficulty in defining form of change ⟶	Catalyst role used to assist company people in defining what they wish to change.
	Change proposed by management quite undesirable for company ⟶	Confronter role used to make Management seek problem definitions outside the ones they have considered.
	Change proposed by management requires drastic change to company ⟶	Imposer role used to perform surgery to accomplish the change.
Most Severe Change		

The severity of the change is a major factor in determining the analyst's role. Making the wrong choice may be fatal both to the project and to his career.

Source: William Feeney and Frea Sladek, "The Systems Analyst as a Change Agent," *Datamation*, November 1977: 87. Reprinted with permission of *Datamation* ® magazine, copyright by Technical Publishing Company, a Dun & Bradstreet Company, 1977. All rights reserved.

questions before introduction so that the important factors will be considered. Examples of these include the following:[18]

1. How will existing departmental procedures be changed?
2. Which jobs will be most affected and in what ways?
3. What will happen to the people affected? How can they be prepared for these changes?
4. What sort of training will people in the department need?
5. What is the time schedule for the change? Startup? Hiring new people? Transferring existing personnel?

As the manager, project director, or systems specialist assumes the role of change agent, several guidelines are best kept in mind. *Keep employees informed:* Good communication is relatively inexpensive, and it can go a long way toward alleviating ill-founded speculation and rumor. *Seek employee participation:* Support and accept-ance will more likely be forthcoming if employees have had a hand in the change. *Consider the timing of the change:* Do not use unreasonable conversion deadlines. People need time to adjust to new technology and ways of doing things.[19] Use objective praise of the existing system as a springboard for acceptance of the new system. Praise the existing system as one which has served well because the people have made it work. The new system will require the same kind of attention if it is to achieve all it is capable of.[20]

IMPROVING SYSTEMS DEVELOPMENT

Understanding the different characteristics of systems users and systems specialists and selecting the type of leader needed to mesh the differences of these two groups is an important step toward the successful implementation of systems development. The change process through which the groups must evolve is also highly significant. It is now important to discuss other specific concerns by which managers, systems specialists, and users can improve implementation based on behavioral knowledge that is available.

User Needs and Involvement.   One of the clearest messages from recent research is that the systems analysts and designers should undertake only those projects which address an *important need* of the intended users. If the users do not think that the proposed systems change addresses a problem they are experiencing, they are not likely to be accommodating.[21] Consequently, it is crucial that specialists encourage, indeed demand, that potential users be involved in the project at the outset and remain involved throughout.

It should be stressed that this *user involvement* mandate is based on experience and research, not just idle speculation. One study, for example, found that "intended users neither initiated nor played an active role in implementing 11 of the 15 systems that suffered significant implementation problems."[22] It was further discovered that "there were relatively few such problems in 27 of the 31 systems in which the users had a hand in initiating and/or played an active role in implementing."[23]

This evidence makes it clear that user involvement as a factor in success is not just conventional wisdom but is based on actual research findings as to results achieved. Of 56 systems studied, it was found that the difference between success and failure was the extent to which managers could use the system to improve their effectiveness and this, therefore, should be a design criterion for the specialists.[24]

Not only is it important that users stay involved throughout the entire change process; specialists must stay involved as well. The odds of successful systems development are improved if the specialists stay involved until the "users are truly able to use the system in their environment." Evidence suggests that a wise systems designer is one who secures management's agreement at the outset that he or she will stay with the project until it is truly implemented.[25]

Though much of what we have said applies to both systems specialists and users, we have frequently implied throughout that the major responsibility falls on the shoulders of the specialists. Successful systems development and implementation also places a heavy burden on users and potential users. Like the analyst and designer, the user must be aware that different projects demand different degrees of change and that a sensitivity to this fact must be developed. In addition, the user must take the time to carefully articulate his or her goals and expectations for the project.[26] The user must recognize that the successful systems development requires time and commitment and that he or she has a major responsibility to work with the specialists if success is to be achieved. Though the project manager may have the leadership and coordination responsibility, heavy duty falls on both the specialists and users if effective implementation is to result.

The Minnesota Experiments.   A recently evolving stream of research focuses on viewing the decision maker, the decision environment, and the characteristics of the information system as three key variables which must be examined in preparation for systems development. The foundation for this research is the belief that it is "wrong to assume that all decision makers are the same and can effectively function with undifferentiated information systems."[27] The message to systems specialists is clear: You must take into consideration the individual differences of the users, the decision environment in which the system will reside, and the characteristics of the system itself in implementing a system development. An examination of some of this research, known as the Minnesota Experiments, will be useful.

The Minnesota Experiments involved a series of experimental games in which various information systems characteristics (for example, CRT-based output or the presence of certain aids to decision making) were evaluated as to their success with particular types of decision makers (based upon quantitative aptitude, cognitive style, and so on) in different simulated decision environments (for example, production, procurement, inventory control). The experiments are too involved to describe here; however a sampling of their results is worth presenting.[28]

One experiment was conducted in an inventory management setting, and the subjects were given different types of output on which to base their decisions. The output included (1) tabular versus graphic output format, (2) decision aids versus non-availability of the aids, (3) exception versus full reporting, and (4) reports giving only "necessary" data versus reports containing "overload" information. Some of the findings of the experiments were as follows:[29]

1. Subjects receiving graphical output and decision aids had the lowest costs (the objective).
2. Subjects receiving decision aids took longer to make decisions.
3. Subjects receiving graphical output used the fewest reports.
4. Subjects receiving the "overload" information requested more reports than those receiving the "necessary" information.

Another experiment focused on the impact of two different forms of information present in operations management decision making. One group received batch processed paper output in a "raw data" format and the other matched group received the data in a statistically summarized format. The results of the experiment were that those with the summary data had the lower total production costs (made better decisions) but took longer to make their decisions and had less confidence in the quality of their decisions.[30]

A number of other experiments were conducted as part of the Minnesota research efforts, and a few of their key findings follow:

1. Systems that have complex or unfamiliar attributes may produce low user confidence and satisfaction even if operating results are better. These attitudes represent a potential barrier to successful implementation.
2. CRT system output can lead to faster decisions and use of less data.
3. Graphic output may have results similar to that of CRT systems and may lead to "better" decision making.
4. Information system designers must be sensitive to individual differences in users.

The point of these findings, of course, is that there are many more attributes of systems development than first meet the eye, and successful systems specialists must become acquainted with these types of findings and use them in their design efforts. Similarly, a burden rests with users to be aware of these characteristics which can make a difference when design efforts are underway.

An illustration of the mistake that can be made when it is assumed that users are basically homogeneous, all having similar goals and expectations for the system, is seen in the case of a large system developed for a group of portfolio managers in a bank. Even though the system was developed by a team that included representatives for the three groups of managers, once the system was in use, their reactions to it fell into three groups:

1. Those who saw very little use for it initially were dissatisfied;
2. Those who saw a need for a system with basic capabilities (which was implemented) were satisfied, and;
3. Those who saw a need for a more advanced system (which was not implemented) were dissatisfied.[31]

Thus, even when user needs are considered, an outcome such as this is a distinct possibility.

Interactive versus Batch Systems. An important consideration in deciding on the type of systems development undertaken is whether the system is designed for the manager to operate in an interactive mode or a batch mode. In an interactive system, managers "can access the computer from a terminal, enter their requests or commands directly, and receive feedback which is virtually immediate."[32] With batch processing, of course, managers get output from the computer but do not themselves interact with the computer.

Over the last decade many progressive commentators on the computer scene have extolled the virtues of "man-machine" interaction as a decision support approach to such an extent that it was implicitly assumed that this should be the model approach to modern-day decision making. The vision of offices of managers, each with their own terminals, carrying on an "interactive" dialogue with the computer was the scenario that many computer experts held as a sacred objective.

While the computer will continue to be popular for on-line accessing of information, questions are being raised about interactive problem solving as the decision making prototype of the future. One of the first to raise the question was Steven Alter, who investigated systems which he thought were specifically designed to support conversational usage.

He observed: "It was surprising that very few situations were encountered which could be described as interactive problem solving, i.e., a process involving a single person (especially a decision maker) sitting at a terminal for a prolonged length of time, adaptively exploring a problem space in an effort to find the best possible action."[33]

This and other findings have led Alter and others to conclude that perhaps the interactive model is not the ideal after all. If, as some evidence suggests, managers do not have the time or the inclination to learn how to solve problems on an interactive basis, perhaps they should be encouraged to use the computer only through staff intermediaries who do understand and enjoy working with the details.[34] Comments from top level managers lend credence to this view. Several executives have responded to the prospect of using computers themselves as follows: "How many executive offices have you been in lately where there's a big box behind the desk with thick computer runs that no one has ever looked at?" "I would rather talk to the people who use the computer and get their judgments." "If I see a computer printout on my desk, I won't read it."

Though interactive problem solving has been viewed as a central tenet of the decision support system movement, arguments are being made which challenge this fundamental assumption. One such challenge comes from Peter Keen who advocates, as a modest proposal, the use of knowledgeable specialists to serve as staff intermediaries. The staff intermediary would necessarily be one who is skilled in programming and computers and who also understands the decision making process from the manager's perspective.[35] Figure 5 illustrates a system which employs a staff intermediary.

Alter summarizes why manager interaction with the computer for its own sake should not be the major issue: ". . . the key issue [is] not whether the user or manager could talk to a computer to get the answers he needed, but rather, whether a combination of people, data, models, and technical tools could provide . . . answers in a convenient, timely, and cost-effective manner."[36]

The key idea for systems development, of course, is that it should not be assumed that an interactive mode is best for an information system. Managers vary in their decision making behaviors and this must be considered in the systems development design. Since systems are developed with multiple users in mind, this poses quite a challenge for the specialists. Nevertheless, consid-

eration of these differences must be given at the outset.

To be successful, systems development requires computer experts in the areas of hardware and software, but these are no more important than the behavioral and process knowledge that is needed to make the systems change process a success. When combined with technical knowledge and other specialized expertise, behavioral knowledge completes the requirements for effective systems development. Indeed, none of the parts can succeed without the whole. This is not just how it should be, but how it is, in successful systems development.

NOTES

1. Edward A. Tomeski, George Stephenson, and B. Man Yoon, "Behavioral Issues and the Computer," *Personnel,* July-August 1978: 66–74, reprinted in

Figure 5.   Interactive System with Staff Intermediary

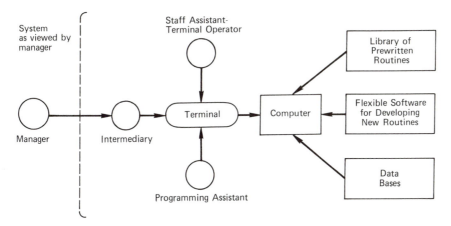

Hugh J. Watson and Archie B. Carroll, eds., *Computers for Business: A Book of Readings* (Dallas, Texas: Business Publications, Inc., 1980): 295.

2. Much of this material comes from Hugh J. Watson and Archie B. Carroll, *Computers for Business: A Managerial Emphasis*, rev. ed. (Dallas, Texas: Business Publications, Inc., 1980), Chapter 12.

3. Ronald S. Kintisch and Marvin R. Weisbord, "Getting Computer People and Users to Understand Each Other," *Advanced Management Journal*, Spring 1977: 5.

4. See Paul R. Lawrence and Jay W. Lorsch, "Differentiation and Integration in Complex Organizations," *Administrative Science Quarterly*, 1967, 12: 1–47.

5. Kintisch and Weisbord: 10–11.

6. Michael J. Ginzberg, "Steps Toward More Effective Implementation of MS and MIS," *Interfaces*, May 1978: 58.

7. Ginzberg: 58.

8. Ginzberg: 58–9.

9. Ginzberg: 58–9.

10. Dale E. Zand and Richard E. Sorensen, "Theory of Change and the Effective Use of Management Science," *Administrative Science Quarterly*, December 1975: 532–545.

11. Ginzberg: 59.

12. Ginzberg: 59.

13. Ginzberg: 60.

14. Donald H. Sanders and Stanley J. Birkin, *Computers and Management*, 3rd ed. (New York: McGraw-Hill, 1980): 282.

15. Ginzberg: 61. For an interesting discussion of the political dimension see Peter G. W. Keen and Elihu M. Gerson, "The Politics of Software Systems Design," *Datamation*, November 1977: 80–84.

16. Ginzberg: 62.

17. William Feeney and Frea Sladek, "The Systems Analyst as a Change Agent," *Datamation*, November 1977: 85.

18. Lester R. Bittel, *What Every Supervisor Should Know*, 3rd ed. (New York: McGraw-Hill, 1974): 430–431.

19. Sanders and Birkin: 283–284.

20. Bittel: 431–432.

21. Ginzberg: 61.

22. Steven L. Alter, "How Effective Managers Use Information Systems," *Harvard Business Review*, November-December 1976: 103.

23. Alter: 103.

24. Alter: 97.

25. Ginzberg: 61.

26. Ginzberg: 62.

27. Gary W. Dickson, James A. Senn, and Norman L. Chervany, "Research in Information Systems: The Minnesota Experiments," *Management Science*, May 1977: 913–923.

28. See Dickson, Senn, and Chervany: 914–917 for a detailed discussion of the methodology.

29. L. Benbasat and R. G. Schroeder, "An Experimental Investigation of Some MIS Design Variables," *The Management Information System Quarterly*, March 1977.

30. N. L. Chervany and G. W. Dickson, "An Experimental Evaluation of Information Overload in a Production Environment," *Management Science*, June 1974: 1335–1344.

31. Ginzberg: 61.

32. Peter G. W. Keen, "Interactive Computer Systems for Managers: A Modest Proposal," *Sloan Management Review*, Fall 1976: 1.

33. Steven A. Alter, "A Study of Computer Aided Decision Making in Organizations," Ph.D. Dissertation, M.I.T., 1975.

34. Steven A. Alter, "Why is Man-Computer Interaction Important for Decision Support Systems?" *Interfaces*, February 1977: 112.

35. Keen: 14.

36. Alter, 1977: 114

QUESTIONS

1. Do users and designers of information systems form different groups within a business firm?

2. Do you agree with the differences between users and specialists as listed in Figure 2?

3. Discuss the *planned change* approach.

4. What is the appropriate role of a systems specialist with respect to a planned change?

5. Who should head a systems development team?

6. What have been the findings with respect to the impacts of changes upon users?

7. Is interactive problem solving by managers a feasible approach?

8. Discuss the behavioral aspects in each phase of the systems development activity conducted at American Imports, Inc. (the firm in the Hax article).

9. Discuss a case in your personal life in which you were forced to consider the behavioral aspects of a major decision.

Strategic Planning
For Information Systems*

There is much evidence to suggest that changes are impacting our society more rapidly than ever before and that the *rate* of change is itself accelerating. This rapidity of change affects, of course, all individuals and institutions. What implications does this increase in the velocity of change hold for the systems manager?

In the past, those responsible for managing the systems function in an organization could, with some confidence, look several years into the future and not envision substantial change in the methodology of their activity. The advent of the electronic computer dealt the first rude blow to the comfortable feeling that, in the systems realm, as elsewhere in the business, things were likely to be much the same in the future as they had been in the past. Today, with the proliferation in the techniques and tools of the systems function an undeniable reality, those managers not capable of introducing a more disciplined planning approach into their area of responsibility will be ill-prepared to cope with the rapidly changing era that lies ahead.

The term "strategic planning" is gaining popularity among systems managers as they become increasingly concerned with more formalized and disciplined approaches to identifying requirements beyond the immediate future. The complexity of today's information systems, and the increasingly large share of company resources earmarked to support them, underscores the need for a more carefully prepared "road map" to the future. This is especially so because of the long lead times that typify today's large system projects.

While it would be difficult to get systems managers to agree upon a precise definition of strategic planning, the concept can be brought into meaningful focus by contrasting such planning with the more conventional type of planning that goes on in an organization.

As borrowed from military parlance, strategic planning has to do with the overall conduct of large-scale operations as contrasted to tactical planning having to do with the immediate problems of maneuvering military units in the field. In a business organization, broad-based strategic planning can be contrasted with planning for the conduct of day-to-day operations such as getting this week's, or this month's, or this year's workload processed in the form of payroll checks produced, demand deposit accounts updated or airline reservations booked.

Regardless of terminology, most organizations have come to recognize that planning is necessary on at least two levels: the tactical level to assure that there is sufficient capacity, personnel and other resources to continue to get the organization's work done; and, at the strategic level, to anticipate what future workloads and workload processing are likely to be.

Typically, the long-range information systems plan encompasses a period at least five years into the future, with eight or ten year planning horizons not uncommon. Where such a long-range planning period has been established, short-range planning is usually characterized as encompassing the current budget year or sometimes the budget year plus one. Thus, short-range plans cover the first year or two of a strategic plan that extends five to ten years into the future.

Strategic plans, being long-range in nature, are concerned principally with goals to be achieved whereas tactical or short-range plans tend to concentrate on objectives. In the strategic planning mileau, goals can be thought of as general statements indicating the basic direction the organization is seeking to take, as suggested by the following examples:

• Provide the telecommunications capability to deliver data to any company computer center from any remote site at reasonable cost.
• Increase the ability to respond to top management requirements for information and facilitate the collection and maintenance of such information.

Goal statements are normally not quantifiable in terms of specific completion dates or resources required. They are, rather, the governing statement from which objectives are derived. Objectives differ from goals in

that they are specific statements of results to be achieved within a given period. Thus, they have associated with them target dates or milestones for accomplishment and an identification of the resource requirements necessary to their achievement. Because objectives are more specific than goals, they can be reflected in the current year budget. (An example of an objective statement is shown in Figure 1.)

The systems planner must seek answers to three basic questions:

• What is the technology going to be like over the planning period?

Figure 1.   Objective Statement

1. **Objective:** Evaluate current and upcoming minicomputer equipment and software capabilities, develop guidelines as to the types of applications for which the mini is technically feasible and cost effective, and evaluate potential costs and benefits of distributed processing systems.
Start date: January 20, 1978 Completion date: November 30, 1978
2. **Background:** With the growth of minicomputer capabilities and the decrease in hardware costs, it is increasingly important to develop policy and guidelines for evaluating their use both as network components and as stand-alone systems.
3. **Principal Milestones:**
   a. Perform a technical review of minicomputer equipment and software capabilities.   March 26, 1978
   b. Survey existing minicomputer and distributed processing installations.   June 28, 1978
   c. Draft of policy and guidelines October 15, 1978
4. **Resource Estimates:**

	12 MONTH
Man-days (Internal)	180
Man-days (Support)	0
Man-day Cost	$16,500
Computer Support	0
Contractual Support	25,000
Other Costs	1,000
TOTAL COST	$42,500
TOTAL MAN-DAYS	180

5. **Constraints:** Schedule and plans depend on approval of consultant support.

• What changes will take place in the environment in which the organization must operate?
• What are the long-range corporate goals?

Despite the acceleration of change, the knowledgeable systems planner can take a fairly accurate fix on what the technology is going to be like over the next few years. It is not easy to take such a reading, not nearly so easy as in the relatively tranquil past, but it can be done. To do so requires much greater awareness of the state of the art with respect to unannounced products than is presently found in most organizations.

Just as the technological capability that may be introduced into the organization over the planning period needs to be identified and, where appropriate, scheduled for introduction, a comparable understanding must be sought of the forces of change at work in the environment within which the business must operate.

These changes are so multitudinous that they almost defy description. They include changes in the purchasing and consuming proclivities of the firm's customers, changes which may in themselves be the result of technological change within the customer organization or business environment. Strategies of competitors also loom importantly as environmental considerations, particularly since we can anticipate that many competitive strategies in the future may be based upon employment of computerized technological tools. The rate of new product introduction that characterizes so many areas of industry, all the way from new customer goods to new financial services and industrial products, strongly underlines the importance of reflecting in the systems plan the characteristics of the environment in which the business must function. For this reason, quantitative estimates must be derived with respect to the business environment — in particular, with respect to

customer relationships and competitive activities — to supplement those dealing with computer technology.

The third major variable affecting the systems plan encompasses the policy dictates of shareholders and top management. What is the firm's competitive strategy going to be over the planning period? Is it to be one of diversification of product line? Are acquisitions, which themselves may have substantial systems capability, contemplated? Will the firm be seeking aggressively to enhance its share of market, or is it content to maintain its current position and defend the status quo? Regardless of whether broad corporate goals such as these are expressly stated or must be inferred from management's present actions and past performance, they have an obvious and fundamental effect on any systems plan.

Systems planning can be a powerful competitive weapon, in the sense that it enables an organization to anticipate technological trends at any early stage and, as a consequence, introduce new technology and develop new systems in advance of the competition.

A basic consideration in systems planning is that such planning must necessarily be done under conditions of uncertainty. Future events affecting the systems plan, whether these be of a technological, environmental or policy nature, cannot be predicted with complete accuracy.

The possibilities of variation in systems characteristics are fairly narrow in the immediate future, since commitments of equipment and personnel have already been made for operational systems and systems development projects. Further along in the planning period, however, the possibilities begin to widen. An organization which does not perform long-range systems planning cannot narrow the possibilities sufficiently to fit within the horn-like enclosure, and consequently is confronted with an overwhelming array of future systems possibilities.

Despite the current emphasis on strategic planning in many companies, the question still arises: "Is such planning necessary in all organizations?" Are there organizations that, either, because of the size or nature of the business, cannot justify the expense of creating and maintaining a strategic plan? The question is especially pertinent, since the investment in planning may be considerable, ranging from a part-time assignment for one professional staff member up to a unit of several people dedicated to planning. Experience indicates that to do an adequate job of strategic planning, at least two man years of effort must be applied initially.

It seems unquestionable that very large organizations, with annual data processing expenditures approaching $100 million, not only can afford an investment in planning, but would be managerially deficient if they failed to do so. It also seems generally accepted that organizations with data processing budgets greater than $10 million per year should engage in some form of strategic planning. Below that level, a careful analysis may be in order to determine what resources should be allocated to the planning function. Given the volatile technological and economic environment in which all firms must operate, it seems doubtful that there are many organizations in which strategic planning is not warranted.

Increasingly, companies are formalizing the corporate planning process — in some instances generating plans covering a 20-year future. In those organizations that have well defined long-range corporate planning procedures, it is obviously desirable to tie the information systems plan into the corporate strategic plan. If there is no formalized corporate planning mechanism, the information systems manager is confronted with a more difficult planning problem. The absence of a corporate long-range plan should not, however, preclude the initiation of strategic information systems planning. There are ways to compensate for such a planning void.

One traditionally employed method of linking systems requirements to corporate strategy is to establish a data processing steering committee composed of top management representatives from line organizations, preferably at the vice presidential level. This is an expedient to compensate in some measure for the absence of corporate planning. One leading management consultant recently stated that the presence of such steering committees in his client companies is a tip-off to weaknesses in overall corporate planning.

Another approach available to the systems planner is to proceed to develop his strategic plan by making assumptions about the company's future direction with respect to such factors as sales volume, product mix, plant location and government regulation. This "bottoms up" approach has been successful in compensating for the absence of strong planning guidance from top management. In fact, information systems planners may find themselves in the position of being the *only* group within the organization engaged in strategic planning, with the result that their planning assumptions become a "de facto" long-range corporate strategy.

In such circumstances, it is especially important to carefully document planning assumptions, so that these can be presented to top management when the occasion arises, as in requests for capital investment funding, and top management given the opportunity to challenge or ratify the assumptions.

Many organizations venturing into strategic planning for the first time tacitly assume that the strategic plan should be updated annually. Where planning is tied in closely to the budget preparation cycle, this may indeed be a logical assumption. But experience has shown that in many cases it is not necessary or even desirable to redo the information systems plan each year.

Because the strategic plan deals with the broad goals of an organization for deployment of information systems, it is unlikely that these goals, once articulated for the first time in the strategic plan, will change markedly in the course of a year. For this reason, an episodic or "ad hoc" plan may prove more suitable, with the plan reviewed and updated whenever events dictate major changes in strategic planning goals.

Given the volatile state of information systems technology, the plan probably should be revised at least every three years. And, of course, major changes in company organization and operations would require updating the plan independent of technological factors. If an annual cycle is not adopted, the systems manager should monitor the state of technology, company goals and environmental factors and initiate action to revise the plan whenever circumstances change significantly.

A compromise method of maintaining currency in the strategic plan would be to issue a basic planning document initially and then to selectively supplement this annually with new material, such as updated forecasts of data processing expenditures. The other parts of the plan would be revised only when needed. A looseleaf notebook format might be appropriate in these circumstances, with some sections of the plan remaining intact and others replaced each year.

Just as the information systems plan should be tied in to the corporate planning process, it should be tied in to the organization's budget mechanism in some way.

One approach is to view the budget either as the first year of the long-range plan and require much more specific cost estimates for this year as well as detailed objectives statements and justification of new project proposals. Some organizations require a high degree of specificity for two years into the future, i.e., budget year plus one.

Some form of zero base budgeting may be appropriate in reviewing both ongoing computer operations as well as planned operations. In many cases, some form of project prioritization may be appropriate for budgeting as well as longer range planning. Here, users might be required to rank their project proposals on the assumption that funding might not be available for all projects. In a decentralized environment, priorities may have to be established by the central management staff based upon a review of all divisional project proposals.

Some companies have adopted a life cycle management concept so that major projects are carefully defined and costs estimated throughout the system life, i.e., from the initial feasibility study phase through system development and into system operations. Before entering each phase, the project is reviewed to assure that it is still consistent with company goals and that cost and schedule commitments are being maintained. Since the life cycle of a project may extend over several years, there is an obvious tie-in between the justification and documentation of individual projects and the broader elements of a strategic plan.

Organizational decentralization and the distribution of systems functions are important factors in developing an information systems plan. In an organization that is completely decentralized, the role of the central planning staff may be largely that of coordinating the development of divisional plans so that they are consistent in format and methodology and perhaps reviewing these plans for adherence to company-wide goals and spending constraints. At minimum, even in highly decentralized organizations, there should be a critical review and challenge of divisional plans.

Many organizations are only partly decentralized, with large-scale computer facilities centrally managed on a service bureau-wide basis but with application development work done by systems staffs in user organizations. With increasing terminal usage for interactive problem solving and information retrieval by end users, this form of decentralization is likely to become increasingly prevalent. Where it exists, there must be close coordination of planning between the computer facility manager and his users so that adequate provision can be made for anticipating and satisfying long-range user requirements.

In all but the most highly centralized organization, there should be control mechanisms to assure that an adequate job of planning is accomplished. Standards for preparing plans and centralized coordination and review of plans are obviously desirable, and there may be other control mechanisms that should be adopted. For example, if corporate approval of capital investments beyond a certain amount is required, proposals for data processing equipment should be referred to the planning staff for review for consistency with overall systems goals.

There are three basic approaches available to an organization seeking to get started in the preparation of a strategic information systems plan: 1) establishment of a task force, 2) employment of an outside consultant, or 3) application of internal staff resources. Any of these can produce results, and the preferred approach is largely a function of the organizational environment in which planning must take place. Frequently,

a combination of methods can prove effective as, for example, using consulting assistance in preparing an initial plan which can then be taken over and maintained by company planners.

A task force comprised of members drawn from the line organizations that are the principal users of information systems products can be a good vehicle for gaining support from users for planning goals. A task force may be especially desirable in a decentralized organizational situation where each operating division controls its own data processing resources and the corporate systems staff is trying to introduce more control over the management of divisional resources.

Another benefit of the task force approach is that it can concentrate the efforts of talented people in the preparation of a plan by applying sustained effort over a limited period. A task force or working committee can be called upon to meet for anywhere from a week to a month or two to put together the initial structure of a strategic plan.

If the task force method is chosen, care should be given to selecting people to serve who have a broad outlook and can contribute to what is essentially a creative endeavor. Major components of the organization should, of course, be represented but it is preferable to keep the group fairly small. A few talented specialists should be invited to participate to keep the group attuned to trends in technology.

When convening a strategic planning task force, it is important to provide the group with a detailed agenda so that they can proceed in a well-organized manner, with assurance that they will produce a meaningful end product. (Figure 2 provides an outline of a typical information systems plan.)

Staff-written plans offer the advantage of having the originators of the plan under the direct control of the systems manager who

Figure 2. Outline of a Systems Plan

The following chapter outline has been adapted from the actual strategic plan of a large organization to illustrate items that should be covered in the preparation of a typical plan.

Chapter 1. The Planning Process

This chapter contains sections summarizing general concepts of information systems planning; a description of the planning cycle for the organization, i.e., deadlines for submission of divisional planning documents to corporate headquarters; and a general description of the procedures to be followed in performing systems planning. Like all chapters in the plan, the discussion is presented in nontechnical terms that a line manager could understand.

Chapter 2. Historical Development

The sections of this chapter describe the history of computer usage in the company. Early experience is summarized in one section describing events up to 1970; a second section covers 1970 through 1975; and a final section discusses events since 1975. The format of this chapter is such that additional summary material can be added without requiring a complete revision.

Chapter 3. Strategic Planning Goals

This is the heart of the strategic plan. It contains a description of the technological environment which the planners expect to prevail over the next five years, followed by goals statements and a discussion of each goal. The chapter is organized into the following sections:

    A. Information Management
    B. Computer Facility Management
    C. Management Science Methods
    D. Application Development
    E. Data Communications
    F. Security and Privacy Protection
    G. Organization and Personnel

Chapter 4. Resource Utilization

This chapter contains a variety of exhibits presenting quantitative data about trends in data processing within the company based on historical data. Included are such items as growth in numbers of terminals; investment in equipment; hardware inventory in terms of large CPUs, terminals and minicomputers; tabulations of average cost per job for each major computer center; and distribution of dollar resources among personnel, equipment, data communications and outside services. Augmenting this historical trend data are five-year projections of expenditures and other indicators of systems growth.

Chapter 5. Divisional Plans

This chapter includes one section for each of the 20 autonomous divisions of the company. Each section contains an organization chart; a planning narrative; an inventory of equipment installed, on order and planned; and five-year projections of numbers of employees in each systems group and the estimated budget of the group.

can interact with them to produce an end result of acceptable quality. If this approach is adopted, it would be beneficial to have the draft plan coordinated with major users by circulating it for review and comment. It may be desirable to assign staff to produce a draft plan which could then be used as input to the meeting of a planning task force.

Because the need for formal systems planning is only now beginning to receive the recognition that it merits, it is not surprising that one can find no general universally accepted principles or methodology for performing such planning. The following points are offered as guidelines in the hope that they may help to delineate further the nature of systems planning, and stimulate thinking and concern about the planning process:

1) Make provision in the systems plan for taking small steps rapidly. This will help to avoid the pitfall of long-range or "ultimate" systems goals that have no immediate targets or operational subphases. It may indeed be desirable to look ahead to the millenium of an "integrated, total, management information system." But the attainment of such an ultimate goal should be a step-by-step process which permits the organization to receive the economic benefits of systems that can be made operational in the immediate future but are consistent with longer-range systems goals.

2) Develop alternative plans when significant contradictory trends are discerned in business objectives or technology. As mentioned previously, the consideration of alternatives becomes almost mandatory in planning beyond a five-year period. Simu-

lation may play a significant role in structuring alternative systems plans, particularly in instances where simulation models are developed to aid policy level management in considering alternative courses of action for the firm.

3) Interface the systems plan with the corporate plan, modifying both appropriately. If there is no explicitly stated corporate plan, as is still frequently the case today, the systems planner must then make planning assumptions about the nature of corporate objectives. These assumptions should be documented as part of the systems plan.

4) Document the systems plan in a format intelligible to top management, and arrange for a personal presentation. One of the voids in the relationship between systems people and executive management is that management is typically approached only to gain approval for the acquisition of a particular piece of hardware or to obtain the go-ahead for a particular systems project. The systems plan, documented in nontechnical jargon and presented to policy level management, can give the "big picture" of the systems function and aid in gaining an appreciation of its importance.

5) Establish a formal mechanism for review and reiteration of the systems plan. Because there is feedback and interaction among the various elements along the time scale of the systems plan, the planning process must be a continuing one. With the rapidity of change so evident in the field of computer technology, modifications will be required, not only because of experiences gained within the company but because of forces at work outside.

6) Develop a system for tabulating and forecasting utilization of installed data processing equipment. This is necessary so that the useful life of such equipment can be reflected in the systems plan.

7) Fix the organizational responsibility for systems planning. In large companies there should be a director of systems planning; in smaller organizations, the responsibility should be assigned to a designated individual, even though this may be only a part-time duty.

8) Rotate the assignment of technical personnel to the planning staff. This enables key people in the systems function to gain new insights and perspectives by exposure to the long-range planning process.

9) Budget for research and development. This is important in order to permit first-hand evaluation of new equipment and systems techniques without the pressure of cost justification that is usually associated with approval of new systems projects or the acquisition of new equipment.

10) Set up a comparative systems intelligence activity. Since systems planning does have importance as a competitive weapon, it is highly desirable to determine the existing capability and the future plans of competitors. This does not require industrial espionage so much as a painstaking review of the public pronouncements of these competitors and their equipment suppliers plus reliance on the time-honored weapon of industry contacts.

There are, no doubt, other points that should be cited as contributory to the development and maintenance of a soundly conceived strategic information systems plan. The most important considerations are that the significance of systems planning be understood by management and that the development of a systems plan, however primitive, be undertaken.

QUESTIONS

1. Discuss the matters that a systems planner must forecast over the life of a strategic plan.
2. Contrast the top-down and bottom-up approaches to systems planning.
3. Contrast goals and objectives, as they pertain to systems planning.
4. What principles should be followed in the development of a strategic plan?
5. What is the relationship between the budget process of a firm and its strategic systems plan?
6. Does a steering committee have useful functions to perform or is it, as the author implies, a "sign of weakness"?
7. How may short-term systems projects be incorporated into the strategic systems plan?

TOPIC TWO

Systems Analysis and Design

Although they should follow adequate systems planning, systems analysis and design comprise the first two major phases of the systems development life cycle. They generally focus upon individual modules of information systems and are conducted within the constraints of specified projects. Although they tend to overlap in real-life situations, each phase will be discussed separately.

SYSTEMS ANALYSIS

Systems analysis results in the definition of functional requirements for a new or revised module of an information system. These requirements generally pertain both (1) to the information to be provided by the information system, and (2) to the capabilities of the system that is to provide the information.

The phase begins with the gathering and organizing of facts concerning the current system and its environment. It next proceeds to an evaluation of the facts. This evaluation should first confirm that an improved information system is both needed and feasible. Then the evaluation should ascertain the information and systems requirements to be designed into an improved information system module. In some cases it also points to

a preferable architecture for the overall information system.

Before examining the collection of analytical concepts and techniques that are available for use in present-day systems analysis, we should consider the reasons for examining the current system and the evolution of systems analysis techniques.

Importance of Examining the Current System. At first glance it may seem unproductive and extravagant to examine the current system. Instead, it may appear to be more productive and prudent to proceed directly to the design of a new or improved system.

Several excellent reasons exist, however, for reviewing and evaluating the current system. In addition to confirming that the system really does need improvement, an examination should clearly define the extent of the present weaknesses and problems. An examination will also provide cost data concerning the current system; these data are needed for developing comparative cost and benefit data, as the basis for evaluating economic feasibility. Furthermore, an examination enables the systems analysts to gain the cooperation and participation of the users, thereby helping to ensure the operational feasibility of the improved information system when it is implemented.

Evolution of Systems Analysis Techniques. Techniques pertaining to the gathering of facts include interviewing employees and managers, observing operations, reviewing documents and records, and circulating questionnaires. Each of these techniques requires practice by systems analysts in order to be effective. While certain of the techniques, such as interviewing, are rather difficult to master, the techniques of data gathering have not significantly evolved over the past 50 years. Numerous management and systems texts discuss their "dos and dont's" at length.

In contrast, the techniques for organizing and analyzing data have evolved dramatically during the past several decades. This evolutionary process is particularly evident with respect to those data-organizing and analyzing techniques that focus on information flows and system logic.

The genesis of information flow techniques was the process flowchart, devised during the early years of the century for use by industrial engineers in tracking the flows of materials. Process flowcharts were modified over the following decades to portray the processing of data and flows of information, whether by manual or electro-mechanical means. In addition, flowcharts that focused on documents were developed. These document flowcharts were applied particularly as an aid in evaluating internal data controls.

When computers were employed in business data processing, beginning during the mid-1950s, other flow-type techniques more suited to computer-based information systems were introduced. The earlier and better-known of these techniques include the following:

1. Computer system flowcharts, which show the use of computer components in collecting, processing, storing, and retrieving data, and in generating information.
2. Computer program flowcharts or block diagrams, which show the logic underlying computer programs.
3. Decision tables, which display matrices of conditions and actions to reflect the logic underlying computer programs.

During the 1960s various organizations began devising formal systems analysis and design methodologies. Among these were National Cash Register's Accurately Defined Systems (ADS), and IBM's Study Organization Plan (SOP) and Time Automated Grid (TAG). These methodologies provided well-organized and integrated approaches to the definition of systems requirements.

Structured analysis techniques were added during the 1970s. These techniques include Softech's Structured Analysis and Design Technique (SADT), Yourdon's Structured Analysis Technique, Sarson and Gane's Structured Systems Analysis, IBM's Hierarchical Input and Processing and Output technique, and Warner and Orr's hierarchical diagramming technique. Elaborate methodologies based on the structured approach, such as IBM's Business Systems Planning (BSP), were also developed. Certain structured methodologies, such as Teichroew's PSL/PSA methodology, involved the assistance of computers in their application. These structured techniques and methodologies provide a top-down approach as well as a step-by-step and integrated approach to systems analysis and design. They are therefore more likely to lead to a sound system analysis and a more tailored and effective system design.

Current Use of Systems Analysis Techniques. Most of the systems analysis techniques identified above are still in use. Certain of the techniques, such as systems flowcharts and decision tables, are extensively described and illustrated in introductory information systems textbooks. The more recently developed techniques, such as the structured analysis techniques, are continually undergoing revisions and improvements.

A particularly effective set of structured analysis techniques are described in the article by Mendes, which also provides references to several of the structured techniques identified earlier. While the five integrated techniques described in the Mendes article are similar to the other structured techniques, the former tend to focus on the business operations and logical information flows rather than the data processing steps and details. Thus, they provide very relevant and sound models from which to develop systems and information requirements.

Analysis of Costs and Benefits. One of the most critical evaluations of an information system concerns the costs and benefits that may be ascribed to the system. The management of an organization must determine whether the benefits gained from the information system exceed the costs that it incurs in collecting, processing, storing, and retrieving data. Similarly, the management must consider whether the benefits that it expects to receive due to a change in an information system will exceed the costs of making the change and operating and maintaining the new system.

A cost/benefit analysis must therefore be performed before a significant systems change is made. This financially-oriented analysis will normally be begun before a systems project is approved. However, the accuracy of the estimates is likely to be quite poor at the inception of the project. Accurate estimates of costs and benefit values cannot be developed until the information and system requirements are known. For instance, the estimators must know the specific requirements with respect to the quality of the information, the comprehensiveness and accessibility of the data base, and the response time of the system, as well as the related tradeoffs. Thus, a more careful analysis must await the gathering of detailed data during the systems analysis phase.

The article by Keim and Janaro reviews the steps of a thorough cost-benefit analysis and the problems in applying the analysis to modern information systems. The authors advocate a phased approach to cost/benefit analysis that extends even into the systems design and implementation phases. They also list several references that enhance an understanding of this difficult area. Two additional references that might be noted are: James Emery, *Cost/Benefit Analysis of Information Systems,* Chicago: The Society for Management Information Systems, 1971; and Fred R. McFadden and James D. Seever, "Costs and Benefits of a Data Base System," *Harvard Business Review,* January–February 1978, pp. 131–39.

SYSTEMS DESIGN

Systems design is the creative phase of the systems development life cycle. It involves the synthesizing of information and system requirements into an efficient, effective, and cohesive framework. This resulting information system framework, or model, is constructed of six building blocks: inputs, processes, controls, data bases, communication links, and outputs.

As might be imagined, systems design is a complex activity. For the information system framework to be effective and cohesive, it must be tailored to the existing organizational structure and foster the organization's objectives and strategies. For the framework to be efficient, its building blocks must be selected and assembled in a logical and cost-effective manner.

Not surprisingly, many current information systems are deficient in one or more respects. Some do not provide adequate information for decision making; others provide too much information, thereby overloading the managers and employees. Some do not provide needed information or documents in a sufficiently timely manner; others provide timely information, but at an exorbitant cost.

Efficient, effective, and cohesive information systems are most likely to result from the application of sound approaches and guidelines. Furthermore, these approaches and guidelines are best applied within the context of a carefully established systems development sequence. That is, the systems design phase is aided when preceded by thorough systems planning and analysis. Through the application of sound approaches and guidelines, systems analysts and designers should select those alternatives among the building blocks that are appropriate to the organization and its situation.

Systems Design Approaches.   Several systems development and design approaches have already been mentioned, either explicitly or implicitly. These include the systems approach, modular approach, bottom-up approach, and top-down approach.

1. *Systems Approach.* The systems approach views a system as an entity of interrelated parts, which is set within an environment to which it must adapt. It states that a system should be designed in a manner that integrates its parts and furthers its objectives. Thus, it emphasizes the cohesiveness criterion of information system design.
2. *Modular Approach.* The modular approach views the system as a collection of parts, called modules. Like the systems approach, it encourages the integration of the modules. This approach also suggests that changes to the system are best achieved by concentrating upon one individual module at a time, since the entire system is likely to be too complex to handle as a single project. However, if this approach is selected, the interfaces between the module under study and adjoining modules should be given particular attention.
3. *Bottom-Up Approach.* This approach concentrates on the operational level of an information system. It emphasizes the efficiency and cost-effectiveness criteria. Thus, the bottom-up approach encourages the development of efficient and cost-effective transaction processing systems.
4. *Top-Down Approach.* This approach centers on the decision-making mission of an information system. It therefore emphasizes the effectiveness criterion of information system design and is particularly relevant to the design of the management information system.

The above approaches are not mutually exclusive. In fact, most system design authorities agree that all four approaches should be employed in most organizations.

Design Guidelines.   Guidelines enable systems analysts to operationalize the above approaches. They may be rather broad or quite specific.

Broad guidelines can be illustrated by reference to the top-down approach. The top-down approach derives from the objectives and strategies established for the organization and the information system. Thus, the first step is for top management to review and confirm these objectives and strategies. The next step is to determine suitable performance measures for the organization, perhaps beginning with the critical success factors mentioned earlier. The third step of the top-down approach is to perform an analysis of managerial decisions; this step may be performed by systems analysts in concert with the managers throughout the various levels of the organization. The fourth step is to determine the information needed to make the decisions.

The above steps of the top-down approach would be performed during the systems planning and analysis phases, using techniques such as those described in the following articles. The remaining steps of the approach, to be performed during the systems design phase, consist of (1) designing the specific reports that are to contain the needed information, and (2) designing and selecting the other building blocks needed to generate the decision-oriented information.

Specific guidelines for designing information systems are available in a variety of published articles and books. For instance, an article by Vincent J. Giovinazzo entitled "Designing Focused Information Systems" (*Management Accounting,* November 1984, pp. 34–41) suggests that managerial reports (the outputs of an information system) should monitor the critical success factors, reflect the 20/80 rule, be concise, be understandable, and be a part of an integrated reporting structure. The article in this section by Hindman and Kettering presents design guidelines through the vehicle of a case study. It illustrates the application of the modular approach by examining detailed modules within two larger modules known as the manufacturing system and the financial accounting/reporting system. This article also illustrates the application of the bottom-up approach by identifying the relationships of the input, processing, data base, and output building blocks within each of the detailed modules. In addition, the article describes numerous managerial reports that are usefully generated by the above information system modules.

Design Alternatives.   Before assembling the building blocks comprising an information system, systems analysts and designers must choose among design options or alternatives. Currently available systems options include the following:

1.   *Inputs* may be entered via terminal keyboards, optical scanners, voice input units, magnetic disk drives, etc.
2.   *Processing* may be performed either in the batch processing mode or online processing mode.
3.   *Data bases* may contain flat files or structured data sets, with the latter being structured according to the hierarchical model, network model, or relational model.
4.   *Outputs* may be provided as hardcopy reports, softcopy displays, voice responses, light signals, etc.

Design alternatives extend to the overall information system architecture and organization. Thus, choices may be made between a centralized system having a single mainframe computer and a distributed system having numerous interconnected microcomputers, minicomputers, and other processors. Also, choices may be made between centralized policy-making and decentralized policy-making.

Alternatives also exist with respect to the relative emphasis of each information system purpose. Thus, the information system of one organization may be designed to emphasize transaction processing at the operational level; the information system of another organization may be designed to emphasize the support of managerial decision making; the information system of a third organization may be designed to provide equal emphasis to both purposes.

The article by Camillus and Lederer discusses several of these design alternatives. It shows that the selection of the appropriate design alternatives depends upon the organization's strategy and overall structure and decision-making style. The authors match the strategy frameworks of illustrative organizations with suitable design alternatives.

Structured Systems Analysis: A Technique to Define Business Requirements*

Growth in the development and use of computer systems has been rapid over the past twenty years. Hardware costs, for a given level of performance, have decreased. Communications technology, an important factor in the advance of computers and information processing, has expanded the capabilities for sharing and coordinating information from many sources. However, software technology — the methods and languages used to develop computer systems — has not shown comparable improvement. As a result, the hardware revolution has driven the demand for computer systems upward by providing increasingly attractive opportunities, but software capability has constrained the ability of system developers to meet this demand.

These hardware and software trends motivated Exxon's computer scientists, in the mid-1970s, to try to improve software methods. Their objective was to devise systems analysis and design techniques that would enhance both the quality of computer applications and the ability of development staffs to deliver systems.

Structured Systems Analysis (SSA) is a member of an integrated set of techniques that resulted from Exxon's research and development in software methods. SSA is a business modeling and communication technique used jointly by users and computer systems analysts to describe business environments and to formulate requirements for computer applications. It gives analysts, for the first time, both a definition of the products to be generated at each stage of a project, and a basis for project planning. Moreover, its application extends beyond the system development environment. It has been used effectively in business improvement studies that do not involve computerized solutions.

This article describes Exxon's SSA, illustrates its usage, and discusses its benefits. It also suggests that SSA, originally developed as an analysis technique for use during the first stages of system building, has evolved into a general purpose modeling technique for describing a business.

BACKGROUND AND DEVELOPMENT

In the past, due to the absence of formal analysis and design techniques, analysts learned through apprenticeship. System developers worked with more experienced people until they developed their own approaches. The first formalization of the system building process introduced the project management disciplines of other engineering and technical areas into computer application projects. These disciplines regarded system development as taking place in four general stages: *Analysis,* in which a business is described and the requirements for a computer system are formulated; *Design,* in which the hardware and software specified in Analysis are configured; *Construction,* in which the software modules are implemented and the hardware is installed; and *Maintenance,* which encompasses a broad range of activities related to keeping the system operational. However, they failed to provide a methodology that could accomplish the objectives of each of the stages of system development.

During the late 1960s, software engineering pioneers, such as Edsgar Dijkstra and Michael Jackson, began fundamental research on formal approaches for system development. Much of the research focused on program design and implementation, key activities in the Construction stage of application building. In the mid-1970s, Exxon began to apply the results of this work to its own environment. Its main purpose was to establish an integrated set of system development techniques. The initial effort led to the introduction of PST (Program Structure Technology) to Exxon's worldwide community of system developers. PST, adapted from Michael Jackson's "Program Design Technique," could provide a precise description of a program and effectively communicate the program's design and behavior.[1] Its graphical notation was a key factor in the widespread usage of PST, and it became a well-established standard within two years.

In the mid-1970s, empirical evidence began to confirm the important role Analysis plays in the building of high quality computer applications. The results of one study indicated that more errors are introduced into a system as a result of failures in Analysis than as a result of failures in any other system building phase.[2] The conclusion of another study was that Analysis errors are more costly to correct and have a greater impact on the effectiveness of the system than errors introduced during either Design or Construction. Significantly, the effects of Analysis errors do not cease with the implementation of the system, but carry over to Maintenance.[3]

Therefore, any methods that improve the quality of Analysis increase the effectiveness of the system development process. Such methods, by contributing to more efficient use of time and by reducing the need to gather additional information as the project progresses, also increase the productivity of systems analysts — usually the most highly paid members of the data processing staff. In the late 1970s, Exxon's computer scientists focused their efforts on developing an Analysis methodology. The purpose of this methodology was to provide a disciplined approach for Analysis, as PST had done for program design and implementation.

Concurrently, application analysts, who were using PST, began to experiment with the flexibility of the notation. They began to use the PST diagramming style during the Analysis stage of system development to specify requirements. Based on the success of this experimental work, Exxon's computer scientists decided to use this approach to formalize system requirements analysis. Thus, the PST notation was brought forward from Construction to Analysis, and it was generalized to provide the basis for the present SSA technique.

Having established a commonality of approach and notation, SSA development proceeded in an evolutionary manner. Existing theory and concepts were drawn upon as needed. They were then adapted and integrated into the technique. At major checkpoints in its development, SSA was tested on pilot projects. This testing contributed significantly to the quality and usability of the present technique.

SSA AND OTHER REQUIREMENTS ANALYSIS TECHNIQUES

The development of a number of requirements analysis and specification techniques during the past several years indicates the importance of these techniques to the data processing industry. Some of the more well-known specification approaches are Softech's SADT ("Structured Analysis and Design Technique"); Yourdon's "Structured Analysis Technique"; Sarson and Gane's "Structured Systems Analysis"; and the University of Michigan's ISDOS ("Information System Development and Optimization System").[4]

The fundamental difference between SSA and these methods is one of orientation. SSA approaches Analysis from the viewpoint of the business. The other techniques approach it from the perspective of data processing. SSA can represent completely in a clear, concise model all respects of the business operation. Other methods are incapable of providing such complete business models.

Another significant difference between SSA and other structured techniques is the graphical notation. The SSA graphical approach consists of several diagram types, while the techniques of Softech, Yourdon, and Sarson and Gane rely upon a single style of diagram. Analysts using SSA have indicated the advantages of its diagrammatic approach. It gives more insight into the business by providing different views, each of which contributes to an integrated business model. Each business entity is described by a notation that is appropriate for that entity's level of decomposition and for its role in the model analysis to follow.

SSA: A DESCRIPTION

SSA is an analysis technique used to understand the business operations of planned computer applications. Its purposes are to model, document, and communicate to users the requirements of computer applications, and to specify the capabilities to be delivered by the recommended system. It consists of a *graphical language* —a precise notation and set of diagrams which collectively are used to model a business—and a *process* — a step-by-step method for building and verifying the model. These components provide a formal, self-documenting approach to the Analysis stage of system development. The graphical language supports information gathering and analysis. The process assists in modeling the operation as it currently exists. The model is then modified to include the new functions provided by the computer application. The revised model and the supporting text replace the traditional specification document.

SSA has been used at Exxon for two years. During this time it has been effective in a wide range of applications that have varied in size, complexity, and orientation. It has been scaled to suit the needs of individual projects, and has been used effectively in a diversity of environments—including both business information systems and technical computing applications.

SSA'S GRAPHICAL LANGUAGE

The SSA graphical language provides a versatile vocabulary for model building and analysis. As shown in Figure 1, the style of the model consists of several diagram types: hierarchies, matrices, and network flows. Figure 1 also illustrates the relationship between the SSA model diagrams and the business entities they describe.

A business model can be represented with the following diagrams and definitions:

— A *Global Model* to describe the overall logical relationships among the business functions in the organization under study.
— A *Function Matrix* to define the responsibilities for each function identified in the Global Model.
— An *Information Flow Diagram* to represent the *flow* of business information.
— A *Detail Activity Model* to describe how *activities,* which correspond to the lowest-level functions in the Global Model, are carried out.
— A *Data Structure Diagram* to describe the logical structure of business information as viewed by the user.
— A *Glossary of Business Terms* to define terminology common to the business operation.

Figure 1.   SSA Graphical Language

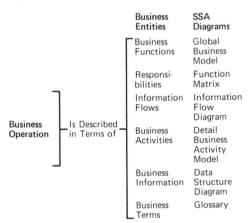

The remainder of this section describes SSA's graphical language. Subsequent sections explain how to build model diagrams and how to use them to identify and specify solutions. Each diagram is discussed in the recommended sequence of construction.

Global Model.   The Global Model of a business is a functional decomposition (a breakdown of *business functions* by purpose) described in a hierarchy of three to five levels. (Figure 2 shows a Global Model of a warehousing business.) In SSA, a *business* is defined as a logical set of functions which exists to provide a product or service (e.g., Warehousing). A *function* is a group of logically related activities (decisions or tasks) required to manage the resources of the business (e.g., Assemble Orders). In addition, a Global Model contains a single-sentence "role statement" capturing the nature of the product or service supplied by the business, the client or market it supports, and its economic commitment. The Global Model concept was developed at Exxon by integrating Constantine and Yourdon's and Myers's functional decomposition techniques with concepts derived from IBM's "Business Systems Planning Methodology."[5]

Function Matrix.   A Function Matrix maps the logical organization of the Global Model to the physical organization chart. (Figure 3 shows a sample Function Matrix which corresponds to the Warehousing Global Model in Figure 2). All of the business functions are listed down the left side of the figure. Across the top are the *responsibilities,* i.e., the job descriptions, organizational units, or personnel accountable for the performance of the function. An "X" at the intersection indicates which functions are performed by each group.

Information Flow Diagram.   A Flow Diagram is a network representation showing the

Figure 2.   Global Business Model

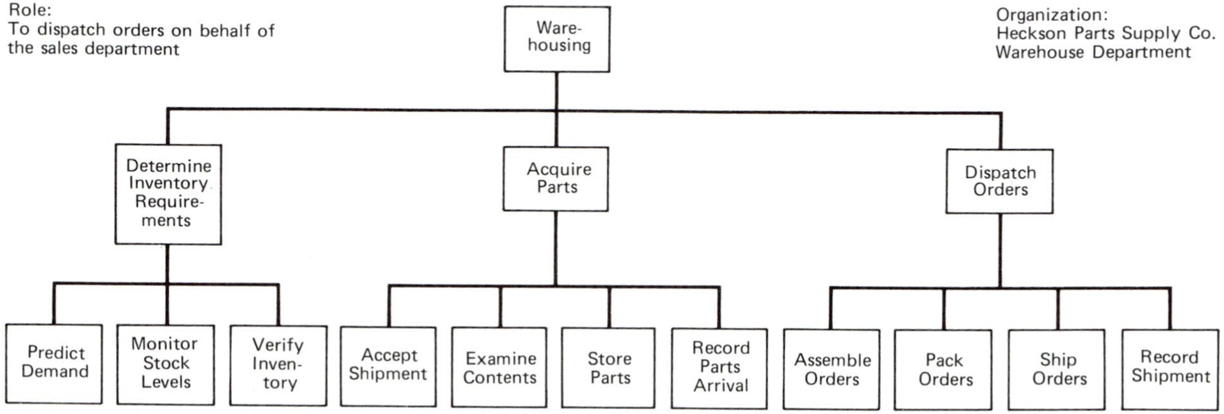

Role:
To dispatch orders on behalf of
the sales department

Organization:
Heckson Parts Supply Co.
Warehouse Department

- Ware-housing
  - Determine Inventory Requirements
    - Predict Demand
    - Monitor Stock Levels
    - Verify Inventory
  - Acquire Parts
    - Accept Shipment
    - Examine Contents
    - Store Parts
    - Record Parts Arrival
  - Dispatch Orders
    - Assemble Orders
    - Pack Orders
    - Ship Orders
    - Record Shipment

Figure 3.   Warehousing Function Matrix

	RESPONSIBILITY					
Function	Warehouse Manager	Receiving Clerk	Forklift Operator	Shipping Clerk	Picker	Stock Clerk
Warehousing	X					
Determine Inventory Requirements	X					
Predict Demand						X
Monitor Stock Levels						X
Verify Inventory						X
Acquire Parts		X				
Accept Shipment			X			
Examine Contents		X				
Store Parts			X			
Record Parts Arrival						X
Dispatch Orders				X		
Assemble Orders					X	
Pack Orders				X		
Ship Orders			X			
Record Shipment						X

flow of business information. A *flow* is the transfer of information or material between business functions. The sources or destinations of these flows can exist within or outside of the business. At a minimum, one Flow Diagram is drawn for the lowest-level functions of each Global Model subtree. Figure 4 is an example of an Information Flow Diagram for the Dispatch Orders subtree of the Warehousing Global Model. It describes where information is used, what it is used for, and how the functions interact. Flow Diagrams can be annotated with statistics on volumes, resource usage, and critical timing. Optionally, Flow Diagrams may be drawn to describe the relationships among the parent functions of the subtrees. These relationships are referred to as high-level flows.

The notation used in Flow Diagrams represents information or material flows; business functions; information stores (passive repositories of information or material which can be either automated or manual); sources or destinations of information or material outside of the business operation; and sources or destinations of information or material outside of the network but inside of the business operation. The basic format of Flow Diagrams derives from the "Data Flow Diagram" concept developed by Yourdon and DeMarco.[6] However, their usage and notation are modified in SSA.

Detail Activity Model.   A Detail Model specifies the relationships between activities and conditions under which activities are performed. An *activity* is a well-defined unit

Figure 4.   Dispatch Orders Information Flow Diagram

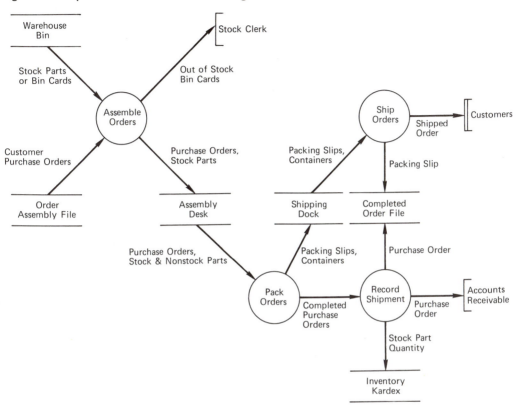

Key:

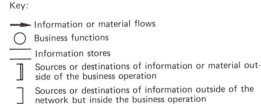

→ Information or material flows
○ Business functions
— Information stores
⌐⌐ Sources or destinations of information or material out-
   side of the business operation
⌐ Sources or destinations of information outside of the
   network but inside the business operation

of work—a task or a decision (e.g., notify stock clerk if part is out of stock). A Detail Model is drawn for each of the lowest-level functions on the Global Model. Figure 5 is an example of a Detail Model for the function, Assemble Orders. It is a hierarchical breakdown by function, which is annotated to describe relationships among activities. Its symbols represent such relationships or conditions as hierarchic membership (with an implied or unspecified sequence); repetition; exclusive alternatives; inclusive alternatives; explicit sequence; parallel activities; release or critical timing condition; and termination activity. The original concept of the annotated hierarchy was de-

Figure 5.   Detail Business Activity Model

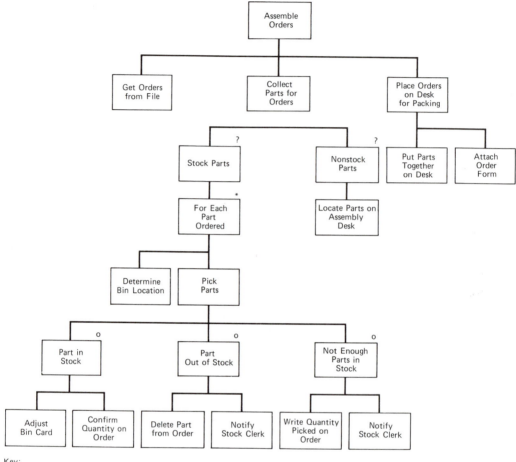

Key:

blank — Hierarchic membership with an
             implied or unspecified sequence
*   — Repetition
o   — Exclusive alternatives
?   — Inclusive alternatives
>   — Explicit sequence
| | — Parallel activities
— Release or critical timing condition
↓   — Termination activity

rived from Michael Jackson's Program Design Technique.[7] Exxon extended Jackson's notation to the Detail Model's description of business processes.

Data Structure Diagram.   A Data Structure Diagram is prepared for each unit of business information that is identified on the Flow Diagrams. *Business information,* as defined in SSA, includes organized data aggregates such as documents, files, products, and intangible forms of information (e.g., order forms, credit criteria). Figure 6 shows an example of a Data Structure Diagram of an order form as viewed by the clerk who takes orders. It is used to gain a deeper understanding of the information required to support the tasks and decisions involved in operating the business. A Data Structure Diagram is a hierarchical data decomposition, which may be annotated with statistics on data volumes and frequencies. It describes the "parent-child" relationship of the

Figure 6.   Data Structure Diagram

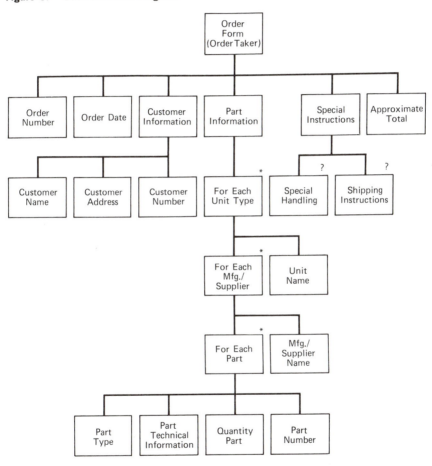

Key:

blank — Hierarchic membership
*   — Repeated occurrence
o   — Mutually exclusive alternatives
?   — Inclusive alternatives
&   — Dimension operator—used in special matrixlike cases

data by indicating hierarchic membership, repeated occurrence, mutually exclusive alternatives, and inclusive alternatives. It also includes a symbol for a dimension operator which is used in special matrixlike cases. Its concept and notation originated from Michael Jackson's Program Design Technique.[8] As used in SSA, it has been generalized and expanded.

Glossary of Business Terms. A Glossary is compiled throughout the model building process. It is used to eliminate multiple definitions and ambiguities, and it serves as a basis for discussion and clear communication between users and analysts.

THE PROCESS OF SSA

The SSA process is a step-by-step approach that guides the analyst and user through systems analysis. It has both the flexibility needed to develop a structure of business operations and the formalism needed to build a model. It also provides criteria for evaluating the model's correctness.

Figure 7 is a schematic representation of the SSA process. It shows the sequence of building the model diagrams. This sequence uses a top-down approach that starts with the most general (the Global Business Model) and proceeds to the most detailed (the Data Model). The figure also shows the recycling

Figure 7. SSA Process

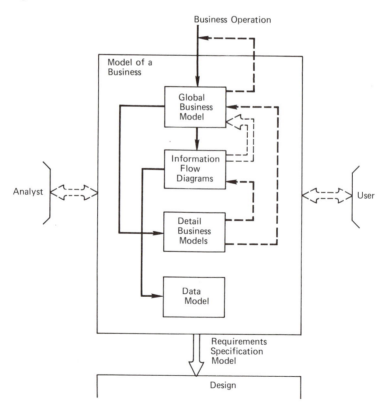

loops needed to refine the diagrammatic representations. During information gathering, the business model is the medium of communication between the user and analyst. The model is completed when it is confirmed that it fits the users' logical views of the business. Once verified, the model becomes the basis for identifying problems and formulating solutions.

SSA moves business and systems analysis from an intuitive to a teachable, structured, and concrete approach. This advance is the result of a well-defined process that assists the analyst in *building, verifying,* and *analyzing* a business model.

Model Building.   Building an SSA business model is a cooperative effort between analyst and user. The diagrams are constructed during fact-gathering interviews, and serve to describe the current business in the project reports. The analyst uses SSA guidelines to elicit the relevant information, record key features, and eliminate irrelevant detail. The interviewing structure fosters consistency in communications between analysts and users. The diagram building approach establishes the set of information to be gathered and thereby provides a framework for each interview. Preestablished questions concerning business objectives, problems, future plans, and business environment forecasts can be drawn upon as needed.

SSA provides procedures to determine the sequence for building diagrams. Model diagrams generally are constructed in the order indicated in Figure 7. However, flexibility exists at the lower levels. For example, in a data-driven business, the Data Model is built before the Detail Model. Nevertheless, the relationships between diagrams always remain intact. Depending upon the size

and objectives of the project, SSA can be used to produce a scaled description of the business. This description includes, at minimum, the Global Model and Information Flow Diagrams.

The rules and syntax for using the SSA notation are the grammatical foundation of the SSA graphical language. For instance, these rules provide that special symbols may not appear on the Global Model; a role statement must be a simple sentence; functions and activities must be described in verb-object form; and error conditions should be excluded from Flow Diagrams.

SSA also provides guidelines for decomposing functions and activities. For example, the following rules determine the functions on the first level of the Global Model hierarchy:

— The first function must cover the requirements aspects of the business; that is, it must show how resource planning and acquisition are carried out (e.g., Determine Inventory Requirements in Figure 2).

— At least one supporting function must be identified that describes the business's provisions for maintaining its service or product (e.g., Acquire Parts in Figure 2).

— The last function must be a disposition function which describes the business's termination of responsibility for a product or service (e.g., Dispatch Orders in Figure 2).

Similar rules apply in the breakdown of the Detail Model. Without criteria such as the above, functional decomposition can be difficult, requiring subjective judgments and experience.

Model Verification.   Building the model diagrams is an iterative process. As such, criteria are applied to the model to determine if and how the model can be improved. Once the criteria have been satisfied, the model is ready for confirmation by all users. Closure is established when all levels of users have verified it.

Criteria to determine whether the model has been decomposed to the appropriate level are applied to the model diagrams. For example, Flow Diagrams that have multipath connections (two functions that pass information back and forth) suggest that further decomposition of the Global Model is required. Or, if a multipurpose function (one with multiple flows in or out and having more than one information transformation) can be identified, then the model requires a further breakdown.

Criteria are also applied in order to test for the correctness of the graphical representation. An analyst can evaluate the model diagram, for instance, by seeing whether or not each function is labeled descriptively. The function should not be defined in terms of its output flow, as described in the Flow Diagram, but should be named to reflect its *purpose*. The analyst also can ask: Have laws of completeness and logical consistency been met? For example, does every information store have an input and output? Are the specified inputs of a function sufficient to produce the indicated output? Is all flow-related information appropriately represented on both Flow Diagrams and Detail Models?

Adherence to the SSA model building and verification process yields a technically correct, self-documenting description of the business operation. Moreover, an analyst's use of SSA leads to models that are the equivalent of those produced by others who use the technique.

Model Analysis.   After the SSA model of the business has been verified by users, it becomes the basis for *diagnosing business problems, identifying computerization op-* *portunities,* and *specifying the requirements model.*

Diagnosing Business Problems

The first step of this analysis addresses those aspects of the business that have been cited as problems by users. In proceeding, it is important to evaluate the organizational and control structure of the business. This analysis can be made by comparing the Global Model and Function Matrix with the organization chart. The comparison shows if the business is organized functionally, if responsibility and control are clearly allocated for each function, and if the geographic distribution of the business makes sense in terms of functional interaction.

It is also important to estimate work loads and peak loads. One can apply simple formulas, using the statistics collected on the Flow Diagrams, to determine if functions are under or overworked; to uncover the source of backlogs; or to trace the cause of high error rates. The Detail Models can be used to find ways to reduce demands on people. Eliminating unnecessary tasks or transferring certain tasks to the computer, for instance, could accomplish this reduction. The Flow Diagrams and Data Structure Diagrams can indicate ways to increase the capacity of staff, such as improving documents, forms, and human-computer interfaces.

Finally, it is important to establish data requirements. The model diagrams can be used to determine the content and structure of the information required for each business function. By contrasting the data actually used by a function (as represented in the Detail Model) with that passed to it (as described in Flow Diagrams and Data Structure Diagrams), one can identify redundant, inconsistent, incomplete, and improperly structured data.

Identifying Computerization Opportunities

It is often necessary, in solving business problems, to determine where the use of computers is feasible and cost-effective. In making this evaluation, SSA applies the concepts of Keen and Scott Morton's "Framework for Information Systems" to the analysis of the SSA Detail Model diagrams.[9] By applying this framework to the Detail Model, the structured activities that are candidates for automation can be readily identified. Moreover, the Detail Model can show where it is possible to implement Decision Support Systems. Thus, the Detail Model is a convenient medium for communicating to the user how the computerized procedures will support the business function.

Specifying the Requirements Model

Generally, the analyst proposes several alternative business solutions and documents them in separate SSA models. After the user has chosen one, the Requirements Specification Model must be prepared in detail. This model is the final product of Analysis. It represents how the business will operate when the new manual or computer procedures are implemented.

The Requirements Specification Model includes organizational requirements that are depicted in the Global Model and Function Matrix; information requirements that are described in the Flow Diagrams and Data Structure Diagrams; and procedural requirements that are detailed in the Flow Diagrams and Detail Models. Thus, it provides a comprehensive set of specifications for use during Design.

A REVIEW OF SSA USAGE

SSA was originally developed as a formal technique for analysts to model both the business environment and the requirements of planned computer systems. However, as users gained experience with SSA, its potential applications increased. It has been proven effective, for instance, in business improvement projects that do not necessarily involve computerized solutions. Since its introduction two years ago, SSA has gained rapid acceptance by users and analysts throughout the worldwide Exxon organization. Its acceptance is attributable to three main factors: business and systems analysts have found its notation and process usable; it can be applied to diverse business environments; and the technique can be adapted to projects of varying sizes and levels of complexity. The following studies illustrate the strengths and versatility of SSA as both a business and a systems analysis technique.

Central Purchasing System.   In this application, SSA was used to specify the requirements for a large-scale purchasing system of an internationally based Exxon affiliate. Analysts used the SSA technique to interview approximately 120 users from diverse business functions. The technique helped to structure the process of gathering information and to improve communications between analysts and users. Its value was evident in the high quality of the requirements specification produced.

Refinery Blending System.   In this study, SSA was applied in a technical computing environment. It was used to describe a process control system which monitored a refinery's blending operation. This case illustrates the power and adaptability of the SSA modeling notation to scientific and engineering applications.

Planning Process Study.   In this project, SSA was used as a business analysis technique. It served as a documentation tool to describe the planning operation of the enterprise. Its analytical capabilities enabled it both to help identify ways of improving the planning process and to determine if the current operations could be extended to support strategic planning.

Financial Modeling System. In this case, a multipurpose financial modeling system that served many different business functions was evaluated. SSA was used to describe the business environment supported by the system and to foster communication among users. It resulted in greater understanding by each user of other users' needs, and in agreements on definitions and calculations to be used in the system.

CONCLUSION

SSA has been used widely in diverse business environments. Based on this experience, it is evident that the technique is valuable in several respects.

— It improves the quality of analysis and of requirements definition. SSA's systematic approach to analysis formalizes what was a very unstructured activity. It enhances the skills of experienced analysts and fosters the involvement of even the most reluctant business users during requirements analysis. Moreover, it enables analysts to prepare Requirements Specification Models that are superior to traditional narrative specifications. The resulting systems are of higher quality than before; they are more capable of representing and adapting to changing business needs.

— SSA facilitates communication between analysts and users. Their interviews are a cooperative effort to construct an SSA model of the business. The analyst does not play the role of interrogator in these interviews; rather, the participants play equal roles. In addition to improving communication during the information-gathering stage, SSA helps to describe to the users the proposed system's effect on the organization.

— SSA increases the productivity of analysts and users, enabling them to use their time more effectively and efficiently. Analysts can learn more about the business in less time. Also, requirements can be documented concurrently with data collection and analysis; SSA does not treat this task as a separate activity. Finally, there is less need to gather additional information as the project progresses, since SSA establishes a comprehensive information base during Analysis.

— SSA provides a basis for identifying opportunities for common systems. Its modeling capabilities enable it to show the potential for generic (or multiuse) systems. SSA models of several business operations can be easily compared or contrasted, and common functions can be readily identified. It is then possible to estimate the degree of tailoring needed to apply the common system to different uses. SSA is a convenient medium for gaining user commitment to the requirements of an application that may serve several user groups.

— SSA is an important tool in project management. Its systematic process provides natural checkpoints for measuring progress. Its notation offers a means of ensuring continuity of effort and consistency in communication even when there is staff turnover. Estimates of the duration, cost, and staffing needs of the project can be obtained earlier in the system building process than would be possible without SSA.

— SSA can adapt to the way in which a system is implemented, even though its specifications are independent of it. SSA is as effective in quickly establishing a set of threshold requirements for an evolutionary or prototyped system as it is in dealing with more traditional system building approaches.

The objective of Exxon's ongoing research efforts has been to develop a compatible set of formal methodologies for building systems — from Analysis to Maintenance. SSA and PST, consistent in their approach and notation, have established a foundation upon which further research will build.

NOTES

1. See M. Jackson, *Principles of Program Design* (London: Academic Press, 1975).
2. See B. Boehm, "Quantitative Assessment," *Datamation*, May 1973, pp. 49–59.
3. M. L. Shooman and M. I. Bolsky, "Types, Distribution, and Test and Correction Times for Programming Errors," *International Conference on Reliable Software Proceedings*, pp. 347–357.
4. D. Ross, "Structured Analysis (SA): A Language for Communicating Ideas," *IEEE Transactions on Software Engineering*, January 1977; "SADT — Structured Analysis and Design Technique Overview" (Waltham, MA: Softech Inc., Form Nos. 9569–4, 956905, 1976); L. Constantine and E. Yourdon, *Structured Design* (Englewood Cliffs, NJ: Prentice-Hall, 1979); G. Myers, *Composite/Structured Design* (New York: Van Nostrand Reinhold, 1978); C. Gane and T. Sarson, *Structured Systems Analysis: Tools and Techniques* (Englewood Cliffs, NJ: Prentice-Hall, 1979); D. Teichroew and E. Hershey III, "PSL/PSA: A Computer Aided Technique for Structured Documentation and Analysis of Information Processing Systems," *IEEE Transactions on Software Engineering*, January 1977; "Problem Statement Language Reference Summary" (Ann Arbor, MI: University of Michigan, ISDOS Project Team, Reference No. 79A51–0174–4, 1979). See also additional ISDOS documentation.
5. See: Constantine and Yourdon (1979); Myers (1978); "Information Systems Planning Guide" (White Plains, NY: International Business Machines Corp., 1978).
6. See T. DeMarco, *Structured Analysis and System Specification* (New York: Yourdon Inc., 1978).
7. See Jackson (1975).
8. Ibid.
9. See P. G. W. Keen and M. S. Scott Morton, *Decision Support Systems: An Organizational Perspective* (Reading, MA: Addison-Wesley, 1978), pp. 79–98.

QUESTIONS

1. How does the structured systems analysis (SSA) technique differ from other structured techniques?

2. Identify several other structured techniques that have been employed during the 1970s and 1980s.

3. What are the benefits of the SSA technique?

4. Briefly describe the five diagrams comprising the SSA technique.

5. Discuss the sequence in which the diagrams are developed during the SSA process.

6. What is the final product of the SSA process?

7. Contrast the use of the SSA technique in diagnosing business problems, identifying computerization opportunities, and specifying system requirements. Give examples for each type of use.

8. Can the SSA technique be employed in the development of decision support systems? Discuss.

9. How can the SSA technique be applied to the later phases, which the author labels as the design, construction, and maintenance stages?

Cost/Benefit Analysis of MIS*

In the early stages of a complex MIS design, the lack of specific requirements, the uncertainty of needed manpower requirements, and the inability to estimate intangibles results in very poor attempts at cost-benefit analysis for information systems. The lack of confidence in these estimates on the part of management has led to suspicion, even outright distrust, of information systems development. This article presents a definition of the design process in such a way as to encourage cost-benefit estimation at each step along the way. This phased approach will result in better estimates, closer user control, and more understanding of the process.

The systems designer is often charged with the task of generating alternative system specifications addressing a spectrum of support levels at the outset of the design process. In the relatively short periods of time allocated for such system specification, if CB analysis is included at all, the result is crude and often inaccurate estimates result.

The problem of developing a cost-benefit analysis methodology to be applied to the design and implementation of information systems must be considered in the context of both the system design activity and the cost-benefit analysis activity. This article will address each context along with a recommendation for a view of cost-benefit analysis, different from the traditional, that can be applied to the design and implementation of information systems.

COST-BENEFIT ANALYSIS

The design of an information system to support management has not been adequately addressed with cost-benefit methodology. "Part of the reason may be the considerable confusion that exists as to how cost-benefit analysis is applicable to the MIS. Opinion ranges from that of advocating profit and loss (P&L) evaluations to those that would not attempt any cost-benefit analysis."[1]

A cost-benefit analysis is composed of five principal steps[2]:

1. *Identification of pertinent measures of effectiveness, i.e., benefits.* Selection of alternatives must be based on quantifiable selection criteria. This is necessary to avoid selections based upon inadequate criteria.

2. *Description of alternatives.* Each alternative system design must be examined in sufficient detail to permit identification of its major characteristics which affect over-all system performance and generate costs. All components of the system which are necessary to perform the desired mission should be included in the analysis.

3. *Expression of performance and cost as functions of the characteristics of each alternative.* A mathematical model is developed to reflect the major relationships. The model will consist of both cost and performance analysis relationships. The primary cost and performance tradeoffs should be obtainable from the model.

4. *Estimation of appropriate values for the equation parameters.* Generate dollar estimates to incorporate in the analysis.

5. *Computation, analysis and presentation of results.* As defined by Hatry, the basis for a cost-benefit analysis is the quantification of a selection criterion for the benefits of the various alternatives. This basic premise is most difficult to address in the proposed information system designs as is the exact description of each alternative.

Unlike a weapon system or a public works project, e.g., a flood protection dam, all major characteristics of an information system cannot be specified in sufficient detail until the actual design is under way. Otherwise, it would mean that all possible alternative information system designs would be completely specified before a decision could be made with respect to the alternative with the most desirable cost-to-benefit ratio.

Any attempt at developing appropriate evaluative criteria for the selection of an information system design requires a redefinition of the traditional cost-benefit model. This redefinition will include the specific characteristics of information systems design which by the nature of its complexity defy detailed specifications at the proposal stage.

INFORMATION SYSTEMS DEFINITION AND DESIGN

According to Tomeski[3], management information systems are "planned and organized approaches to supplying executives with intelligence aids that facilitate the managerial process." In an attempt to further define this concept, the managerial process can be viewed in terms of the major activities faced by organizations as defined by Anthony[4]:

1. Strategic Planning — the process of deciding on the objectives of the organization, on changes in these objectives, and the resources used to attain these objectives, and on the policies that are to govern the acquisition, use and disposition of these resources.

2. Management Control — the process by which managers assure that resources are obtained and used effectively and efficiently in the accomplishment of the organization's objectives.

3. Operational Control — the process of assuring that specific tasks are carried out efficiently and effectively.

The early definitions of MIS tended to focus on the information to support the strategic and tactical planning activities. However, through application, this concept has come to be used to refer to information systems that primarily support the managerial control activities that focus on the use and review of information generated by the data processing of transaction activities of an organization.[5]

The original concept of MIS to support the planning activity has been further defined and is now often referred to as Decision Support Systems (DSS). The distinctions drawn between the Data Processing System (DPS) on one extreme and DSS at the other are well defined. Figure 1 contrasts these two concepts on a number of characteristics.[6]

Since both extremes of this spectrum can be referred to under the general heading of information systems, it is not an easy task to specify a cost-benefit methodology to evaluate all possible alternatives that a systems designer can be asked to propose. Fundamental to the philosophy of information systems is that information is the catalyst of management, and is the unifying ingredient of the management functions of planning, operating, decision-making, and controlling. Therefore, a fundamental consideration in the design and development of an information system is determining which is the vital information needed for maintaining and extending the organization at desired levels of stability and growth. Lyles[7] presented a framework of planning for MIS that provides a structured and systematic approach that addressed many of the organizational issues.

An important consideration in the design of a system is cost-effectiveness. High quality data, large quantities of data, and rapidly available data involve higher costs for the management information system. However, the cost of the information must be balanced against the resulting reduction of uncertainty, increased predictability of events, and more responsive managerial decision-making[8].

The selection of a particular level of information system for an organization is not always specified by management. The decision is often made as a result of a systems design study undertaken by the organization and managed by the systems analysts. The study is often charged with the specification of alternative system configurations as well as the evaluation of the costs and benefits to be associated with each alternative.

The design of information systems follows a life-cycle pattern that includes: definition, physical design, implementation, and evaluation. Each phase of this life-cycle pattern has associated costs and benefits.

COSTS OF THE INFORMATION SYSTEM

Information can be considered to be a resource in modern organizations, and there are costs associated with its use that must be taken into account in the design of a system. The costs of the acquisition, processing, storage, retention, and transmission of information are most apparent in those parts of the information system which have become formalized. For example, the formal descriptions of information processing operations in a completely specified system such as a basic data processing system would allow precise estimates to be made of the cost of these systems in normal everyday use. By com-

Figure 1.   Data Processing Systems (DPS) versus Decision Support Systems (DSS)

CHARACTERISTICS	DPS	DSS
Problem-solving Structure	Programmable	Non-Programmable
Orientation	Clerical Transactions	Intelligence
Time-focus	Historical	Futuristic
Scope	Internal	External and Internal
Design Criteria	Mechanistic	Behavioristic
Computational Focus	Basic	Complex
Output Orientation	Managerial Control	Planning, Forecasting

puting forms cost, data preparation, records retention, output requirements and distribution costs, a well specified accounting process, like payroll, can be accurately costed.

In many organizations, the cost of a completely specified system is taken as the total cost of the information system. The other elements of the system such as the common data base, the management reporting system, and the strategic planning modules are much less developed. The costs of the embryonic versions of these elements that do exist are often included in other budgets. Development of more formal versions of these elements is sometimes taken as an additional cost to the information system. The greatest proportion of the cost of operating a completely-specified system is that of the computer support and the associated personnel.

BENEFITS OF AN INFORMATION SYSTEM

The objective of some systems is cost reduction, while in other cases the aim is to replace a labor-intensive operation with a capital-intensive one[9]. The benefits of the capital-intensive projects are clearly measurable in terms of the cost reductions achieved or the services maintained per unit of human effort expended. The benefits to be obtained from implementation of a completely-specified system are similarly easy to assess. However, the benefits that may be obtained from other parts of the organizational information system are less tangible and much more difficult to measure.

The parts of the information system other than a completely-specified system serve managerial decision-making in management control and the strategic direction of the organization. The benefits from the decision support portion of the information system are in terms of a greater awareness and alertness on the part of the members of the organization to both external and internal environments in which they are working. Therefore, the major benefit of the information system is the value of the information it makes available. But, how can we measure that value — how can we quantify it for our cost-benefit analysis?

VALUE OF INFORMATION

According to Hirsch[10], any item of information is needed if without it a decision would be different; leading to the conclusion that an item of information has no value if it cannot at least potentially influence a decision. Since perfect information would allow us to foretell or control the future, and since this obviously does not happen, then it is safe to assume that we make decisions with imperfect information. Reasons for using imperfect information:

1. The needed information is unavailable.
2. The effort to get the information may be unrealistically great or costly.
3. There is no knowledge of the availability of the information.
4. The information is not available in the form needed.

Following Hirsch's reasoning, decisions are made with imperfect information for all of these reasons. Therefore, additional or different information always has value, which must be analyzed to determine whether the costs of providing it are justified.

VALUE JUSTIFICATION WITH CALCULABLE BENEFITS

According to Hirsch, the justification yardstick for information can be stated as follows: If its cost is less than its contribution to profit or reduction of other costs, the information is justified. This yardstick is useful in cases where the information has a concrete measurable objective, and although these cases are probably in the minority, many of them do exist.

One conventional instance of measurable information value would be changes in accounting systems permitting earlier billings and hence earlier payments. Calculation of how much faster payments are then received and of the resulting interest implications is an easy matter. Value justification of information is an easy matter in cases such as this, where objectives are clear-cut and the extent to which they are achieved can be determined. Unfortunately, this holds true in only a minority of cases.

VALUE JUSTIFICATION WITHOUT CALCULABLE BENEFITS

Most cases of information value determination are less clear-cut than the previous example. Typically, improvements in information systems are designed to bring benefits such as faster order processing. Changes such as this are intended to be beneficial and usually are, but it is difficult and in most cases impossible to make a firm calculation of their dollar impact. An example of this noted by Hirsch would be the major airlines at the time of his article, most of which had or were about to install computer-based reservation systems. Though costly, no attempt was made to profit-justify them. Their justification was instead that they would enable the airlines (1) to continue operating in the face of rapidly increasing passenger volumes, and (2) to prevent competing airlines from gaining a competitive advantage.

The problem in these cases is that the estimation of benefits obtained cannot be a concrete matter, and thus contains an element of risk. Since it takes a long time to determine whether or not the expected benefits are being obtained, an information system may be operated for a long time before it can be decided to discontinue it.

Andrus[11], and Feltham[12], and Mock[13] all discuss methods for determining the value of information. These methods range from theoretical utility approaches to Bayesian (expected value) approaches. The models are logically sound, based on the limiting assumptions, but the assumptions are not realistic. At this point, we are faced with the question: Can we quantify an intangible?

CAN AN INTANGIBLE BENEFIT BE QUANTIFIED?

Although models for determining the value of information have been developed, the complexity of the various designs of information systems preclude their application. It is not possible to accurately determine or quantify the value of all information system design alternatives. To even begin building a cost-benefit model for this type of analysis for information systems design requires situation specific models that depend upon many unrealistic assumptions. Many of these assumptions rely upon subjective probability distributions.

Information is an intangible resource for which a value cannot be accurately nor reliably determined. But, this does not mean that cost-benefit analysis cannot be used in determining which system to develop. It can be a useful tool, but from a slightly different perspective. Litecky[14] suggested that the systems study team use an estimation or "guess-work" basis that must be fully explained to the management who will evaluate the proposal.

A PHASED APPROACH FOR APPLYING COST-BENEFIT ANALYSIS TO INFORMATION SYSTEMS DESIGN

In order to assist the system developers and the management decision-makers, cost-benefit analysis can be a useful tool if evaluated within the context of the design process. We will now present a system design methodology that includes a CB technique that becomes more specific as the system design is more concretely specified.

The initial design stages of an effort to specify information systems for the management of an organization will by the nature of systems design specify a range of alternatives. For each alternative the basic components of the system are specified at a level that is appropriate for cost analysis. The initial estimates will be very general. As the system is more definitely specified, the cost analysis becomes more accurate. The components of cost include hardware, software and operating expenses.

Addressing the benefits of the various system alternatives requires a different perspective. Instead of computing reduction of personnel, forms savings, etc., the benefits might be considered relative to the level of decision support provided by the individual alternative. The estimates will be the responsibility of the management to be served by the system. They will be asked to assign a dollar figure to the benefits for each system alternative.

If management learns to evaluate the various information system alternatives relative to the level of output or decision support provided by each alternative, the choice can be made without artificially quantifying intangible concepts. This method of evaluation can be operationalized by an evolutionary concept for system specification that would have a form of cost-benefit analysis embedded in its life cycle.

Such a systems design life cycle would include the following steps:

1. Definition — the range of alternative system descriptions would be defined in general terms with associated gross costs estimates. PERT/CPM cost techniques as applied to a decision analysis could be used at this level.

2. Specification — given the desired output level the management would select a particular cost range along with a system alternative.

3. Detailed definition — at this point since more procedures and requirements will be specified, additional cost estimates and benefits can be determined. At this point the number of alternatives should be limited to a manageable number for the systems analyst to specify. A more detailed, formal cost-benefit analysis can then be carried out. However, the application of traditional cost-benefit analysis will be lengthy and expensive even with a small range of alternatives.

4. Selection — given the alternatives and some best estimates of costs and relative benefits the management, along with the systems analysts, can select the alternative best meeting the planning, controlling and decision making requirements for the organization within a reasonably estimated cost.

5. Detailed design — proceeds along with the detailed design using some form of budget or project management controls to apprise the system sponsors of increasing or decreasing cost and benefit trade-offs.

6. Implementation — the actual installation, training and initial input activities to cut over to the new system.

7. Evaluation — the planned audit and performance criteria applied to the system to foresee the need for system modification or redesign.

The last two life cycle activities mentioned are really the basis of this entire methodology. The activity of implementation is not merely installing a set of computer programs on a computer and giving the users a set of instructions on how to use it. Rather, it is the ongoing activity of keeping the users and sponsors of the system apprised of its impact throughout the life cycle. This is both a behavioral and mechanical process that makes users aware of what is going on and the sponsors are kept up to date on cost estimates.

The system design process is described along with the cost-benefit analysis output and management action in Figure 2.

FORM OF COST-BENEFIT ANALYSIS

The traditional cost-benefit analysis methodology can and has been applied to information systems analysis and design. However, due to the evolutionary nature of the final system configuration the original estimates are often grossly distorted. The only way to make evaluations reasonable is to compare relative cost-benefit scenarios for the range of alternatives under consideration.

As with systems design, the approaches to making relative estimates vary. This approach calls for assumptions that distort the actual figures but will come up with adequate relative cost estimates. Since there exist no acceptable unit costs for development, design and operation, the method will have to accept some arbitrary standard and factor it into the analysis.

The top-down approach would start with the product or desired output of the system and factor it into units of programming and operations based upon the experience of the organization and the systems analysts. By applying units to the accepted standard costs a relative system cost can be estimated.

The overall benefits of the system will be estimated by the system sponsor prior to making an action decision at each stage in the life cycle. The costs will necessarily be evaluated in this stage as an impact or negative benefit as it relates to the output of the system and impact on the rest of the organization. Another benefit from using this approach is to involve management in the design at every stage of development. However, this approach will add time and cost to the design process, but the resulting system will meet management expectations that have been raised throughout the process.

CONCLUSIONS

The reduction of uncertainty about the impact of a major project upon an organization in terms of costs and benefits is a desirable factor in decision-making. In many instances cost-benefit analysis has provided this reduction of uncertainty to decision makers in the private and public areas. However, as projects become more complex the long term results of cost-benefit analysis have not been very accurate.

The design, development and implementation of an information system is a very complex activity characterized by a large number of alternatives. This activity has also been notorious for cost overruns and reduced levels of projected design capabilities.

This article has presented a phased design methodology whose application can make the use of cost-benefit analysis an effective tool even for complex information system projects. This approach takes account of the system design life cycle and applies a flexible and evolutionary cost-benefit analy-

Figure 2.   The Phased Approach to Cost-Benefit Analysis

SYSTEM DESIGN STEP	NATURE OF CB ANALYSIS	MANAGEMENT ACTION
1. Definition	Identify relative costs and benefits of a range of alternative system configurations.	Select an alternative or limit range of alternatives for further specification.
2. Specification	At this step, the associated time estimates should be more clear. Identify hardware cost ranges for each alternative and estimate manpower requirements for associated support levels. Benefits will be descriptively identified.	Since costs are more specific, management can begin to budget for further development. Target a specific alternative to meet desired support level. Iterate through this step until a single alternative is agreed upon.
3. Detailed Definition	The level of system specification is complete enough to provide detailed cost estimates and many quantifiable benefits can be specified.	At this point, the CB analysis should be complete enough to determine if the system specification meets management requirements within available resources. If it does not, iterate back to Step 2 and select another alternative.
4. Selection	Specify cost-benefit tradeoffs within the alternative and present figures.	Select actual configuration for detailed design. Prepare project tracking techniques to maintain cost control.
5. Detailed Design	Throughout this step, project progress reports to management should include detailed tracking against project schedule.	This level of reporting should apprise management of potential cost overruns or delays that will impact later design steps.
6. Implementation	When the system is ready for installation, management will have complete cost information along with a clear understanding of the benefits.	Formal acceptance and checkoff as each module or portion of the system is installed.
7. Evaluation	Throughout the stages of the design process, the accuracy and specificity of the CB should increase. At this time, operating costs and realized benefits should be available.	The evaluation of the overall project at this time will provide a more effective CB methodology for future projects.

sis throughout the life cycle. As each stage in the system design defines a more specific system configuration, the updated CB analysis is completed using increasingly specific and quantifiable information and evaluation. Such a phased approach will avoid the traditional, unrealistic and inaccurate CB analyses that rely on a single application at a very early stage of the MIS design.

REFERENCES

1. D. V. Mathusz, "The Value of Information Concept Applied to Data Systems," *OMEGA,* Vol. 5, No. 5, 1977, p. 594.
2. H. P. Hatry, op. cit.
3. E. A. Tomeski, "Management Information Systems," *The Encyclopedia of Management,* Carl Heyel (ed.), New York: Van Nostrand Reinhold Co., 1972, pp. 496–498.
4. R. N. Anthony, *Planning and Control Systems: A Framework for Analysis,* Boston, MA: Howard Business School, 1965.
5. G. B. Davis, *Management Information Systems: Conceptual Foundations, Structure and Development,* New York: McGraw-Hill, 1974.
6. P. G. W. Keen and M. S. Morton, *Decision Support Systems: An Organizational Perspective,* Reading, MA: Addison-Wesley, 1978.
7. M. A. Lyles, "Making Operational Long-Range Planning for Information Systems," *MIS Quarterly,* Vol. 3, No. 2, 1979, pp. 9–19.
8. E. A. Tomeski, op. cit.
9. K. J. Radford, *Information Systems for Strategic Decisions,* Reston, VA: Reston Publishing Co., Inc., 1978.
10. R. E. Hirsch, "The Value of Information," *The Journal of Accountancy,* 1968, pp. 41–45.
11. R. R. Andrus, "Approaches to Information Evaluation," *MSU Business Topics,* Vol. 19, pp. 40–46.
12. G. A. Feltham, "The Value of Information," *The Accounting Review,* Vol. 43, pp. 684–696.
13. T. J. Mock, "Concepts of Information Value and Accounting," *The Accounting Review,* Vol. 96, pp. 765–778.
14. C. P. Litecky, "Intangibles in Cost/Benefit Analysis," *Journal of Systems Management,* Vol. 32, No. 2, 1981, pp. 15–17.

QUESTIONS

1. Discuss the steps in a cost/benefit analysis.
2. What are several factors that give value to information?
3. At what point, measured in terms of values and costs, is the optimal quality of information produced by an information system?
4. What tend to be the impacts of information technology upon the value and cost of information?
5. Discuss the costs and values of each of the following:
   a. Very detailed data to be stored in the data base.
   b. Very short response times to be provided by the information system.
   c. Very accurate information to be provided by the information system.
6. What difficulties are generally encountered in attempting to estimate the benefits of a planned information system?
7. In what ways can estimates of (a) tangible benefits and (b) intangible benefits be improved?
8. What are the implications of employing a phased approach to cost-benefit analysis?
9. Describe several cost/benefit analysis models or methods that are available for determining the economic feasibility of systems projects.

Integrated MIS: A Case Study*

Effectively planning, controlling, and evaluating the activities of a large corporation requires considerable information. In the "one-man show" business organization, the owner has complete knowledge of operations and can effectively plan and control the enterprise. But when business activities reach the point where reliance on memory is an insecure basis for action, the need for data processing arises. The business' information must be recorded, manipulated, and reported first in manual systems and then in complex automated systems. Finally, the complexities in processing the data become subservient to the basic information needs of the business. Without integration of this data, management may not have access to adequate and consistent information required to plan and control the business effectively.

An integrated management information system (MIS) serves as a substitute or replacement for the personal observations of the "one-man show." It combines the roles of diverse disciplines including marketing, engineering, research and development, manufacturing, accounting, data processing, and management sciences. MIS will never replace the totally integrated information system represented by the "one-man show." An individual's information data base cannot be economically or realistically duplicated because it contains all experience stored since his birth. Nevertheless, an integrated MIS can synthesize a data base, using the most pertinent information available, to supply management information needed for making decisions.

INTEGRATION FACTORS

The "one-man show" information system is totally integrated because the data base and decision-making procedures are limited to a whole unit. In the larger organization, however, the data base and decision-making procedures develop into complex systems, and unless carefully worked out, separation may result in incomplete information and misunderstandings among executives. The information system must be integrated to facilitate coordination of all segments of the business with corporate objectives. The integration of information is requisite for

*By William R. Hindman and Floyd F. Kettering, Jr., *Management Accounting* (August 1973).

enabling effective communication of ideas, plans, and results among management functions.

In MIS, two factors, human and technical, must be considered. Human integration cannot be accomplished without acceptance of the MIS concept by the different functional users. Once achieved, human integration can help establish common ground for mutual understanding of the corporate business. Technical integration is implemented through generation and manipulation of a statistical data base and multiple uses of common data. The data base includes information bearing on all functions within the company — production, marketing, engineering, and accounting. An example of such mutual or multiple uses is labor reporting for use in production control, job scheduling, job cost analysis, standards evaluation, market and product profitability analysis, and accounting records.

An illustration of integrated operations is the consolidation of information for the payroll and personnel functions. An actual program typically would consolidate related functions (e.g., payroll and personnel who worked cooperatively but independently) by creating a master file containing all basic personnel and payroll information which serves personnel, accounting, and payroll. Integration offers opportunities for many additional applications, such as answering "what if" questions. In this example, the new employee file may be used to test the consequences of payroll changes related, for example, to labor union negotiations. In other words, integrated MIS provides an ability to develop a clear picture of the probable financial results of actions before they are taken.

This discussion has considered the "one-man show" and the factors of integration but has neglected a significant question for management accountants: What is accounting's relationship to an integrated management information system? A primary role and responsibility of accounting is to keep score of the company's performance and to provide useful quality information to management. The following case study of the manufacturing and financial segments of a management information system presents accounting's relationship to an integrated management information system and shows how MIS works.

CASE STUDY

The company manufactures major components and supplies them to municipal and industrial contractors. Its two plants, approximately 70 miles apart, mainly conduct machining, fabricating, and assembly operations. The corporate offices are at one of the plant sites where the staff is developing an integrated management information system.

Company management recognizes that the scope of its business has expanded beyond the point where reliance upon memory and verbal communication are adequate management techniques. The business is becoming more difficult to understand, plan for, and control. These are the primary reasons behind the move into MIS. Management recognizes that to achieve an integrated management system, it must tailor the concepts to the business at hand. In designing the manufacturing segment of the management information system, management expended effort to develop:

1. A definition of management objectives
2. Adequate definitions of management responsibilities for planning and controlling operating activities
3. Profit plans and budgets by function
4. A definition of management information needs including determination of reporting needs, timing, and frequency

5. Product definitions
6. Up-to-date bills of material
7. Complete product routings by operation
8. Standard labor hours by operation
9. Improved controlling and reporting of physical flow of material in the plants
10. Controlled production and labor reporting
11. Current standard material price lists

These items are elements of one or more subsystems within the MIS. It is essential for the collection and reporting of valid data that production reporting accurately reflect actual activity and measurement standards and budgets are current and accurate. Therefore, early effort must be expended to improve or develop the basic elements.

To facilitate the implementation of MIS, the company decided to integrate through the use of a computer. Therefore, management took pains to convert existing manual systems to computer systems and to place bill of material processing, route sheet processing, inventory records, and purchased and processed parts requirements determination on the computer.

Now that we have identified the work performed on the foundations, let us look at the general plan for this segment of the company's MIS. The system can be split into two major building blocks—the manufacturing information system and the financial accounting/reporting system.

Manufacturing Information System

The manufacturing information system, Exhibit 1, is a series of modular subsystems. These modules are small building blocks, each block representing a manual, computerized, or combined information processing subsystem. The exhibit identifies how the subsystems interrelate and fit into the manufacturing planning-controlling-reporting system.

To understand how the system works, let us examine one module in more detail. Within the manufacturing overview, the bill of material update subsystem includes input from:

1. Engineering—Change notices and part numbers, new inventory item master information, product structure changes, and standard engineering costs, if any
2. Methods and Standards—Process sheets and standard labor hours by operation
3. Cost Accounting and Manufacturing—Standard labor and overhead rates by work center
4. Purchasing—Standard purchase prices by part

This detail input is processed against the bill of material processor (BOMP) master files to update the files and automatically produce:

1. Edit listings—used by production control to validate accuracy of file update transactions and correct errors
2. Bills of material—used by engineering and production control as formal documentation and for scheduling production
3. Process sheets—used by methods and standards for release to the shop as part of the production package
4. "Where used" lists—used by engineering in identifying common parts usage and to achieve standardization of parts.

As another example the labor control subsystem receives daily labor cards and corrections of prior day's transactions as input. The daily labor activity is processed against the BOMP master files, primarily for labor standards, to make performance calculations and update labor performance files. The automatically produced output includes:

1. Daily labor proof list—used as audit list and for re-input of corrections for labor

Exhibit 1. Manufacturing Information System

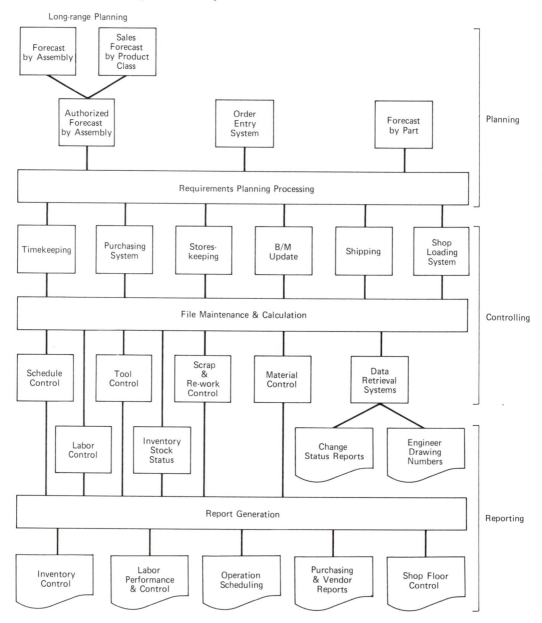

transactions not passing the edit tests of the labor control system

2. Daily labor performance report — distributed to all factory supervisors, it details individual and departmental efficiency against the predetermined labor standards for measurement of performance

3. Weekly manufacturing labor utilization report — used by factory supervisors to measure the ratio of direct to indirect plant personnel

4. Weekly indirect labor utilization report — used by plant managers to analyze the activities of indirect labor

5. Quarterly standards analysis — used by methods and standards personnel to determine accuracy of standards and to identify any trends of improved or deteriorated performance on specific operations and machines

Financial Accounting/Reporting System

The financial accounting/reporting system, Exhibit 2, is also designed in modular subsystems. In addition to the relationships shown in the exhibit, these subsystems integrate into subsystems in the manufacturing information system.

For example, the cost/price estimating subsystem within the financial overview includes input from many sources:

1. Costs — from cost accounting records
2. Assemblies, components, and parts cost lists — as developed using the BOMP master files
3. Standard cost history — from the BOMP update and vouchers payable subsystems
4. Variance analysis by product and job — from job cost files
5. Requests for quotations — from marketing

For new or improved products or unique combinations of components, this input is processed manually to price the request for quotations.

The proposed new prices of standard items are computed using guidelines established by marketing and the updated BOMP files. An updated standard product and component price list is generated and submitted to marketing for review and analysis with market conditions. This approach helps ensure that all standard cost increases have been taken into consideration in setting prices.

As another example, the work-in-process subsystem uses input common to other subsystems within both the financial and manufacturing information systems including:

1. Daily labor cards — from labor control subsystem
2. Material requisitions — from inventory control subsystem
3. Standard maintenance — from bill of material update subsystem

This input is processed utilizing files common to both the financial manufacturing information systems: standards — BOMP master files of purchase price, labor hours, labor rates, and overhead rates — and job cost at standard and actual.

The application of these inputs and files to the work-in-process subsystem maintains the work-in-process files, which, in this case, are actually a component of job cost files. In addition, this subsystem produces accounting distributions of labor and material costs as input to the general ledger subsystem. A subsequent interface of the job cost files, the sales and margin reporting subsystem, and the general ledger subsystem results in the preparation of performance reports and margin and contribution reports.

We have summarized a few of the manufacturing and related accounting elements of the integrated management information system being developed by the company. We will now detail one of the major components, the cost system.

Exhibit 2.   Financial Accounting/Reporting System

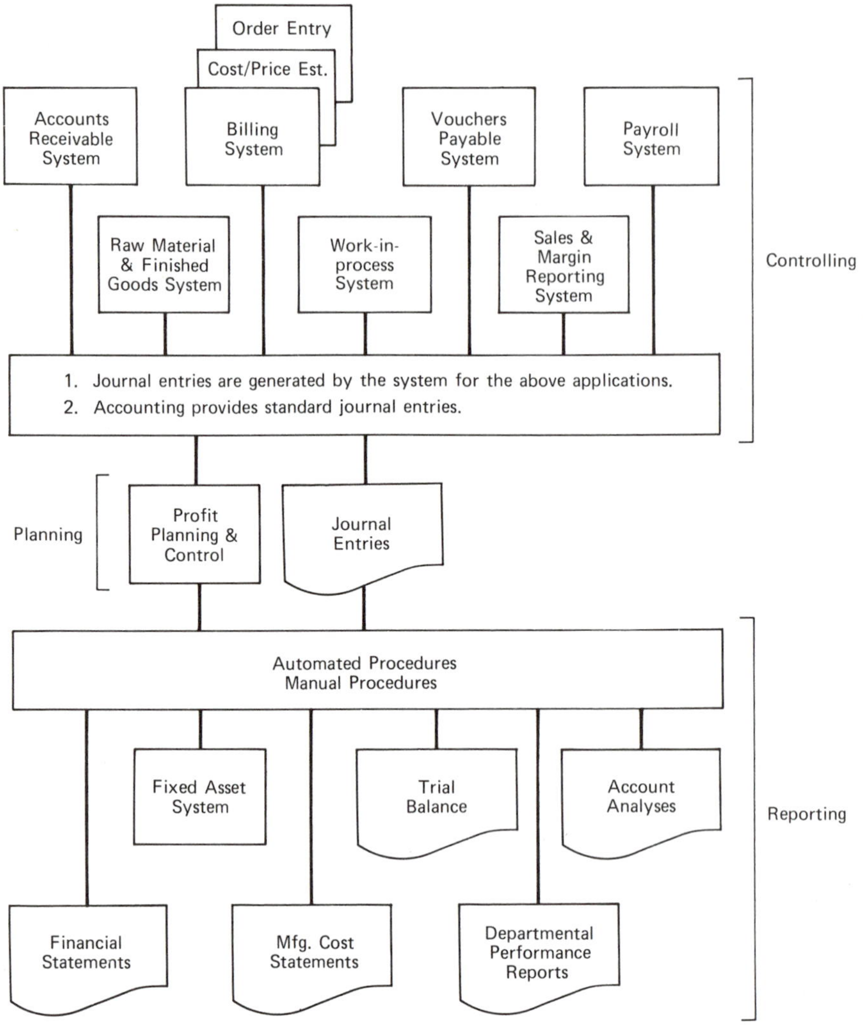

Cost System

The cost system is woven through several subsystems in the financial accounting/reporting system and the manufacturing information system. These related subsystems include:

1.   Raw material and finished goods system
2.   Work-in-process system
3.   Sales and margin reporting system
4.   Storekeeping reporting
5.   Shipping reporting
6.   Timekeeping reporting
7.   Labor control
8.   Material control
9.   B/M update

The cost system is built on interfaces of these subsystems and files maintained by these subsystems.

The explanation of the complex inter-relationships in the new cost system will follow, but first let us consider why this complex system is being developed. The company's old cost accounting procedures accumulated and recorded historical material and labor costs by job. These costs were compared to the estimates originally made in quoting the job but were not utilized as automatic feedback into the estimating system to improve procedures and the quality of estimates. In old cost procedures, standard material prices were used to provide purchasing guidelines, but the standards were not used for costing purposes and had limited use in estimation procedures. The old cost procedures applied burden on a total plantwide rate full absorption basis. These procedures did not reflect differences in overhead between departments. As a result, costs of product groups, which flow through departments in a different manner, were not accurately accumulated. These inaccurate historical costs were subsequently used to determine the gross margin earned by job after the fact. The system of costing did not lend itself to analysis of variances by type and cause.

The Mis Cost System

A standard-direct-job cost system was developed at the company. One purpose of this improved cost system was to provide the company with a foundation for the development of a profit plan. The basic elements of a profit plan include a sound cost system which distinguishes:

1. Directly variable costs, in this case direct material, direct labor, and direct work center overhead, which vary directly with volume.

2. Managed capacity costs, often called controllable or manageable costs, exemplified in the number of clerks needed in relation to the volume of orders processed (They do not vary directly with volume but may vary with significant changes in volume and may be controlled by a responsible manager.)

3. Committed capacity costs, almost completely fixed during the short-run situation and therefore controllable only by long-range planning (They are also termed noncontrollable costs, standby costs, or pure fixed costs. Executive salaries, building depreciation, and insurance are examples of committed costs.)

The "standard-direct-job cost system" provides the company with separation of directly variable, managed capacity and committed capacity costs. The system also measures direct costs — namely labor, material, and overhead — against predetermined standards for:

1. Labor hours/piece — operation routing file
2. Labor rate/hour — work center file
3. Material price/unit — item master file
4. Material usage — product structure file
5. Overhead rate/direct labor hour — work center file

Direct costs such as labor and material are generally readily identifiable. It is much more difficult, however, to determine which elements of direct overhead cost are directly variable, managed or committed. The approach used to identify directly variable costs may be a combination of techniques:

1. Scatter charts — A simple plotting of expenses against some measure of production volume such as direct labor hours to identify patterns
2. Discussion and questionnaires — Operating personnel, factory foremen, and general supervisors have a vast knowledge of the relationships of expenses and

production volume which can often be helpful in deciding which expenses should be classified as directly variable or as managed capacity. This knowledge, however, requires careful interpretation for accounting purposes.

3. Functional classification — Measuring costs where they arise fixes responsibility for cost incurrence and determines the causes of cost incurred. This often helps in deciding degree of variability.

4. Correlation/regression analysis — A statistical analysis of cost behavior using computer programs available on most time-sharing computer systems often provides a rapid and accurate determination of cost elements to be included in direct overhead.

Advantages of the correlation/regression analysis approach where larger volumes of data are involved include:

1. Reduction of study time and costs
2. Improvement in study accuracy
3. Determination of cost behavior in relation to several measures of production volume
4. Identification of the measure of production volume having the highest correlation to the cost studied (in this case, direct labor hours)

The analysis of overhead costs at the company produced two levels of directly variable costs: the department level and the plant level. Departmental overhead costs vary closely with direct productive labor hours within the department. Such costs are assigned to the department and become its responsibility. Each factory department is assigned a unique rate. Plant overhead costs vary closely with direct productive labor hours for the entire plant. Such costs are plantwide and the responsibility of the plant manager. The plant has an overhead rate in addition to the overhead rate specified for each plant department.

Variance Reports. The cost system provides for measuring and reporting variances from labor, material, and overhead standards by assigned responsibility.

Departmental performance reports are issued monthly to each production department supervisor, comparing actual performance against standards and budgets. These reports detail expenses incurred by type — direct, managed, or committed.

Departments without direct productive activities receive only a report of managed and committed expenses. These expenses are reported by assigned responsibility and are measured against predetermined budgets, flexible budgets for managed costs and fixed budgets for committed costs.

The performance reports issued by department provide the company with improved cost control and measurements of performance.

The departmental results are summarized and sent to the next higher level of responsibility. For example, factory departmental results are summarized in plant performance reports for each of the two plants. These reports are combined at the manufacturing level with other manufacturing departments, such as purchasing and inventory control, that serve both plants.

Contribution Reports. To provide improved measurements of profitability and pricing for the company, a set of reports measures contribution to income from operations. An example is the product contribution report, which identifies sales by product group and provides a series of measurements:

1. Product sales as a percent of total sales
2. Amount and percent of variance from budgeted sales
3. Gross margin at standard and gross margin after deducting identifiable direct cost variances

4. Amount and percent of net contribution after deducting distributed costs, capacity costs identified as having some relationship to sales volume
5. Net contribution by product as a percent of total net contribution

The set of contribution reports also includes a more detailed report by job and reports by customer type. Additional reports may also be presented by product group, customer, salesman, and sales territory depending on how profitability is to be analyzed. The performance and contribution reports are summarized in the company's statement of income, which presents companywide measurements of performance, cost control, and profitability. Performance and cost control are measured by variances, in amount and percent, from budget and by percentage variance from the prior year's actual.

Distributed Costs. The measurements in this case study take into account distributed costs. These costs are actually capacity (managed and committed) costs which have some apparent relationship to sales. The purpose for distributing capacity costs is to recognize as many costs as can be reasonably associated with a product in determining net contribution for analysis of profitability. The analysis of profitability after distribution of capacity costs may be performed on any reporting period desired, monthly, quarterly or annually. A contribution report should be prepared monthly to measure gross margin at standard and gross margin after deducting identifiable direct costs variances. For this case it was decided to perform distribution of capacity costs on a monthly basis. Many companies perform such an analysis only on a semiannual or annual basis.

The techniques used to identify direct overhead are also used to determine if there is some reasonable basis for distributing capacity costs. The possible allocation bases considered in this instance were sales dollars, direct material costs, and direct engineering costs.

The capacity costs analyzed to determine if they were distributable included costs from manufacturing, marketing, engineering, and also from administration.

Costs which are not direct or distributed to specified products are deducted from the total net contribution of all products to arrive at the net income from operations as presented on the company's statement of income.

The Overall System

Now, let us see where the cost system fits in the overall corporate information system (Exhibit 3). First, there must be planning by engineering, manufacturing, and marketing; in fact, everyone gets into the planning act. Accounting should plan for the expenditures for which it is directly responsible and for the financing required by all corporate expenditures. For the other areas, accounting should serve mainly as the scorekeeper and controller, reflecting, reviewing, and challenging the figures associated with the plans prepared by the other functions.

Once plans are established, information must flow, and the cost systems interact (as shown in Exhibit 3) with:

1. Material reporting system — actual material requisitions
2. Labor reporting system — actual labor hours spent
3. Costed B/M processor system — planned material and labor
4. Payroll system — actual pay earned
5. Billing system — actual sales made
6. Accounts payable system — actual material prices
7. General ledger system — budgeted operating results

Now the management information system is at work, collecting and recording

Exhibit 3. The Cost System in MIS

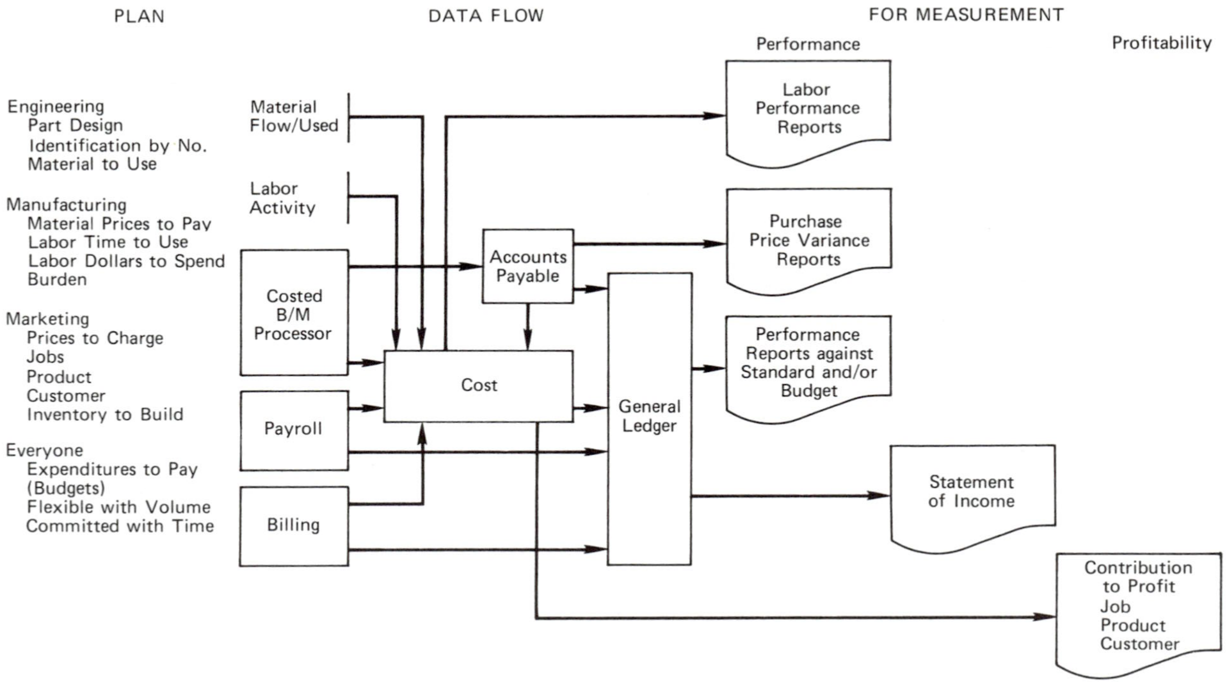

PLAN

DATA FLOW

FOR MEASUREMENT

Performance

Profitability

Engineering
Part Design
Identification by No.
Material to Use

Manufacturing
Material Prices to Pay
Labor Time to Use
Labor Dollars to Spend
Burden

Marketing
Prices to Charge
Jobs
Product
Customer
Inventory to Build

Everyone
Expenditures to Pay
(Budgets)
Flexible with Volume
Committed with Time

Material Flow/Used

Labor Activity

Costed B/M Processor

Payroll

Billing

Accounts Payable

Cost

General Ledger

Labor Performance Reports

Purchase Price Variance Reports

Performance Reports against Standard and/or Budget

Statement of Income

Contribution to Profit
Job
Product
Customer

actual results from day-to-day business transactions and comparing these to predetermined plans for measurement of performance and profitability.

The improved cost system is fundamental to the management information system. It furnishes the company with a foundation for the construction of a profit plan and provides control for the profit plan through improved measurement of performance, cost control, profitability, and pricing. In general, management's understanding of its business is improved and flexibility is provided to allow changes to the business and its operating system. The company's integrated MIS for manufacturing will supply:

1. Information for manufacturing cost control by comparing actual direct and indirect costs with planned and standard costs by area of responsibility
2. Exception reporting by identifying variances from predetermined plans or standards
3. Guidelines for sound pricing policies, reliable cost estimating, and product-mix production decisions
4. Guidelines for standardizing production by identifying common parts usage and generally improving the availability of adequate product information
5. Information for evaluating the effect of varying capacities on product costs and other "what if" production alternatives
6. Profitability measurements by products, customers, jobs and company

COMMUNICATION FACTORS

Achieving benefits through the implementation of the integrated management information system requires total commitment, participation, involvement, and understanding by all management personnel. They must communicate clearly with each other, especially when using special terms such as "standard" in referring to a standard product, a standard part, a standard operation, or a performance standard. These terms require complete, clear, and concise definitions to prevent confusion in design of the MIS.

Good communication also demands clearly understood identification of various items such as: part numbers, account numbers, or operation numbers. Whatever the item, the rules for identification must be carefully set down and followed.

The project to implement MIS must have strong direction, coordination, and control to prevent floundering and wheel-spinning in the design and implementation phases. Such direction must come from the top of the organization. Although implementation responsibilities may be delegated, the desire to achieve the implementation of a good MIS must be communicated to the entire management team.

CONCLUSION

We have just described the development of an important major segment of the MIS. The MIS program does not stop once a manufacturing system is implemented. The cost system is integrated into the accounting and manufacturing information system, and these systems must be integrated with the marketing and engineering information systems. Once this complete integration is achieved, what follows?

The integrated management information system can become more sophisticated through the addition of terminals to capture and transmit data to a central processing location and by changing from batch processing to direct computer entry or "on-line" processing. This operation could lead to an executive information service. The executive may have a keyboard console and visual display screen with instant access to information and the ability to request complex analyses, correlations, and "what if" situations. Regular reporting, then, could be substantially reduced since the executive would call, as required, for whatever information he needed.

QUESTIONS

1. By what means is a management information system integrated?
2. What are the major modules of a manufacturing information system?
3. What basic informational items must be developed before the manufacturing segment of a management information system may be implemented?
4. Describe the inputs, processing, and outputs of a typical module within the manufacturing information system.
5. What are the major modules of a financial accounting/reporting system?
6. How does the cost system link together the manufacturing information system and the financial accounting/reporting system?
7. Describe several key reports that are produced by the management information system of a manufacturing firm.
8. How may the presentation of reports to managers be made more effective by the use of current systems technology?
9. By what means may information overload be avoided?

Corporate Strategy and the Design of Computerized Information Systems*

The implications for strategic management of computerized information systems (CIS) have been the focus of much speculation in both practitioner and research journals. It has been argued, for instance, that the explosive improvements in computer hardware technology and related software design have made it possible for senior managers to exercise close supervision and control of subordinates whose performances they would not otherwise have been able to track in a timely and detailed fashion.[1] For instance, senior managers can now directly access the data bases of managers reporting to them and can develop their own measures of performance in addition to those that are formally reported. The reliability of the information they obtain is also presumably enhanced as a consequence.

On the other hand, convincing arguments have been presented that advances in the design of decision support systems (DSS) and the availability of computer terminals and personal computers to a broad spectrum of managers decentralize decision making to an unprecedented, and unexpected, degree. For example, plant managers can exercise control over labor utilization and production scheduling with minimal involvement from corporate or division management.

A third perspective that has recently been offered is that despite all the excitement and the apparently stunning breakthroughs, the impact of computerized information systems on top management has been and will continue to be negligible.[2]

These three highly disparate points of view have been advanced in a most convincing fashion with apparently unassailable logic and are supported by empirical, albeit somewhat anecdotal, evidence. It is not the intention of this article to champion or denigrate any one of these points of view. In fact, we consider all three perspectives to be valid. The first two points of view, that both centralization and decentralization are supported by CIS, suggest that alternatives that vary a great deal are offered by CIS. The third point of view, that the impact of CIS on the nature of top management responsibility has been and will continue to be insignificant, is not inconsistent with the contention that the way in which this responsibility is discharged can be influenced by the design of the CIS.

We interpret the empirical evidence as indicating that very different alternative designs and purposes of CIS exist. Here we discuss how to select and orient the design of the CIS in order to obtain the desired impact upon the strategic management processes of the organization.

THE IMPACT OF CIS ON STRATEGIC MANAGEMENT

CIS design that is chosen to be consonant with the strategy, structure, and style components of an organization's administrative system will contribute to more effective management.[3] The rationale underlying this proposition is that the CIS, as an element of the organization's planning and control system, should meet with the consistency imperative of effective administrative system design. The experiences of companies that have been proactive and pioneering in CIS design tend to support this proposition. There have been instances of both gratifying success[4] and dismal failure,[5] thus strongly corroborating the importance of appropriate design.

CIS capabilities presently offer management more choices in terms of alternatives than those previously available to organizations. That CIS capabilities offer new options and strategic advantages has been amply demonstrated. For instance, the war between Walden Books and B. Dalton has been fought mostly on the CIS battlefield.[6]

Based on these propositions, it follows that identifying the range of CIS options and selecting the most suitable is of critical importance. We identify here what we view as key dimensions of choice with regard to the design of the CIS that managers should consider. Furthermore, we offer guidelines with regard to how to best tailor and exploit CIS capabilities from the perspective of alternative management viewpoints. These key dimensions and guidelines are discussed below.

KEY DIMENSIONS OF CIS DESIGN

The designers of the organization's administrative system have begun to recognize the fundamental differences between computer systems that have been set up to process a large number of transactions (record-keeping) efficiently and accurately and systems that are intended to aid managerial decision making.[7] While it is not entirely impractical to implement both transaction processing systems (TPS) and decision support systems effectively, it must be recognized that the hardware, software, expert personnel and, most importantly, management style needed to perform each of these two tasks efficiently are vastly different.[8]

Trade-offs will almost inevitably have to be made and it is better for them to be conscious rather than arrived at by default. A key design choice, therefore, is where on the TPS–DSS spectrum the organization should position itself in terms of hardware, software, and personnel choices. The TPS is inherently oriented toward programmed decisions,[9] whereas the DSS is more appropriate to semi-structured problems and nonprogrammable decisions.[10]

It is important to note that the practical extremes of the TPS-DSS continuum do not entirely exclude either capability. There is a minimum or threshold TPS capability that all CIS should possess. A similar argument might be made for DSS capability. One might go a step further and maintain that, in fact, if TPS are inadequate or not at critical mass, then DSS are not possible because of the lack of essential data in electronic form. However, the relative importance given to either orientation is what is at issue, in the universal context of scarce resources.

A second key decision related to TPS/DSS posture is the choice of hardware configurations. At one end of the spectrum one can visualize mutually independent microcomputers and, at the other end, a single mainframe, possibly with remote terminals. Between these extremes lies a wide variety of options, such as networked minicomputers connected to a central, host mainframe.

The independent microcomputer extreme may be appropriate, for example, for an organization engaged in engineering consulting, with dedicated micros in the various departments such as civil, electrical, and chemical engineering, whose strategy is based on the distinctive competence of the professionals in these departments. Each engineering department, it could be argued, needs to have immediate access to its own data without necessarily having to share it with other departments. At the other extreme is an airline emphasizing efficiency and customer service with a large mainframe hooked up to numerous remote terminals. Reservations must be current and accurate while being shared by all agents throughout the country. In between these two extremes would lie the manufacturer of a large variety of automotive parts in different locations throughout the country whose viability depends on the ability to maintain quality, control costs, and manage inventories in each of its nationwide manufacturing locations. Slight inaccurancies, however, may be tolerable in order to achieve larger savings. In this last case, a headquarters mainframe and distributed minicomputers may best serve the organization's strategy.

The third key dimension is not as readily obvious as the previous two. A subtle, but significant, influence on CIS design is the nature of the related policies adopted by the organization. These policies could address, among other issues, the following:

— The criteria for acquisition of hardware and software. For example, should all new microcomputers be required to be compatible with a particular mainframe?
— The locus of authority for data entry and retrieval. For example, who may retrieve confidential computerized marketing information?
— The appropriate use of consultants.[11] For example, may functional departments hire their own computer consultants?

A flexible approach to these CIS-related policies would foster different managerial responses and attitudes than would a rigorous and strict set of policies.[12] In organizations where strategies demand creativity, independence, and adaptive behavior among managers, as in innovative consulting organizations, a flexible approach to policy formulation is probably appropriate. On the other hand, where the efficient execution of clearly defined responsibilities is at the heart of an organization's strategy, a bias toward a comprehensive and strict articulation of policies is probably warranted.

The preceding three dimensions are perhaps the most important determinants of the appropriate design of the CIS. Several other dimensions can be identified, some of which will be discussed later; however, it does appear as though choices made with regard to the TPS/DSS posture, the micro/mini/mainframe configuration, and the flexible/strict policy stance are crucial. Once these choices are made, the pattern of decisions with regard to the other characteristics of CIS's appear to be largely determined.

Granting, for the moment, that this assertion regarding the dominance of these three dimensions is essentially correct, it follows that the choices with regard to the CIS are defined by a three-dimensional space. This conceptualization of the feasible (and vital) space for decision making regarding the design of the CIS is diagrammed in Figure 1.

Figure 1.   Key Dimensions of Strategic Choice in CIS Design

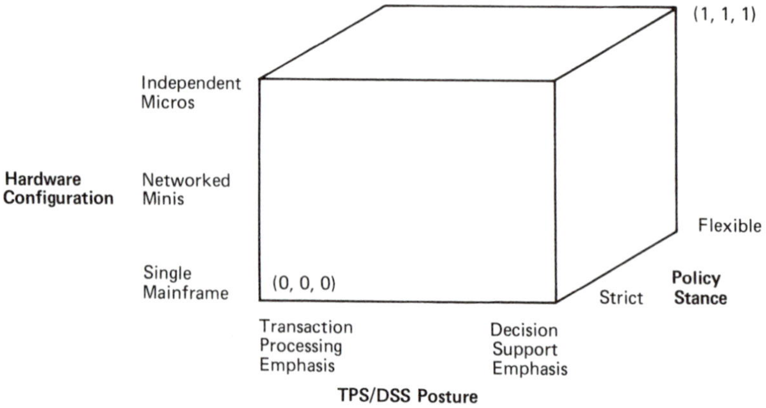

The significance of these three dimensions of choice in CIS design is readily apparent in Figure 1. Organizations appropriately positioning themselves at one extreme, (0, 0, 0) would of necessity be vastly different in strategic characteristics than organizations that justifiably select the other extreme (1, 1, 1). On the one hand, one can visualize a large, centralized, efficiency-oriented, stable organization with a top-down approach to decision making. On the other hand, one can conjecture a smaller, decentralized, effectiveness-oriented, growing organization with a bottom-up decision making style.

Organizations positioned at the (0, 0, 0) corner of the matrix would appear to be "transactional" in character. The (1, 1, 1) corner of the matrix, in contrast, would appear to be the appropriate location of organizations that can be characterized as "decisional." To facilitate further discussion, we shall, therefore, refer to the (0, 0, 0) corner as "transactional" and the (1, 1, 1) as "decisional."

ADDITIONAL DIMENSIONS OF CIS DESIGN

A variety of other decisions relating to CIS design appear to be closely linked to the organization's administrative system. These decisions, however, are substantially driven by the choices made with regard to the TPS/DSS posture, hardware configuration, and policy stance. Consequently they are perhaps best made following a determination of the organization's preferred positioning along the three key dimensions. The endeavor in the context of the additional dimensions identified below is to ensure that consistent decisions are made. An erroneous decision or an undesirable situation resulting from the failure to make a decision with regard to these dimensions could lessen the positive impact of correct, mutually consistent decisions along the three key dimensions.

These additional dimensions essentially reflect aspects of the structure of the MIS function in the organization:

— The emphasis on personnel who are "dedicated" functional specialists with close ties to particular user departments.[13] Examples of these specialists would be the accounting systems analysts and personnel data base administrators. Alternatively, the emphasis would be on personnel whose capabilities are in the areas of information technology in general, and who are primarily associated with the corporate headquarters rather than departments or functional areas. The dedicated, functional specialists would fit in with a more decentralized, flexible, decision-support-oriented approach. The other extreme would be more in keeping with the choice of centralized information technologists.

— The existence of CIS/MIS departments in the subunits of the organization, possibly in addition to a centralized department in the corporate office. The obvious extreme alternative here is to have only a single centralized CIS/MIS department.

— The reporting relationship of the head of the CIS/MIS department to corporate management. The department could report to a "line" general manager (CEO/COO/Executive VP) in the situation where decision support is given a great deal of importance. Alternatively, where transaction processing dominates, the CIS/MIS department head could report to a corporate-level staff executive such as the Controller or Financial Vice-President. This possibility was often adopted in the early days of CIS/MIS development.

The proposed relationship between these three structure-oriented dimensions of CIS design and the original three key dimensions of choice is illustrated in Figure 2. As the preceding discussion of the structural aspects of the CIS function suggests, the choices that are made vis-à-vis the key dimensions identified earlier can greatly facilitate the making of effective and consistent decisions in other aspects of CIS design.

GENERIC STRATEGIES AND CIS DESIGN

The significance and conceptual validity of the three key dimensions can perhaps be assessed by evaluating the relationship between these dimensions and the concepts of generic strategy that have earned widespread credence in recent years. Three of these accepted definitions of generic strategy have been developed by Glueck (1976), Miles and Snow (1978), and Porter (1980).[14]

Glueck identifies growth, stability, and retrenchment as basic alternatives between which organizations should choose. A growth strategy makes a decision-support, flexible orientation imperative in order to provide the

Figure 2. Key Design Dimensions and the CIS Departmental Structure

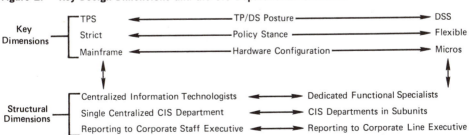

information base and climate that can sustain organizational growth. Stability, on the other hand, mandates an efficiency orientation that can enhance profits without an increase in volume of activity.

The relationship of retrenchment strategies to the key dimensions is possibly less clear-cut. Retrenchment that focuses on determining which business segments or product lines should be eliminated from the corporate portfolios would require a continuing emphasis on decision support. Transaction processing in relation to the components of the business that are dropped can be eliminated, thus reducing the absolute magnitude of the TPS component of the CIS. On the other hand, retrenchment that relies on merely reducing the volume of activity across the board places few demands on the DSS component of the CIS. The TPS component should probably receive more attention in this mode of retrenchment, as volume reductions will have to be accompanied by increases in efficiency if the organization is to enhance or regain profitability.

Porter's three generic strategies also appear to map quite well onto the three dimensions of CIS design. Cost-efficiency strategies demand a transactional (0, 0, 0) (Figure 1) posture while the need to identify and maintain differentiation strategies can

be readily linked to the decisional (1, 1, 1) end of the spectrum. A strategy of focus, however, does not *a priori* suggest a bias in favor of one or the other extreme along the dimensions of CIS design. If focus means doing a few things well, a transactional emphasis may be appropriate. If focus means identifying niches on an on-going basis, because the organization wishes to grow, the bias could be more toward the decisional extreme.

Finally, the Miles and Snow typology displays a logically supportable relationship with the key dimensions. An organization that is a defender would clearly be best served by a transactional emphasis in CIS design. A prospector, on the other hand, almost by definition, requires a decisional orientation. An analyzer requires a more balanced posture that can vary depending on top management's decision-making style.

The relationship between these generic strategies and the key dimensions is illustrated in Figure 3.

APPLYING THE FRAMEWORK

The practical significance of this framework can be assessed by reviewing its applicability to two different corporate contexts. For example, a company in the business of overnight pick-up and delivery of small packages

Figure 3.   Generic Strategies and the Key Dimensions of CIS Design

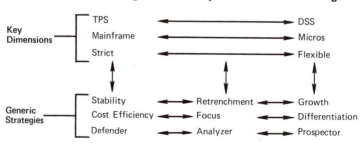

illustrates the "stability, cost efficiency, and defender" (Figure 3) end of the spectrum of generic strategies. At the "growth, differentiation, and prospector" end of the spectrum would be an acquisition-oriented conglomerate.

In the overnight, small-package business, reliability and cost efficiency are the key requirements for survival and success. Both reliability and cost efficiency in this business are obtained by selecting the most appropriate equipment (aircraft, communications, trucks, etc.), by taking advantage of economies of scale, and by careful routing of the daily itinerary of individual aircraft. These imperatives should, therefore, drive the choice of integrated communications and computer equipment and practices. For instance, one of the most successful companies in this business recognized the implications of these basic requirements for organizational success when computerizing the daily, real-time routing of its pick-up vans.

At first glance, the obvious avenue to accomplishing the computerization of its van routing appeared to be a decentralized, flexible, DSS-oriented approach with microcomputers located at each office or airport with voice communication to individual van drivers, as done by taxicab companies. A closer examination of the situation suggested, however, that a strict, centralized, TPS-oriented approach using mainframe computers and satellite-based communications, with identical dumb terminals in vans, would be preferable for a variety of reasons.

First and foremost, the key to reliability and cost efficiency in terms of daily operations was seen to lie in the routing decisions for aircraft. These decisions could best be made centrally with a real-time awareness of package volume at each airport location. This volume results from thousands of individual transactions aggregated at hundreds of airports. Second, voice communication with individual drivers of vans was severely impeded by the fact that, unlike taxi drivers, these drivers were out of their vans for substantial periods of time in order to pick up and hand-deliver packages. The use of satellite-based communications, between a central computer facility and terminals in vans, was seen as desirable. The terminals would receive updated routings even when the driver was out of the van. Centralized receipt of pick-up requests would also enable more efficient routing of vans to locations served by more than one local office, thus ruling out the use of microcomputers in the individual offices. Third, the algorithms for optimal routing of aircraft and even of vans were complex and required mainframe capacities and speeds for timely operations. Fourth, and finally, these algorithms were constantly being improved and it was simpler to test and introduce innovations in one central location, as opposed to dozens or hundreds of decentralized computing facilities.

The relevance and value of the framework that we propose is corroborated by this example. Application of the framework suggests apparently counterintuitive solutions to a key problem in a particular strategic context. These solutions upon further examination, however, appear to be the correct approach to adopt in this context.

In the second example, at the other end of the spectrum, the decision as to appropriate acquisition targets for a conglomerate appears to require a flexible, DSS-oriented approach, using microcomputers. The acquisition analysis carried out at the corporate level would initially require the use of microcomputers as terminals to access external data bases and pull out information for subsequent analysis using the internally developed search routines. This exercise would result in the development of a preliminary list of acquisition candidates. This list would then be subject to further intensive, spreadsheet-oriented analyses.

In this growth-oriented context, where the mode is one of prospecting for new opportunities, the CIS decisions suggested by the framework developed in this article again appear to be valid. Both examples reinforce the validity and utility of the framework. The utility of the framework is particularly evident in the first example where the counterintuitive solution suggested by the framework was shown upon further analysis to be justified.

CONCLUSION

The basic thrust of our article, that there should be a match between the design of the CIS and the strategic management choices of the organization, has been explored from a pragmatic perspective. The key dimensions of the design of the CIS that have been identified define possible alternatives that display vastly different characteristics. These very different characteristics are related to particular strategies. Managers with strategic responsibilities and CIS designers thus have the beginnings of a framework for a fruitful dialogue. This article, it is hoped, offers preliminary guidelines as to the nature and direction of the decisions that are likely to promote a mutually supportive relationship between the design of the CIS and the strategic management of the organization.

NOTES

1. See: *Wall Street Journal*, "Direct Data," 12 January 1983; *Wall Street Journal*, "Automated Self-Service Machines Spread after Their Success in Banks," 21 July 1983.

2. See J. Dearden, "Will the Computer Change the Job of Top Management?" *Sloan Management Review*, Fall 1983, pp. 57–60.
3. See: L. M. R. Calingo, J. C. Camillus, P. Jenster, and T. S. Raghunathan, "Strategic Management and Organizational Action: A Conceptual Synthesis" (University of Pittsburgh: Working Paper Series, WP-527); J. C. Camillus, "Strategic Management: Reflections on an Alternative Paradigm" (University of Pittsburgh: Working Paper Series, WP-476).
4. See *Data Management*, "SABRE — Realtime Benchmark Has the Winning Ticket," September 1981, p. 26.
5. See *Sun Oil Company* (A) and (B) (Boston: HBS Case Services #9-170-033/034, 1970).
6. See: W. R. King, "Strategic Planning for Management Information Systems," *MIS Quarterly*, March 1978, pp. 27–37; *Business Week*, "Walden Books: Countering B. Dalton by Aping Its Computer Operations," 8 October 1979, p. 116.
7. See Camillus (WP-476).
8. See P. G. W. Keen and M. S. Scott Morton, *Decision Support Systems: An Organizational Perspective* (Reading, MA: Addison-Wesley, 1978).
9. See H. A. Simon, *The New Science of Management Decision* (New York: Harper and Row, 1960).
10. See Keen and Scott Morton (1978).
11. See A. L. Lederer, "Going Outside or 'Why Buy a Programmer when You Can Rent One for Less?'" *Proceedings of the Eighteenth Annual Computer Personnel Research Conference of the ACM*, 1981, pp. 351–370.
12. See D. McGregor, *The Human Side of Enterprise* (New York: McGraw-Hill, 1960).
13. See J. C. Camillus, "Designing a Capital Budgeting System That Works," *Long Range Planning*, April 1984, pp. 57–60.
14. See: W. Glueck, *Business Policy, Strategy Formation and Management Action* (New York: McGraw-Hill, 1976); R. E. Miles and C. C. Snow, *Organizational Strategy: Structure and Process* (New York: McGraw-Hill, 1978); M. E. Porter, *Competitive Strategy* (New York: The Free Press, 1980).

QUESTIONS

1. What are three points of view with respect to the impacts of computerized information systems upon an organization's strategic management?

2. Describe three key dimensions of computerized information system design.

3. Describe other important but less critical dimensions of computerized information system design.

4. The mode of processing (i.e., batch versus online) is not mentioned in the article. Does it represent an additional dimension of computerized information system design?

5. Identify and define the generic strategies that are mentioned in the article.

6. Describe the relationships among the generic strategies and the key dimensions of computerized information system design.

7. Describe one example of a firm that illustrates the "stability, cost-efficiency, defender" end of the spectrum of generic strategies; and discuss the key choices of computerized information system design that pertain to your example.

8. Describe an example of a firm that illustrates the "growth, differentiation, prospector" end of the spectrum of generic strategies; and discuss the key choices of computerized information system design that pertain to your example.

9. Describe an example of a firm that illustrates the "retrenchment, focus, analyzer" center of the spectrum of generic strategies, and discuss the key choices of computerized information system design that pertain to your example.

TOPIC THREE

Systems Implementation, Management, and Evaluation

NATURE OF SYSTEMS IMPLEMENTATION

Systems implementation consists of transforming requirements and design specifications into an operational information system. The system on paper becomes a system of physical resources. If the implemented information system is computer-based, it will be composed of computer hardware, computer software, supplies, facilities, data, and people.

The systems implementation phase is generally viewed as following the systems design phase and preceding the systems operations phase. However, a broader view is that the implementation phase extends back into the systems analysis phase and projects forward into the systems operations phase.

Systems implementation projects span a wide spectrum. On one end of the spectrum is a project that involves a minor change, such as a revised transaction processing procedure, and does not require additional resources. On the other end of the spectrum is a project that requires the revision of the entire information system and the acquisition of major additional resources, e.g., a new computer system.

Most systems implementation projects within this spectrum exhibit certain common characteristics. They tend to involve very lengthy periods of time, as compared to the periods devoted to systems analysis and design. Thus, the costs for implementation generally far exceed those for analysis and design. Also, systems implementation projects often have a direct and weighty impact upon the users.

ACTIVITIES DURING THE SYSTEMS IMPLEMENTATION PHASE

A variety of activities are performed during the implementation phase of a typical systems project. While the particular set of activities varies from project to project, it often includes the following:

1. Selection of personnel to operate the new system
2. Training of personnel to operate the new system
3. Detailed design of the new system, including programming and development of printer spacing diagrams
4. Documentation of the design of the new system
5. Testing of newly written programs

100

6. Mailing of requests to computer hardware and software vendors for proposals concerning the new system
7. Evaluation of proposals from vendors
8. Acquisition of computer hardware and software resources from selected vendors
9. Physical installation of computer hardware and other facilities
10. Conversion of files to newly acquired storage media
11. Preparation of standards concerning the operation of the new system

These varied activities may in turn give rise to additional activities having the purpose of controlling and coordinating their use. One instance is the activity of communication. Other examples are noted in a later section.

FEASIBILITY REQUIREMENTS

Underlying most implementation projects are feasibility concerns. While these concerns first arise during the earlier phases of systems development, they are most acute during the implementation phase. The major feasibility concerns can be expressed by the following questions:

1. Will the existing state of information technology be adequate to satisfy the requirements and specifications of the system to be implemented, i.e., is it *technically feasible?*
2. Will the realized economic benefits exceed the expected costs, i.e., is the system *economically feasible?*
3. Will the system be accepted and effectively used by the personnel for whom it is designed, i.e., is the system *operationally feasible?*
4. Will the system be completed within the expected implementation period, i.e., is the system *schedule feasible?*

FAILURES OF SYSTEMS IMPLEMENTATION PROJECTS

Each systems project carries the seeds of possible failure as well as the hopes of success. As suggested by the above feasibility concerns, failures can be classified as technical, economic, or people-related.

Technical failures often occur because the system design is inadequate. For instance, the designed information system may not provide appropriate decision-oriented information to managerial decision makers, or may not provide the information in a sufficiently timely manner. Another type of technical failure occurs because the designed information system is technically infeasible. The computer capabilities specified in the design may not be currently available, for example. A third type of technical failure occurs because of schedule infeasibility. That is, a new system cannot be implemented within a needed time period.

Economic failures occur because the economic benefits do not exceed the costs. Failures of this type may be due to the fact that suitable economic feasibility analyses were not applied. They may also be due to the fact that managers grossly overestimated the system's intangible benefits or underestimated its development or operating costs. For instance, managers may expect a newly designed data base system to provide considerable benefits through improved decision making; however, the resulting benefits may be marginal at best. They may expect a newly acquired transaction processing software package to be instantly useable when acquired; however, the package may require extensive modification costs before it can be used satisfactorily.

People related failures occur because of operational infeasibility. Sometimes the employees or managers who are to use the new system simply do not understand fully how to use it; sometimes they become afflicted with "computer mystique." More often they offer resistance, usually due to fears that the new system will downgrade or eliminate their jobs.

STRATEGIES FOR SUCCESSFUL IMPLEMENTATION

Many of the foregoing failures can be prevented by the use of sound implementation procedures or strategies. Two of the articles included in this section suggest a variety of implementation strategies.

The article by Multinovich and Vlahovich divides implementation strategies into two categories: people-related strategies and system-related strategies. Because people-related problems are the more numerous, the primary emphasis is upon the former. Thus, the authors discuss several ways of establishing effective communication with the intended users of new systems, ways of involving users in the implementation process, and ways of providing simple and understandable interfaces between the users and the system. With respect to system-related strategies, the authors stress the need to plan the implementation beforehand and to evaluate the implemented system after the implementation activities have been completed.

The article by Boer and Barcus presents a case study of a systems implementation project, focusing upon the technical and economic concerns. This case study clearly shows the relationship of the implementation phase to the system and information requirements developed during the systems analysis phase. It emphasizes the evaluation of vendors, a key implementation activity, in terms of a variety of specific requirements.

OPERATION AND MANAGEMENT OF INFORMATION SYSTEMS

At the end of the implementation phase a new or improved information subsystem enters the operational phase. It joins the remainder of the information system in serving the users of the organization of which it is a part.

An organization must devote almost as much attention to the major body of the information system that is currently in operational status as it does to the portion currently undergoing development. A variety of activities must be performed. Also, certain issues must be confronted on a continuing basis. Most of these activities and issues are organizational and/or managerial in nature.

Systems Organization Activities and Issues. The information system function, like other functions within any enterprise, must be organized in order to fulfill its several roles. With respect to its systems development role, as we have seen, the function must organize to conduct systems development projects. Typically these organizational units consist of transitory project teams that are focused on particular application areas, such as the accounts payable transaction processing system. In some cases they are focused on a system component, such as the organization's data base, or on a key management activity, such as strategic decision support. These teams are generally comprised of professional systems analysts and users; often they are supervised by systems development managers and supported by staff specialists.

With respect to the operational information system, the information system function has the traditional role of providing computer service to users. It also has the role of providing technical advice and assistance to users and to top management. The former role has been described as its "manufacturing" role, while the latter role has been characterized as its "distribution and technology transfer" role.

During the process of organization to fulfill these roles, such issues as the following arise:

1. What specific responsibility units should be established within the information system function?
2. How should the information system units be structured in relationship to each other, in order to reflect sound principles of organizational independence and to achieve optimal efficiency?
3. To what extent should the information system function be decentralized throughout the organizational structure of the enterprise? What degree of authority should the central corporate system group exercise over the decentralized units?
4. To whom should the information system director report?
5. Should the information system function be organized as a service center or a profit center?
6. What should be the relationship of the information system function to such policy-making groups as the systems steering committee?
7. What should be the formal organizational relationship of the information system function, if any, to the various key users and user groups throughout the enterprise?

System Management Activities and Issues. While the management of systems development consists primarily of project management activities, the management of operational systems includes such activities as developing operational budgets, control-

ling the use of system-related resources, accounting for system-related costs, hiring needed systems personnel and providing their training, providing desired information technology services and training to users, maintaining the operational systems in good working condition, and supervising all aspects of computer-based information system operations.

During the attempt to perform these management activities, such issues as the following arise:

1. What should be the level of the information system budget in terms of gross sales or some other measure?
2. How can participative budget procedures be best employed?
3. What measures should be employed to measure the efficiency and effectiveness of system-related resources such as personnel and equipment?
4. What reports are needed to adequately evaluate and control the use of system-related resources?
5. Should users be charged for the costs of providing information system services?
6. If the answer to Question 5 is yes, should the charge-out rate (transfer price) be established on the basis of actual costs, standard costs, rates charged by commercial services, or some other basis?
7. What qualifications should be established for the hiring of systems analysts, programmers, and other systems personnel?
8. What training programs should be conducted in-house, and what training should be acquired from outside sources?
9. What array of services should be made available to users (e.g., aid in acquiring user department microcomputers)?
10. Through what means should services be provided to users (e.g., information centers)?

11. To what extent should users maintain control over systems resources such as microcomputers and data bases?
12. How should systems maintenance programs be conducted?
13. What supervisory and operating procedures should be established?

ALTERNATIVE STRATEGIES FOR EFFECTIVE SYSTEMS ORGANIZATION AND MANAGEMENT

Two articles have been selected that focus on the organization and management of operational systems. Although they do not attempt to deal with all of the foregoing issues, they do point out significant evolving developments, examine a number of key issues, and suggest strategies for resolving those issues.

The article by Zmud considers the evolving nature of the information system (IS) function and the growing domination of many activities by end users. The author identifies the various traditional organizational designs and proposes prototypal designs for the future that promote innovativeness and adaptability. In these proposals he emphasizes the various managerial tasks and activities to be performed by the respective units within the information systems function.

The article by McFarlan and McKenney discusses the conflicting pressures that many organizations are feeling as they integrate emerging information technologies. In particular they contrast the benefits to be gained through a highly centralized information system function with those to be gained through the decentralized control of systems resources by localized users. The authors suggest a strategy that provides an effective balance of managerial and operational responsibilities between the centralized information system function and decentralized users.

A Strategy for a Successful MIS/DSS Implementation*

Implementation entails bringing a system or subsystem into operational use and turning it over to the end user. The implementation phase in a Management Information System and Decision Support System (MIS/DSS) is the culmination of the design process. Traditionally, implementation has been viewed as beginning after the system analysis and design effort and ending as soon as the system becomes operational and the outputs are produced [Schultz and Slevin, 1975]. We share the view of authors who believe that this definition is too narrow and that implementation is part of the total system design effort, which begins with system analysis and concludes with testing phases [Alter, 1980; Ginzberg, 1975].

With the exception of MIS/DSS and OR/MS disciplines, there is a paucity of literature on implementation. Unfortunately, existing knowledge is far from comprehensive and sheds little insight on the nature of implementation. Keen and Morton (1978), two notable observers, state that:

> The most obvious point is that we do not understand the *dynamics* of implementation. This is really an extraordinary fact; implementation is the avowed purpose of a large number of highly skilled and experienced professionals in the computer field, but while many of them are certainly successful implementers, they seem unable to pin down any general principles underlying their success. Hordes of researchers have analyzed millions of questionnaire responses and the best they can conclude is that top management support is essential. If we assume that the practitioners are competent and the researchers intelligent, then *we must suggest either that implementation is impossibly difficult or that there are some key barriers to implementation that arise from the nature of the technology itself or the personality, training, and behavior of the implementer and/or client.* [Italics by the authors, pp. 196–197.]

These conclusions are by no means unique to the field of MIS/DSS and OR/MIS. In very different areas, including those where the body of literature is far less developed, conclusions are essentially the same.

MIS/DSS designers, if they want to achieve status, professional standing, and respect, should stand back and take honest looks at their failures as well as their successes. Failures can sometimes tell more than successes. The exclusion of some positive factors may not be the cause of an MIS/DSS failure, but the inclusion of certain negative factors may spell failure in many cases. Much more research should be done and seen from the viewpoints of the user and management as to why it failed, not from the viewpoint of MIS/DSS implementers on why they think it failed. Until this research can be done effectively, MIS/DSS systems will probably continue to have problems in achieving good implementation results.

This article will discuss a strategy that will help successful implementation of an MIS/DSS. This strategy is presented as a number of steps management and system designers should take into consideration during the implementation process. These steps are presented in Table 1, clustered into people and system related strategies. All steps, policies, and procedures listed should not be considered all-inclusive, nor should any significance be placed on the order.

PEOPLE RELATED STRATEGIES

Get Management Involved

Management must be involved in the implementation for several reasons. First, subordinates are much more prone to act when their superiors are interested in the outcome. Second, the capital resources required for system implementation are increasing significantly, and management must approve these expenditures. Lastly, highly placed management support helps in crossing organizational boundaries and in restructuring activities [Multinovich and Phatak, 1981].

Management commitment and support are critical and essential for successful implementation of MIS/DSS [Alter, 1980; Ein-Dor & Segev, 1981; Ginzberg, 1981; Robey, 1978; Schultz & Slevin, 1975]. While

Table 1.   Steps to be Considered During the Implementation Process

People Related Strategies
- Get Management Involved
- Ascertain That There Is a Felt Need for the System
- Get User Involvement
- Provide Training and Education
- Consider User Requirements
- Consider User Attitudes
- Establish Effective Communication
- Keep Interface Simple
- Let Management Determine Information Usefulness

System Related Strategies
- Identify the Problem
- Plan the Implementation
- Control the Implementation Process
- Do Post Implementation Evaluation

this is one area that almost all experts say is significant, few provide any insights on how to gain management support. Management support should be analyzed in the political and hierarchical organizational framework of the organizational environment. If true support is lacking, it would be wise for the MIS/DSS effort to be aborted before it is even begun. Multinovich and Phatak (1981) listed barriers to management involvement and presented a list of 14 pragmatic ways to remove these barriers and involve management.

However, if the support is misread and the MIS/DSS is begun, there are certain things which can be done which may help. First, the system must be sold to management, i.e., management must be apprised of the benefits of the MIS/DSS and convinced that it would be to their advantage to support and implement the system. If this fails and top management strongly opposes the system, it would be prudent to abort the system design effort before more time and money are wasted. By knowing when to abort rather than pushing onward in the face of almost sure failure, the MIS/DSS personnel can save their reputations and conserve their energies for those projects which are better received.

If management does not openly oppose the system, but is only lukewarm in its support, and the MIS/DSS for some reason can not be shelved, other methods must be tried. It is sometimes possible to create the illusion of support and even generate support by sending a copy of all reviews to top management, particularly action memos. In this manner, others not aware of management's lukewarm support may be led to believe top management supports the MIS/DSS effort and will in turn support it. Also, if top management reads the memos, they may change their opinion and support the system. For example, in a trucking company the new president opposed the new MIS system, but when he started to see the results, he became an ardent supporter of the new system.

Ascertain That There Is a Felt Need for the System

This is an area where implementation fails in the predesign phase. The system designer should analyze the user environment to determine the felt need for the proposed system. An analysis of this type should not be restricted to the person proposing the system and his peers but should extend to the ultimate end users and those who must give inputs to the system [Lucas, 1973; Narasimnah & Schroder, 1979]. The person proposing the system obviously feels a need for the system. However, a system cannot be successful unless the ultimate users and those who must provide data for the system feel the need [Alter, 1980; Barnett, 1978; Ein-Dor & Segev, 1981; Maish, 1979; Robey, 1979].

In a Great Eastern Bank the outside consultant did not analyze whether the ultimate users felt a need for the system. When the system was put into operation, the portfolio managers who had to use it did not feel it was needed and either ignored it or stopped using it as the first problems developed [Keen and Morton, 1978].

Fortunately, this is not always an insurmountable problem, as the case cited above demonstrates. After the system was initially underutilized by the portfolio managers, a series of meetings was held to review successful applications of the system by some portfolio managers. Top management's clear signal that the new DSS was there to stay, as well as successful use of the new system by some portfolio managers, generated new ideas and put peer pressure on reluctant nonusers.

The key factors in creating a need for a system are:

- *Identify the problem to be worked on.* If the homework has been properly done and the groundwork laid, there should be plenty of support in this area from other departments who are involved with the problem. In fact, identification of the problem may precede you to management. Just make sure you are not the problem.
- *Show how the system can help.* This is perhaps the most important part of selling the system. A clear-cut concise explanation as to how the system can help should be given in non-technical terms. The explanation should be in areas of management's concern (e.g., return on investment, improved efficiency, improved effectiveness, etc.). Homework must be done to identify the areas of management's concern and take maximum advantage of these concerns.

Get User Involvement

The users must actively be involved from the initiation of the system project through its life cycle [Ein-Dor & Segev, 1981; Murdick & Ross, 1974; Thierauf, 1982]. A systems team should be formed with systems personnel and full time or part time user members [Barnett, 1978]. This user participation cannot be token or lip service participation; it must be meaningful and genuine. Talk to everyone concerned with the problem and the solution. Discuss your ideas with them and listen to their ideas. Enlist their aid in designing the system. Very often they know much more than you can learn in a short time. They have probably been through several solutions that didn't work, maybe even one identical to yours. They may have also been through a solution that almost worked and even would have if the users had had direct and meaningful input into its design.

Reports should be made available to users to whom they are pertinent [Ginzberg, 1978]. This helps them to feel that they are a part of the implementation and encourages involvement. Also all user suggestions should be elicited and considered for applicability. They should be given reasons for rejection if their idea is not implemented. Managers must remember that a lot of people make decisions based on emotions, and if personnel have negative feelings about a system because of unexplained rejection of their input, problems will occur. The advantages of the system to the user should be explained. Many users are noncommital to systems because they do not know what it can do for them [Guimaraes, 1981]. Finally, the system should be integrated into the user's working environment. This will reduce the user's feelings of aloofness toward the system.

One of the major obstacles to user involvement which must be overcome in any system implementation is fear — fear caused by imagined threats, fear of the unknown, and fear of the complex. Fear can be reduced by well developed and thought out indoctrination and training programs.

Provide Training and Education

Many systems fail because of inadequate training. The importance of adequate training is often overlooked. Training does not merely mean teaching a user how to input data to the system or how to get answers from the system. Training also means educating the user in the overall purpose of the system: what it is supposed to do, how does it do it, why do we want or need it done, and who must do it. Proper training does not just tell the users how important their contributions are, it lets them see that they are an important integral part in the entire process and that the success of the system depends on how well they do their job. Training should be given to all people associated with the new MIS/DSS system [Alter, 1979; Ein-Dor & Segev, 1981; Lucas, 1973; Maish, 1979; Scheve, 1976; Robey, 1979; Zmud, 1979].

A properly devised training system should follow the example of the Training Path System used frequently by the U.S. Navy. This system breaks training down into three levels.

1. *Top management level* — A broad brush treatment to acquaint top management with the capabilities and limitations of the system and how to use the system in practice. This is a broad stroke approach and may relate to overall organizational goals and policies.
2. *Line management level* — A deeper level for those who must supervise those who input data to the system and also must use the outputs of the system. This level should be deep enough to permit a thorough understanding of the system, what it does, and how it does it.
3. *Operator level* — This level should provide the operators with the necessary skills and knowledge to input data to the

system, manipulate the data, and keep the system performing the function it was designed for.

In training, as in all other interchanges with the users, jargon should be avoided. Remember, the users are not usually trained systems people, and they can easily be scared or confused by jargon. The KISS principle (Keep It Short and Simple) should be adhered to as much as is consistent with adequate exchange of knowledge.

A case in a California aerospace firm illustrates this point. An information data-gathering system was installed for the purpose of generating daily reports indicating the exact production status of each aircraft. Each worker was issued a coded plastic card which he was to insert into the computer data gathering terminals on the production floor. He/she inserted the card and punched in job codes at the beginning and completion of each job. Each worker was *trained* in the mechanical operation of the terminals but was not *educated* about the purposes of the system. The lack of knowledge produced fears that the computer was being used to spy on each man by monitoring his work efficiency. Fearing job loss the workers tried to destroy the computer terminals in many subtle and untraceable ways. It took two years and an extensive education program to get the users to fully accept the new system. This short-sightedness resulted in time delays and cost overruns.

Consider User Requirements

User requirements must be taken into account while implementing an MIS/DSS system in order for the system selected to be compatible with a user's need and organization. Some primary systems requirements are flexibility, simplicity, reliability, economy, accuracy, compatibility, security, etc. A new system should satisfy a particular user's

requirements without adversely affecting the information requirements of other users in the system [Awad, 1979; Ein-Dor & Segev, 1981; King, 1979; Semprevivo, 1982].

User requirements which must be considered are not related to what is required from the system but rather to what is required of the system. For this aspect, the implementer must know both the present and future company plans as well as the personnel who are going to use the system. If the users are highly technical people, then ease of use is not a major user requirement. However, if the users are to be clerks and other regular office employees, then ease must be planned for in the system. If the company has plans to expand, then the manager should plan to have a flexible system that can be expanded to meet the additional demands the user will put on the system. For example, once the system is in use and the company outgrows it, changeover to a larger computer is difficult and expensive unless the system and software are planned to facilitate the switch and expansion.

Consider User Attitudes

"MIS can and does fail where user psychological reactions and organizational factors are ignored by system designers." This quote by Robey (1979) sums up the importance of considering user attitude when preparing to manage with a computer. Studies have shown the relationship of user attitudes and effective system use [King and Rodriquez, 1978; Lucas, 1978; Zmud, 1979]. Studies have also shown that where use of the system is not optional with the user that user satisfaction is a meaningful criteria for system success. Figure 1 shows a simplified model of user behavior by Robey (1979) which can be applied in designing a system. It shows that a user's assessment that rewards, intrinsic or extrinsic, are a re-

Figure 1.   Simplified Model of User Behavior

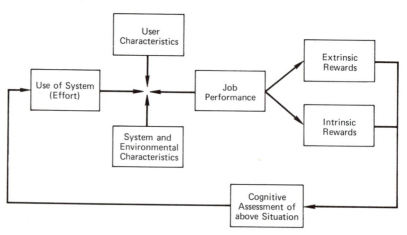

sult of job performance, and job performance is a result of use of the system. This shows an area where the designer can influence the user's attitude toward the system. If the system is well planned and designed, system use will result in increased job performance and increased rewards. This will result in increased system use. The converse, however, is also true. Poor system design usually results in poor job performance and reduced rewards, and reduced system use. It is evident from the above that users' attitudes can be influenced by proper preparation in the planning stage. Establish rewards, which do not have to be monetary, but which can be in the form of recognition or even the satisfaction of having achieved a clearly defined goal. The rewards or goal accomplishment can result in increased user satisfaction and an increased chance of system success.

Establish Effective Communication

Opportunities to enhance the probability of successful implementation are provided through effective use of communication. Considering that the primary mode of transferring decision information is obvi-

ously via communications, this area is strategically important in the MIS/DSS implementation process [Edstrom, 1977; Ginzberg, 1981; Narasimhan & Schroeder, 1979; Zmud, 1979].

Two primary functions of communication are motivation and information transfer. Studies on leadership stress the fact that it is an influential process by which supervisors attempt to control the behavior and performance of subordinates. Communication is the major vehicle of such control available to project leaders and implementers. Communications are involved in the processes of issuing directives, reviewing and evaluating the system, making system assignments, and training and developing subordinates. In addition to motivational functions, communication serves as a vital information function for decision-making.

Although communication appears to be an over-researched field, it is amazing how many managers ignore the findings. Especially significant in a system implementation, where many people of diverse backgrounds are meshed together, is avoiding the establishment of barriers to communication. These barriers include distortion and information overload. In general, communications can be improved in two ways. The manager must sharpen skills in encoding and consider the receiver's environment. Several techniques to accomplish these ends include followup and feedback (making communication a two way street), use of parallel channels to insure correct interpretation, proper timing, setting aside "retreats" that block out distracting sources of communication, and the use of grapevines to clarify messages.

Finally, the implementer must analyze the communication network within the organization. The functional effectiveness must be objectively evaluated, and if necessary, the organizational design adjusted to increase receiver (user) involvement. For example, there should be a system manager drawn from the organization who is in charge of education and coordination efforts. This person serves as an organizational linkage or communications center. Keen and Morton (1978) illustrated with the Brand-aid case that application of this philosophy successfully facilitated implementation of the system.

Keep Interface Simple

One of the most commonly offered bits of implementation advice is to keep the interface simple. From most viewpoints, the appeal of simplicity is quite direct: simple solutions are easier to understand, easier to implement, and usually easier to control and modify than complicated solutions. The rub, of course, is that many business problems are not really amenable to simple solution.

The above is basically good advice given by Alter (1980) and Hammond (1974), but it needs further clarification to be more useful. Alter comes a little closer to the truth when he describes two data analysis systems which encountered difficulties because they became too complicated mechanically. The first, which was developed for commercial use, went through a stage in its development when it was necessary to "put in too many numbers to get a few numbers out" when requesting simple reports. In order to make system usage more convenient, parts of the user interface were revamped. The second, a generalized planning system, "had so many options that you had to be very knowledgeable to use it" [Alter, 1980, p. 171]. This system gets more to the crux of the problem; keeping the interface simple, not the solution. The creativity of the designer should not be stifled in coming up with the solution. However, the creativity, innovation, and complexity should be kept within the flowcharting and programming; the areas that the user does not see. The users will not ordinarily appreciate the genius of the designer; they will only appreciate results. Interface is the area that is seen and interacted with by the user. This must be kept simple so as not to scare or confuse the user. Creative genius must be exercised to achieve the complex solution, but it should be confined to areas not treated on by the non-indoctrinated user. In short, the user interface should be as simple as possible, with ingenuity and creativity applied in such a way as to develop a simple interface for a complex solution.

Let Management Determine Information Usefulness

The perceived usefulness of the information to be provided is an important aspect to be considered when implementing a system. If the information is considered to be neither useful nor important in making a decision, the system implementation will likely fail. The designer should remember that it is not just what he thinks is important, but what the ultimate users think is important. The objective of an MIS/DSS is to provide information which facilitates the managerial decision making process. The ability of the manager to determine whether the information to be presented in the system output is perceived as useful or important to the users is instrumental to the success or failure of the system [Barnett, 1978; Dutta & King, 1980; King, 1979].

SYSTEM RELATED STRATEGIES

Identify the Problem

One of the early things to be done to aid in implementation is to identify the problem to be worked on [Alter, 1979; Ein-Dor & Segev, 1981; Ginzberg, 1981]. One of the most wasteful things is to come up with a beautiful designed system to solve a problem that does not exist. Many a person has lost face by announcing, "I have worked long and hard, and here is the solution to the problem," only to have someone else say, "That never was a problem, we handled it very simply this way . . . ." Keen and Morton (1978) also offer evidence to support the view that logically defining the problem increases the likelihood of implementation success in their discussion of the portfolio management system in the Great Eastern Bank case. One of the primary reasons for successful implementation was the logical definition of the problem facing portfolio managers.

Before assuming that there is a problem and working hard to design a solution, there are two simple steps which should be taken:

- Check with all the managers involved to see if they think that there is a problem or if they already have a solution for the problem.
- Check all employees involved in any way with the suspected problem to see if they have a solution to the problem. Frequently employ-

ees have solutions and work around problems managers are not aware of.

Sometimes it is easy to identify the problem but it is difficult to find the root cause. All we can see at the beginning are symptoms which are often misleading. They may lead a person to suspect one part of the system when, in fact, another defective component which is perhaps less visible is producing the problem. The person who solves the symptom rather than the real problem will get only temporary relief. The real problem not being solved will cause the same symptoms to re-occur later in the MIS/DSS system.

It is also very useful to identify potential problems before and during the implementation process in order to eliminate headaches usually facing implementers. Use of a formal problem analysis technique, such as the problem analysis chart presented in Figure 2, can help prevent disasters before they occur. The simple act of listing the potential problems forces the designer to think of them. In addition, after looking at the problems written down, other problems may come to mind. Also, this technique forces a look at problems, their causes, and prevention, which is better than having to worry about a solution after the problem arises. Use of a technique such as this can minimize the risks involved with successful implementation of an MIS/DSS.

Plan the Implementation

The process of implementation takes place in series with many parallel operations occurring simultaneously. This is in order to minimize start up time. This leads to another step during the implementation phase which is to plan the implementation [Murdick and Ross, 1975]. We do strategic planning for business and even plan personal schedules for the upcoming weeks, so the least that can

Figure 2. An Example of a Problem Analysis Chart

PROJECT:

DATE:

Potential Problems	Likely Causes	Preventive Actions	Preventive Action Responsibility	Post-Action Contingency Plan	Information Reporting Points
Poor user involvement	Authoritative system designers; lack of motivation	Meeting with system designers; motivate employees to participate	System designers, all levels of management	Change designers to ones who will consider users	Grumblings among future users during design and implementation phases
Poor subsystem design	Analyst working alone; lack of management inputs	System designers and managers work together	System designers and all levels of management	Change designers and managers who will not cooperate; sign off every phase	Reporting after each major phase and 25%, 50% and 100% completion

113

be done is to plan for the implementation process. This should be done near the end of the design phase so that the planning efforts to implement the plan are tied together closely. Also, the system design and the typical start up urgency influence the plan. Finally, the system analysts can prepare plans, yet managers must have the final say. Realizing that managers prefer making decisions on recent information also supports the contention of planning directly prior to the actual implementation [Gibson, 1975; Ein-Dor & Segev, 1981; Semprevivo, 1982; Zmud, 1979].

Control the Implementation Process

Successful implementation must involve the development of a strategy for controlling the implementation process. Management control of systems implementation is exercised typically by setting of goals, approving specific plans, and measuring performance against budget. This control requires four major activities [Davis, 1974]:

1. Overall planning and direction
2. Project planning and control
3. Cost control
4. Review and audit

The value of planning and audit cannot be underestimated. Companies that plan system activities and audit results against plan tend to have more successful implementations [The McKinsey Quarterly, 1968].

One of the strategies in the overall planning and direction activity is to assign a system manager. This need was clearly illustrated in the analysis of the Portfolio Management and Brandaid systems [Keen and Morton, 1978]. When these systems were implemented in several companies, one of the foundations for success was noted to be the existence of an organizational linkage and "home" for the system. This system

manager should be drawn from the potential user group (i.e. a functional manager). This insures that the system belongs to the organization and facilitates institutionalization of the system and encourages user participation. The system manager must be involved in the planning, priority setting, and major decision making. Many requests will arise from different functional areas, and the manager will be responsible for assigning priorities so as to avoid conflict.

Do Post Implementation Evaluation

The last phase of the implementation process is a post audit/evaluation. However, not only is it a very neglected step, but in MIS/DSS implementation, evaluation is perhaps the most difficult aspect [Keen and Morton, 1978]. It is virtually impossible to determine implementation success without a thorough evaluation [Cerullo, 1979].

The review should be done by an audit task force composed of a user representative, an internal auditor, a MIS/DSS representative and a project team member. Their determination of success should be based on three factors.

1. A prior definition of "improvement."
2. A means of monitoring progress toward the predefined goal.
3. A formal review process to determine when the system is complete.

All three of these areas are aspects of implementation as well as evaluation. The key to a successful evaluation is the existence of a plan developed in the initial planning step. The audit group reviews the objectives and resource estimates made before the project was approved and compares these to actual performance and resource requirements. It also reviews the operational characteristics of the system to determine if they are satisfactory. If not, system modifications should be made. This process should be repeated at regular intervals following cutover.

A project evaluation should also be done. This is concerned with the efficiency with which the overall project was completed. Similar questions are asked in this evaluation as in the first type described. The benefits of evaluation include a more complete definition of criteria for implementation, better monitoring of the implementation process, and opportunities for learning. The results of post audit should be presented in a report. The recommendations should assist in improving implementation success of future projects.

Summary and Conclusions

Thirteen steps were identified as keys to successful implementation strategy. Nine are people related and four are MIS/DSS system related. This is certainly not an exhaustive list and was not intended to be one. Successful implementation is a very important research topic and deserves more attention than it has received in the past. Virtually all industries use some type of MIS/DSS system, but, unfortunately, many of the intrinsic benefits are not accrued due to poor implementation. We suspect that more research will be done in this important area within the next decade, especially in the areas of problem definition, user commitment, top management support, implementation environment, and education. Also, there should be more studies on successful systems and why they are successful.

During the preparation of this article, the following became obvious concerning the implementation steps.

- The implementation steps are not independent; they are interrelated. One step may lay the groundwork for another step or the extension of still another step.

- The steps are not sequential and several steps may be done simultaneously.
- The steps are not a one-time function, but are iterative. One step may feed back and improve or reinforce another step. The results of one step may require revision or improvement of a previous step.
- The steps for implementation must be an ongoing process. As long as the system is in use, the steps must be reviewed, reevaluated, revised, and used to improve or maintain system performance.

REFERENCES

1. ALTER, S. L., 1980, *Decision Support Systems,* Addison-Wesley, Reading, MA.
2. ALTER, S. L., 1979, "Implementation Risk Analysis," *TIMS Studies in the Management Sciences,* Vol. 13, pp. 103–119.
3. AWAD, E. M., 1979, *Systems Analysis and Design,* Irwin, Homewood, IL.
4. BARNETT, A., 1978, "Securing User Involvement," *Data Management,* Vol. 16, No. 1, pp. 52–57.
5. CERULLO, M. J., 1979, "Determining Post-Implementation Audit Success," *Journal of Systems Management,* Vol. 30, No. 3, pp. 27–31.
6. DAVIS, G. B., 1974, *Management Information Systems: Conceptual Foundation, Structure, and Development,* McGraw-Hill, NY.
7. DUTTA, B.K. and KING, W. R., "A Competitive Scenario Modeling System," *Management Science,* Vol. 26, No. 3, pp. 261–273.
8. EDSTROM, A., 1977, "User Influence and the Success of MIS Projects: A Con-

tingency Approach," *Human Relations,* Vol. 30, No. 7, pp. 589–607.

9. EIN-DOR, P. and SEGEV, E., 1981, *A Paradigm for Management Information Systems,* Praeger, New York.

10. GINZBERG, M. J., 1975, *A Process Approach to Management Science Implementation,* Doctoral dissertaton, MIT, MA.

11. GINZBERG, M. J., 1981, "Key Recurrent Issues in the MIS Implementation Problem," *MIS Quarterly,* Vol. 5, No. 2, pp. 47–59.

12. GINZBERG, M. J., 1978, "Steps Toward More Effective Implementation of MS and MIS," *Interfaces,* Vol. 8, No. 3, pp. 57–63.

13. GUIMARAES, T., 1981, "Understanding Implementation Failure," *Journal of Systems Management,* Vol. 32, No. 3, pp. 12–17.

14. HAMMOND, J. S., 1974, "The Roles of the Manager and Management Scientist in Successful Implementation," *Sloan Management Review,* Vol. 15, No. 2, pp. 1–24.

15. KEEN, P. G. W. and MORTON, M. S. SCOTT, 1978, *Decision Support Systems: An Organizational Perspective,* Addison-Wesley, Reading, MA.

16. KING, W. R. and RODRIQUEZ, J. I., 1978, "Evaluating Management Systems," *MIS Quarterly,* Vol. 2, No. 3, pp. 43–51.

17. KING, W. R., 1979, "Strategies for Success in Management Information Systems," *Management Decisions,* Vol. 17, No. 6, pp. 417–428.

18. LUCAS, H. C., JR., 1978, "Empirical Evidence for a Descriptive Model A Implementation," *MIS Quarterly,* Vol. 2, No. 2, pp. 27–52.

19. LUCAS, H. C., 1981, *Implementation: The Key to Successful Information Systems,* Columbia University Press, New York.

20. LUCAS, H. C., 1973, "User Reactions and the Management of Information Services," *Management Informatics,* Vol. 2, No. 4.

21. MAISH, A. M., 1979, "A User's Behavior Toward His MIS," *MIS Quarterly,* Vol. 3, No. 1, pp. 39–52.

22. *The McKinsey Quarterly,* 1968, *Unlocking The Computer's Profit Potential: A Research Report to Management,* pp. 17–31.

23. MULTINOVICH, J. S. and PHATAK, A. V., 1981, "How to Involve Top Management in an MIS Implementation Effort," Paper presented at The Joint National ORSA/TIMS Meeting, Houston, TX.

24. MURDICK, R. G. and ROSS, J. E., 1975, *Information Systems for Modern Management,* Prentice-Hall, NJ.

25. NARASIMHAN, R. J. and SCHROEDER, R. G., 1979, "An Empirical Investigation of Implementation as a Changing Process," *TIMS Studies in the Management Sciences,* Vol. 13, pp. 63–68.

26. ROBEY, D., 1979, "User Attitudes and Management Information System Use," *Academy of Management Journal,* Vol. 22, No. 3, pp. 527–538.

27. SCHEVE, C. D., 1976, "The Management Information System User: An Exploratory Behavioral Analysis," *Academy of Management Journal,* Vol. 19, No. 4, pp. 577–590.

28. SCHULTZ, R. L. and SLEVIN, D. P., 1975, *Implementing Operations Research, Management Science,* American Elsevier, New York.

29. SEMPREVIVO, P. C., 1982, *Systems Analysis: Definition, Process, and Design,* SRA, Chicago, IL.

30. THIERAUF, R. J., 1982, *Decision Support Systems for Effective Planning and Control,* Prentice-Hall, Englewood Cliffs, NJ.

31. ZMUD, R. W., 1979, "Individual Differences and MIS Success: Review of Empirical Literature," *Management Science,* Vol. 25, No. 10, pp. 966–979.

QUESTIONS

1. Contrast two alternative views of the place of implementation activities within the systems development life cycle.

2. Identify people related strategies that should be considered during the implementation phase.

3. Identify system related strategies that should be considered during the implementation phase.

4. How can systems analysts obtain the involvement of management before and during the implementation phase?

5. How can systems analysts overcome the resistance of employees to the implementation of a new information system?

6. Contrast the types of training that are appropriate at the various levels of the organization.

7. What are the purposes of a post-implementation evaluation?

8. Should the strategies for implementing a centralized data base differ from those for implementing a transaction processing system such as the general ledger system?

How a Small Company Evaluates Acquisition of a Minicomputer*

With increasing clerical costs, rising fees from computer service bureaus, greater pressure for timely information on key business activities, and the falling price of minicomputers, small companies are increasingly turning to computer ownership as a means of survival in today's competitive economic environment. Choosing the right computer from the bewildering array of machines, manufacturers, and the alternative configurations of system components can be a frustrating (and, if improperly handled, expensive) experience for a company.

To help managers and accountants deal with this important decision, we describe here the process followed by an automobile leasing company (which we call ABC Leasing) in making this crucial decision. We have altered information that would reveal the identity of the company, but the basic facts remain true to the actual case.

ABC LEASING

ABC Leasing is a licensee for a major auto rental company; its location in a resort city near the ocean brings it both business and vacation customers. Annual sales volume is approximately $6 million, and the company has 60 full-time employees. Sales are expected to increase to $9 million over the next three years. The company has rental offices at the local airport, in several downtown locations, and in two neighboring towns. A local service bureau has been satisfying all its data processing needs, but this operation recently increased its charges to ABC to $2,000 per month. At this price the company decided it might pay to purchase its own computer.

To get some idea of how to approach the problem, ABC managers attended a seminar on small business minicomputer systems where they talked to some managers from small businesses who recently had acquired computers. They learned two important things from these conversations: (1) approximately one-half the total costs of the system would cover the hardware, and the remaining half would pay for the necessary software, supplies, consulting help, and assorted start-up costs; (2) they needed help in gathering the right information, asking the right questions of vendors, presenting the appropriate information to the vendors, and specifying the exact output they wanted from the

*By Germain B. Boer and Sam W. Barcus, III. Copyright © 1981 by the National Association of Accountants, Montvale, N.J., *Management Accounting* (March 1981). Reprinted by permission. All rights reserved.

system. ABC management approached its accounting firm for help in gathering and evaluating information for the computer purchase decision. The firm's consultant suggested ABC should:

1. Study the present data flow within the company.
2. Compile and classify information requirements.
3. Get computer system proposals from vendors.
4. Analyze the proposals and then select the best proposal from those submitted.

DATA FLOW WITHIN THE COMPANY

After several weeks of data gathering by the clerical staff at ABC, the company was able to compile the relevant information necessary for specifying the parameters of the system the company needed (Table 1). The data were important not only to ABC but also to the companies that would write the pro-

grams for the system because company management wanted all software developed by outside software vendors. The company president felt strongly that ABC should not create a data processing department; therefore, the company would have to buy all its software from outside suppliers. This decision also meant that programs and machines acquired by the company would have to be readily usable by the existing clerical staff.

Finding out what information company managers need is no easy task, but ABC was able to identify some obvious needs by looking at existing problems. For example, monthly accounting reports useful for controlling operations and for projecting cash flows arrived from the service bureau two or three weeks after the close of the month. The clerical staff was gradually getting behind in its preparation of operational analyses, with each sales increase putting them further behind. Given that sales would increase about 50% over the next three years, it was clear

Table I.   System Statistics

General ledger accounts	133
Digits per account number	6
Entries per month to all accounts	900
Contracts outstanding on any day	1,600
Payments received each month	1,400
Number of contracts processed monthly	7,900
Number of contracts in rental revenue master file	50,000
Payment vouchers per month	240
Number of entries per voucher	8
Number of vendors serving ABC Leasing	200
Journal entries per month for all disbursements	1
Automobiles bought and sold each month	250
Automobiles on hand	1,200
Number of digits in automobile number	6
Number of digits in automobile serial number	6
Unidentified payments per month	250
Outstanding billable items	900
Unapplied cash items at any time	1,500
Payroll checks per week	100
Full time employees	60

the company had to automate existing procedures just to enable the staff to keep on performing its present activities.

At the beginning of the output definition process, company managers were convinced that automation of accounting procedures was the most important reason for buying a computer, but as they worked with defining system outputs they began to realize the profit potential of a computerized rental revenue file. Their current system showed a single number for sales revenue; however, the computerized rental revenue application could show rental revenue at a level as detailed as a specific automobile.

Such revenue detail would enable managers to evaluate the profitability of alternative mixes of corporation versus individual renters and small versus large automobiles. It also would allow them to evaluate the relative profitability of their rental locations and to assess the profit impact of various pricing strategies, strategies that involve alternative prices for mileage and day charges. Finally, managers realized that information about the most popular cars would enable them to alter the mix of automobiles they owned by selling less popular cars and replacing them with the more popular ones. In this case, then, output definition activities caused managers to shift their attention from the automation of clerical tasks to consideration of the profit potential of rental revenue information.

After their detailed review of management requirements, the company managers decided to implement the six applications listed below. They decided to start with the general ledger application because doing so would allow company personnel to get acquainted with the system using familiar data before they tried using the new information from the rental revenue system:

1.   General ledger and financial reporting
2.   Rental revenue

3.   Cash payments and bank reconciliation
4.   Fleet fixed assets
5.   Unapplied cash and items billable
6.   Payroll

These applications formed what management considered the basic components of the system the company needed. The information required by each application and the information flows among these applications were illustrated in a visual overview of the system, which was most helpful in enhancing communication between managers and technical personnel. It also forced technical personnel to constantly be aware that no system component stands alone. The general ledger application served as the unifying element in the total system.

Not only did ABC managers have to specify the overall information flows, they also had to select those computer systems features compatible with their policy of using the present clerical staff to operate the new system. Working again with its consultant, the company prepared the following list of computer techniques that would satisfy company needs:

1.   On-line interactive processing
2.   Menu selection and program prompting for data entry, inquiry, file update, and report generation
3.   Multi-programming capabilities
4.   Printer spooling concurrent with other functions
5.   Program prompting for such functions as paper changing and file mounting
6.   Preparation of special reports by users through report writing software
7.   Multiple security levels to limit file access to authorized individuals

On-line interactive processing with program prompting fit the company requirements well because input station operators need little experience in computer operations. They simply respond to the questions appearing on the screen, and the system accepts only answers that fit a rigid set of constraints. The third requirement, which allows the computer to perform several activities simultaneously, was included at the suggestion of the consultant who felt the feature would be important for the company. Printer spooling allows operators to continue using terminals while the system prints reports; i.e., running the printer does not tie up the entire system so nobody can enter data during printing operations.

Requirements five and six are important because of the limited data processing knowledge of the personnel operating the computers. Prompting for paper and file changes requires less sophisticated personnel than a nonprompting system. Likewise, report writing software generally can be quickly mastered by nonprogramming personnel who can then create nonstandard reports from the data files whenever the company needs them.

The final requirement arose out of management concern about system controls. Large data processing operations employ enough people so that various duties can be segregated to maintain adequate internal control. ABC, however, simply planned to put the computer in a room where present clerical personnel would operate it. This room would be open to all employees, and data entry personnel would also print reports; in short, segregation of duties would be nonexistent. To compensate for this lack of separation, the company wanted to use computer controls to the extent technologically feasible. Purchasing software from an outside vendor helped remove one severe control problem usually present in small companies: program preparation and data entry by the same individuals. Use of a hierarchy of security levels, each higher level giving access to larger portions of the system, allowed the company to carefully control which personnel would

have access to specific portions of the computer system.

To make sure accurate data entered the system, ABC decided it wanted editing procedures on data input that included both field and multiple field tests. Specifically, the company wanted the system to edit for format, perform range tests on data items, compare values to master file elements, and verify logical relationships between and among fields. Field tests in an interactive system catch data errors while the operator enters data, a feature that increases accuracy and allows inexperienced personnel to correct mistakes before the input data becomes part of the data files. Both these features were important to ABC because it wanted to use its present clerical staff to operate the system. In addition to these input data editing tests, ABC wanted input data, transaction files, and master files processed under system control with each batch of data processed generating control or audit trail reports for user review.

One other feature the company considered that fits roughly under the heading of information requirements is that of documentation. System documentation refers to the procedure manuals, program listings, flow charts, listings of test data used to debug programs, and so on. ABC management especially was concerned about this feature because it planned to operate the system with no specialized data processing employees. This meant the instructions for using the programs and hardware would have to be written in clear, precise terms understandable to the present clerical staff; it meant ABC management would have to carefully scrutinize the material provided by the vendors before accepting it, and it meant that ABC would have to specify to the vendors in blunt terms that programs and hardware would be accepted only upon the receipt of documentation suitable for ABC personnel. Documentation is important in companies that have a fully staffed data processing department, but for ABC it wasn't just important — it was absolutely essential. Those factors for which the company decided it needed clear documentation were: systems, programs, equipment and systems operation, user procedures, and data control and error correction procedures.

SOLICITATION OF VENDOR PROPOSALS

After it completed the study of data flow and management information requirements, the company moved to the next step in the computer acquisition process: solicitation of vendor proposal with a request for proposal (RFP). A request for proposal tells hardware vendors and, in the case of ABC Leasing, software vendors what the company wants from its system. The document describes in detail the specific company requirements for output, performance, and control procedures. In addition, it provides information such as company size, number of employees, and geographic location which helps vendors match their products with the company's needs.

Vendors, however, are not the only ones who benefit from a carefully prepared RFP; company managers benefit, too. Preparing an RFP forces them to define just what they want from the system. They cannot use vague objectives like "better decisions" or "improved customer service"; they must articulate specific system objectives. For example, instead of saying "we want a computer that will solve our payroll problem," managers must explicitly describe the payroll problem. They must specify the number of paychecks they want produced weekly, or monthly, the kinds of payroll records they want, the types of management reports they want, and the

degree of accessibility different employees have to payroll data. For example, at ABC top managers got directly involved in defining system output. Even the company president spent at least one full day reviewing line by line every proposed report for the system.

Preparation of a detailed RFP draws managers into the early stages of computer acquisition decisions by making them specifically state what they want from the system *before* the company buys a particular system. Managers have to face up to difficult questions about information needs, the relation of company goals and the information system, and the kinds of input media they want. They do all this while they still have time to think through the answers. Involvement in the RFP preparation also helps top managers to learn about the complexity of the computer acquisition decision and to develop healthier, more realistic expectations about system results than if the entire decision were delegated to accountants and data processing personnel. Their involvement exposes them to the risks and limitations of computerized systems. For example, at ABC Leasing lengthy discussions ensued about who would have responsibility for the computer. The company considered assigning it to the vice president of administration, the accountant or to an individual who reported to one of these managers. Top management eventually selected the accountant because he was the focal point of most company information flows.

Keep in mind that top managers do not always have to be as involved as the president of ABC Leasing was, but they do have to make policy decisions on the kinds of information the system must produce, the technical competence of personnel the company will hire to run the system, the resources the company will commit for system controls, and the acceptable operating changes the company will make to accommodate the computer system. As a result of this participation, top managers come face to face with the policy implications of automated data processing; therefore, they can address these policy issues before they buy a computer system instead of after it is already in the office.

Because ABC Leasing wanted both software and hardware vendors to provide services, the company prepared a lengthy and detailed RFP. It contained a section setting forth detailed input and output specifications for each application and a set of instructions telling vendors how they should respond to the RFP. Because of the length of this RFP (approximately 200 pages), we have included just the specifications for the application of the fleet fixed assets and a selection of excerpts from the instructions for the vendors.

DETAILED SPECIFICATIONS FOR FLEET FIXED ASSETS

The company described in a separate section of the RFP the requirements for each application it wanted to implement, so the RFP contained six sections of specifications. Each one began with an overall flowchart of the specific application, followed by introductory comments describing the purpose and objectives of the application, a scope section that described the specific things the application should accomplish, a set of desired application features, a listing of specific elements making up the master file, and sample input screen formats and output report formats.

Figure 1 shows the overall flowchart for the fleet fixed assets application. This flowchart provides an overview of the system highlighting the inputs, major files, and the

Figure 1.   Fleet Fixed Assets

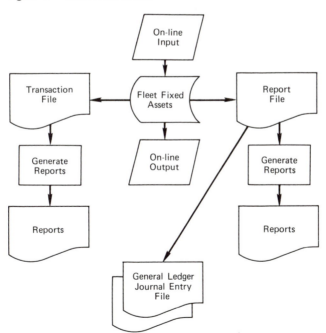

outputs generated by this application. Such a flowchart enables readers of the RFP to grasp quickly the overall structure of the specific application; it can also show management and nontechnical personnel just what this particular application accomplishes.

Table 2 shows the information that describes the fleet fixed assets application. The introduction gives a verbal overview corresponding to the flowchart in Figure 1, and the scope section lists the specific activities ABC wants the application to perform. Notice how specifically each function is described to make clear to the software vendor precisely what the company needs from this application. The same degree of precision shows up in the description of system features and operating statistics. Here again ABC Leasing describes exactly what it wants this application to do, and it gives statistics about the transaction volume, number of cars in the file, and the size of both the car numbers and serial numbers. ABC Leasing provides data on each element in the master file in such detail that the reader of this RFP can quickly calculate the storage space required for this master file.

The next set of information on this application describes the input for the fleet fixed assets application. Figure 2 shows this information. Notice how the screen formats illustrate the prompting messages that guide data entry operators through the file maintenance steps for fleet fixed assets.

Table 3 shows the output instructions for the fleet fixed assets application. Observe how ABC Leasing first gave a verbal description of each report and then drafted a report format to illustrate its description. Such a presentation leaves little room for misunderstandings with the software vendor who will prepare the programs to generate these reports. ABC Leasing, however, mentioned in its RFP that vendors who could provide im-

provements on the input prompting messages or the output reports were welcome to offer such improvements provided they could show why their approach was superior to that in the RFP.

The information in each section for the six applications was organized like that for fleet fixed assets and included the same degree of detail. Obviously, it takes a great deal of time for managers to prepare this information, but it gives them a chance to think about the exact form, content, and character of the system they want for their company. At ABC Leasing the president spent about 50 hours working on the RFP, the vice president of administration about 120 hours, and the accountant 200 hours. In addition, the consultant from the accounting firm devoted another 200 hours to the project. Managers have to go through this kind of detailed analysis to create an effective system, and doing the analysis before buying a computer enables them to buy a system that fits company needs instead of trying to make company needs fit an already purchased system. Also, specific details like these helped ABC to evaluate the adequacy of vendor responses because the vendor who cannot provide what the company wants stands out clearly. As an added benefit, the analysis educated managers to the point that they could confidently discuss their needs with the various vendors.

To help insure that responses to the RFP would be easy to analyze, ABC Leasing provided vendor instructions, some of which are illustrated at the first part of Table 4 (note the use of a bidders conference to clear up misunderstandings), and a detailed questionnaire which the vendor was asked to use for responding to the RFP. The second part of Table 4 shows two excerpts from this questionnaire. Such a device greatly enhances the comparative analysis of the vendor responses, an analysis that allows company

Table 2.   Functional Specifications for Fixed Assets Application

INTRODUCTION

The fleet fixed system calculates monthly depreciation expense and book gain or loss on fixed asset disposals. Straight-line depreciation is used for risk cars and a negotiated depreciation rate is used for buy-back cars. The system also produces periodic management and distribution reports. Transactions such as Inventory Master File changes, additions, and deletions are entered from a CRT screen and immediately affect the appropriate file if edit and validation criteria are satisfied.

SCOPE

The fleet fixed assets system should include all the processing necessary to perform the following functions:

1. Maintain a current file of all automobiles, including a complete description of each car.
2. Process on-line inquiries by car number and display car description, original cost, accumulated depreciation and net book value.
3. Process additions to the car inventory.
4. Process sales from the car inventory and calculate book gain or loss on disposal.
5. Process changes to the inventory master file in order to modify records.
6. Prepare addition, sales and depreciation reports for management.

SYSTEM FEATURES AND STATISTICS

1. System Features

- On-line inquiry to the inventory master file
- Calculate book gains and losses
- Transactions cannot be processed without selected data elements
- Interfaces with general ledger system
- Provide facility for extraordinary depreciation due to special circumstances

2. Statistics

	Current	Projected
• Additions and deletions avg./month	250	400
• Cars on file at any one time	1,200	2,000
• 6 digit car numbers		
• 6 digit serial number		

MASTER FILE DATA

Three files must be set up to run the fleet fixed assets system:

1. Fleet Fixed Assets File

Car number (6 digit)
Account number (6 digit)
Car serial number (6 digit)
Car description, including:
   Year (2 digit)
   Color exterior (4 digits)   Color interior (4 digits)
   Type interior (4 digits)   # doors (1 digit)
   Engine type (4 digits)   # cylinders (1 digit)
   Accessories (5 fields of 2 digits with alphanumeric coding)
Year of purchase (vintage year) (2 digit)   Original cost (7 digit)
YTD accumulated depreciation (6 digit)   Book value (6 digit)
Monthly depreciation (5 digit)
Proceeds from sale (7 digit)   Book gain or loss (7 digit)
Active/sold status (1 digit)
Date added (6 digit)   Date sold (6 digit)
Type of purchase tag (1 digit)
Rental/consignment tag (1 digit)

2. Transaction Log

Record of all maintenance to the inventory master file.

3. Report File

Contains data to be transmitted to the general ledger system.

125

Table 3. Output Description and Report Formats for Fixed Assets

Output Documents and Reports and Screen Layouts

The specific output reports are described below. Following these brief descriptions are examples of report formats.

1. Active Fleet Inventory

   This report is sorted by fleet status, account number and purchase year end and includes a full description of each car in the fleet inventory. This same data may also be requested sorted by type of purchase tag or rental/consigned tag or by car number. Reports will have subtotals at control breaks.

2. Vehicle Deletions

   This is a monthly report listing all cars disposed of by car number. It includes original cost, accumulated depreciation, vintage year, proceeds and book gain or loss on disposal. It also accumulates depreciation and proceeds for all cars disposed of within each vintage year. The report is sorted by rental/consigned and includes subtotals at control breaks.

3. Extraordinary Depreciation Report

   This is a monthly report listing all cars disposed of by car number using extraordinary depreciation.

ABC LEASING ACTIVE FLEET INVENTORY

Unit/Acct/Serial No.	Pur/Mod Yr.	Make/Model	Accessories	Orig. Cost	Month Depr.
XXXX XXXX XXXX	XX XX	XXX XXXXX	XX XX XX XX	XXXX.XX	XXX.XX
XXXX XXXX XXXX	XX XX	XXX XXXXX	XX XX XX XX	XXXX.XX	XXX.XX

ABC LEASING VEHICLE DELETIONS MONTH, YEAR

Type of Purchase	Active Sold	Rental/Consign Tag	Serial. No.	Vint. Year	Orig. Cost	Accum. Deprec.	Proceeds	Gain (Loss)	Number of Units
X	X	X	XXXXXX	XX	XXXX.XX	XXXXX.XX	XXXXX.XX	XXXXXX.XXX	
X	X	X	XXXXXX	XX	XXXX.XX	XXXXX.XX	XXXXX.XX	XXXXXX.XXX	
Totals for location					XXXX.XX	XXXXX.XX	XXXXX.XX	XXXXXX.XXX	XXX
YTD total for xx					XXXX.XX	XXXXX.XX	XXXX.XX	XXXXXX.XXX	XXX

Table 3. (continued)

	Orig. Cost	Accum. Deprec.	Number of Units
YTD total for yy	XXXX.XX		XXX
YTD total for zz	XXXX.XX		XXX
YTD total for aa	XXXX.XX		XXX
YTD total for all years	XXXX.XX		XXX
Grand total	XXXXX.XX	XXXXX.XX	XXX
YTD total xx		XXXXX.XX	XXX
YTD total yy		XXXXX.XX	XXX
YTD total zz		XXXXX.XX	XXX
YTD total aa		XXXXX.XX	XXX
YTD grand total		XXXXX.XX	XXX

ABC Leasing Extraordinary Depreciation Month, Year

Unit No.	Serial No.	Vint. Year	Orig. Cost	Accum. Deprec.	Proceeds	Gain (Loss)	Number of Units
XXXXX	XXXXXX	XX	XXXX.XX	XXXXX.XX	XXXXX.XX	XXXXXX.XXX	XXX
XXXXX	XXXXXX	XX	XXXX.XX	XXXXX.XX	XXXXX.XX	XXXXXX.XXX	XXX
Totals for location			XXXX.XX	XXXXX.XX	XXXXX.XX	XXXXXX.XXX	XXX
YTD total for xx					XXXXX.XX		XXX
YTD total for yy					XXXXX.XX		XXX
YTD total for zz					XXXXX.XX		XXX
YTD total for aa					XXXXX.XX		XXX
YTD total for all years					XXXXX.XX		XXX
Grand total			XXXXX.XX	XXXXX.XX	XXXXX.XX		XXX
YTD total xx					XXXXX.XX		XXX
YTD total yy					XXXXX.XX		XXX
YTD total zz					XXXXX.XX		XXX
YTD total aa					XXXXX.XX		XXX
YTD grand total					XXXXX.XX		XXX

Figure 2. Input Description and Screen Formats

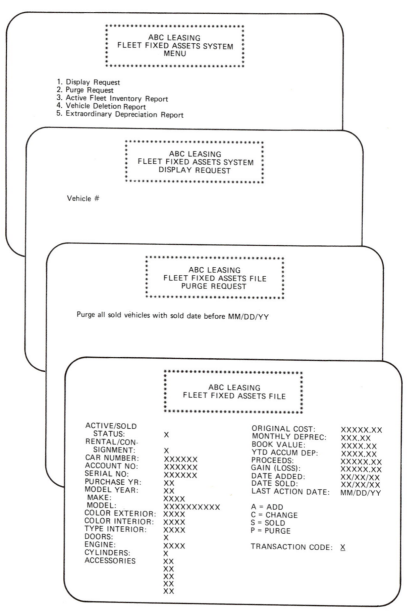

```
..............................
:       ABC LEASING          :
: FLEET FIXED ASSETS SYSTEM  :
:          MENU              :
..............................

1. Display Request
2. Purge Request
3. Active Fleet Inventory Report
4. Vehicle Deletion Report
5. Extraordinary Depreciation Report
```

```
..............................
:       ABC LEASING          :
: FLEET FIXED ASSETS SYSTEM  :
:      DISPLAY REQUEST       :
..............................

Vehicle #
```

```
..............................
:       ABC LEASING          :
:  FLEET FIXED ASSETS FILE   :
:       PURGE REQUEST        :
..............................

Purge all sold vehicles with sold date before MM/DD/YY
```

```
..............................
:       ABC LEASING          :
:  FLEET FIXED ASSETS FILE   :
..............................

ACTIVE/SOLD                          ORIGINAL COST:      XXXXX.XX
   STATUS:           X                MONTHLY DEPREC:     XXX.XX
RENTAL/CON-                           BOOK VALUE:         XXXX.XX
   SIGNMENT:         X                YTD ACCUM DEP:      XXXX.XX
CAR NUMBER:          XXXXXX           PROCEEDS:           XXXXX.XX
ACCOUNT NO:          XXXXXX           GAIN (LOSS):        XXXXX.XX
SERIAL NO:           XXXXXX           DATE ADDED:         XX/XX/XX
PURCHASE YR:         XX               DATE SOLD:          XX/XX/XX
MODEL YEAR:          XX               LAST ACTION DATE:   MM/DD/YY
 MAKE:               XXXX
 MODEL:              XXXXXXXXXX        A = ADD
COLOR EXTERIOR:      XXXX              C = CHANGE
COLOR INTERIOR:      XXXX              S = SOLD
TYPE INTERIOR:       XXXX              P = PURGE
DOORS:               X
ENGINE:              XXXX              TRANSACTION CODE:  X
CYLINDERS:           X
ACCESSORIES          XX
                     XX
                     XX
                     XX
                     XX
```

FLEET FIXED ASSETS

V. Sources of Input
The sources of input for the fleet fixed assets system follow. Sample screens are shown on the following pages.

1. Vehicle Information Addition or Change
   This form is used to add a new car to the fleet fixed assets master file or to change data elements pertaining to a car already on file. Additional information concerning specific features of each car will also be added to the file.

2. Report of Vehicle Sale - This form lists information on vehicles that are sold.

3. Purge Request - This is a request to purge vehicles deleted and inactivated before a specific date. The purpose of the request is to rid the file of unnecessary information.

managers to look at the relative costs and benefits of each system. A standard data format facilitates this comparison because the same information about each vendor is located in the same place on each response. Managers don't have to search through pages of information about the system to find the total price of the system — the price is in a location dictated by the company buying the computer. The RFP and accompanying instructions were delivered to six vendors whom the company thought would be able to provide the system it wanted. ABC Leasing sent RFPs to only those vendors its accounting firm consultant identified as having the ability to satisfy the company's needs.

EVALUATING VENDOR PROPOSALS

The final step in the computer acquisition process deals with choosing a system from those proposed by the vendors. ABC management began this final phase by carefully reviewing the proposals for completeness and for responsiveness to the RFP. A list of questions was prepared for vendors submitting proposals with deficiencies such as missing data or incomplete responses to specific points in the RFP. Vendors were asked to answer these questions to clarify the ambiguities in their proposal. Unsatisfactory responses to these questions provided grounds for dropping a vendor because company management felt such unresponsiveness was a good indication of the service it could expect from this vendor in the future. After clarifying these points the company summarized the vendor proposal data in a format that facilitated vendor comparisons. To do this summary, ABC management simply created a large spread sheet that assigned columns to each vendor and rows to the specific elements related to each vendor. Table 2 contains excerpts from this analysis illustrating comparisons for hardware and software.

Consider the data on memory, for example. Vendor A offers only 64K of main memory while three of the other vendors propose twice that amount. Also, all machines have the capability of expanding main memory to 256K except Vendor D who can expand to 512K. The importance of main memory size hinges on its constraint on application program size, number of programs running concurrently, and the speed of system operation. Disk storage was also important to ABC Leasing because its rental revenue file required at least 50 million characters of storage, and the company wanted the ability to add more disk storage without moving to a different minicomputer.

A comparison of disk storage proposed by the various vendors shows that they varied from as little as 32 million characters for Vendor B to as much as 160 million characters for Vendor E. Additional disk drives can easily be added to Vendor B and Vendor C computers, and Vendor D and Vendor E provide removable disk packs which allow the company to add as many more disk packs as they want for storage although these systems provide direct access to only two disk packs at any one time. The company planned to use tape storage for backup only, so all vendor tape systems were adequate for ABC needs; however, Vendor A proposed a floppy disk system instead of tape for this purpose. Disk access time and main memory time were important for this system; but all the proposed systems were approximately equal on these elements making them unimportant in the vendor selection decision.

In evaluating software, ABC management was interested in the features available with standard accounting packages — the greater the number of features available from a standard package, the better — and it was concerned with both the time required to complete the custom software programming and the understanding of ABC requirements

Table 4. Instructions Sent to Selected Vendors

Proposal instructions

Proposals must include all of the following elements in order to be considered:

1. A *management summary* in non-technical language describing the total system, services, and capabilities offered to ABC Leasing.

2. *Completed questionnaires* describing hardware configuration and cost, software design and cost, and general information. These questionnaires must be completed in the prescribed format and should be supplemented by additional information required to describe the proposed systems or to explain deviations from the system specifications.

A bidder's conference will be held approximately one week after bids are issued to allow vendors to question details outlined in the RFP. Vendors will be notified of the time and place as early as possible. It is the desire of ABC Leasing management that demonstrations be deferred until after proposals are evaluated.

Hardware multiply/divide? _____
Number of concurrent tasks _____
2. On-line data input/output
Model of CRT _____
Number of units-proposed _____
-expandable to _____
Rated speed (BAUD) _____
Model _____
Screen size and format: lines _____ characters/line _____
Keyboard _____
Ten key pad? _____
Special features _____
3. Other hardware features:
Virtual memory? _____
Response time (sec) with 4 terminals active:
logon _____
data entry _____
Approximate time to sort a 3,000 record file of 200 character records on a 20 character (alphanumeric) key in ascending sequence _____

130

Table 4. *(continued)*

Hardware Vendor Questionnaire

Vendor name: _____

Vendor address: _____

Telephone _____

Local contact _____

Name or model designation of
proposed system _____

Date first announced _____

Date first delivered _____

Number installed-Total _____

-Locally _____

Projected delivery date _____

Proposed hardware configuration

1. Central processor

Model _____

Word size (bits/word) _____

Main memory size (K words)-proposed _____

-expandable to _____

Main memory not available to user _____

Cycle time (microseconds) _____

Arithmetic precision (99,999,999.99 required) _____

The sort disk work space required for the above operation _____

Special hardware features _____

4. Training

User Instruction method _____

Class location _____

24 hour system help? _____

Additional training cost/hr _____

5. Maintenance

Service center location _____

Ratio customers/technicians _____

Preventive maintenance period _____

Average service call response time _____

Maintenance hours _____

Parts inventory location _____

Backup location _____

Software/hardware enhancement cost _____

6. Environmental

Temperature/humidity range _____

Power _____

Floor weights (heaviest piece) _____

demonstrated by the vendor. Vendor A can complete custom software faster than the others, but speed without quality would not help the company. Consequently, ABC management visited current users of Vendor A software, looked at the number of technical personnel on the staff, and assessed the company "track record". Table 3 gives a cost summary for the various vendors. Note the level of cost detail. Costs are shown for individual system components for both hardware and software, and this breakdown helps management make decisions on cost trade-offs among different components. For example, management may consider shifting from disk storage to tape storage. With the cost detail shown here it can quickly estimate the cost impact of these changes.

ALL FACTORS ARE RELEVANT

Cost, of course, doesn't give the full picture. For instance, ABC Leasing looked at factors such as current user satisfaction with a vendor, the number of systems sold to date, the total years the software vendors had been in business, and the number of companies using the software produced by the software vendor. Company managers also asked these questions: Is a terminal "locked up" while the printer is running? Are data items protected from erroneous update when two or more programs request that item simultaneously? How much does response time slow down when one additional terminal is added to the system? They looked, too, at the expandability of the system to make sure the system could grow with the business. More importantly, they looked at whether the system could produce reports on time, i.e., regardless of the amount of main memory or the access speed of the disks, management wanted a system that delivered information on time.

Finally, the managers considered how fast the vendors could fix a machine if it breaks down; that is, they evaluated the location of maintenance personnel, their hours of availability, the number available, and the comments of present customers on vendor maintenance service. ABC managers visited user installations and attended company demonstrations. They actually used the equipment to see how easily errors could be corrected, screens could be read, and paper could be loaded into a printer. Numerous other factors received the attention of ABC Leasing management, but this sampling of factors gives an indication of the care and deliberation that went into the computer selection process.

Choosing a minicomputer is a significant decision which has an impact on all phases of a company's operation. Accordingly, this decision deserves the care that any major expenditure of $100,000 receives in most companies. The analysis presented here illustrates the elements, factors, and processes one company used to study this decision. Any company embarking on this process can learn from the detailed analysis this company performed in order to make its decision.

QUESTIONS

1. Describe the steps by which the data shown in Table 1 would be developed by systems analysts, including the sources of the data and the techniques that might be applied.
2. Identify the specific contents of the RFP developed by ABC Leasing, and speculate on the need for an RFP of 200 pages.

3. How does the acquisition of a mini-computer differ from the acquisition of a mainframe computer?

4. Identify key systems and information requirements established by ABC Leasing during the systems analysis phase, and suggest other requirements that might be desirable.

5. What aspects of systems design did ABC Leasing perform, and what aspects of a designed system did the firm expect to acquire from the selected vendor?

6. Identify the capabilities and features by which each of the vendors was evaluated.

7. Describe two methodologies by which the proposals of vendors may be evaluated and rank-ordered.

8. Minicomputers introduce potential security issues, such as ease of access and lack of separation of duties among the systems personnel. Identify several security exposures in a minicomputer environment and suggest one or more control measures for each exposure.

Design Alternatives for Organizing Information Systems Activities*

INTRODUCTION

Information systems activities (those tasks associated with acquiring, deploying, and managing information technologies) are in a considerable state of flux in many organizations. Recent articles have concluded that changes must occur in how information systems activities are *organized* in order to meet the challenges of an information society [1, 2, 3, 4, 17, 25].

Two major forces are behind much of this turmoil. First, a substantial increase in computing has occurred over the last decade because of the phenomenal advances achieved in computer hardware and software [3, 19]. As a consequence, individuals responsible for directing an organization's use of information resources face an expanding user base and an exploding portfolio of information services. Second, resource scarcities have led many organizations to stress the improvement of existing services rather than the provision of new services [2]. This, in turn, has led many end users to act independently of the centralized information systems authority in deciding when and how to exploit information technologies [17]. The recent availability of high quality, fourth-generation software products has heightened this trend. Managing information resources within such an environment is considerably more difficult than the environments of the 1960s and 1970s, where an intimidating, relatively inflexible, but generally stable, technology-base resulted in the centralized information systems authority maintaining a virtual monopoly as a provider of information services.

The main reaction of leading information systems organizations to these external and internal challenges has been to decentralize information systems responsibilities. Generally, this decentralization has been limited to the acquisition and deployment of relatively simple, stand-alone applications. However, as information technologies become more deeply embedded within an organization's operational, tactical, and strategic activities, line managers will be increasingly motivated to gain authority over applications. For example, managers with bottom-line profit and loss responsibilities who depend on the availability of reliable, on-line transaction processing systems are increasingly demanding

*By Robert W. Zmud. Reprinted by special permission of the *MIS Quarterly*, Volume 8, No. 2, June 1984. Copyright © 1984 by the Society for Information and the Management Information Systems Research Center.

full control over the computer systems providing these services. Such authority transferals result in much more than simply changing the location of information processing activities. Significant changes are increasingly being observed in both the ownership of information resources and the stewardship of information activities.

It is the intent of this article to describe and discuss alternative designs for organizing information systems activities for the information resource environments expected throughout the 1980s and 1990s. Practitioners need to be actively considering their options for managing this transition period. A final objective of this article then, is to stimulate research programs that critically assess the viability of the options available to information systems managers.

EVOLVING NATURE OF INFORMATION SYSTEMS ACTIVITIES

Throughout the 1960s and 1970s, information systems activities in most organizations were handled by a centralized information systems authority primarily serving a *manufacturing* role. This typically involved configuring and operating a production facility consisting of large-scale hardware and systems software as well as establishing and maintaining a sizeable in-house application software development group [17].

This central authority was most often organized with four information systems subfunctions [11, 14, 17, 26, 33]: systems development, operations, technical services, and administration. Table 1 provides a summary of the information systems activities included within each of these subunits. This strategy for partitioning an organization's information systems activities recognized that the task environments of each of these infor-

mation systems activities would benefit from quite different management styles and practices. Large-scale application systems development, for example, involves a series of interdependent tasks, emphasizes organizational effectiveness, and benefits from a high degree of end user involvement. Operations involves a series of interdependent tasks, emphasizes efficiency and reliability, requires a moderate degree of end user interaction, and involves short time horizons. Technical services involve relatively independent tasks of a highly technical nature requiring minimal end user interactions. Finally, administration involves a wide variety of tasks primarily directed toward coordinating and controlling other information systems activities.

While this manufacturing role remains important today, two emerging roles — distribution and technology transfer — may soon account for a majority of information systems activities within most organizations [13, 17].

The distribution role arises in recognition of the multiple channels through which information services can be obtained. Application software, for example, can be acquired through an internal development group, fourth-generation end user development tools, software package vendors, time-sharing services, systems houses, etc. Given the expense of in-house software development and the scarcity of talent for developing sophisticated applications software, it is usually advantageous to acquire externally-produced information products and services. However, locating available products and services and then assessing their quality and appropriateness can consume a significant amount of time unless the effort is effectively managed.

The technology transfer role is associated with organizational efforts to keep abreast of

Table 1.   Traditional Information System Roles

SUBFUNCTION	ACTIVITIES
Operations	data preparation and data entry input and output controls machine operation file storage and control hardware maintenance job scheduling
Systems Development	feasibility studies systems analysis and design software development packaged software acquisition system conversions user training application software maintenance
Technical Services	systems software maintenance telecommunications support database support
Administration	capacity planning systems planning budgeting systems personnel management systems personnel training standards development

innovative information technologies by identifying and experimenting with new technologies, by developing a technical and social infrastructure such that appropriate technologies can be absorbed, and by managing the introduction of new technologies into the work units. Many organizations have recently established office automation and microcomputer subfunctions to develop plans, policies, and support services to facilitate the organizational diffusion of these technologies.

Table 2 suggests a partitioning of information systems activities that accounts for these new roles. Here, delivery systems and systems development represent the traditional manufacturing role of assuring that mainstream information systems are cor-

rectly implemented, efficiently operated, and effectively maintained. The support center and the information center represent a distribution role that serves to unite end users, end user development tools, and external products and services. Research and development along with technology diffusion, represent the technology transfer roles concerned with (1) ensuring that technological innovations are recognized and assessed with regard to their organizational relevance and (2) facilitating the diffusion of appropriate technologies into the work units. Finally, planning, internal auditing, and administration represent an administrative function responsible for the overall planning, control, and coordination of information systems activities.

Table 2.   Evolving Information System Roles

SUBFUNCTION	ACTIVITIES
Delivery Systems	operations as described in Table 1 end user facility operations support database support telecommunications support maintenance (hardware, systems software and applications software) end user liaison and quality assurance for production systems capacity planning
Systems Development	system design and software development for production systems, for critical systems, for sensitive systems, for corporate-wide systems, and for software tools
Support Center	internal consulting service for organizational analyses, modeling, feasibility studies, and systems analysis broker for packaged software, external data services, word processors, and microcomputers end user and systems personnel training
Information Center	internal consulting service and support facilities for end user applications development via microcomputers, decision support systems, modeling languages, data inquiry systems, and automatic applications generators
Research and Development	monitor technological developments develop technical infrastructure technological forecasting
Technology Diffusion	develop organizational infrastructure investigate potential for applying new technologies within organizational areas plan and manage system implementations plan and manage pilot studies
Planning	overall information planning liaison with corporate strategic planning overall evaluation of organizational use of information systems establishing information policies
Internal Auditing	standards development evaluation of adherance to controls
Administration	budgeting personnel management document management

As the set of information system activities given in Table 2 also involve different task environments, they are likely to benefit from differing management styles and practices. Considerable variation exists with regard to issues such as efficiency versus effectiveness, reliability versus flexibility, pragmatics versus technical elegance, and dependability versus innovation. Furthermore, desired work behaviors within these subunits might, at times, be contradictory. Consider the following characteristics recently proposed for software development groups [24]: innovative, technologically current, adaptable, and highly productive while producing quality software products that are reliable, maintainable, and portable. Devising an organizational design that promotes such a demanding set of work behaviors is clearly not a simple, straightforward chore.

ORGANIZATIONAL DESIGN ALTERNATIVES

Organizational design involves specifying relationships between tasks and work groups such that work behaviors will be consistent with the performance criteria characterizing that particular task environment: (e.g., effectiveness, efficiency, reliability, flexibility, innovativeness, etc.). Efforts to arrive at an appropriate organizational design should attend to a variety of issues [6, 9]: selecting appropriate organizational structures and processes, establishing appropriate management and motivational systems, and facilitating required interpersonal interactions.

It would be extremely difficult to adequately cover all these organizational design issues within a single paper. This section will limit its focus to those issues relating to organizational form: the structures through which subunits are established, the processes through which subunits are directed, and the coordination mechanisms through which subunits are integrated.

Structural Forms

As any organization grows in size, a point is invariably reached where communication problems require that its activities be parti-

tioned. The two most basic partitioning strategies are to form work groups on a functional or product basis. Each of these structures possesses certain advantages and disadvantages. A third form, the matrix organization, was devised to simultaneously capture the strengths of both the functional and product structures.

With the functional form, work groups are organized according to the nature of the tasks undertaken with concern primarily directed toward achieving economies of scale and work specialization. The objective is that of internal efficiency [7, 16, 30]: functional skill development is actively promoted, standards for performing activities are devised and a long-term perspective is developed within work groups ('Let's discover the best way to perform this task'). As each functional work unit performs only a portion of the tasks associated with an organization's mission, tight hierarchical control is necessary to ensure overall work success. Performance problems often arise, nonetheless, because of incomplete or inaccurate information flows between work groups and the limited number of employees who hold a global understanding of the organization's mission.

The product form, on the other hand, finds subunits organized around end products or services. Because total mission responsibilities are given to the subunit, decisions can be made more quickly and with a more complete grasp of client/customer needs [7, 16, 30]. Attention is directed toward external effectiveness, local responses to problems are promoted, global perspectives are encouraged, and a medium-term perspective is developed within work groups ('Let's provide the best product/service we can'). Certain disadvantages accompany these advantages: economies of scale and skill specialization are not exploited, and work groups tend to act independent of the global organization.

With the matrix structure, employees are officially housed within functional subunits but are assigned to product work groups in performing their duties. The result— constantly shifting assignments, authority relationships, and interpersonal ties along with a project-oriented interweaving of reporting relationships—provides a very flexible organization able to adapt to changing work circumstances [6, 7, 10, 16, 23]. The informal communication flows and simple control relationship associated with the matrix structure make it particularly well suited for turbulent environments: personnel skills are broadened, adaption is promoted, compromise is encouraged, and a short-term perspective is developed ('Let's perform this task to the best of our abilities given the current situation'). Matrix forms are the most difficult structure to establish and nurture. A considerable investment in administrative overhead is usually required. The dual reporting structure can produce individual role ambiguity, job anxiety and stress, and the potential for work group conflicts and power struggles. Employees must develop political skills along with a sense of trust and a willingness to compromise.

Basic Process Forms

As used here, organization processes refer to the patterns of authority and responsibility that influence the behaviors of individual employees within subunits. A popular view of these issues locates work environments along an organic-mechanistic continuum. High levels of employee discretion and few work policies and procedures characterize organic processes. Low levels of employee discretion and many policies and procedures characterize mechanistic processes [5].

Individuals in organic work groups are allowed considerable discretion regarding the manner in which work is performed. As a result, behavioral reactions to evolving demands tend to be quick and well-targeted to client/customer needs. Mechanistic work groups, on the other hand, are generally very efficient and reliable through the tight control that results from routinization of work behaviors.

Basic Coordination Forms

It is impossible, when partitioning an organization into subunits, to allocate work such that a perfect fit occurs between work group responsibilities and required organizational activities. Many tasks must be passed between work groups, thus increasing task uncertainty. Coordination mechanisms are used to facilitate handling these joint assignments by establishing channels for information exchanges.

An indication of the wide variety of coordination mechanisms that can be applied is provided in Figure 1 [8, 16, 21]. Here, the mechanisms are roughly classified according to their capability to enable work units to cope with task uncertainties. While limited to the coordination of well-understood and routine activities, formal, static, and uni-directional mechanisms promote consistency and predictability. The more informal, dynamic, and multi-directional mechanisms, as they promote both behavioral flexibility and work group interaction, are especially useful when poorly understood or nonroutine activities predominate.

SUMMARY OF BASIC DESIGN ALTERNATIVES

Table 3 contrasts basic design alternatives by indicating the task environments that each is most suited for, as well as the major

Figure 1.   Basic Coordination Mechanisms

Formal, Static, Uni-directional

direct supervision
formal rules and procedures
planning and control systems
committees, task forces, liaison roles
continual, interactive planning between work groups
physical work group rearrangements
manipulation of work group power relationships

Informal, Dynamic, Multi-directional

Table 3.   Major Distinctions Among the Basic Design Alternatives

Design Alternative	Task Environment	Work Behaviors
Structural		
functional	stable routine	efficiency consistency reliability
product	dynamic segmented market	effectiveness rapid response
matrix	turbulent	effectiveness flexibility
Process		
mechanistic	simple stable	efficiency dependability
organic	complex dynamic	effectiveness adaptability
Coordination		
formal	stable routine independent tasks	consistency reliability
informal	dynamic uncertainty interdependent tasks	adaptability rapid response cooperation

work behaviors each promotes. As a further means of illustrating these basic designs, Table 4 indicates those forms typically used in organizing the traditional information systems subunits given in Table 1. It should be recognized that most 'real' organizational designs are hybrid forms rather than pure representations of these basic forms.

Table 4.   Traditional Organizational Designs

Information Systems Subunit	Structure	Process	Coordination
Systems Development	product	mechanistic	informal
Operations	functional	mechanistic	formal
Technical Services	functional	mechanistic	informal
Administration	functional	mechanistic	formal

ORGANIZATIONAL DESIGNS FOR EVOLVING INFORMATION SYSTEMS ACTIVITIES

While these basic organizational designs provide a useful starting point, they are not sufficient given the nature of the work objectives desired in today's information systems task environments. Certain information systems activities, particularly those associated with distributor and technology transfer roles, require considerable innovativeness and adaptability. Innovativeness refers to a work group's creativity in approaching problems and opportunities as well as the work group's willingness to experiment with new methods for performing work. Adaptability refers to a work group's ability to recognize the need for change and to successfully implement a change program.

Designs Promoting Innovativeness and Adaptability

Generally, innovativeness and adaptability can be enhanced by broadening the knowledge, perspectives, and interests of a work group's members. This can be achieved through increasing the diversity of the work group [22, 28], through organic processes [5, 28, 32], and through informal coordination mechanisms [9]. The willingness of a work group to adopt and accept change does not always follow these prescriptions, however [22, 32]. For example, the adoption of

new work methodologies occurs most readily in mechanistic organizations, and acceptance of new work methodologies can be facilitated with either mechanistic or organic processes, depending on a work group's attitudes toward the new methods. This last point introduces the important notion that innovativeness and adaptability can be promoted through seemingly contradictory organizational designs.

Quite different organizational designs can adequately confront change depending on the nature of the change effort. When change is localized to a single subunit, or when a change effort can be incrementally pursued, designs that both isolate a work group and allow for considerable discretion in handling the change effort can be very effective [9, 29]. Such a strategy enables the work group to engage in continuous, improvised, highly-localized change actions without impacting other work groups or disrupting organization-wide operations. This approach may prove effective, for example, when introducing a stand-alone microcomputer into an organization's work units. Even here, however, individual work units cannot be allowed total discretion; some standards will have to be enforced regarding microcomputer acquisition in order to ensure a desired level of organization-wide compatibility regarding hardware, software, support, training, etc.

With radical or large-scale change, it might be best to blur rather than define work group boundaries [20]. Here, the simultaneous recognition of a need for change by multiple work groups, along with the inevitable boundary disputes between work groups, can encourage productive intergroup negotiations as well as collaborative problem-solving efforts. This strategy, then, is aimed at providing integrated solutions to global change events. Accordingly, it might very well be employed when implementing a corporate DSS to support an interactive planning process throughout an entire organization.

It is also necessary for most organizations to simultaneously demonstrate stability and flexibility in their work behaviors in order to exploit current and future opportunities [9, 29]. By effectively applying the notion of an organizational *overlay* [28], it becomes possible to employ a single organizational form characterized by both stability and flexibility. With an organizational overlay, a secondary organizational form is used along with a primary organizational form such that certain limitations of the dominant form are overcome. A recent study found that software groups that employed overlays were more innovative than software groups that did not employ overlays [32]. For example, mechanistic software groups that had established R & D subunits to identify and then introduce new software methods made greater use of these methods than mechanistic software groups without such R & D subunits. Similarly organic software groups that assigned their analysts and programmers to projects as fixed teams (through which new software methods could be channeled) made greater use of these methods than did organic software groups that assigned their analysts and programmers to projects on a more ad hoc basis.

This discussion, oriented toward promoting innovativeness and adaptability, suggests that any organizational designs facilitating information systems activities must themselves be flexible. The appropriateness of any given organizational form will vary, however, depending on the technology being applied, the organizational unit being supported, and the activities currently being taken in applying the technology.

The Need for Multiple Forms. While the tasks involved might appear very similar, information systems activities, even within the same subunit, may require different organizational forms because of specific task environments. For example, software provided to maintain financial ledgers are quite distinct from that supporting on-line inquiry into customer files by clerical personnel [13, 15, 17]. Project team structures for these two applications are likely to be quite different in order that design criteria such as reliability, auditability, error control, ease-of-use, and 'natural' and user interactions can be reinforced. Technology transfer efforts (office automation, flexible manufacturing systems, programmer's workbench, end user development, etc.), can present a variety of task environments depending on the degree of change required within the target unit, the target unit's readiness to accept this change, and whether these uncertainties are technological or organizational in nature.

The Need for Dynamic Forms. Information system activities often consist of lengthy task sequences requiring different participants and different work orientations at each stage [12, 19, 23, 31, 34]. While such an activity might have a single project administration, organizational form is likely to vary with each successive stage. A critical design element here involves establishing coordination mechanisms that not only apply across a variety of organizational forms but also enable work to flow smoothly to each succeeding stage.

The Need for Disintegrating Forms.   Three forces are at play that periodically require the destruction of information systems work groups. First, as software development and technology transfer efforts possess finite time horizons, work groups responsible for such activities undergo periodic restructuring as old projects are completed and new projects are begun. Second, given the dynamic nature of information technologies, the appropriateness of specific products, services, or technical skills lessens over time. As the organizational relevance of any work group erodes, the group itself should disband. Finally, much information systems activity involves organizational learning through the transfer of new technologies. For example, the intent of establishing a centralized information center might be to have similar units formed throughout the organization. If the staff of such an information center is successful in establishing spin-off centers serving local needs, the central staff may eventually erode the justification for its own existence. Together, these forces suggest that many information systems work groups should adopt a life cycle perspective in which a continual stream of work group births and deaths is viewed as one measure of information systems success. However, as Pettigrew [27] has pointed out through his analysis of influence shifts between programmers and systems analysts in Britain, it can prove very difficult to reduce, let alone remove, a work group's organizational role.

The Need for Umbrella Forms.   Whenever organizational activities are dispersed throughout work units whose interrelations themselves evolve over time, the need emerges for a managerial superstructure that provides overall coordination, that sets directions, and that resolves the disputes that will invariably arise among subunits [20, 23, 25]. Devising suitable structural mechanisms (committees, task forces, review boards, planning groups, etc.) is clearly going to be a critically important task in organizing information systems activities.

Prototypal Designs

Building on the concepts which have been developed, Table 5 provides a prototypal collection of design alternatives for organizing the information systems function. An awareness of the changes occurring within many of today's information systems organizations, particularly those making innovative uses of information technologies, will indicate that these prescriptions are not simply idle speculation. Even so, it would be unusual to find these designs fully implemented as specified. Actual design efforts must necessarily consider a number of factors not brought out here, e.g., an organization's dominant structural form, leadership styles of key managers, organizational priorities and strategies, etc.

Delivery System.   As it is likely that efficiency concerns will dominate other objectives, a mechanistic product structure based upon processing environments, such as batch, interactive, high security, etc., might be preferred. This product structure would be aligned with functional technical support groups responsible for services such as database management, telecommunications, and systems programming. Coordination mechanisms would likely differ with the degree of end user interaction encountered with particular processing environments.

Systems Development.   This technical service subunit is primarily responsible for developing large, well-defined but complex

Table 5.   Prototypal Organizational Designs

INFORMATION SYSTEMS SUBUNIT	STRUCTURE	PROCESS	COORDINATION	OTHER ISSUES
Delivery System	product some functional	mechanistic	formal some informal	
Systems Development	functional	mechanistic some organic	informal some formal	multiple dynamic
Support Center	matrix	organic	informal (external) formal (internal)	overlapped dynamic
Information Center	functional product	organic	informal	overlapped disintegrating
Research and Development	product	organic	informal	isolated
Technology Diffusion	matrix	organic	informal	dynamic disintegrating overlapped
Planning	functional some product	organic	informal (internal) formal (external)	dynamic overlapped umbrella disintegrating
Internal Auditing	functional	mechanistic	formal	overlapped
Administration	functional	mechanistic	formal	umbrella

information systems requiring disciplined behaviors to ensure adherence to end-user specifications and to organization-wide software standards. Given such a task environment, a very tight organization stressing technical proficiency and high productivity might, in general, be preferred.

Support Center. As support center personnel act in a variety of roles, such as broker, consultant, advisor, or systems analyst, the preferred organizational form is likely to be a matrix structure emphasizing specialized skills as well as knowledge of end user application areas. While mechanisms linking the support center to end users should be

informal, internal coordination of the support center might benefit from more formal mechanisms to ensure consistency regarding project selection criteria, hardware/software acquisition, etc. One might also expect that as end users gained sufficient expertise they would begin to incorporate these activities within their own task domains with the support center eventually serving as a coordinating body for these local support centers.

Information Center. The pure consulting service provided by an information center might benefit from an organic hybrid form using both functional work groups skilled in the application of end user development tools and product work groups knowledge-able of specific end user areas. An organic climate is preferred because of the short life of many projects, the desirability of flexible internal relationships, and the benefits to be derived from adaptable end user relation-ships. Finally, a major aim of the information center should be to encourage networking among end users such that information cen-ter responsibilities could eventually be spun off to end users.

Research and Development.   This sub-unit primarily serves to maintain an organiza-tion's technical infrastructure by scanning the environment for new information techno-logies, assessing their appropriateness, and communicating this information to others. One might expect that an organic structure, isolated from other work units, might perform best. A product orientation, where personnel expertise was maintained along technological lines, would also seem desirable.

Technology Diffusion.   As this subunit performs a range of activities requiring quite different skills, it would seem that a matrix form combining skill specialization along with end user familiarity under a project man-agement umbrella would be preferred. Given that most projects would involve numerous stages, flexibility and adaptability regarding project structures, processes, and coordi-nating mechanisms would be mandatory.

Planning.   The planning subunit might best be viewed as occurring at two distinct organizational levels—a senior level where organization-wide concerns are handled, and a lower level where specialized concerns are handled. While the senior-level activity might best be performed through a single umbrella-like executive steering committee [25], the lower-level work groups would be composed of dynamic, eventually disinte-grating task forces formally reporting to the senior-level committee.

Internal Auditing.   In order that it per-form its responsibilities in a consistent and objective manner, this subunit should ideally have few linkages with other organizational work units. The rigorous, disciplined, and specialized nature of its task environment clearly suggests that a mechanistic, func-tional form might be preferred.

Administration.   As this subunit serves a housekeeping role in providing and managing the resources necessary for all other informa-tion systems activities, the task environment should promote behaviors emphasizing effi-ciency, consistency, and reliability.

IMPLICATIONS

Movement toward the organizational forms just described will require substantial changes in the perspectives, activities, and styles of many information systems managers. Two critical issues in particular must be directly confronted: recognizing that information resources can be owned, operated, and man-aged by all of an organization's work units; and, recognizing that power losses will in-variably be felt by the information systems function as this transition to end user com-puting unfolds.

As information technologies become em-bedded deep within the fabric of organiza-tions, responsibility for information resources will increasingly be given to line and staff management. As a consequence, the manu-facturing role of the information systems function is likely to take on a custodial or advisory nature. In order for their influence to be felt, information systems specialists and managers must demonstrate an organizational as well as technical expertise such that they are perceived as the catalysts behind the organization's innovative uses of information technologies.

Even if information systems specialists and managers actively support this democratization of organizational computing, the influence that information systems personnel exert in their organizations is likely to be initially reduced. The severity and tenacity of this power loss will follow one of two paths depending on the directions taken by information systems managers. If an effort is made to hold on to the manufacturing role, this power loss could very well be substantial and irreversible. If evolution toward the distributor and technology transfer roles occurs, however, a substantial increase in power could result.

The following anecdote illustrates how an information systems manager's long-term power position can actually be increased through end user computing [18]. The information systems director in a large consumer goods firm diffused office automation technologies through the use of joint (user and information systems personnel) pilot projects which, over time, became fully user managed. This director then established an umbrella organization, a Standards Review Board composed of information systems office technology specialists and key users, which now exerts a significant influence within the organization. By developing this business-dominated but technically competent organizational unit, the information systems director assumed a new and necessary organizational role. Information systems personnel should, if they can combine their understanding of information technologies with an understanding of organizational purpose, find their influence growing with any increase in an organization's reliance on information resources.

These fluctuations in the organizational influence maintained by information systems managers should be tempered by two additional thoughts. First, a broad understanding of information technologies may very well prove requisite for line management responsibility in those operating units where information resources are the primary vehicle through which organizational activities occur. Thus, information systems management experience might become a necessity for promotion into senior management positions. Second, information systems managers serving under line managers not technologically conversant may find themselves with considerable influence because of their ability to reduce organizational uncertainty regarding the technology.

Such scenarios are not common today for the simple reason that most organizations are just beginning their transition toward end user domination of information systems activities. While successfully managing through this transition period is likely to be a trying experience for *all* managers, it will prove especially difficult for the information systems manager, as the information systems function itself will be drastically reorganized. To ease this experience, information systems managers and researchers must commit themselves to undertake a number of important tasks for the redesigning of the information systems function.

Information Systems Manager Tasks

Redesigning the information systems function would require four actions. First, assess the current situation regarding the assignment of information systems responsibilities throughout the organization. How is the information systems function currently organized? To what extent are other organizational units responsible for information resources or activities? How are organization-wide information responsibilities being addressed?

Second, work with corporate planners in specifying short- as well as long-term scenarios depicting the manner with which information technologies will be applied to perform and support organizational activities. These scenarios are necessary as it is through them that one begins to envision the likely shifts regarding both information systems activities and organization-wide responsibilities.

Third, begin to evaluate the various organizational forms with regard to their capability to provide these activities and responsibilities. This effort should ultimately result in the development of a few future organizational designs along with the steps to be taken in implementing each.

Finally, experiment with the various organizational forms in order that their strengths and weaknesses become apparent. Such experimentation should mesh well with the pilot project or task force operations that often accompany the use of new information technologies.

Information Systems Researcher Tasks

Researchers can provide extremely valuable services to those managers addressing the question of organizing for these new information systems activities and responsibilities. First, it seems clear that the appropriateness of a particular organization form for a specific information systems activity will be contingent upon a variety of factors. Exactly what these factors are and how they relate to particular organizational forms, however, have yet to be determined. Research projects aimed at developing a contingency theory for organizing information systems activities are strongly advocated. Second, it also seems clear that many impediments are likely to arise as organizational redesign programs are implemented.

Research is needed that both identifies likely problems and prescribes strategies for managing around, or through, these problems.

Joint Manager-Researcher Tasks

A final set of tasks will be required that are likely to be accomplished only through the cooperative efforts of information systems managers and researchers via active research programs. If the notions behind the prescriptions given in Table 5 are accepted, it seems likely that information systems designs will involve a mixed-bag of organizational thrusts. How exactly does one *manage* such an organization? Not only is it comprised of many different work groups, but these work groups are likely to be characterized by quite distinct cultures. What are effective management systems, e.g., planning, control, and evaluation processes, for such an organization? How are these units staffed? What type of career path can be established to provide for both skill development and personal advancement? As this type of organization does not exist today, conjectures regarding its nature are fraught with uncertainty. Research must take place along with the early experimentation by innovative information systems organizations.

CONCLUSION

These views on organizing the information systems function are primarily directed toward large, complex organizations making sophisticated use of information resources. Organizations of all sizes, nevertheless, might very well benefit from applying these notions in examining their own practices for organizing information systems activities. While it is unlikely that the prescriptions offered here will ever be fully applied, the information systems function in most organizations must evolve if it is to remain a potent organizational force. An information systems function continuing to serve a primarily manufacturing role will eventually find its influence regarding information resources preempted by other organizational units. If these other organizational units do not have the expertise to successfully manage information technologies, the overall loss to the organization may be severe. It is hoped that the ideas expressed in this paper will encourage experimentation with different but appropriate organization forms such that this transition to the distributor and technology transfer roles not only occurs but transpires smoothly.

REFERENCES

1. ALLEN, B. "Computer Strategy: A Philosophy for Managing Information Processing Resources," in R. Goldberg and H. Lorin, eds., *The Economics of Information Processing,* Volume 1, Wiley-Interscience, New York, New York, 1982.

2. ALLEN, B. "An Unmanaged Computer System Can Stop You Dead," *Harvard Business Review,* Volume 60, Number 6, November-December 1982, pp. 76–87.

3. BENJAMIN, R. I. "Information Technology in the 1990's: A Long Range Planning Scenario," *MIS Quarterly,* Volume 6, Number 2, June 1982, pp. 11–31.

4. BUCHANAN, J. R. and LINOWES, R. G. "Understanding Distributed Data Processing," *Harvard Business Review,* Volume 58, Number 4, July-August 1980, pp. 143–153.

5. BURNS, T. and STALKER, G. *The Management of Innovation,* Tavistock, London, England, 1961.

6. CLELAND, D. I. "The Human Side of Project Management," in A. J. Kelley, ed., *New Dimensions of Project Management,* Lexington Books, Lexington, Massachusetts, 1982.

7. DALY, E. B. "Organizational Philosophies Used in Software Development," in R. Goldberg and H. Lorin, eds., *The Economics of Information Processing,* Volume 2, Wiley-Interscience, New York, New York, 1982.

8. GALBRAITH, J. R. "Organization Design: An Information Processing View," *Interfaces,* Volume 4, Number 3, May 1974, pp. 28–36.

9. GALBRAITH, J. R. "Designing the Innovating Organization," *Organizational Dynamics,* Volume 10, Number 3, Winter 1982, pp. 5–25.

10. HEMSLEY, J. R. "Matrix Organizational Structures in Brazilian Organizations," in D. Soen, ed., *Industrial Development and Technology Transfer,* George Godwin Ltd., London, England, 1981.

11. JENKINS, J. M. and SANTOS, R. F. "Centralization vs. Decentralization of Data Processing Functions," in R. Goldberg and H. Lorin, eds., *The Economics of Information Processing,* Volume 2, Wiley-Interscience, New York, New York, 1982.

12. KEEN, J. S. *Managing Systems Development,* John Wiley, Chichester, England, 1981.

13. LIENTZ, B. P. *An Introduction to Distributed Systems,* Addison-Wesley, Reading, Massachusetts, 1981.

14. LUCAS, H. C., JR. "Alternative Structures for the Management of Information Processing," in R. Goldberg and H. Lorin, eds., *The Economics of Information Processing,* Volume 2, Wiley-Interscience, New York, New York, 1982.

15. MANTEI, M. "The Effect of Programming Team Structures on Programming Tasks," *Communications of the ACM,* Volume 24, Number 3, March 1981, pp. 106–113.

16. McCANN, J. and GALBRAITH, J. R. "Interdepartmental Relations," in P. C. Nystrom and W. H. Starbuck, eds., *Handbook of Organizational Design,* Volume 2, Oxford University Press, Oxford, England, 1981.

17. McFARLAN, F. W. and McKENNEY, J. L. *Information Systems Management: A Senior Management Perspective,* Richard D. Irwin, Inc., Homewood, Illinois, 1982.

18. McKENNEY, J. L. "User Domination Means DPer Must Know Business," *Information System News,* September 19, 1983, pp. 17, 20.

19. McKENNEY, J. L. and McFARLAN, F. W. "The Information Archipelago — Maps and Bridges," *Harvard Business Review,* Volume 60, Number 5, September-October 1982, pp. 109–119.

20. METCALF, L. "Designing Precarious Partnerships," in P. C. Nystrom and W. H. Starbuck, eds., *Handbook of Organizational Design,* Volume 2, Oxford University Press, Oxford, England, 1981.

21. MINTZBERG, H. "Structures in 5's: A Synthesis of the Research on Organization Design," *Management Science,* Volume 26, Number 3, March 1980, pp. 322–341.

22. MOCH, M. K. and MORSE, E. V. "Size, Centralization and Organizational Adoption of Innovations," *American Sociological Review,* Volume 42, Number 5, 1977, pp. 716–725.

23. MORRIS, P. W. G. "Project Organizations: Structures for Managing Change," in A. J. Kelley, ed., *New Dimensions of Project Management,* Lexington Books, Lexington, Massachusetts, 1982.

24. MUNSON, J. B. and YEH, R. T. "Report by the IEEE Software Engineering Productivity Workshop," Proceedings, 15th Hawaii International Conference on System Science, 1982, pp. 249–282.

25. NOLAN, R. L. "Managing Information Systems by Committee," *Harvard Business Review,* Volume 60, Number 4, July-August 1982, pp. 72–79.

26. OLSON, M. H. *Organization of Information Services: Alternative Approaches,* University Microfilms International, Ann Arbor, Michigan, 1980.

27. PETTIGREW, A. M. *The Politics of Organizational Decision Making,* Tavistock Publications, London, England, 1973.

28. PIERCE, J. L. and DELBECQ, A. L. "Organization Structure, Individual Attitudes and Innovation," *Academy of Management Review,* Volume 2, Number 1, January 1977, pp. 27–37.

29. WEICK, K. E., "The Management of Organizational Change Among Loosely Coupled Elements," in P. Goodman, ed., *Change in Organizations,* Jossey-Bass, San Francisco, California, 1982.

30. WILLIAMSON, O. E. *Markets and Hierarchies,* Free Press, New York, New York, 1975.

31. ZMUD, R. W. "Management of Large Software Development Efforts," *MIS Quarterly,* Volume 4, Number 2, June 1980, pp. 45–56.

32. ZMUD, R. W. "Diffusion of Modern Software Practices: Influences of Centralization and Formalization," *Manage-*

ment Science, Volume 28, Number 12, December 1982, pp. 1421–1431.

33. ZMUD, R. W. *Information Systems in Organizations,* Scott, Foresman & Co., Glenview, Illinois, 1983.

34. ZMUD, R. W. and COX, J. F. "The Implementation Process: A Change Approach," *MIS Quarterly,* Volume 3, Number 2, June 1979, pp. 35–43.

QUESTIONS

1. What subfunctions are performed within traditional information system functions, and what are the activities and responsibilities of each subfunction?

2. Describe the organizational structure of a traditional information system function in a large organization, including in the description an organization chart.

3. What recent forces are creating pressures for changing the traditional organizational structure of the information system function?

4. Discuss each of the following roles of the information system function, and state the evolutionary trends of each:
   a. Manufacturing role
   b. Distribution role
   c. Technology transfer role

5. What implications do the evolving roles of the information system function hold for the roles of individual information system personnel such as systems analysts and information system directors?

6. Contrast the basic alternatives with respect to each of the following organizational forms:
   a. Structure
   b. Process
   c. Coordination

7. Since the information system function seems to be evolving in the direction of decentralized authority and user orientation, what organizational designs can enhance the innovativeness and adaptability that are their hallmarks?

8. What organizational subunits are likely to comprise the information system function of the future, and what organizational design features is each likely to exhibit?

The Information Archipelago— Governing the New World*

In the future, information services operations will include a central hub of operations linked by telecommunications to remote devices that may or may not have their own extensive data files and processing power. The balance between work done at the hub and at distributed locations will vary from one organization to another. To make their information systems evolve to that point, companies will have to integrate, at least at a policy level, the separate technologies of computers, telecommunications, and word processors.

During this evolution, organizations will simultaneously manage a blend of systems, some of which will be familiar, such as batch data processing, and some of which will not, such as electronic mail. Each new system will need a management structure quite different from those needed merely to expand the uses of older technologies. The corporation will have to encourage innovation by both information systems specialists and users in the newer systems while it focuses on control and efficiency of those that are more mature.

In formulating their policies for the deployment of information services (IS) in the 1980s, managers must deal with two main conflicts. The first involves the tension between innovation and control. How far a particular company goes in encouraging either of these will depend on the particular phase the organization is in with regard to the technology. As we saw in the previous articles of this series, companies in the early phases of using a new system should be learning about its operations and exploring its implications for the corporation. The importance a company places on aggressive innovation early on will vary widely depending on the role of IS technology in the company's strategy, the corporate willingness to take risks, and the status the IS portfolio has in the organization. In later phases, the emphasis is on implementing the new system efficiently.

The second conflict is that between the IS department and users in developing skills for dealing with the new technology and in setting priorities. The user often has a predilection for meeting short-term needs at the expense of orderly long-term development.

IS, on the other hand, can become preoccupied with mastering the technology and establishing a development plan at the expense of fast response to the legitimate needs of users.

Effectively balancing these two groups' roles is a complicated chore that must take into account such factors as organization culture, potential strategic impact of IS technology, organization structure, and geography. Very different application portfolios and operating problems result from domination by either group. (*Exhibit 1* shows some consequences of IS and user domination.) Further, this balance may have to shift over time.

Throughout this article we emphasize the need for experimentation because most organizations have been unable to foresee the implications of their entry into a new technology. The experiences of four companies, described in the following paragraphs, illustrate this problem:

The top priority of a large machine tool manufacturer's engineering department is computer-aided design (CAD). Early success with CAD has led the company to expand the effort by modifying the digital information design output to enable it to control computer-driven machine tools. This work has been done independently of the bill-of-materials cost system, which is in a data base maintained by the IS unit. Although staff was not available to deal with integrating the new system in the company's data base structure—which IS management in objecting pointed out—users pushed the decision to go ahead. Despite the prospects of serious system integration problems, the engineering department received full support from senior management to proceed because the project promised to shorten the product development life cycle.

Exhibit 1.   Possible Implications of Excessive Dominance of Systems Development and Use by IS or Users

IS DOMINATES	USER DOMINATES
Too much emphasis on data base hygiene.	Too much emphasis on problem focus.
No recent new supplier or new distinct services (too busy with maintenance).	IS claims lack of control. Explosive growth in number of new systems and supporting staff.
New systems always must fit data structure of existing system.	Multiple suppliers delivering services. Frequent change in supplier of specific service.
All requests for service require system study with benefit identification.	Lack of standardization and control over data hygiene and system.
Standardization dominates; few exceptions.	Hard evidence of benefits nonexistent.
IS designs and/or constructs everything.	Soft evidence of benefits not organized.
Benefits of user control over development discussed but never implemented.	Few measurements and/or objectives for new systems.
Study always shows construction costs less than outside purchase.	Technical advice of IS not sought or, if received, considered irrelevant.
Head count of distributed minis and development staff growing surreptitiously.	User buying design, construction, maintenance services, and even operations from outside.
IS specializing in technical frontiers, not user-oriented markets.	User building networks to own—not corporate—needs.

Exhibit 1.   (continued)

IS DOMINATES	USER DOMINATES
IS spending 80% on maintenance, 20% on development.	While some users are growing rapidly in experience and use, other users feel nothing is relevant because they do not understand.
IS thinks they are in control of all.	No coordinated effort for technology transfer or learning from experience between users.
Users express unhappiness.	Growth in duplication of technical staffs.
Portfolio of development opportunities firmly under IS control.	Communications costs rising dramatically through redundancy.
No strong user group exists.	
General management not involved but concerned.	

A division of a large consumer products manufacturer undertook a large investment in office automation with only modest cost-benefit justification. The IS department encouraged managers and administrative support personnel to use the system after a little instruction and some introductory training on a word processor. In four months' time, three product managers had developed independent networks for their activities to support sales, and two had automated some of their word processing—at substantial savings. Two others did little to encourage their support staffs to try out the system, so although their staffs were enthusiastic, they had gained no measurable benefits to date.

After six months, IS was given the job of developing an approach to integrating these seven "experienced" users. The IS manager estimates that it will take roughly two years to achieve this. Both he and divisional management agree, however, that it would have been impossible to proceed so rapidly with office automation with a standard IS systems study and that the expense of rationalizing the system after the fact was an acceptable price for the benefits. This particular program was in sharp contrast to the company's mature DP technologies, over which IS was exerting strong control.

A large grocery chain acquired a system of point-of-sales terminals. The retail division bought these terminals (with the support of the IS manager) to help store managers control inventory. Once installed, however, the systems evolved quickly into links to central headquarters, which used the data to modify forecasting, measure advertising effectiveness, and manage warehouse stock levels for the whole chain. This linkage is seen by all involved as providing significant value added.

This unplanned linkage was very expensive because the communication protocols in the terminals were incompatible with those in the computer at headquarters. No planning for compatibility had been undertaken, since the retail division had not intended to use the computers in this way when it had bought its terminals. Further, even if the organization had considered such use, management probably would have seen the costs of the resulting system as prohibitive.

A large bank separately introduced both an electronic mail system and a word processor system to facilitate bank loan paperwork. From the two systems a new service of on-line loan portfolio management emerged with exception reports on the state of each portfolio. This system was the result of conversations between a loan officer and a member of the trust department, who discovered that the loan word processor system could be used for investment analysis and could be easily accessed by trust personnel through the electronic mail system.

After three months, the costs of both systems were rising unexpectedly, yet the bank had no formal means of evaluating this "experimental" use of the systems by participants who had not been involved. And the fact that this use was draining work away from the central IS unit caused hard feelings. Eventually a senior management review committee gave the project ad hoc support, even though such use of the system was not what the bank had originally intended.

These examples illustrate that it is often impossible to foresee and plan for the full range of consequences before introducing IS technology and that excessive control and a focus on quick results in the early stages can inhibit learning about a system. Neither IS departments nor users have had outstanding records in predicting all the consequences and potential of a new technology.

PRESSURES TOWARD USER DOMINANCE

The forces that encourage user control over the acquisition and development of stand-alone mini- or microcomputers fall into five main categories. (Throughout this article, unless otherwise stated, the word *minicomputer* refers to both mini- and microcomputers.)

Pent-up Demand

The backlog of development work facing an information services department is often too great for its staff resources (three- to five-year backlogs are the norm). Staffing

crunches occur, first, because established systems require maintenance to deal with changing regulatory and other business requirements; as more systems are automated, maintenance needs rise. Also, systems design philosophy has shifted from incorporation of data into programs in the early 1970s to clear separation of data base management from processing procedures now. Effecting this one-time conversion of data systems is expensive in terms of staff resources.

Further, the most challenging, highest status IS jobs tend to be with computer vendors and software houses. This makes it hard for in-company IS departments to attract, keep, and promote talented people. Further, when the IS support staff is closely linked to the user organization, promotion of employees from IS to other functions becomes easier.

Finally, the protocols for interfacing with a network and conforming to corporate control standards can be time consuming and complex. A stand-alone system that a user develops independent of the network can simplify a job and permit the use of less-skilled staff.

For all these reasons, IS management appears to be unresponsive to user demands. These views of IS as not being helpful and focusing too much on detail, though often inaccurate, make user-developed systems and stand-alone minicomputers an attractive and expedient way of getting work done.

Available Service

Minicomputer-based software packages, available for specific applications, offer easy, and sometimes deceptively easy, solutions to short-term problems. These packages, marketed by hardware or software vendors to end-user managers, emphasize functional features and downplay technical and software problems. Use of a stand-alone minicomputer is seen as particularly desirable because of its faster and more consistent on-line response time. The minicomputer gives easy access to on-line systems, and its stand-alone feature permits the user to avoid being one of many users of a system with a highly variable volume and an equally variable response time.

Also, the distributed system appears to be simple operationally, needing only one operator to run it. Users do not consider problems of air conditioning, maintenance, and power availability. Often, the local solution appears to be more cost-effective than the work done by the central IS development group. Further, there is no cumbersome project proposal to be defended before IS technicians, who have their own agendas.

However, there is a rapidly growing set of decision support applications, such as interactive financial planning models, that require a new approach. In these cases, the software makes it genuinely easier for users to develop the application without enlisting the technical support for programming and running it on a mainframe computer.

User Control

For users, the notion of regaining control over a part of their operation, particularly if IS technology is crucial to their unit's success, is very appealing. Such a move away from IS domination often reverses a trend that began years ago with very different technology: that of the large mainframe computer. Control by users has at least three important implications.

First, employing either their own staff or a software house, users often believe they can get a system up and running more quickly than if they tried to navigate through the priority-setting process in the corporate IS department, let alone get staff assigned to the project. Users also think that the re-

sulting systems will be more responsive to their particular needs. It is easier to accept one's own mistakes than those made by a remote group.

Today, because users have had experience with computer systems, especially with home computers, they are more confident in this ability to manage a computer project successfully, and clever computer vendor marketing has helped increase their confidence. Often such experience is superficial, however, and users have unjustified confidence.

Problems of communication among IS departments and users are especially acute when one moves to the international environment, where different languages, operating protocols (including government relations), and quality of support by individual vendors—as well as vast distances—come into play. These problems can be alleviated by distributing development to these units. Limited expertise and lack of experience in developing sophisticated systems, however, restrain local control, especially in the less industrialized parts of the world.

The second result of user control is that users see themselves as able to set maintenance priorities, either by doing the work themselves or contracting with a supplier.

The third result is that users see themselves as gaining control over day-to-day operations and becoming insulated from the vicissitudes of corporate computer scheduling. This is particularly important to small, marginal users of data centers with heavy and volatile loads.

Greater Innovation

As the four examples at the beginning of this article show, it is hard to predict all the ramifications of the introduction of a new technology. First-hand, enthusiastic experimentation by the user can unlock creativity and stimulate new approaches to solving troublesome problems, whereas systems developed by an IS unit often generate resistance. This is an example in the IS area of the application of the idea that organization by multiple profit centers instead of by function stimulates creativity.[1]

Fit to Organization

As a company becomes more decentralized and geographically spread out, a distributed function for development of IS systems will help to avoid heavy expenses for introducing and coordinating any new system. Only a few conglomerates have tried to centralize development. Another advantage of distributing development is that the divestiture of a unit is easier when its IS activities are less integrated with the rest of the company.

In aggregate, the foregoing considerations represent a powerful argument in favor of a strong role for users in systems development and provide some clues as to when users ought to dominate. They further suggest that users seek minicomputer-based systems to fill short-term needs. The stand-alone minicomputer offers users an immediate solution and gives them the control they want. Buying a minicomputer with packaged software represents a reaction to the current shift in costs from expensive hardware to low-cost technology and expensive people. Our experience suggests that the policies needed to deal with locally developed systems must focus on this changed reality. In the information service industry, people no longer wait on expensive computers; now computers wait on the expensive people of the central IS services department.

The availability of well-trained people to work in the cottage software industry lags behind the need and will continue to lag, thus intensifying this problem over time. This trend is forcing greater reliance on new forms of outside software support for information services ranging from purchased services, systems, software, and occasionally even contracting for project management.

PRESSURES TOWARD IS CONTROL

The internal pressures are strong to consolidate or keep consolidated the development resources for IS in one or more large clusters. These forces, which we discuss in the following paragraphs, range from the relative ease of developing and enforcing IS standards to the ability to produce realistic cost estimates.

Staff Professionalism

A large support staff furnishes an opportunity to attract and continually challenge technical experts. The chance to both work on interesting problems and share expertise with other professionals is appealing. For the organization, having these skills permits the undertaking of complex tasks without undue risk. Further, keeping these persons in a single unit permits the company to make the best use of them in meeting the problems it considers most important, and the central unit can provide support for small divisions or functions that lack their own systems development staffs but occasionally need them.

A large IS group is an important weapon in postponing so-called burn-out and slowing turnover because it provides more avenues for career development. As the average age of IS experts continues to climb (what some call "the graying of IS"), providing opportunities is essential to improved productivity. In addition, salary levels, individual interests, and possible communication problems with nontechnical persons make lateral movement out of the department for some IS staff an infeasible option.

It is also easier to develop and enforce standards of IS management in a large group. Documentation procedures, project management skills, and disciplined approaches to maintenance are critical for a development department. In 1971 a large financial services organization, faced with a poor relationship between its central development department and key users, split the development department into a number of smaller units and distributed them around the company, thereby changing both reporting responsibility and office location. Although at first this stimulated new ideas and better relationships with users (many development people identified more readily with users' needs than with technical issues), by 1977 the level of IS professionalism had dropped so low through neglect that the company had to call an outside service organization to straighten out several project fiascoes. The company has again centralized important parts of the development function and has installed much tighter controls over management practices in the remaining distributed development groups.

User-designed or user-selected minicomputer-based systems are particularly vulnerable to a deterioration in standards. Lacking practical systems design experience and standards for purchased software, the user may ignore normal data control procedures, documentation standards, and conventional costing practices. Consequently, purchasing from several suppliers or incrementally from one produces a clumsy system design that is hard to maintain.

Managers in one large financial organization were surprised to discover that all the people involved in the design and purchase of software of three of its stand-alone minicomputer systems had left the company, that no formal documentation or operating instructions had been prepared, and that all source programs had been lost. Only disk files with object programs on them remained. The system ran but no one knew why. Even if its survival depended on it, the company could not make changes quickly.

Further, unless great care is taken in the initial hardware selection and system design process to allow for growth, expansion can disrupt business and require very expensive software modifications. Feasibility studies by users may contain serious mistakes if inexperienced staff underestimate both the complexity of the software needed to do the job and the growth in the number of transactions the system will handle. The risk rises if users do not understand the company's most important business needs.

Such a feasibility study fails to recognize that a successful first application generates an unexpected second application, then a third, and so forth. Each application appears to require only a modest purchase and therefore may not get a comprehensive cost review. The result can be a hardware configuration that is unable to handle the work.

Implementing a user feasibility study may be quite impractical because of vendor instability. As it reaches maturity, the rapidly growing software sector will experience the same trends that characterized the pocket calculator and digital watch industries in the late 1970s, and many vendors will leave the market. This can be vital to the user because a department's operations may become completely dependent on a system.

Since such investments are software intensive, failure of the vendor will disrupt the service the department gives and necessitate conversion of software to another machine. Both of these consequences are expensive. These concerns apply also to the packages and services provided by software suppliers. As some companies have learned, a single experience with a product from a failed software vendor can be painful. But user groups often have a tendency to buy systems tailored to their situations, which may lead to rigid, hard-to-maintain systems. Further technology transfer between users is often poor.

For example, when a systems-minded regional manager and an aggressive, growth-oriented IS manager worked in the same regional division of a large forest-products company, their budget for IS doubled that of a comparable region, but they had exported only one application to other regions. Review of the unit's work revealed that nearly half of its developments could have helped solve companywide problems.

Corporate Data Base System

A company that wants to develop a corporate data base often needs a collection of files at a central location for reference by multiple users. Availability of staff in a central unit provides a focal point for conceptualization and development of such systems. Moreover, a central department can best distribute these systems to users or manage the development process in a company where local units are building the data base.

Inevitably, the first concern of managers in discussing stand-alone minicomputers is whether the company will lose the opportunity to control its data flows. They worry that data of significance to many people other than those in the originating unit will be locked up in a nonstandard format in inaccessible locations. Although this fear has some validity, several mitigating factors exist.

The first is timing. In many cases managers argue against acquisition of a minicomputer because they want to preserve flexibility for future data base design. Often, however, it turns out that this flexibility will not be needed until three or more years later. Therefore, using a system of minicomputers may be an equally good (if not better) means of moving toward longer term systems as making the leap to them now.

Second, at planned and frequent intervals, users can abstract data from a minicomputer and send it directly to the main computer. And of course not all information in the minicomputer's files is relevant to other users — indeed, often only a small percentage is.

On the other hand, maintenance and linkage of uniquely designed data handling systems can prove expensive. This problem is typified by word and data processing systems, which generate voluminous records in electronic format. Unless well designed, these files may become too full, lock up key data from potential users, and pose security problems. A mail-order house recently discovered that each customer representative was using more than 200 disks per day and storing them in boxes by date of order receipt; this made aggregate customer information impossible to obtain in a timely manner. A new procedure reduced the number of disks to five. Not only does proper organization of and access to electronic files often require central storage but, security is often easier to maintain when all files are in one place.

Center for New Ideas

A central unit helps to identify new technologies of potential value to the company and to inform prospective users about them. It can also function as a research unit and take financial and implementation responsibility for leading-edge projects that might be too venturesome for an individual user to undertake. Several organizations use such groups to initiate and manage corporately mandated productivity improvement programs. In these cases, senior management saw user departments as needing productivity improvements but incapable of implementing them. The central unit became a catalyst for initiating these improvements, with full authority to compel users to follow.

In its role of expert and leader, however, the central development group may push for "make" decisions when it should "buy": their high level of professionalism can make them overcritical of any purchased package as being too general and incorporating inappropriate features.

Recently, following a reduction in personnel, the IS staff of a large government agency ended up with highly trained persons who had suffered through the early stages of a complex "standard system" installation. Staff members met a request for a new data retrieval system for the entire agency by insisting on an expensive in-house development project instead. This project took up all available systems expertise, which forced user management into buying, at its own expense, several outside services to meet immediate operational needs. Later, when the development group tested the retrieval system, it discovered that the unmanaged proliferation of new services made key data files inaccessible to their "efficient" system, which would not have occurred with an "inefficient" package from outside.

Fit to Corporate Structure

The development role of centralized IS is clearest in organizations where planning and operational control are centrally directed. A large manufacturer of farm equipment, which has a tradition of controlling functions from corporate headquarters, has implemented a program relatively easily whereby its corporate systems group develops all software for factories and distribution units worldwide. As a company decentralizes its structure to be effective, central systems development groups need more generous budgets to integrate their activities with users. It is becoming increasingly common for centralized development groups in decentralized companies to have a defined internal "marketing" activity to accomplish this transition to greater user control.

Cost Analysis

Through its experience in other systems efforts, a centralized IS group has a big edge in its ability to produce a realistic estimate for software development costs that takes into account the interests of the whole company. The situation with user feasibility studies has often turned out to be just the opposite for two reasons:

The first is that in most cases a new system is more software intensive than hardware intensive. In fact, software costs running from 75% to 85% of the total costs for a customized system are not unheard of. Since the user often has had little or no experience in estimating software development costs, an order-of-magnitude mistake in a feasibility study, particularly if it is an individually developed system and not a "turnkey" package, is not unknown.

The second factor is the charge-out system. Many corporate charge-out systems show calculations in computer resource units that are unintelligible to the user. So each month or quarter a meaningless and unpredictable bill arrives. This can be frustrating to users whose companies hold them responsible for their variance from budget. For some users, a solution is a locally developed minicomputer system to ensure that costs are intelligible, predictable, and thus controllable. Further, many companies design their charge-out systems on a full-cost basis. Consequently, the charges from the corporate center often seem high to the user. Since corporate information systems centers have many fixed-cost elements, particularly in the short run, what appears to the user as a chance to reduce costs may actually mean a cost increase for the company.

These are essentially long-term operational problems. They are not evident at the time the system is installed, and they tend to grow in importance over time.

DEVELOPMENT POLICIES

As a company seeks to balance the pressures between central and local IS development of systems, it must retain certain systems support policies and procedures at the central IS hub and give users certain responsibilities.

Central Hub Policies

The IS hub should retain procedures to ensure a comparison of the cost of internal development versus purchase of IS projects of any size. The comparison must take into account the fact that user-developed minicomputer systems pose quite different problems from those of systems to be run on mainframe computers. Professional standards for project control and documentation for projects implemented either outside or by the users should therefore be flexible.

The central group should also maintain an inventory of installed or planned information services. In addition, the central group should establish: mandatory telecommunication standards, standard languages for all acquired equipment, documentation procedures for different types of systems, and a corporate data dictionary (clearly defining what types of data elements are to be included and describing file maintenance standards and procedures). The group should examine systems developed as independent islands to ensure that they conform to corporate needs and that they have any necessary interfaces with other systems.

Determining and providing appropriate career paths for IS development staff throughout the organization are proper tasks for the central group. These can be achieved by sideways transfer within and between IS units as well as upward movement within IS and outward movement to other functional units. Although this is more difficult in distributed units, it can be done.

The group should establish appropriate internal integration efforts for IS support activities. The aim is to coach and exert pressure on units that are lagging and slow down the units that are proceeding too fast.

The central group should maintain a detailed checklist of questions to be answered in any hardware or software acquisition, to ensure that relevant technical and managerial issues are raised, including how the proposed system meets corporate communication standards. For word processing systems, IS should raise questions on upward growth potential and built-in data processing capability; for data processing systems, on availability of languages to support its systems growth potential, available word processing features, and so forth; and for communication systems, on data transfer capabilities, available services, storage capacity, and so on.

A list of preferred systems suppliers and conditions for entertaining exceptions to the list should come from the central group. Finally, the group should establish education programs for users to both communicate the potential and warn of the pitfalls of new technologies and to define users' roles in ensuring a system's successful introduction.

If the situation warrants, companies can expand these functions with tighter and more formal controls. In this regard, the diagnostic framework presented by Jack R. Buchanan and Richard G. Linowes is particularly useful in assessing both the current position of an organization and the direction it should move in.[2]

User Responsibilities

Users should also have some irrevocable responsibilities in developing an IS system. These include keeping aware of financial expenditures made in IS-type activities on their behalf. The more progressive organizations now use more understandable IS charge-out systems. Users ought to be fully aware of the level of their staff investment that is required in the short and long runs to ensure systems success and be willing to commit this level of their staff resources.

Users should fully participate in the development of a support plan for the systems they will use. This includes helping to determine network architecture, data base policies, standards as they affect the user, and user training programs for both staff and managers. The users should also concur on the forms of service to be used to support their operations. The mix of central site, packaged programs, and outside contracts should be approved by users, as should the appropriateness of system reliability standards and security requirements.

These activities are the very minimum for users. Depending on the company's location, management style, stage of IS development, and mix of technology development phases, greater involvement of users may be appropriate, including acquisition of their own staffs.

GENERAL POLICIES

Distinct from issues in the distribution of hardware and development resources are the broad policies and direction that require senior management involvement. Such responsibilities can be built into the structure of a central IS organization but, because they involve a longer time span and thus a more strategic orientation, they are often separate. A major oil company recently reorganized to create a 300-person systems and operations department reporting directly to the head of administrative services. This department does the operational IS work of the company.

At the same time, an eight- to ten-person IS policy group reports directly to the head of corporate planning, who formulates overall policy and long-range strategy. A major conglomerate in which all development and hardware is distributed to key users also has a group at headquarters level.

Such a corporate policy group should ensure that there is an appropriate balance between IS and user inputs in the different technologies so that one side does not dominate the other. It should initiate appropriate staff and organizational changes, such as establishment of an executive steering committee.

Through its understanding of the total role of information systems in the company, the group should also ensure that the company has a comprehensive IS corporate strategy. In particular where IS resources are widely distributed, a comprehensive overview of technology, corporate use of that technology, and the fit with overall corporate goals is vital. The resources a company will devote to this group will vary widely from organization to organization depending on, among other things, the contribution of IS to corporate strategy.

To maintain control in the establishment of purchasing relationships and contracts, the group should audit the hardware and software resources. In some companies, this group will be the appropriate place to initiate standard vendor policies. It should develop and monitor standards for both development and operations activities. In this regard, the group plays a combined role of consultant and auditor, particularly if the IS auditing function is weak or nonexistent. Carrying out this role requires both technical competence and sensitivity.

Acting as a center to encourage joint projects and common systems among units, the group can, for example, visit different operating units often, organize periodic corporate MIS conferences, and develop an information systems newsletter. It can also identify and encourage promising technical experimentation. A limited research program is a very appropriate part of the IS function, and an important role of the corporate policy group is to ensure that the press of urgent operational issues does not sweep away such activities. Further, this body is in a position to encourage patterns of experimentation that smaller units might see as unduly risky.

Finally, the corporate group can encourage the proper development of planning and control systems to link IS to the company's goals. Working closely, for example, with an executive steering committee, the group can monitor and encourage planning, charge-out, and project management processes.

These roles suggest that the group needs a staff that in aggregate represents both technical backgrounds and extensive IS administrative experience. Usually it is not a good department for new staff members.

Determining the best pattern of distribution of IS resources within the organization is complicated. The final resolution of the organization and planning issues raised here is inextricably tied to the corporate environment outside IS.

The leadership style at the top of the organization and the chief executive's view of the future obviously affect the path of redirection. A goal of tighter central control sets a direction for these decisions different from one that emphasizes autonomy for operating units. Other important considerations in deploying IS resources are the corporate organization structure and culture and the trends that are occurring there. The geographic spread of the business units also determines what is possible. The large headquarters of an insurance company poses problems different from the multiple international plants and markets of an automobile manufacturer such as General Motors.

In short, there is a right series of questions to ask, though the answers will differ among companies and among individual units in an organization. Analyzing the identifiable but complex forces will help determine the best answers for each organizational unit—at least for the present.

NOTES

1. For a general discussion of this type of organization, see Richard E. Vancil, *Decentralization: Ambiguity by Design* (Homewood, Ill.: Dow Jones-Irwin, 1979).

2. Jack R. Buchanan and Richard G. Linowes, "Understanding Distributed Data Processing," HBR July-August 1980, p. 143, and "Making Distributed Data Processing Work," *HBR* September-October 1980, p. 143.

QUESTIONS

1. What three emerging technologies need to be integrated by an organization in order that a workable balance may be achieved between its localized users and the centralized information system function?
2. What are the possible implications of excessive domination of systems development and operation by the centralized information system function?
3. What are the possible implications of excessive domination of systems development and operation by the localized users?
4. What pressures and forces are encouraging the centralized control of systems development and operation within an organization?
5. What pressures and forces are encouraging the localized user control of systems development and operation within an organization?
6. Describe a workable balance or blend of responsibilities among the centralized information system function, the local users, and the top management of an organization with respect to systems development and operation.
7. Does the answer to Question 6, as suggested by the authors in this article, agree with the roles that the Zmud article proposes for the evolving user-oriented and decentralized information system function?
8. Richard L. Nolen hypothesizes that information system organizations evolve through six stages of growth (see "Managing the Crises in Data Processing," *Harvard Business Review*, March-April 1979, pp. 115–26). He calls these six stages initiation, contagion, control, integration, data administration, and maturity. Signs of a maturing information system include end-user participation in systems development, a balance between centralized and decentralized applications, a value-added user chargeback procedure, and an emphasis on data and information (rather than computer) resource management. Which of these signs accord with the strategies advocated by the authors of this article? Should those organizations just beginning the use of computer-based information systems attempt to bypass the early stages of growth, as listed by Nolen, and move directly to the strategies that are suitable to an organization with a mature computer-based information system?

TOPIC FOUR

Networking, Telecommunications, and Distributed Data Processing

The management debate regarding the centralization versus decentralization of an MIS is an unresolvable issue. The pros and cons of each philosophy have been discussed for years and are well understood. However, within the last decade, a strong call for decentralization, or *distributed data processing* (DDP), has surfaced from a new force to reckon with—the end-users.

Traditionally, the initiative for organizational change has originated in upper management philosophical shifts. Such a perspective is top-down in that upper management notions then proceed to reshape the organizational structure. However, the proliferation of microcomputers has generated the impetus for end-users to call for increased localized data-processing autonomy. Consider that many business professionals may go home at night to find their ten-year-old children playing with relational data bases! Seeing the power of a micro, these individuals may then return to work frustrated by the rigidity of the centralized mainframe data-processing facility which dictates report format and delivery date, file content, and acceptable file queries. In short, the end-user may "know better" the capability of a computing system and

become quite disenchanted with that of his or her firm. The movement toward DDP is, then, an end-user bottom-up call for organizational change.

SYSTEMS EVOLUTION— A MATTER OF DEGREES

The evolution of information systems design mirrors the technological advances in electronic data processing, as outlined here.

Stage 1: Dispersed, stand-alone computers with no electronic link. Each facility ran in a dedicated batch environment, using machine language.

Stage 2: Centralized main frame to achieve economics of scale. No electronic link to outlying ports. Remote I/O via U.S. Mail. Overlapped processing in a stacked job shop. Programming in Fortran and Mnemonic Assembler.

Stage 3: Centralized main frame with simple electronic network. Remote job entry and I/O, with multiprocessing and multiprogramming operating system capabilities. Programming in Basic, Cobol, and RPG.

Stage 4: Centralized versus dispersed processing with localized minicomputers acting as I/O ports and intelligent machines. Centralized files with local query and update capabilities. Programming in Pascal. Online real time applications.

Stage 5: DDP. End-user partial to full control over files, processing and network power. A reallocation of the data processing staff throughout the organization.

Remember that DDP is end-user driven. Given that upper management makes the ultimate decision to philosophically restructure the organization, what signals should management be cognizant of from the end-users? What are the organizational implications of DDP? Certainly the future needs of the *organization* must be of primary consideration. Long- and short-range objectives must be stated as goals, and then the strategic and tactical planning occurs. Consideration must also be given to technological advances and personnel needs.

Grayce Booth,[1] a special projects manager for Honeywell, proposes ten questions to assist in determining an appropriate MIS structure. The questions and their related directional implications are summarized as follows:

1. Are the capacity requirements of the application too great to be implemented in a single computer system? The needed capacity is determined by the total number of users to be served, the number of users who will access the system simultaneously, the volume of transactions to be handled, the response-time requirements, the size and complexity of the data base, and the complexity of the processing functions. It is also prudent to include a cushion of unused capacity to allow for rapid and unpredictable growth.

2. Is a high degree of flexibility for change and/or capacity expansion required? One of the basic rules of information

systems is that complexity reduces flexibility. A centralized system with a large number of possible unrelated applications would be much less flexible than a distributed system.

3. Are there requirements for a high level of availability and/or a high degree of resilience to failures? Distributed and decentralized systems typically are dispersed over multiple sites and, therefore, are less vulnerable to single point failures than centralized systems.

4. Which mode of processing will predominate: interactive or batch? The more inactive the system, the greater the likelihood that the distribution of at least some functions will be advantageous.

5. Are there clusters of shared functions, each of which serves a separate group of users? The clustering of functions, in effect, defines the distributed systems structure.

6. Are there user groups that need somewhat different functions, methods, interfaces, and/or reports than other similar groups? Customization in a centralized system typically results in increased complexity which limits the flexibility needed for change. A distributed system can be highly customized without reducing flexibility.

7. Will the system handle data and/or functions that require tight protection for security or privacy reasons? The physical protection provided by a restricted access computer center makes it easier to handle sensitive data or functions. There are ways to partition sensitive data or functions from nonsensitive ones in a distributed system, but they are costly.

8. Are the users widely dispersed geographically? A distributed system will lower the cost of communications and may also improve the speed of response to terminal users.

9. Does the system consist of a set of loosely related functions or of functions whose requirements are not well de-

fined? Office systems, in particular, are made up of clusters of related functions. A distributed system provides greater flexibility than a centralized system to change each of the functions as needed.

10. Will a distributed system result in lower total life-cycle costs for the system? If the cost of communications facilities in a centralized system can be reduced by using local satellite processors, total life-cycle costs will be lower. However, in general, distributed systems have a somewhat higher expected cost than centralized systems.

Obviously DDP systems are unique to the needs of the individual organization. Yet a DDP systems designer must be well trained in certain "nuts and bolts" telecommunications concepts.

NETWORKING AND TELECOMMUNICATION TOPOLOGIES

The technology of computer networking is steadily advancing. *Digital transmission* has replaced analog as the preferred "pure" data transfer technique. Digital transmission offers significantly higher transfer speeds *and* lower error rates than analog. *Packet switching* networks, such as X.25, are available for dial-up users to send standard size "packets" of information in an extremely efficient manner. In fact these packets, viewed as little boxcars of data, may move through a congested system via multiple paths with the last portion of the message arriving at the destination before the front portion! The technology exists to then reconstruct the message. Standard handshake *protocols* have been developed to the point where the network utilized is transparent of the user. Well developed protocols and message design contain all the necessary parameters such as error detection and correction codes,

routing instructions, audit check bits, encryption keys, and acknowledgment tracers.

An interesting design question in networking is the MIS *topology* or configuration. Consider the conceptual management structure of a typical organization, as depicted in Figure 4.1. It is not difficult to bridge from the philosophical structure of a centralized organization to the centralized mainframe topology of Figure 4.2. DDP introduces one or more intermediate "levels" of processing power and autonomy. Figures 4.3 through 4.5 reveal the most popular DDP topologies: hierarchy (tree), star, and ring. The design of

Figure 4.1.

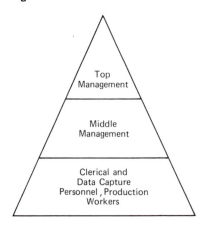

Figure 4.2.

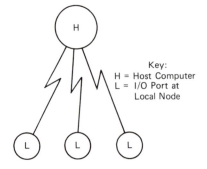

Figure 4.3.   Hierarchy

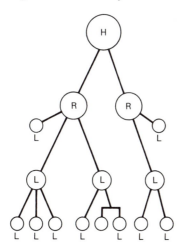

Figure 4.4.   Star

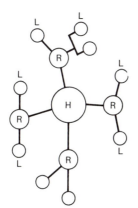

Figure 4.5.   Ring

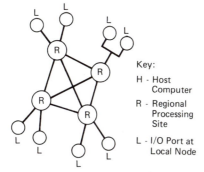

Key:

H - Host
   Computer

R - Regional
   Processing
   Site

L - I/O Port at
   Local Node

a DDP network encourages the dispersion of power throughout the network. However, as will be discussed later in this introduction (and in a subsequent article), the distribution of computing power is not without its drawbacks.

The hierarchical or tree configuration has gained the most support to date. Such a statement is not surprising in that upper management remains comfortable with a system designed to layer the power within each level. That is, the tree network forms a set of *master/slave* relationships thereby providing well-defined lines of responsibility and reporting at each level. Although processing is distributed, there remains a highly structured, central planning and coordination facility which retains ultimate control over the tree network.

The star topology, while found in most textbooks, is not really found in practice. Look again at the drawing of a star. Now "bend" all the arms down and notice that a star becomes a tree configuration. Consequently it is difficult in practice to differentiate between star and tree.

A ring network most closely mirrors the philosophy of DDP. That is, in a true ring no host exists, and thus no true master/slave relationship prevails. A literal interpretation of Figure 4.5 is that each regional site "has no boss." Ring topologies exist in actual practice, an example of such being the ARPANET research network. Commercial for-profit business examples of rings have been uncommon as the master/slave notion remains most easily facilitated in a tree structure. However, an increasing number of ring topologies are starting to emerge.

The reader now possesses fundamental knowledge of teleprocessing and network topologies. Let us now confront the definition of "true DDP" and address the related design implications.

TRUE DDP

The following is a rough working definition:

> DDP is an approach to business data processing in which the primary processing is placed on multiple smaller computer units, with increased control and authority provided to end-users of information.

The reader is encouraged to compare this definition with his or her own preconceived notion of DDP.

Hal Becker, of Honeywell, has been a pioneer in the design issues relating to DDP. Becker developed a theory of DDP based upon the notion that every business system, centralized or dispersed, is composed of three processing functions: information or data processing, network processing, and data base processing. The first function reflects computing power and authority over access, query, and update. The second function, network processing, addresses the ability to have a say in network design and transfer paths. That is, in true DDP end-users should have input into the design of a "session" (person-to-person, person-to-machine, person-to-file) and such concepts as acknowledgement and message prioritization. The file processing function concerns the location of files, and a determination of file organization structure and content. File replication and partitioning are issues regarding the file processing function somewhat driven by DDP.

Becker postulates that *true DDP* requires the distribution of all three functions. He further notes that the first two functions have been distributed in many firms, but file control seems to remain a centralized concept.

IBM has advanced the concept of true DDP by the development of software to facilitate a hierarchical network. IBM's software, called Systems Network Architecture (SNA), incorporates a hierarchy of "layers"

of hardware and software. Master/slave relationships exist in a tree-type network, with "domains" of responsibility established throughout the system. A domain is a conceptual monarchy with its designated "host" computer. The host computer is attached to a front-end processor which acts as a clearing-house for message approval, logging, and transmission throughout the network.

DDP is certainly a "user-friendly" system in that end-users see DDP as highly desirable. Yet DDP is a Pandora's box of control problems, as will now be seen.

DDP Control Issues

DDP is a movement to grant processing autonomy throughout the network. How can centralized management control the structure or format of decentralized power? Several items easy to control in a centralized mainframe shop become hazards in DDP. For instance uncontrolled local data processing growth could result in nonstandard file structures, different hardware, and unsimilar processing methods. Separation of duties and other classic internal controls may disappear as a local port may well be a one man/woman data processing facility. File location is another debatable issue. Additionally, if local machines are small, the opportunity to load large audit software and password schemes becomes lost. The article by Summers, Fernandez and Wood (Topic Seven) will expound upon DDP control issues and solutions.

Articles

The first article is viewed as introductory material. Brown develops a solid introduction to DDP while raising several design issues. Fundamental concepts, such as autonomy file distribution and DDP components, are discussed early in the paper with hardware diagrams provided to act as a bridge between his conceptual discussion and real-world application. Finally, the author provides a lengthy listing of DDP pros and cons which should entertain and challenge the reader's viewpoint of the centralize/distribute paradigm.

The article by Van Rensselaer, although written in 1979, was selected for several reasons. First, the author is the corporate CIS director for a major firm and thus he speaks from experience. Second, the author is employed by an IBM competitor thereby offering a contrasting perspective to the "IBM approach." Third, several business applications are categorized as centralized, decentralized, or distributed. Thus the author proves his firm's philosophy to fit

the MIS structure to the application, and not vice versa.

Topic Four introduces networking, telecommunications, and the movement to DDP. MIS designers will continually be confronted by the design and the philosophical and organizational ramifications of these issues throughout the systems development life cycle.

NOTES

1. See G. M. Booth, "Centralize, Decentralize, Distribute?" *Computerized Special Report,* February 22, 1982, pp. SR 5–6.

Defining Distributed Data Processing*

This article takes a look at distributed data processing (DDP); what it is conceived to be as well as what it is. To gain an understanding of the concept of DDP and when it is attained, its goals, advantages, and hazards are considered. Some current examples of both nearly-distributed and fully-distributed systems are presented, along with an outlook on the future growth of both the concept and the highly-competitive marketing industry which has grown around DDP at an even faster rate.

While no one author is likely to end the controversy about the nature of a distributed data processing system, it is hoped that this article will bring managers to a fuller appreciation of the need for a common definition and a better understanding of what DDP is.

WHAT DOES DDP MEAN TO TODAY'S MANAGERS?

Most managers will agree that, simply stated, distributed data processing is a hybrid between centralized and decentralized processing systems. Which functions are distributed will depend upon the particular benefits expected. The four components which might be distributed are:

a.   hardware or processing logic,
b.   the data,
c.   the processing itself, and
d.   the control (operating systems).

Note that there can be no distribution of the processing function if there is no distribution of the hardware.

One author, Jean LaPrairie, believes most managers will agree that DDP includes at least these two elements:

1.   the transfer of certain information processing functions from a central system to small, dedicated processors in the functional area (department, branch, remote site) where that information is used; and
2.   interconnection of the components of a system, permitting shared resources and data bases.[1]

Such an organizational approach suggests that the end user should be responsible for local, non-technically complex operations and applications and that the high level of technical responsibility should be centralized within the organization. Yet all computing facilities (referred to as "nodes")

*By Larry C. Brown. Reprinted from an article appearing in *Cost and Management* by Larry C. Brown, November/December 1981, by permission of The Society of Management Accountants of Canada.

which constitute the distributed data processing system are interconnected on a coordinated basis to all other computing facilities as *users* of the total communications facility, not merely as *parts* of the communications facility. The suggestion here is that multilateral communication, where each node may communicate at will directly with other nodes, is a criterion for a distributed system.

This differs from dispersed data processing where stand-alone, semi-autonomous computer facilities are distant from a central computing facility, but:

1. mini- or microprocessors are employed rather than classic mainframes,
2. little or no staff is devoted on a full-time basis,
3. few data professionals are required at the end-user site, and
4. limited local services are provided.[2]

Current managerial views and opinions about distributed data processing differ widely. A survey by the Auerbach editorial staff illustrates the confusion that exists about the nature of DDP within the professional community itself. Here are some of the survey responses to the question, "As I understand it, distributed processing can briefly be described as..."[3]

In relation to processors:

"Satellite processors functioning semi-independently but using a large host for primary storage."

"Minicomputers installed at other locations or within large departments to do some things on their own."

"Multiple processors in communication with each other."

"Decentralized computer processing."

In relation to functions:

"Decentralizing data collection and local computing with communications to a central data base host system."

In relation to users:

"Providing to users the resources needed to meet local needs while providing centralized control."

"Farming out processing to users."

In relation to input/output:

"Processing data where the transaction occurs and communicating the results to the mainframe."

"Enabling each branch to perform its own input and receive related output."

WHAT IS DISTRIBUTED DATA PROCESSING?

It is clear that a simple definition of DDP may not be possible. In this section, the reader may develop his/her own definition of DDP by considering its goals, its criteria, and some nearly-distributed systems.

Often the best definition of a subject is a description of what the subject is to accomplish. The many achievements expected of a DDP system include:[4]

* high systems performance, fast response, and high throughput;
* high availability;
* high reliability;
* reduced network costs;
* failsoft capability (see following note);
* use of modular, incremental growth and configuration flexibility;
* resource sharing;
* automatic load sharing;
* high adaptability to changes in work loads;
* easy expansion of capacity and function;
* easy adaptations to new functions;
* good response to temporary overloads; and
* incremental replacement and/or upgrading of components (both hardware and software).

NOTE: "The failsoft capability of distributed systems for communication or central node failure arises because files and records are normally distributed on the basis of record activity. The records that are most active for a given node are generally stored at that node. If the central node becomes available, the high activity records can still be processed."[5]

The term distributed system has been used to describe anything from a centralized star network to a totally decentralized system. As soon as any *one* of the four components (hardware, data, processing, control) is distributed, the label of a "distributed system" has been readily applied. But Enslow states that the definition of a DDP system, if it is to attain the aforementioned achievements, should include all of the following five operational requirements.[6]

1. A multiplicity of general-purpose components, including physical and logical resources, that can be assigned specific tasks on a dynamic basis.

Here, a homogeneity of resources is not essential, but without a multiplicity of resources, there can be no distribution of processing. Such a situation is essential for high availability, reliability, and failsoft capabilities. The attainment of these goals contributes, in turn, to greater flexibility, adaptability, and incremental expansion. Special-purpose components add only to the range of functions satisfied by the system and not to overall systems performance, which is why general-purpose components must be stressed.

2. Physical distribution of physical and logical systems components that interact through a communications network.

A network uses a two-party cooperative protocol to control the transfer of information. As opposed to a "gated" transfer where the master (i.e., central facility) has full authority to force a slave (i.e., distributed facility) to accept any and all messages, the two-party protocol exists where the two parties cooperate to complete a transfer. Thus,

a second-party destination can refuse to accept a message by answering "BUSY" or "NOT READY." This makes the request from the first-party facility a *request*, not a *signal*; and produces the high degree of autonomy which contributes to the high availability of resources. Of course, this requirement must apply to logical resources as well as physical resources.

3. A high-level operating system that unifies and integrates control of the distributed components.

Each individual distributed processor may have its own unique operating system but that system must be governed by well defined policies that, in effect, produce a higher level operating system to govern the integration of components and operations for the benefit of the total system.

Local operating systems used need not be homogeneous, though a variety of interfaces does complicate the problem of systems design, and there must be no *strong* hierarchy between the high-level operating system and the local operating system. A strong hierarchy would violate the autonomy of distributed facilities and can produce critical paths; but, a lack of any hierarchy would produce anarchy.

The high-level operating system is probably the most important requirement. It is complex and requires extensive research in its design in order to mould a collection of hardware into a coherently functioning system. Another author states, "(System) Software makes the difference between a cluster of computers that act independently and that same cluster integrated into a smooth-working, cost-effective DDP operation."[7]

4. Systems transparency that permits services to be requested by name only; the server does not have to be identified.

The user must be able to specify the service to be rendered without specifying which physical or logical component is to supply that service. Thus, the distributed system is transparent to the user and it appears as a single, centralized system.

5. Cooperative autonomy that characterizes the operation and interaction of physical and logical resources.

This coincides with requirements 2 and 3 that all resources must be highly autonomous but following the master plan of the higher operating system.

Absolute DDP is difficult to attain. Some examples will be considered later. Here are some concepts that are not truly DDP systems and why they are not.

Distribution Within a Single Mainframe. The architecture of several modern processors, including independent I/O channels has been described as "incorporating distributed processors since it contains separate I/O processors, arithmetic and logic processors, and possibly diagnostic processors."[8] But there is a permanent binding of tasks to various components here.

Single or Multiple Host Processors. A single host processor with a number of remote terminals that simply collect and transmit data does not qualify as a DDP system even if the terminals are intelligent and do some editing and formatting.

Multiple hosts in a network interconnection structure do not necessarily make a distributed system (except in regard to switching), as overall control is usually centralized. Such systems do not have the capability for dynamic reallocation or reassignment of tasks in the event of hardware failure.

Intelligent Terminals. Systems using several terminals connected to a local processor which have secondary storage capabilities (usually discs or cassettes) and which can edit data entries are often presented as distributed systems. But these systems have shared file access only to local files and communicate with the main processor by having the local processor emulate a "dumb" terminal. They process no distribution of control as the distribution of work is fixed and local terminals cannot affect it.

In summation, intelligent terminals can only be considered as representative of a DDP system if they are "a) smart enough to do some real work, and b) able to recognize when they cannot accomplish the assigned work and can pass it on to another appropriate service component (off-loading of work)."[9]

HOW DISTRIBUTED DATA PROCESSING EVOLVED

Distributed data processing evolved from the decentralized system philosophy of installing mini-microcomputers at remote locations to interface with a host computer at a central site. DDP is much more than that, though, and requires an intelligent, systematic approach as well as a high level of managerial and technical skills.

Interest in DDP was initially sparked (especially for Canadian firms) through the problems encountered by the geographically distributed organization requiring a unified, information-sharing and processing system. DDP should be considered when failsoft needs are important, when the data base can be distributed according to activity (partitioned), or when performance requirements (transactions/second) are high.

APPROACHES TO FILE DISTRIBUTION

A unified information-sharing system can be implemented through three approaches (see Figure 1):

Figure 1. File Distribution Approaches[10]

EXCEPTION RATE	FILE SIZE	DISTRIBUTION METHOD
–	small	replication
small	large	partition
high	large	centralization

1. centralization of files,
2. replication of files, and
3. partitioning of files.

Centralization exists where all files are centralized and accessed by remote terminals. It is desirable when there are economies of operations, hardware economies of scale, unified control, easy intrafile communications, and easy update and retrieval. If the files are large and the number of transactions which are exceptions to local processing is high (i.e., 50 per cent of activity), then centralization of files is a more attractive approach.

Replication of files is the duplication of the total file at all locations. Updates are propagated to all locations. This approach is desirable where file sizes are small.

Partitioned files are desirable where the files are large but can be segmented, each section being held at the node which has the highest activity for that record. The exception rate here should be low (i.e., 25 per cent of activity).

VARIATIONS IN DDP SYSTEMS DESIGNS

DDP systems designs vary with the degree to which they evolve into fully-distributed networks. The following is a look at five such variations.[11] The first four are centralized designs with some distributed functions as each of the four has a single processor playing a central role.

1. *Distributed processing with a central data base.* In this example (see Figure 2), some local processing occurs without local data bases. Auxiliary storage is limited to storing routines, input formulas, and edited transactions. Edit checks, such as range and mode, do not require access to the central data base.

2. *Hierarchical system with non-shared local data bases.* This design (see Figure 3) is especially attractive if local data bases contain data that is not required elsewhere in the system and is updated from local transactions. Examples of this include localized plant inventories, production schedules, employee work hours, and transaction-level accounting data.

3. *Distributed, segmented (partitioned) data base with remote access.* This design is for transactions originating in one location and requiring access to data maintained at another location. It is attractive only if such a probability is low. Problems exist of a) which data bases to access (i.e., all bases until the correct one is found or directly through a rigid identification number), b) synchronization of data bases, and c) file security and privacy.

Figure 2. Distributed Processors with Central Data Base

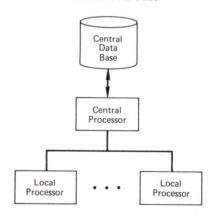

Figure 3.   Distributed Processors with Non-shared Local Data Bases

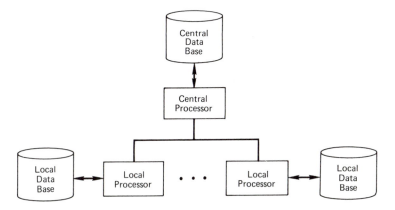

In this *Digital Equipment* information system, departmental computers are interconnected into a network, and the network communicates with a central mainframe.

4. *Multiple-level hierarchical distributed system.* Under this system (see Figure 4),[12] a processor can be made a node of a lower-level distributed subsystem but each facility is not equally autonomous.

5. *Fully-distributed network.* A fully-distributed network (see Figure 5) has no central focus, but is composed of multiple autonomous processors that have equal control status, though they may vary widely in their computing abilities.

EXAMPLES OF FULLY-DISTRIBUTED SYSTEMS

The following six examples represent unique approaches[13] to distributed data base systems and all are now operational.

1. SITA (Société Internationale de Tele-communications Aeronautiques) provides a system for communication between airline data bases for the purpose of making passenger reservations on airplanes in Europe and Asia. It is a partitioned system, with ex-

ception transactions handled by a directory at the master node.

2. Celanese is a large U.S. textile manufacturer with a number of geographically distributed facilities in Charlotte, S.C. and Shelby, N.C. Each location has its own computer which serves as a node. Replicated files are maintained with periodic updates of the data from both locations.

3. Bank of America is a large financial institution headquartered in California with over 1,000 branches and 11 million accounts; 209 branches have 2,100 terminals. The data base is partitioned between the two data centers (San Francisco and Los Angeles), with exception transactions from one node forwarded to the other for processing. Each node is also fully redundant so that processing can continue in spite of hardware failure.

4. ARPANET is a distributed system that includes the software system entitled RSEXEC (Resource Sharing Executive System). RSEXEC is a distributed file capability

Figure 4.   Multiple Hierarchical Distributed System

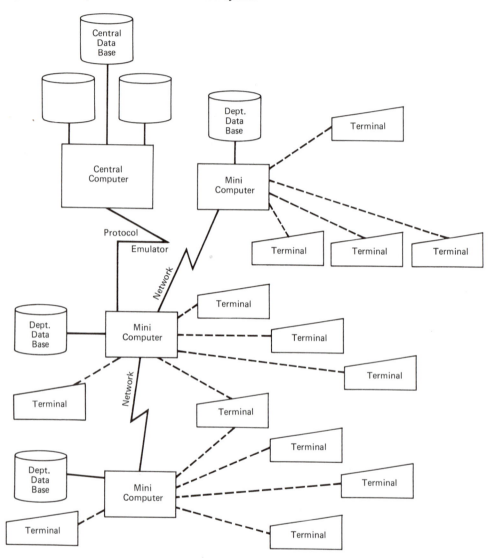

which spans host computers (nodes) and supports uniform file access and automatic maintenance of replicated files. ARPANET is accessed by such a diverse user community that all design approaches may be currently in use.

5. Lowes Companies, Inc. is a chain of 140 retail lumber/hardware stores located in the southeastern United States. A mini-computer with disk and up to 16 terminals at each store were implemented. Each store is connected to a central system by data

Figure 5.   Full-blown Distributed Processing

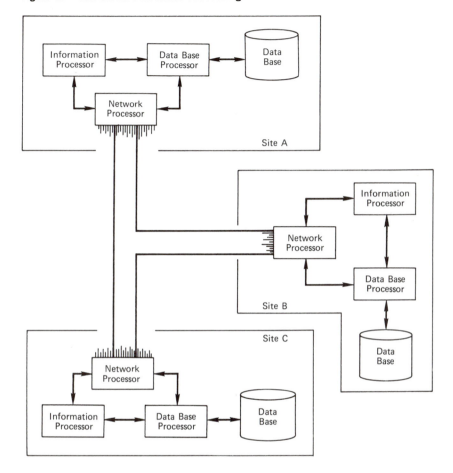

communications lines with inventory and sales summary information processed automatically each night. In turn, each node receives information such as new prices from the central facility. Thus, the Lowes system is a partitioned data base with all files and transactions handled locally.

6. Aeroquip Corporation is a manufacturer of fluid power components with plants scattered from Georgia to Oregon. This system selected intelligent terminals supported by a local data base or disk. Each node main-

tains a local subset of the master data base that is needed by that node. The complete copy of the file at the master node handles exception transactions.

ADVANTAGES OF DISTRIBUTED SYSTEMS

Being a hybrid of centralized and decentralized systems, the distributed system can operate along much of the continuum to gain the advantages of both concepts and adapt to varying organizational needs. A central staff is still essential, though, to produce standard communications lines, common software packages, and control of distributed operations regarding growth and undesirable duplication.

The following are the advantages that can reasonably be expected from DDP systems:

* High systems performance resulting from high availability of resources upon demand.
* Reduced response time for interactive functions performed locally.
* Increased efficiency through techniques such as intermittent high-speed transmission of stored transactions and spooling until off-peak periods.
* Demand smoothing by shifting work between processors.
* Failsoft capability, especially in many highly-intensive transaction applications such as financial institutions.
* Reliability is provided by having multiple assignable resources.
* Reduced communications costs due to reduced volume of data traffic, as much processing is done at the local level.
* Simplification achieved by breaking systems into relatively small sub-units.
* Ease of incremental growth, replacement, and/or alteration of systems configuration offers an overall systems flexibility.
* Increased predictability of costs at local levels.
* Economies of scale and powerful facilities for applications requiring a large, full-service machine such as is often provided at the central facility.
* Increased efficiency of the central facility due to transfers to distributed processors of those jobs for which they are best suited.
* Integration of organizational activities through exchange of summary data among hierarchical levels of the system.
* Integration of information processing (sharing common data and programs) on a central facility for applications for which it is more cost-effective than local processing.

* Incorporation of user-related experiences and technical expertise through joint development of applications by users and central technical staff.
* Economics of specialization within segmented components that comprise the system.

HAZARDS OF DISTRIBUTED SYSTEMS

DDP systems are not without their hazards. The potential problems include:

* Creeping escalation of capabilities and applications occurs by additions of applications and components on the grounds of low incremental costs to the distributed facility. Such accumulated costs can prove to be a serious burden to the total EDP system. Managers must begin to think of effective and cost-sensitive means of controlling both the external and the internal demand for processing services.
* The allocation of full average cost for additional applications performed by the central facility may exceed the distributed facility's incremental costs of expansion, causing the latter to add to its facilities even though the total cost to the organization is greater.
* Undesirable duplication and incompatibility can result from independently developed systems which lack common software, data bases, back-up facilities, repair parts, and maintenance personnel.
* The simplicity of distributed systems is lost if design sophistication becomes excessive and produces strong interaction between facilities.
* Systems design and implementation personnel can be incompetent as the smaller centre finds it difficult to attract and support experienced staff. Thus, each facility will commit common errors and duplicate the woes to the total EDP environment.
* Hidden costs exist, such as increased user roles in design and operations, that are not allocated to developmental costs and yet pro-

duce "bootlegged" time from defined job specifications.

FUTURE OUTLOOK OF DDP

The distributed data processing trend began in Canada as late as 1977. With its population concentrated along a 3,000 mile-long, narrow band, Canada is a good prospective customer in the DDP sales industry. Moreover, the essential communications channels required by DDP users are readily available and well developed in Canada through such highly visible and technically innovative leaders as Bell Canada and CN/CP.

One Canadian marketing firm of data systems estimates that the percentage of decentralized processing will rise from a current 20 per cent to at least 50 per cent.[14] Digital Equipment of Canada has predicted an annual growth rate of 40 per cent while Prime Computer forecasts a compounded annual growth rate of 60 per cent.[15]

The technological environment does nothing to discourage these figures. Here are some of the predicted technological gains supporting DDP growth.[16]

* Central processor and primary storage costs will continue to decrease by about 25 per cent per year to become a small percentage of the total system cost. Thus, distributed "intelligence" will be an insignificant cost factor.
* Auxiliary storage shows similar improvements in cost/performance ratios suitable for small, local data bases.
* Systems software will become increasingly large, complex, reliable, and powerful, especially for general-purpose computers.
* Data base management will be enhanced and widely applied, fostering a strong trend toward greater sharing of common data and a higher degree of integration of processing tasks.
* Applications will become increasingly complex as we move into new areas; intelligent

terminals will become more cost-effective; and computing languages will become more powerful.
* Communications services will improve in reliability, effectiveness, and flexibility in linking host computers with improved switching packages. Costs will decrease at 10 per cent per year and utilize distance-independent pricing.

Distributed data processing is certainly in an enviable position to become the primary systems architecture of the future. But managers must come to a common understanding about the nature of DDP. Unless this transpires, they will encounter even more difficulties as they are called upon to assist in the evaluation and implementation of such systems in their own backyards.

Each DDP system must be considered individually and planned for meticulously. Current operating systems are evolved from the centralized philosophy and are not prepared to recognize an "equal" within the same network. Co-existence of operating systems and acceptable levels of interaction will require more than trivial rewrites of existing operating systems. And many of the tools and experiences possessed today by divisional managers, who have operated successfully within the framework of conflicting autonomies, will be essential in tomorrow's DDP environment.

NOTES

1. Jean LaPrairie, "Distributed Data Processing: Annual Growth Rate Forecast at 40 to 60 per cent," *Computer Data* (Toronto, Ont.: Whitsed Publishing Ltd., Jan. 1979), p. 23.

2. August L. Kelsch, "Dispersed and Distributed Data," *Journal of Systems Management* (Cleveland Ohio: Assn. for Systems Management, March 1978), p. 32.

3. Auerbach Editorial Staff, "Now That You've Told Us...", *General Management: DP Planning* (Auerbach Publishers, Inc., 1978), pp. 4–5.

4. Philip A. Enslow, "What Is a Distributed Data Processing System?" *Technology: Computers* (Auerbach Publishers, Inc., 1978), p. 2.

5. G. A. Champine, "Six Approaches To Distributed Data Bases," *Datamation* (Barrington, Ill.: Technical Publishing Co., May 1977), pp. 67–70.

6. Enslow, *op. cit.*, pp. 2–6.

7. Stephen A. Kallis, Jr., "Network and Distributed Processing," *Mini-Micro Systems* (March 1977).

8. Jules H. Gilder, "Distributed Processing: Keyword for Tomorrow's Supersystems," *Computer Decisions* (April 1976), p. 14.

9. Enslow, *op. cit.*, p. 7.

10. Champine, *op. cit.*, p. 7.

11. James C. Emery, "Managerial and Economic Issues in Distributed Computing," *General Management: Management Planning* (Auerbach Publishers Inc., 1978), pp. 5–8.

12. LaPrairie, *op. cit.*, p. 23.

13. Champine, *op. cit.*, p. 70–72.

14. LaPrairie, *loc. cit.*

15. LaPrairie, *loc. cit.*

16. Emery, *op. cit.*, pp. 2–3.

QUESTIONS

1. Do you agree with the author's four components of DDP "which might be distributed," as described on the first page of the article? Compare these four to Becker's statement in the introductory bridge.

2. What is a "gated" transfer as opposed to a "two-party cooperative protocol"? Who cares? Or is a philosophical statement being made based upon which MIS design method is utilized?

3. Develop your own definition of DDP and compare it to those of your classmates. Is your definition hardware, processing, or file oriented?

4. The word "autonomy" is mentioned throughout the article. Define autonomy in a DDP environment. Are there levels or degrees of autonomy?

5. The author presents three methods of file distribution. Are all three realistic? Which method approaches do you prefer, and why?

6. Various DDP design topologies are depicted in the preceding article by words and drawings. Can you state that one of the designs "best" reflects DDP, or is the answer more situation-specific?

7. A list of advantages and disadvantages of DDP is presented near the end of the article. Interestingly there are more "pluses" listed than "minuses." Is DDP a movement that is here to stay? Or will we see a negative reaction to DDP someday when systems crash, or develop in an uncontrolled manner?

8. Of the listed DDP advantages and disadvantages, which three of each concern you the most? How would you reduce or eliminate your concern?

Centralize? Decentralize? Distribute?*

Hewlett-Packard Co. has been extremely successful in using large and small computers to handle its administrative data processing in whatever environment was necessary: centralized, decentralized, or distributed. We think that what we've learned can be useful to other worldwide multi-divisional companies with broad product lines, and so we've gone to some effort to share our experience. Describing something as complicated as how a company operates is not an easy task, however, especially given the added confusion that comes from an unsettled data processing vocabulary, so it seems best to trace what we have done with specific examples.

Basically, we have evolved from a purely centralized operation to our present mix by riding on the coattails of advancing technology. Our first computer experience in the late '50s and early '60s was with large standalone processors (and we still have some of those). As the company grew, we developed a central data processing facility at our corporate headquarters in Palo Alto, Calif. This facility served a number of San Francisco Bay area users in a batch environment, in which input and output was transferred by messenger or taxi.

In the early '70s, this center became too cumbersome to manage. It became increasingly difficult to respond adequately to the diverse needs of a large number of users. The short term answer was to go to an RJE environment—while still retaining a centralized computing facility—where control of the operation of application systems would be transferred to the users.

During the same period, we began to use time-sharing for interactive systems requiring geographically dispersed terminals, and to install a worldwide data communication network with local data entry to support our sales and service activities. The time-sharing and remote data entry applications gave us confidence in the effectiveness of minicomputers, and the development of the communications net was to be the groundwork for what has followed.

About five years ago we realized that our standalone installations outside the Bay area were more responsive to local management needs than our common RJE systems were. As a result, we began to decentralize a large portion of our previously centralized data processing.

Finally, our data communications network and decentralized computers together made it possible to experiment with distributed systems, where data storage and processing functions are shared across a mix of computers and lines, and where nontrivial operations are performed at more than one place. This activity has grown very rapidly, and several of our major data processing applications systems now operate in a distributed mode.

Thus far our experience with distributed processing has been positive. Distributed processing has made it possible for us to adapt to a constantly expanding geographic operation, and a constantly changing organizational structure, while maintaining consistent administrative support. It has permitted us to meet the reporting requirements of our own management and those of the governments of the various countries where we operate, in a timely and cost-effective manner. And it has improved the accuracy of administrative data by moving a significant portion of the processing to the source of information.

The most significant lesson we have learned from our experience, however, is that there is no one best way to process data. Information systems must be designed to match the organization they support. Thus our decentralized organization with its strong central management requires both decentralized and centrally managed systems. (See Table 1.) Understanding why this is true requires a short explanation of our business.

THE BASICS OF THE BUSINESS

Hewlett-Packard manufactures more than 4,000 products for wide-ranging markets which are primarily in manufacturing-related industries. We have 38 manufacturing facilities and 172 sales and service offices around the world, and together these employ about 45,000 people. We have experienced a very rapid growth of about 20% per year, culminating in sales of $1.7 billion in 1978.

To support this business, we currently have some 1,400 computers (not including desktop units or handheld calculators). Of these, 85% are used to support engineering and production applications, are usually dedicated to specific tasks, and often are arranged

Table 1.   After Nearly 20 Years of Evolution, HP has Come to the Conclusion That There Is No One Best Way to Process Data, and the Company Does Some Processing in Each Kind of Environment.

CENTRALIZED	DECENTRALIZED	DISTRIBUTED
Materials services	General accounting	Production information
Vendor contracting	Cost accounting	Customer information
Consolidated statements	Customer service	Orders & changes
Legal reporting	Production	Accounts receivable
Employee benefits	Shipments	Payroll & personnel
	Purchasing	(85%)
	Inventorying	
	Product assurance	
	Payroll & personnel	
	(15%)	

in networks. A number of them are also used in computer-aided design applications as front-end processors for large mainframes.

The remaining 200 computers are used to support business applications. The largest is an Amdahl 470/V6 located in Palo Alto, and there are nine medium-sized IBM systems in other large facilities. Seventy HP 3000s are used in our factories and larger sales offices, and 125 HP 1000s are scattered about for data entry, data retrieval, and data communications work.

Generally speaking, the HP computers are oriented toward on-line applications, and the large mainframes toward batch processing (although three also support on-line applications). In additions, HP uses about 2,500 crt terminals in business applications alone.

The network tying all this together consists of 110 data communications facilities located at sales and service offices, at manufacturing plants, and at corporate offices in northern California and Switzerland.

Some long-standing management traditions have contributed to the successful application of all this hardware. For example, for the past 20 years HP has been oriented toward decentralized management responsibility at the operating level with strong central management coordination. Local managers have been accustomed both to making their own decisions and to reporting to management on a frequent and detailed basis.

Another important tradition has been the adoption of companywide coding standards. Universal conventions for product number, account number, part number, entity code, employee number, and others were established to meet business requirements long before computer systems were extensively employed.

But perhaps the most important systems-related management tradition has been the existence of functional advisory councils.

These groups were established to resolve common local problems in such areas as order processing, materials management, cost accounting, and quality assurance. Today, these councils provide a forum in which to arrive at a consensus for dp related problems and to achieve user support.

We have found the decentralized management, the companywide standards, and existence of the councils all to be invaluable in building and managing our complex, dispersed systems.

TEN BIG PROBLEMS

Yet, for all our built-in advantages, progress hasn't always come easily. As our use of computers has evolved, we have faced a number of continuing challenges, some of the most important of which are:

1. Establishing a central planning and management program for company-wide information systems activities so that decentralized development work could be coordinated.
2. Designing systems which could respond easily to constant geographic expansion, organizational change, and the addition of new operating units.
3. · Coping with ever-increasing needs for detailed and accurate information to meet management and government reporting requirements while controlling administrative costs.
4. Designing systems which could be adapted to respond to specific local needs while maintaining companywide compatibility.
5. Getting user-managers to accept responsibility for the specification and operation of their systems.
6. Convincing users in different functional areas that data is an organizational resource to be shared by all, and that individual transactions should simultaneously update the records of all functions.

7. Avoiding unnecessary duplication of effort in designing and supporting systems.
8. Developing the skills of data processing staff members to meet the needs of a growing organization, and assigning priorities to their activities.
9. Establishing, maintaining, and promoting the use of standards for hardware, software, documentation, project management, data, and auditability and control as a foundation for well-coordinated worldwide applications systems.
10. Controlling security, and privacy in an on-line, decentralized, and distributed multinational environment.

Although we have made a great deal of progress in solving many of these problems, candidly, a number of them are still unresolved.

We began to seriously address the first and most important challenge — establishing management control over companywide systems developments — about two years ago. We saw then that a large amount of data processing hardware had been installed in decentralized locations and that many potentially incompatible systems were being designed. Furthermore, we realized that the plans for hardware installation were not well-coordinated with the needs of systems being developed centrally. In an attempt to deal with these matters we established an Information Systems Planning Office. This in turn led to the creation of an Information Systems Planning Task Force (similar to the advisory councils discussed earlier), which was assigned responsibility for defining how HP's information systems activities should be managed.

The task force first identified three organizational areas which required different approaches to system design and operation: sales and service, manufacturing, and corporate administration.

HP's fundamental organizational unit is the manufacturing division profit center.

There are 38 of these. Each occupies a single plant location, and performs a full range of business functions (including research and development, manufacturing, and marketing) as well as support functions (financial control, personnel administration, and product assurance). In many respects, each division resembles an independent company.

We practice management by objectives and attempt to have decisions made by the people who are closest to the problems. From an organizational viewpoint, this means that manufacturing support systems must be *decentralized*. The exceptions are centrally managed distributed systems such as those for payroll and personnel.

With such decentralization, there is an unfortunate tendency for redundancy in system design. To minimize this, HP has established a sharing policy for common programs, which has been quite successful.

HP's worldwide sales and service organization employs a different type of system. Customers are served by a single organization which just happens to be geographically dispersed. Sales and service activities related to specific product lines are performed by specialists; and these specialists are supported by a *distributed* marketing administration system which ties the sales and services offices to the company headquarters and to the factories.

The third entity, corporate, provides those services such as product assurance, payroll, and employee benefits, financial and legal reporting, which are best handled in a *centralized* manner.

The planning team studied how existing information systems supported these various company operations. During this analysis, it became clear that our most successful systems were those which matched the company's organization and management philosophy. This led to the conclusion that systems should be centralized, decentralized, or distributed depending on management needs.

The following four examples describe specific HP information systems or facilities and show how they match our organization. The first deals with the communication system, which is the heart of our minicomputer network. The second and third examples are of two systems having distributed data bases, one with central master files (at two locations) and the other with both central and dispersed masters. The final example deals with decentralized systems which interface some distributed systems.

110-NODE NETWORK

The communications system which supports our computing network employs minicomputers at 110 worldwide locations. These minis take care of a number of data communication functions. They handle data entry, format data for transmission, automatically detect and correct errors, and adapt transmission protocols to meet the requirements of various countries. In addition, the minis support on-line access to local data bases.

We started to build this network in the late '60s when we were using paper tape, which was slow, very expensive and—even more important—extremely error prone. In 1968, HP introduced a minicomputer oriented primarily toward scientific applications. To see if we could use this machine in business applications, we started using it to support a communications network with intelligent terminals. The network was successful right from the start, and we've been continuously adding to the locations served. Five years ago we began to install display terminals on the network. More recently we've been adding distributed data bases and an inquiry capability.

The network operates in a store and forward mode. In Europe, for example, local sites may perform data base inquiry and update their own files, but must batch all data for files maintained in Geneva. Similarly, Geneva batches data bound for Palo Alto files. The Geneva office handles both sales and manufacturing orders for products produced in Europe, sending only summary information to Palo Alto. For products manufactured outside of Europe, Geneva ships orders directly to Palo Alto; order status files for those sales are maintained simultaneously in Palo Alto and Geneva. The communications system uses the standard dial-up worldwide telephone network over most routes. This greatly reduces the cost, since we pay only for the actual time used. For example, it takes about one minute a day to transmit all the information back and forth to New Zealand. A single dial-up call to New Zealand is clearly a lot less costly than having a dedicated line.

The average worldwide data volume is about 140 million characters per day. This translates into about 100,000 messages. Still the line cost runs under $50,000 per month, which is very economical compared with the communication costs of other companies using on-line systems at similar data volumes.

The largest communication system applications are for marketing (60% of the traffic), accounting (15%), employee information (10%), and administrative messages (15%). We transmit about a million orders per year over the network, almost 50% of which originate outside the U.S., and about three million invoices. The network is also used extensively for file transmission.

The system has provided an excellent means for transmitting administrative messages (electronic mail) and has been particularly effective for overseas communication, where the telephone is costly and inconvenient because of time zone differences. Using the system, the cost of transmitting a letter-size message overseas is typically 30¢. This low cost, coupled with the system's speed and convenience, has resulted in a large increase in day to day communication between people at the operations level in our U.S. and overseas offices.

As the largest user of the communications system, the marketing administration group is responsible for planning and implementing systems enhancements, which are developed by a small central team of programmer analysts. New releases are transmitted as data to the remote locations and put into operation at a prearranged time. The installation of these periodic system enhancements normally goes smoothly, but a fair amount of expertise is required at the remote locations to cope with unexpected bugs which occur due to slight hardware differences, special local modems, and other incompatilbilities

MARKETING ADMINISTRATION SYSTEM

The second application system example is the distributed marketing administration system, which supports the sales and service organization. The primary objective of the marketing system is to provide accurate and consistent information to support our customers on a worldwide basis. To do this requires a centrally managed distributed system.

The marketing administration system (Figure 1) suggests how centralized, decentralized, and distributed processing all go on simultaneously.

Decentralized processing is used for production planning, product configuring, and shipment scheduling at the manufacturing

sites, and for order entry and service scheduling at the sales and service offices.

Centralized processing comes in for such functions as financial and legal reporting and administration of the employee benefits program at corporate.

Some forms of distributed processing are employed for maintaining and accessing distributed data bases. The data for customer records all originates at the sales offices, for example, and slices of the customer data base are kept in each sales office, but a complete customer data base is simultaneously maintained at corporate and slices of the data base also exist at the manufacturing plants.

The data for product records all originates at the sales offices, for another example, and slices of the product data base are kept at each plant, but complete product data bases are simultaneously maintained at corporate and at each sales office.

Orders and changes are entered at the sales and service offices, transmitted to headquarters where they are entered on central files, and then sent on to the factories for acceptance and delivery acknowledgement. Company order, shipment, and backlog status is maintained centrally to provide information to top management. Delivery information is transmitted from the manufacturing divisions back to the sales offices where orders are acknowledged.

Invoices are centrally processed in Palo Alto and Geneva. The credit and collection functions are decentralized to the sales offices, with central reporting of receivables status to provide financial control.

Files of European open orders are maintained in both Geneva and Palo Alto. An order from a European sales office containing items to be supplied from a European factory and a U.S. factory is processed in Geneva. Complete detail pertaining to the U.S.-sup-

Figure 1.   Marketing Administration System

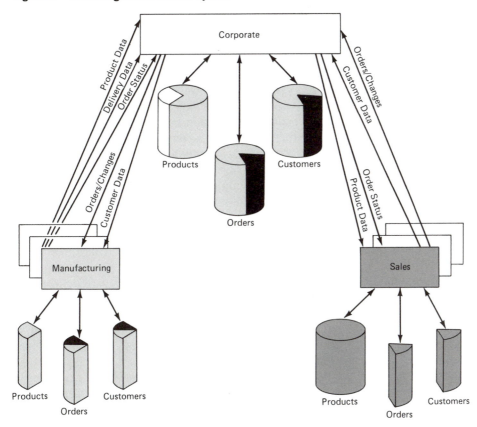

plied items is transmitted to Palo Alto; however, only order statistics are sent to Palo Alto for the European-supplied items. Order status information is transmitted back and forth daily to keep the two files in sync, and a monthly audit procedure insures that nothing has been overlooked in the daily updates.

Up-to-date order status change information is transmitted daily from the Palo Alto headquarters to the larger U.S. sales offices to provide on-line access for response to customer inquiries. The remote files are kept in sync with the master files by computer con-

trol. That is, the update program requires each batch update to be performed in the right order. (The Jan. 17 update cannot be performed before the Jan. 16 update.) Local files can be recreated from the central files should recovery be necessary.

Although data communication is handled in a batch mode, the system operates in the same manner as an on-line distributed system in which a significant portion of the data processing is done at more than one location. Data is batch communicated because this is the most economical method to employ with currently available communication facilities.

The use of display terminals in the sales offices to access order status information produces a labor saving of close to 20% over the former methods. In the past, HP used microfiche reports, produced once a week and mailed to the sales offices. Data retrieval was awkward and time-consuming. In addition, reports were usually received late, so we had to transmit printed information daily to update the microfiche. Now, having this information directly available also cuts costs, since fewer telephone calls to the factories are necessary for order status inquiries.

Managing the marketing administration system is a continual challenge. Because of its wide geographic and applications scope, changes must be made slowly and carefully to avoid upsetting existing features. Individual HP organizations and functions have a continuing need for enhancements and want these to be installed quickly. Functional councils such as the Information Systems Task Force, the Order Processing Council and the Customer Service Council, have played important roles in prioritizing these needs and obtaining support for overall system development plans. Needless to say, differences of opinion are strongly expressed in meetings of these councils.

Another management challenge is the coordination of international dp system activities. Europe, in particular, has important and unique system needs which are best developed and supported locally. These needs, however, must be closely coordinated with the main system because of the close interrelationship of transactions and files. A great deal of overseas travel, along with rotation of knowledgeable personnel, is needed to keep these efforts properly coordinated. To accomplish this coordination, three U.S. systems people are currently assigned in Europe, and two Europeans in the United States.

PERSONNEL/PAYROLL SYSTEM

In order to comply with local laws and customs, an independent personnel/payroll system is maintained by HP in each country in which we have operations. In the United States we have a distributed system which pays about 25,000 employees. The pay information is entered on display terminals at about 30 remote locations, each with its own daily updated disk file. The data is transmitted to Palo Alto monthly, where the payroll is processed. The pay checks are either transmitted back to the originating locations for printing or they may be directly deposited in the employee's bank account.

Why do we process our payroll in Palo Alto, rather than at the remote locations? We do this for two main reasons. First, to help administer overall HP benefits. For example, we have a nationwide insurance plan, a retirement program, cash profit sharing, and a stock purchase plan; all of these must be administered out of a central file.

Second, many government reports must be made on a centralized basis: retirement legislation reports, equal opportunity reports, withholding taxes, etc. By producing the information needed for benefit administration and government reporting a by-product of the payroll system, the information need only be entered into the computer system once.

The distributed data base which supports the payroll/personnel system operates in a different mode from that which is used for the sales and service system. Each division is responsible for the accuracy of the data relating to its employees. The data is kept on local HP 3000 disk files updated daily. Changes made to these files are transmitted to Palo Alto several times a month, where they are used to update the central file prior to payroll processing.

Characteristics of Application Systems

ACTIVITY	FACTORY MANAGEMENT SYSTEM	MARKETING ADMINISTRATION SYSTEM	PAYROLL/PERSONNEL SYSTEM
Development	Joint effort between divisions and corporate on modular basis	Various operational units working under centrally coordinated plan	Corporate
Operation	Decentralized (use is optional)	Distributed	Distributed
Data Base	Locally maintained, serves all manufacturing facility departments	Centrally and locally maintained, local sales office data bases updated daily	Locally and centrally maintained, central data base updated before each payroll run
Support	Sharable systems centrally supported	Central support of basic systems, local support of alterations	Central support

The audit and control procedure which ensures that the central and remote files are in sync works in the following manner. After the central file is updated, the modified records are transmitted back to the local entity for comparison. Any discrepancies are then reported.

Discrepancies can arise from two causes. First, somewhat more stringent edit routines can be applied centrally, so an unedited error is occasionally detected. Second, certain changes to employees' records can be made centrally and these are sometimes not recorded in the local files. A small, but significant number of errors are detected by this audit and control procedure.

The payroll/personnel system serves a number of departments: finance, accounting, personnel, and tax. An advisory board consisting of members of each of those departments reviews and approves changes to the system's programs, which number several hundred per year.

Eighty-five percent of HP's U.S. employees are paid by this system. The other 15% are located in manufacturing divisions which have elected to run their payrolls locally. Personnel data for this 15% must still be maintained in the central file to take care of the centrally administered benefit programs. Keeping this independently prepared data accurate and consistent with that prepared centrally is a significant challenge. This experience has dramatized the advantage of sharing common data used by different functions. The discipline of the payroll system has proven to be invaluable in keeping central personnel records up to date and accurate.

The remote personnel files of both kinds permit local entities to produce reports on their employees. In addition, they provide a timely interface to local systems such as cost accounting. The remotely used software is centrally supported, and changes are released periodically.

FACTORY MANAGEMENT SYSTEM

The last application system to be described is the factory management system, which is implemented on HP 3000 hardware. This decentralized system supports the functions of order processing, materials management and purchasing, production planning, product assurance, service support and accounting.

The factory management system consists of a group of functional modules which access a central data base which serves as an information resource for the division. As mentioned earlier, most systems used by our manufacturing divisions are decentralized and locally managed. Although each HP division has unique requirements which must be satisified by its local support systems, there is a remarkable similarity between the needs of the different divisions. Most HP divisions are oriented largely toward assembly operations, so manufacturing support systems are designed around a bill of materials processor. As a general rule, 80% of a division's needs can be satisfied with the basic system. We developed the factory management system to multiply the return on development and support costs by sharing systems between these decentralized locations.

The factory management system has been developed over the last five years, one module at a time. (An example of a system module would be materials management, production planning, or cost accounting.) The development has been done by joint development teams consisting of division personnel responsible for providing the specifications and ensuring that the system meets their functional needs, and of central data processing specialists who make sure that the modules operate efficiently and properly interface other system modules. On completion each module can be shared by other divisions on a voluntary basis.

We have not attempted to solve all system problems in each module, We have followed the 80-20 rule, taking care of major requirements that are common to a number of divisions. In fact, we have encouraged sharing divisions to add unique features required to meet their local needs. Quite often these unique features are of value to other divisions and later get incorporated into the "standard" modules.

This approach to sharable system design has been very successful. We find that the shared modules save up to 75% over the cost of local development and that they can be implemented in a fraction of the time. So far, over half of HP's 38 divisions have elected to participate in this program, and nearly all have plans eventually to use some parts of the system.

The factory management system has been especially useful to new divisions (which are being added at a rate of about three per year). It has permitted managers in these divisions to have a high level of systems support capability early in their growth cycle. On the other hand, the system has been much less useful to older, established divisions with mature systems. These entities have found it difficult to justify the cost of change (especially retraining people), even though on-line operation and other enhancements would be desirable.

The factory management system architecture permits divisions to utilize either the complete system or individual modules to support specific functions. Many divisions have installed modules to automate activities which previously were handled manually.

Often these modules are interfaced with existing systems implemented on IBM (or IBM-compatible) hardware.

With the large number of divisions using the factory management systems, we have found it profitable to establish a central support facility. This group installs enhancements to the system on an on-going basis, makes modifications as required to match changes in interfacing systems (such as companywide distributed systems), and helps the divisions install modules. Several functional advisory boards have been established to facilitate priority setting and to keep the central group tuned in to user needs. One of the important problems considered by the advisory boards is whether to enhance existing systems to achieve short-term benefits, or to put the effort on additional systems capability to satisfy future needs.

The factory management system provides an interesting management challenge. Since it uses within one facility a data base supporting all using functions, managers must rely on the accuracy of one another's data. This can be difficult to implement in an organization accustomed to individual departmental control of systems resources, but it pays off by providing consistent information and eliminating the classic argument over whose numbers are right.

For access to those numbers, HP is making wide use of display terminals in factory applications, as well as in sales and service work. The primary advantage of these on-line terminals is usually thought to be that access to data, but there is an important secondary justification: paper saving. Terminal availability greatly reduces the number of printed reports required. In one study (involving another manufacturer's hardware), we found that half the cost of installing on-line displays was justified by a direct reduction in printed reports which the users agreed to give up in return for on-line access to data.

FOUR STRINGS TO TIE IT TOGETHER

An important activity of managing systems in a large worldwide company is the central systems support which ties the whole process together. Four main functions or aspects are involved at HP: (1) long-range planning, (2) "visibility and leverage," (3) personnel, and (4) standards and guidelines.

The preparation and maintenance of *an overall plan* for systems evolution and development is essential. This involves the combined efforts of manufacturing, sales and service, and companywide personnel. To accomplish this, we've established three planning teams. The manufacturing planning team is headed by the vice president of corporate services and his staff. The marketing team consists of members of the staff of the vice president of marketing. Companywide planning is handled by the office of the controller. The central management job is to consolidate the results of the planning efforts by these three teams and then communicate these plans throughout the company and to upper level management for approval or for suggested modification.

The aspect we call *"visibility and leverage"* has played an important role in the success of our systems. We believe that good managers will make good decisions if they have the right information. A great deal of needless duplication of effort has been avoided by communicating information about information system activities taking place throughout the company. For one thing, this has highlighted existing sharing opportunities.

Information systems *personnel* are very important in this scheme, and growth of the number of people in this function parallels that of the company's dollar growth: 20% per year. Most of the hiring and development of these people is decentralized, but the central activity provides an overall framework to improve consistency.

Another important function of Central Information Systems Services is user management education. Training programs are conducted regularly covering the role of users in system design and operation.

The final area, *standards and guidelines,* is essential to the success of all our systems. As mentioned earlier, we have some well-established, companywide coding standards which arose out of non-dp activities. In addition, the dp systems themselves have helped create and maintain standards. For example, our worldwide order processing system imposes a strong data standards discipline. Factories and sales offices must follow the rules in order to communicate with one another and to ensure that orders are processed.

We have put a lot of effort into standardizing our documentation procedures as well. Documentation is of great importance as a project management tool during system design. It is also a key ingredient of our systems sharing program, as it helps a prospective user evaluate the utility of systems under consideration.

In contrast, hardware and software standards have probably been of less importance to HP. Nearly all of our computers are manufactured by HP or IBM, and have compatible communication protocols at the hardware interface level. Magnetic tapes can be readily interchanged, for one thing. Then too, HP minis emulate HASP workstations for IBM mainframes. Data is transmitted using standard protocols. We have adopted COBOL as the standard language for application programs, and we use the HP Image data base management system extensively in our HP 3000 applications. There aren't too many pieces to coordinate.

In summary, our minicomputer systems have helped us find workable solutions to the 10 challenges listed earlier. These systems have helped us provide consistent support for our administrative activities under conditions of rapid growth and change. They have kept our sales organization supplied with the up to date information necessary to provide full service to our customers in all of our worldwide sales and service offices. They have helped our management keep score by providing key information when needed. And they have helped us cope with ever-increasing government reporting requirements.

HP's internal business systems are continually being improved to meet changing requirements. As this goes on, and as we evaluate the results, it seems that several characteristics emerge over and over again as the most significant.

Successful systems put the control of the data close to the source of the information and the control of processing close to the manager responsible for the function being performed. In an organization like Hewlett-Packard, this will frequently imply distributing the processing, but not always. When distributed processing is called for, there are additional criteria for success. Among these are an existing set of standards and coding conventions, some mechanism whereby disagreements among users and developers can be resolved, and some facility for sharing programs and procedures among the participants.

When all of these things can be combined, as they have at Hewlett-Packard, user managers are satisfied, corporate managers have the data they need when they need it, and administrative productivity is increased —

and those have been the goals all along, haven't they?

QUESTIONS

1. Hewlett-Packard (HP) utilizes three differing methods of data processing, as reflected in Table I. Is such an approach practical?

2. Explain "decentralized management responsibility at the operating level with strong central management coordination" (first page).

3. Ten "big problems" are enumerated by HP. Rank these ten problems in terms of how critical you believe they are.

4. Do you feel that HP should have designed their system around their basic organizational unit (the manufacturing division profit center)? Or should they consider an organizational shift in definition of the basic unit to be measured?

5. The author mentions that the payroll application is a "centrally managed distributed system." Can such a design really exist, or is this system really a centralized one with remote I/O?

6. Which design topology (star, ring, or tree) is utilized in the four specific systems examples presented in the article?

7. React to the four listed "main functions" of the central systems support group. How would you rank order these four tasks?

8. HP takes a global approach to problem solving via the central systems support function, yet it is mentioned that many newly hired personnel are being decentralized. Organizationally, how does the HP approach achieve success?

TOPIC FIVE

Data Bases and Data Base Management Systems

The notion of "data" was introduced on page one of the Topic One overview. Data, when properly captured and assimilated, provides the basis for business decision making. Thus we can deduce that data has a benefit factor and is desirable. Yet data is extremely expensive. Consider the following tasks performed upon millions or billions of data documents in a business year:

Data capture
Data recording
Data transmission
Data edit and/or validation
Data structuring
Data storage
Data retrieval
Data analysis
Data reporting
Data security (access)
Data migration
Data recovery

The above tasks clearly indicate a huge cost associated with the benefit of possessing data.

Prior chapters in this book have highlighted the importance of systems planning analysis, design, and implementation. All four concepts are relevant for consideration in the data base area as corporate data reflects a microcosm of the firm. Data base planning requires the elicitation of user informational needs while analysis more clearly focuses on the available resources and constraints of the data base and encourages the consideration of multiple data base designs. The data base design phase narrows the consideration of various architectures into a clear conceptual scheme of the data base, while the implementation step carries the logical data design into physical reality.

The concept of a "data base management system" (DBMS) has elevated the importance of data management due to improved software architecture and user friendliness. Unfortunately, DBMSs have spawned a new genre of techno-babble phraseology, which the data base novice must master. For instance, what is a "tuple" or "3^{ed} normal form"?

A discussion of data bases reads much like a journey through time. That is, an evolution has occurred regarding the metamorphosis of file management sophistication. Let us embark upon the journey to better appreciate the data base technology of the 1990s.

EVOLUTION OF FILES

Back in the days of exclusively magnetic tape or punched card systems, files were viewed as bundles of data to be accessed, read, and updated in a sequential manner. An example of a flat file would be a student records file as shown below. A flat file can be thought of as

State	Stu ID#
MI	2168
MI	2171
MI	2172

on a tape file, one must still sequentially read the entire file.

RECORD	STUDENT ID	STUDENT'S HOME STATE	STUDENT'S GRADE POINT AVERAGE
1	2168	MI	3.68
2	2169	NJ	2.91
3	2170	IN	1.44
4	2171	MI	4.00
5	2172	MI	2.85

a two-dimensional array. The "flatness" of the file is derived from the fact that data retrieval is sequential, meaning that you cannot "hop" over records which have no interest to you. A file normally contains one record for each *entity* (employee, part, location, student, asset) and each entity may possess one or more *attributes* (data items in the record or entity). The unique identifier in the record (in this case it would be the Student ID no.), is the *primary key* for access, with other attributes being called *secondary* keys. Primary keys must be unique; thus only one student has the number 2170. However, several students may possess the same home state attribute.

One design advancement to alleviate the unnecessary sequential search through the entire file is the concept of *inverted files*. Inverted files are separate tables which list records by a similar secondary key. Thus if a typical file query was "List all students from Michigan," an inverted file based upon the state attribute would be appropriate. Although inverted files are an improvement over pure flat files, recognize that to read the records for the State = Michigan students

The invention of direct access storage devices (computer hard disks) dramatically boosted the evolution of file management. Disks allow the data user the *option* of direct record access, thus changing the concept of file from a two-dimensional array into a three-dimensional (or n-dimensional) cube. In short, the topology of a flat file was forever altered in the minds of advanced data managers. Concurrent with the shift from magnetic tape to disk storage was the philosophical shift from batch to online processing.

Disks allow the user the advantage of "hopping" over records which have no interest. Consider the following five student records stored randomly on a disk. If the typical query was "List all students from State = X," *pointers* (links) could be placed in individual records to form *chains* (lists) of records with a related secondary key listed in front of each record as its physical disk address. The chain for all Michigan students would be formed by placing the disk physical address of the next Michigan student into the record of the previous Michigan student. Thus to access all Michigan students, one need not traverse nor read all

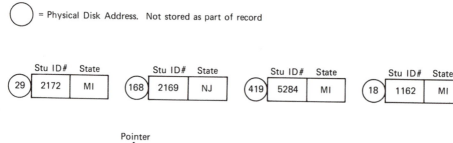

records. Similarly, a second pointer could be placed in each record to link all students with a GPA of 3.00 or better. From a data retrieval standpoint, link-listing was a tremendous advancement in data management. It is important for you to know that most commercial database management systems are architecturally based upon inverted files and/or link-listing.

DBMSs≠BASE OF DATA

The concept of link-listing, although an advancement, did not necessarily infer that a business had a true DBMS. In fact, unfortunately, the phrase "data base" is one of the most misused and misunderstood terms in the business world. Many corporations have enormous banks of data to draw upon, but their files remain unintegrated *and* redundant. Such files are indeed a *base of data,* but fall far short of a true *data base.* A true DBMS must meet all of the following conditions:

Comprehensiveness — The database must contain all of the data of the business. Such data may go far beyond merely financial information. For instance, limits of measure may include dollars, time, or quantities, while valuation may be at both historic and replacement cost.

Nonredundancy — Consider the advantage of the elimination of redundant data, from the perspective of file compression and space saving. The pay rate of a student employed at a university under a work-study program could be contained in at least three files: payroll, student records, and the department of his/her employment. Why should such a kernel of data be in all three files? (Similarly, an employee in a manufacturing firm could have his/her pay rate stored in a personnel file, a job cost file, and a pension file.) The elimination of redundant files also reduces the tendencies for individual departments to view data as "their" data with exclusive territorial rights. Data "monarchies" are indeed a dangerous thing from the long-term perspective of comprehensive business planning.

Consistency — An excellent design feature of a true DBMS is that, if data kernels exist only once, any kernel update is a true *global* update, Thus you are never faced with the ridiculous situation of a kernel of information (Pay rate of J. Jones) being recorded at different values in different files at the same time! Of course if the value you record for J. Jones is incorrect, it's universally incorrect. However, consistency is still a fundamental MIS virtue.

Flexibility — A true DBMS allows multiple users to "see" the same data base in different formats. Each user's view of the data is called his/her *subschema* of the files. The *schema* is the overall logical design of the

DBMS. For instance, in a student record DBMS, each student record may be 500 bytes long, containing both academic information (GPA, class enrollment) and financial information (work-study wages, library fines). Should a career counselor be allowed to access the student record and read pay information? Should a payroll clerk be allowed to see the student's GPA? The beauty of a true DBMS is that you may develop separate subschemas for these two user groups so that they view the same data in differing contexts. In fact, a major advantage of DBMS is its flexible design nature which allows you to *model the data around business needs — and not vice versa.*

Data Independence — The final condition of a DBMS is that the data be independent of the application programs. The notion here is that users need only know the logical design of the file, via the subschemas. The physical design of the file and file access is controlled by the DBMS itself. Thus the physical structure of the data and its overall schema may change architecturally, without necessitating a change in any user's application program.

Pictured in Figure 5.1 is a drawing of a DBMS. Remember that a DBMS is, basically, a piece of *software.* Each user accesses the DBMS via his/her "host" application program written in some conventional programming language (Cobol, PL/1, Basic).

The interface between the application program and the DBMS is referred to as the data manipulation language (DML). Typical DML commands are: FIND, INSERT, MODIFY, DELETE, and STORE. The DML, in short, allows file processing. The DML calls upon the data description language (DDL) to build the user's view from the logical schema. Finally, the operating system and the database control system (DBCS) provide the bridge from logical design to physical data linkage.

An interesting question at this point is "Who designs the logical subschemas, selects the appropriate DBMS architecture, and controls the physical data?" The answer is God — a.k.a. the data base administrator (DBA). He/she sits in the position of ultimate power for only he/she may add new attributes to the data dictionary. The DBA also maintains responsibility for DBMS backup and recovery, and for security issues. (DBMS control and security will be addressed in Topic Seven.)

DBMSs have evolved into three structures, or architectures: *tree* or *hierarchical, network,* and *relational.* The philosophy of the tree approach is that a file has a dominant *root* or singularly important method of access. For instance, a student data base may utilize STU ID# as the key for any query.

Figure 5.1.

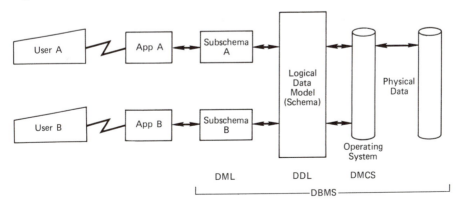

Figure 5.2.   Tree

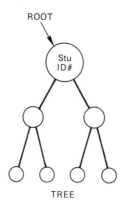

TREE

Figure 5.3.   Network

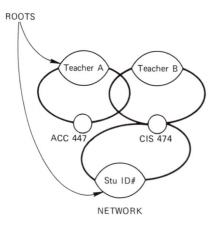

NETWORK

Figure 5.4.   Relational

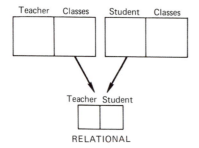

RELATIONAL

The benefit of a tree is that it is a one-to-many relationship—if you access the proper root it explodes into a great deal of information (all siblings of the parent or root record). A network architecture holds the perspective that a single dominant root is unhealthy. That is, two or three roots (points of access) are appropriate because different users perceive data differently. Some users may ask the query "Which classes is Student 2169 taking?" yet administrators may query the file with "Which classes is Teacher A teaching?" Networks are called many-to-many or *shared record* relationships because both the student and teacher "share" the class they have in common. The most recent DBMS design is the relation (table or entity) approach. The relational model says, in effect, that any or all data attributes are root candidates for primary access. Relations (tables) for teachers and students could be established. Then a JOIN operation would merge these two tables into a third table to find which teachers have a class in common. Thus, relational DBMSs are based upon relational algebra operations.

We have now completed the introduction to DBMSs via a walk through the evolution from flat files to n-dimensional file topology. It is appropriate now to get "back to basics" regarding file design. The classic systems development life cycle (SDLC) was presented in Topics Two and Three. The SDLC phases present guidance for the consideration and design of DBMSs. The conceptual design phase reflects an identification of systems needs on a corporate-wide basis, while detailed subschema design is a fine tuning of systems needs to individual user groups, with user feedback. Logical and physical design address architectural and implementation considerations which ultimately result in the physical loading of the data. The database design cycle, much like the SDLC, is an

SDLC PHASES	DATABASE DESIGN PHASES
1 Planning	1 Conceptual Design
2 Analysis	2 Detailed Subschema Design
3 Design	3 Logical Design
4 Implementation	4 Physical Data Design

iterative process predicated upon constant feedback from the analyst, DBA, and user.

ARTICLES

The paper by Herman brings DBMSs into sharper focus by developing a robust hierarchical application. Herman deals at quite a level of specificity, introducing several DBMS terms such as *entities, attributes, tuple,* and *normalization.* The reader is encouraged to maintain a list (3" × 5" cards) of DBMS terms for future reference. A final caveat is offered regarding the Herman paper. There is a movement afoot due to the "trendiness" of relational DBMSs, which states that any DBMS other than a relational one is unquestionably inappropriate and archaic. On the contrary, the Herman paper reveals a perfectly appropriate application of a tree DBMS.

The second paper (McCarthy) is a conceptual discussion of the Entity-Relationship model of accounting. This groundbreaking work blends accounting and relational theory, and actually extends relational architecture. An accounting information system is integrated into DBMS technology as the author calls for creative thinking from the reader to eliminate several accounting "artifacts." Terms such as *objects, agents, events,* and *artifacts* are developed in the E-R model.

After reading the two articles in this section, you should possess a working knowledge of the DBMS design cycle, architectures, and terminology. Careful consideration on your behalf will now allow you to design the DBMS around the needs of the corporation.

A Database Design Methodology for an Integrated Database Environment*

The design methodology described in this paper is used by the Wholesale Data Administration function at Manufacturers Hanover Trust Company, the fourth largest U.S. commercial bank. The Wholesale Data Administration function provides database administration support to Wholesale Banking Systems, one of four decentralized data processing functions within the bank.

Most of the application supported by the Wholesale Data Base Administration function are on-line, real-time applications which are part of a large integrated on-line system. Each application can be thought of as a sub-application of the larger application. At any one point in time several of the sub-applications may be in development. In addition several unrelated applications may simultaneously be undergoing development. CICS is the standard teleprocessing monitor, and IMS is the standard database management system. The IBM DB/DC dictionary is used to support application development and the database administration function.

The database design methodology used by the Wholesale Data Base Administration function is performed in conjunction with the standard data processing Project Life Cycle used at Manufacturers Hanover. The standard Project Life Cycle consists of the following phases:

Feasibility: The scope of the project is defined and various alternative approaches are discussed. One approach is recommended, and a general estimate of overall development costs is prepared.

Functional Analysis Phase: During the functional analysis phase, the application project works closely with the end-user to determine the business requirements of the project, and to define all input, output, and processing requirements.

Design Phase: During the design phase, a general design for the system is developed and documented.

Implementation Phase: During the implementation phase, detailed program specifications are prepared. The programs are coded, unit tested, system tested, acceptance tested by the user, and finally environment tested and installed.

THE WHOLESALE DATA ADMINISTRATION DATA BASE DESIGN METHODOLOGY

As mentioned earlier, the Wholesale Data Base Design Methodology phases correspond to the phases of the standard project life cycle. The correspondence is as follows:

PROJECT LIFE CYCLE PHASE	DATABASE DESIGN PHASE
Feasibility	Conceptual Design
Functional Analysis	Detailed Conceptual Design
Design	Logical Design
Implementation	Physical Design

Each data base design phase will next be described.

CONCEPTUAL DESIGN PHASE

During this phase the data required to support a proposed application is identified, and the fundamental structure of the data is determined. Identification of required data and its structure is accomplished by identifying the business functions to be supported by the application and then assessing the data required by the business functions to perform their specific objectives. Business functions represent actions or processes which the system must perform; the data represents that on which the actions or processes operate.

In the first step of the conceptual design phase the application analysts identify the business functions to be supported by the application via a series of interviews with the end-users. The business functions are then decomposed using standard functional decomposition techniques to 2-4 levels depending on the complexity of the function.

Next the applications analysts identify the entities required to support the business functions. An entity is a person, place, object or thing that is relevant to the business function. From the entire universe of entities relevant to the business functions, the analyst extracts those which are required to support the new computer system.

Entities required to support the new application are represented by data classes — the informational representations of entities. That is, data classes consist of the specific information which the computer system will need to maintain about the entity which the data class represents. One or more data classes may be required to represent an entity.

For each data class the following descriptive information is collected and documented:

- *Definition.* A data class definition is a narrative describing the purpose, use, and volume of a data class.
- *Attributes.* Attributes are specific items of information that describe a data class, e.g., customer name and address information or customer balance information. The items that make up the attributes of a data class are used to further distinguish the keys. During the Conceptual Design Phase only the major attributes of each data class, such as keys are identified.
- *Indicative Key.* In most cases, data classes are capable of being uniquely identified, i.e., each occurrence can be distinguished from all other occurrences. The indicative key is the key which uniquely identifies the data class.
- *Cross Reference Key.* A cross reference key is an attribute of a data class that relates it to another data class. For example in a Customer Information File system, a DDA account number might be the indicative key for the data class "account" but the cross reference key for the data class "customer".
- *Retrieval Key.* A retrieval key is an attribute used to retrieve or access a data class. A data class can have several retrieval keys. Unlike indicative keys, retrieval keys need not be unique.

During the Conceptual Design Phase, emphasis is put on identification and analysis of all keys. Other attributes of the data class may be identified during the conceptual phase but will be more fully identified and analyzed during the Detailed Conceptual Design Phase.

Finally, the relationships between the data classes, 1-1, 1-many, or many-many are analyzed, and a data structure diagram is drawn. To assist in drawing the data structure diagram and in reviewing it during the design review, a Data Class Relationship Matrix and/or a Data Class/Business Function Matrix may be prepared.

The data class relationships are normally analyzed in one or more working sessions conducted between the application analysts and the database analysts. The data structure diagram is prepared, however, by the database analyst.

The following documentation is prepared during the Conceptual Design Phase:

Business Functions:

A *Business Function Input Form,* which names and describes each business function and identifies all data classes used by the business function, is prepared for each business function. Information from this form is entered to the Data Dictionary. A Functional Decomposition Diagram, a hierarchical diagram of all business functions and their subfunctions decomposed to 2-3 levels, is prepared for the entire system. An example is shown in Figure 1.

A *Data Class Input Form* is prepared for each data class. It names and describes each data class, identifies the indicative, cross reference and retrieval keys for the data class, and identifies relationships to other data classes. The Data Class Input form is entered to the Data Dictionary.

A *Data Class Relationship Matrix,* showing relationships between data classes, may be prepared; a Data Class/Business Function Cross Reference Matrix is prepared. The Data Class/ Business Function Cross Reference Matrix shows all business functions and data classes

Figure 1.   Functional Decomposition Diagram

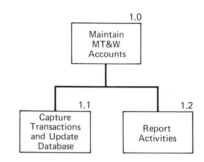

used by the system, and which data classes are used by each business function. Finally a *Data Structure Diagram* is drawn, which pictorially documents all data classes and their interrelationships. See Figure 2. Responsibilities for each type of documentation are shown in Figure 3.

When all elements of the conceptual design phase have been collected and documented, the review procedures are initiated. The review is normally conducted in three stages:
- DBA
- Application Project Team
- End User

DBA Review.   The DBA group must make certain that:
- Business functions are completely defined and documented.
- Data classes are unambiguous and consistent.
- Relationships between data classes have been correctly analyzed and documented.
- Naming conventions have been followed.

Application Project Team Review.   The application project team is responsible for reviewing the Conceptual Design for completeness and accuracy. As such, all forms used to document the design are reviewed. After reviewing the documentation, the application project team is required to sign off

Figure 2.   Data Structure Diagram

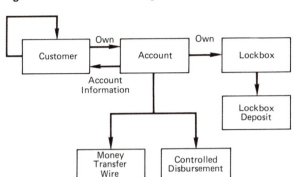

Figure 3.   Conceptual Design Responsibility Matrix

TASK DESCRIPTION	TASK RESPONSIBILITY		DOCUMENTATION RESPONSIBILITY	FORM ID.
	Primary	Assisted By:		
Collect and Describe Business Functions	APT		APT	II-2
Decompose Business Functions	APT		APT	III-3
Identify and Describe Data Classes	APT	WDA	APT, WDA	II-5a, II-5b
Data Structure Diagram	WDA		WDA	II-8
Data Class Relationships	WDA	APT	WDA	II-6
Data Classes/Business Functions	WDA	APT	WDA	II-7

Notes

or present written comments on the conceptual design.

User Review. Finally, the Conceptual Design must be presented to the user. The user must verify and approve all business functions, entities, data classes, and data class relationships. The goal of this review is to reach a clear understanding between users and analysts as to the scope, functions, and data class requirements of the proposed application system. Any discrepancies or conflicts are normally resolved before the completion of the Conceptual Design phase.

In certain cases, such as minor conflicts, the analyst may proceed to the next phase, i.e., Detailed Conceptual Design. However, the exact nature of the conflict must be documented and subsequently resolved in the next phase.

DETAILED CONCEPTUAL DESIGN PHASE

During the Detailed Conceptual Design phase the business functions identified during the conceptual design phases are further decomposed into logical transactions. Data classes and their associated data elements are identified.

By the end of the detailed conceptual design phase, most of the attributes (data elements) have been identified for each data class. The Detailed Conceptual Phase is performed during the Functional Analysis Phase of the application project. The specific steps in the data collection and analysis process are as follows:

Logical Transactions.   Data collection is accomplished by expanding and further analyzing the outputs obtained in the Conceptual Design Phase. The business functions identified in the WDA Functional Decomposition Diagram are further decomposed into logical transactions. A logical transaction is a complete unit of work, such as "Update Account Balance." The application analysts are responsible for identifying and specifying all logical transactions that support each business function, the expected transaction volume, required response time, data classes used, and the input and output documents or forms used.

Data Elements.   After identifying all logical transactions, the application analyst must specify the data elements required for the processing of each transaction. The analyst begins by searching the Data Dictionary for data elements already defined. If the search produces a list of data elements with the same or similar name, each of these elements must be checked against elements of the proposed system. For elements with identical definitions or attributes, only the relationships to the components (categories) of the proposed system are specified for documentation in the Data Dictionary. Thus, the duplication of data elements is eliminated. If, however, definitions and/or attributes of elements of the proposed system

differ from or conflict with those elements of existing systems, the application analyst is responsible for identifying these conflicts.

The final responsibility for identifying any conflicts of this nature *always* resides with the DBA group. Thus, responsibility for identifying conflicts should be viewed as part of the standard review process which occurs after the application area has completed its data documentation procedures. A brief description of the nature of the conflict is prepared.

Finally, the database analysts must assist the application analysts in associating the identified data elements with the appropriate data classes. This process is performed for each logical transaction. The database analyst also must ensure that there are no ambiguities or inconsistencies in this process. The end result of the Detailed Conceptual Design Phase is the formulation of an integrated interrelationship between the data classes, data elements, and logical transactions that support the business functions which were identified in the Conceptual Design Phase.

Documentation of the logical transactions is via the Logical Transaction Input Form. Documentation of new elements is via the Data Element Input Form. The Logical Transaction Input Form names and describes the Logical Transaction, identifies which data classes are used by the Logical Transaction, and gives processing information about the Logical Transaction, such as maximum and peak volume and processing mode. The Data Element Input Form names and describes the Data Element, specifies its edit criteria, and identifies related data elements. Both the Logical Transaction and Data Element Input Forms are entered to the Data Dictionary. Where existing data elements will be used by a new application, a connection is made to the system's data dictionary description to facilitate data dictionary cross-reference reporting.

In addition, the documentation produced during the Conceptual Design Phase is updated to reflect any new information collected during the Detailed Conceptual Phase. For example, new data classes may be discovered during the Detailed Conceptual Phase. Data classes identified during the Conceptual Design Phase may be further broken down into additional data classes. The Data Structure Diagram must be updated accordingly.

Responsibilities for each type of documentation are shown in Figure 4.

As in the Conceptual Design Phase, a three-step review procedure is followed: DBA, Application Project, and User.

DBA Review. The DBA group is responsible for conducting a thorough examination and review of the data elements and associated information entered into the Data Dictionary by the systems analysts. In this review, the data elements and associated information are scrutinized for accuracy and adherence to standards.

A major function in the review process to identify and assess the impact of any conflicts which result from the input of new elements into an existing system. For example, such a conflict could involve a discrepancy in the number of digits or range of values for a data element. The DBA group is solely responsible for guiding the review process through to definition of the conflict and a resolution of the problem.

Application Project Team Review. The application project team is responsible for reviewing the result of the detailed Conceptual Design Phase for completeness and accuracy. After reviewing this documentation, the application project team is required to sign off or present written comments on the Detailed Conceptual Design.

User Review. The user is responsible for reviewing the Detailed Conceptual Design documentation. The user must agree to the Detailed Conceptual Design model and make certain that the data classes and data elements are compatible with the business functions of the application system, and that all data classes and data elements have been correctly defined and documented. Emphasis is placed on developing business-oriented definitions for business functions, data classes, and data elements.

LOGICAL DESIGN PHASE

Although the first two phases of our database design methodology are independent of the database management system, the last two

Figure 4.   Detailed Conceptual Design Responsibility Matrix

Task Description	Task Responsibility Primary	Task Responsibility Assisted By:	Documentation Responsibility	Form ID.
Decompose Business Functions to Transactions	APT		APT	II-3
Supply Transaction Information	APT			II-12
Identification of Data Elements	APT		APT and User	II-14

Notes

phases are not. During the Logical Design Phase, the outputs of the Detailed Conceptual Design Phase are translated into IMS logical structures.

The major tasks to be performed consist of:

- Determining how many physical and logical databases are required by the application,
- Specifying the IMS segments for each hierarchy,
- Specifying all primary keys, secondary keys, and search fields.

The Logical Design Phase is performed during the Design Phase of the application project.

Data Collection and Analysis. No additional information is collected during the Logical Design Phase. However, all previously collected information is reviewed, completed, or possibly revised. Additional data elements, for example, may be defined during the Logical Design Phase.

The Logical Design Phase is performed by the database analysts. Although in the previous two design phases a good deal of the input used for data analysis is collected and documented by the application analysts, the Logical Design Phase is nearly exclusively the purview of the database analysts.

Following the review of previously collected documentation and completion of any missing parts of the documentation, access requirements for each data class are analyzed.

The access requirement for a data class is merely the total number of accesses by each key, and assists in showing where the major access paths to the data bases must be provided. The access requirements will show which keys should be primary keys, which secondary, and which search fields. The access requirements will also show which data classes should be root segments in physical

or logical hierarchies, since the most frequently accessed data classes should be the root segments of the physical data bases.

Following analysis of the access requirements, the data bases are identified and their segments are laid out. Generally, one segment will be used for each data class. All keys and search fields are indicated.

Finally, an analysis of relationships from the original Data Structure Diagram is done, and an implementation method for each relationship is determined. In IMS 1-1 and 1-N relationships can be directly represented in a hierarchical structure; N-N relationships can be represented via logical relationships.

At the end of the Logical Design Phase all segment layouts are made available to the application programmers so that detailed program specifications and program coding can begin.

Documentation Segments. Each segment is documented via a Segment Input Form and Segment-Element Input Form and is entered into the Data Dictionary. The Segment Input Form names and describes the segment, relates it to its parent segment, and relates it to the logical transactions which use it. The Segment-Element Input Form relates the segment to the data elements which compose it. Both forms are entered into the Data Dictionary.

In addition a Segment Structure Diagram is drawn for each physical or logical database. The Segment Structure Diagram shows each hierarchy with the root segment at the top. An example is shown in Figure 5. Additional diagramming conventions are used to indicate secondary indices and logical relationships.

Review Procedures:

DBA. The DBA group reviews the logical design to determine that all access require-

Figure 5.   Segment Structure Diagram

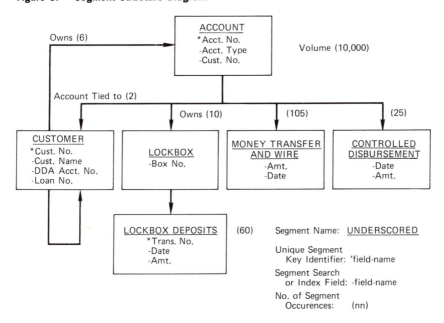

ments can be met and that efficient access to the data base can be obtained.

Application Review.   The application project team next reviews the Logical Design to insure that all data classes and data elements have been included, all required access paths have been implemented, and all relationships are accurately represented.

No user review is conducted: additional technical reviews of the Logical Design may be performed for a complex design. In these cases the IMS Systems Programming group or IBM may be asked to serve as reviewers.

PHYSICAL DESIGN PHASE

During the Physical Design Phase the details of the IMS implementation are worked out. The following major tasks are performed:

- IMS access methods and pointer options are selected.
- The implementation method for any logical relationships and secondary indices is selected.
- Physical data set options and placement of segments onto data sets is determined.
- DBDs and PSBs, the control blocks which define data bases to IMS and enable application programs to gain access to the data bases, respectively, are coded and generated.

All physical database design tasks are performed solely by the database analysts, with the assistance of IBM and IMS systems programmers for more complex designs. The Physical Design Phase is performed during the Implementation Phase of the Project Life Cycle.

The physical design is almost always done in two stages. The first physical design is done in order to create test data bases as quickly as possible for unit testing the application programs. The objective for the first physical design is merely to implement the logical design. Once the physical design for the initial test data bases has been done, various options are more carefully thought out for the implementation into production. Performance simulations may be done in order to determine optimal placement of data onto data sets and to experiment with various physical design parameters, such as pointer options. The physical design for the production system is implemented preferably during the System Test phase and no later than the User Acceptance test phase.

Documentation. The physical design is documented via the physical control blocks, the DBDs and PSBs. In addition design rationale are documented in written format.

Review Procedures. An internal DBA review is followed by a review by IBM and/or the IMS systems programming group. The review determines whether the logical structure has been accurately implemented, whether performance objectives can be achieved, and whether the generally accepted principles of IMS physical design have been followed.

Following implementation, performance both of the data bases themselves and of the system are monitored. Adjustments to the design may be made if indicated, although in actual practice it has never been done.

WHOLESALE EXPERIENCE WITH THE METHODOLOGY

When the design methodology described in this paper was first introduced, it was unclear how much resistance to its use would be encountered. Generally, the reaction to the methodology has been favorable. A number of factors are responsible for its favorable reception.

First, the bank has a highly structured data processing organization that is used to forms, regulations, and procedures. Usage of a standard Project Life Cycle and Structured Programming techniques are fairly widespread. Introducing a formal database design methodology did not require introducing a revolution in the way the data processing organization does business.

Next, since database supported systems were new to the bank, no one had a clear concept about what special techniques should be used to assist in developing a database application. It was generally known that database applications are more complex than non-database, and it wasn't startling that new methodologies would be needed.

A major concern when this methodology was first introduced was how easily it could be learned, applied, and understood by those who would use it. Our experience has shown that it isn't difficult. The methodology was first introduced by a series of formal presentations to applications analysts and database analysts. Content of the presentations was oriented somewhat differently for application analysts than for database analysts. Users were given brief explanation of the terminology and the various diagramming techniques as design review sessions were conducted.

Although development of the first application was difficult due to lack of experience with the methodology and with database systems in general, by the second application it was second nature. Even the users quickly became accustomed to the terminology and the different types of documentation produced so that now it isn't uncommon to hear end-users referring to "data classes."

On a continuing basis, training in the methodology has been conducted on a less formal basis but seems to have propagated itself based on the accumulated knowledge of the database analysts, application analysts, and end users.

Usage of the methodology has produced concrete benefits for the applications to which it has been applied. It has provided a standard for consistent documentation of actual database contents and of the global data structures which underlie the physical structures. Standard documentation techniques are extremely important in an environment like the bank's where new personnel are frequently introduced both to the Wholesale Data Base Administration Group and the various application projects.

The standard documentation provides a common method for communicating the existing data structures and thus provides a starting point for analyzing new data requirements. New staff who are assigned to support the existing production system are also easily introduced to the current system.

From the standpoint of a Data Base Manager, the methodology provides a vehicle for guiding database designs in such a way that higher quality, more stable database designs can be achieved. Specific design principles are set forth in the methodology; the methodology implicitly guides the database design towards a physical implementation based on the conceptual structure, which leads to stable data structures. In practice this has proved to be the case. Major design changes have not been necessary following implementation—an important feature in a highly integrated environment where there is a large investment in application code supported by specific data structures.

At its current stage of development the methodology has some weaknesses. The design review component of the methodology needs to be formalized so that each participant can document any issues identified, and more precise feedback can be given to management. Data element analysis, though it indirectly leads to normalization, has not

always led to correct placement of data elements within segments.

Lastly, the methodology works best for application-by-application development and does not adequately address data integration of several applications that are being concurrently developed. Recently, however, the Conceptual Design methodology was extended for a Data Planning project. It is premature at this point to evaluate the effectiveness of that effort.

As with any other standard, our Data Base Design methodology is meant to be a living tool that will be adapted to meet changes brought about by our changing application environment and by changing technology. The foundation that has been laid to date will provide a base from which we can grow into the future.

QUESTIONS

1. Comment on the four database design phases mentioned on the first page of the article. Are these the most appropriate design classifications? Is the ordering correct?

2. (a) Several DBMS terms are introduced in this paper. How does Herman define the following?
   Entities
   Definitions
   Attributes
   Indicative Key
   Cross-Reference Key
   Retrieval Key
   (b) Are Herman's definitions consistent with your understanding of DMMSs?

3. Herman suggests several forms (Figs. 1, 2, and 3) for assistance in the con-

ceptual design phase. Comment on the desirability of her forms.

4. What is the purpose of a DBA? How much power does he/she possess?

5. Define "logical transactions."

6. Herman states early in the paper that "the first two phases of database design are independent of the DBMS." Could we infer then that DBMS selec-

tion should not occur until these first two phases are complete?

7. How was the bank able to obtain employee acceptance of the database methodology?

8. Is the database design methodology an integrated approach? If not, will it ultimately prove to be a poor MIS concept?

An Entity-Relationship View of Accounting Models*

A number of recent studies have addressed the issue of integrating accounting information systems and computer database technology. Colantoni, Manes and Whinston [1971], Lieberman and Whinston [1975], and Haseman and Whinston [1976] used aspects of Sorter's [1969] "events" accounting theory and incorporated them into a hierarchical database model. More recently, Everest and Weber [1977] suggested the use of Codd's [1970] relational framework to overcome the hierarchical model's lack of data independence. Finally, Haseman and Whinston [1977] constructed an accounting system using the network or CODASYL [1971] approach.

This paper reviews the same process of integrating accounting with database models, but on a more general level that does not necessitate commitment to any particular system. In lieu of debating the comparative advantages of the hierarchical, relational, or network approaches, the contention will be made here that an accounting system is most naturally modeled in a database environment as a collection of (1) real world *entities* and (2) *relationships* among those entities. Using methodology conceived by Chen [1976], an entity-relationship model of an account-ing system will be developed that will overcome some of the difficulties encountered by the authors mentioned above, such as the use of accounting "artifacts." Additionally, readers will see that this method of development will allow a system designer to incorporate explicitly into an accounting model aspects of measurement theory proposed recently by Mock [1976] and causal double-entry advocated by Ijiri [1975].

DATABASE ABSTRACTION PROCESS

The data in any information system is an abstraction of some aspect of reality. The more recently developed *database* information systems require that this data representing a particular slice of reality be organized in a structured manner that will remain consistent with itself and maintain its integrity over time.

Incorporating methodologies suggested by Chen [1976], Sundgren [1974], Date [1977], and Will [1974], Figure 1 portrays this structured abstraction process as it applies to an accounting system.

Beginning with LEVEL 1, note that a database system is intended to model some part of the real world or some reality. In an ac-

Figure 1.   Database Abstraction Process

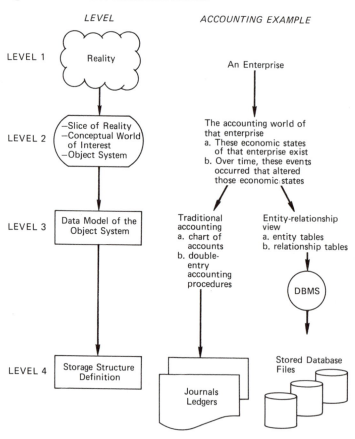

counting context, this reality is an economic enterprise defined by the business entity principle [Yu, 1976, p. 245].

At LEVEL 2, the description of reality narrows to those aspects that are of interest to intended database users. Sundgren [1974, p. 61] refers to this slice of reality as the "object system," and for the accounting example, it includes information about two matters of substance: (1) the economic states of the enterprise and (2) the events occurring over time that alter those economic states.

As the abstraction process moves to LEVEL 3, it passes from the world of reali-

ties, or principals as they are called by Ijiri [1975, Ch. 3], to the world of data models or surrogates. A data model is intended to be a description of the logical structure of the object system as seen by the community of database users. It is a scheme that represents, with data, the organization of the conceptual world of interest.

In traditional accounting, it is here that the "artifacts" (such as the chart of accounts) deplored by Everest and Weber are encountered. Those authors characterize many traditional accounting structures as "useful taxonomies, classification schemes, or naming conventions rather than real entities" [Everest and Weber, 1977, p. 342] and consequently conclude that database systems are not able to accommodate them easily.

This paper proposes to depart from traditional accounting at LEVEL 3, and to use instead an entity-relationship view of an enterprise to construct its accounting data model. Additionally, the scheme to be developed will not be limited by the principles of double-entry and monetary measurement, but will be allowed instead to assume more of the multidimensional and disaggregated aspects proposed by "events" accounting theorists [Sorter, 1969].

LEVEL 4, the storage structure definition, will not be of interest in the treatment here. However, note that once an object system has been modeled on an entity-relationship basis, it is possible to translate the data model of LEVEL 3 to the storage structure definitions of LEVEL 4, using the definition language and facilities of most existing database management systems (DBMS).

LEVEL 3 of the database abstraction process — development of an accounting data model for an enterprise — will now be treated in detail.

AN ACCOUNTING DATA MODEL

A chart of accounts and its accompanying double-entry procedures might be viewed simply as a scheme for organizing, classifying, and aggregating financial data. Additionally, however, it represents the imposition upon an accountant of a particular mode of thinking about the economic affairs of an entity. For example, when queried about the "things" that accounting deals with, an accountant might list items such as "prepaid revenues," "retained earnings," or "liabilities" because these, among others, constitute the elements in his/her predefined world of interest. Collectively, these account names

and double-entry procedures represent a data model of an enterprise's economic aspects.

This predisposition toward certain types of "things" of interest will be discarded here. Instead, this paper will view an object financial system without "traditional-accounting colored" glasses and use the following steps to construct an accounting data model [Chen, 1976].:

1. Identify (a) the *entity* sets such as classes of objects, agents, and events that exist in the conceptual world and (b) the *relationship* sets that connect those entities;
2. Construct an *Entity-Relationship* (E-R) diagram that will exhibit the semantic nature of identified relationships;
3. Define the characteristics of entity and relationship sets that will be of interest to particular system users, and specify mappings that will identify those characteristics; and
4. Organize the results of steps 1, 2, and 3 into entity/relationship tables and identify a key (unique characteristic) for each entity/relationship set.

As each of these steps is considered in the following sections, its application to accounting will be made more concrete by using a small retail enterprise as an example.

Identification of Entity/Relationship Sets

The process of viewing an object system and identifying its relevant entities and relationships cannot be described exactly, because it will normally include a wide variety of systems analysis techniques (such as those detailed by Taggart and Tharp [1977]). The particular list of entities and relationships that any one person produces might differ quite legitimately from another person's list, depending upon their differing backgrounds and perceived uses of information. A guiding principle here for accountants is that in enumerating entities they limit themselves to real phenomena that can be distinctly identified and remain clear of accounting "artifacts." Everest and Weber [1977, p. 356] supply direction in this process by warning designers to avoid the use of "naming tree" entities (that is, accounts used for presentation or accumulation purposes only).

For a small retail enterprise, the entity sets (groups of objects, agents, events) of interest in the accounting object system might include those 16 items shown in Figure 2 (a). For simplicity, only this limited list will be used in the rest of the discussion here. A modeling of a real enterprise would probably produce a larger and more exhaustive group of entities, including such additional objects as buildings, such additional agents as federal and state governments, and such additional events as equipment disposals and purchase orders.

Once the entity sets have been identified, system design proceeds to specification of sets of relevant relationships that may exist among them. A partial list (a more complete diagram is given later) for the retail enterprise is shown in Figure 2 (b).

The bases for explicitly recognizing relationships between the various entities will again be peculiar to the person constructing the data model, but it is of interest to note at

Figure 2.

	OBJECTS		AGENTS
	Equipment		Stockholder
	Inventory		Employee
	Cash		Customer
			Vendor

EVENTS

Order	Cash Receipt	Capital Transaction
Sale	Cash Disbursement	General and Administrative Service
Purchase	Equipment Acquisition	Personnel Service

(a) Entity sets in an accounting data model

Event (- - - -) Event
Sale (fills) Order
Cash Receipt (payment for) Sale
Cash Disbursement (payment for) Personnel Service
Agent (- - - -) Event
Employee (employed in) Personnel Service
Vendor (supplier of) General and Administrative Service
Customer (made to) Sale
Object (- - - -) Event
Cash (flow of) Cash Receipt
Inventory (line item) Sale
General and Administrative Service (allocate cost of) Equipment

(b) Some relationahip sets (not complete listing)

this point the rationale for connecting some of the *Event* entities with each other. With the exception of the "order" event which is not, traditionally speaking, an accounting event at all, the *Event* (- - -) *Event* links represent explicit manifestations of Ijiri's [1975, Ch. 5] causal double-entry conventions; that is, each change in the resource set of the enterprise is linked explicitly to another change by means of a causal relationship. In Mattessich's terms, these events would be called "a pair of required transactions [where] . . . one transaction is the legal or economic consideration of the other" [1964, p. 450].

Again, there is no claim to absolute "truth" in the entity/relationship sets given in Figure 2. They are not intended to be exhaustive enumerations, only illustrations of Chen's initial design stage.

Construction of an Entity-Relationship Diagram

After identification of appropriate entity and relationship sets in an object system is completed, data modeling continues with a further analysis of how these concepts fit together. The semantic nature (or real world character) of a relationship is examined at this stage and is portrayed through the use of Entity-Relationship (E-R) diagrams. Again for simplicity, this paper will illustrate only a portion of the real world possibilities, in this case binary relationships. Such relationships concern associations between just two entity sets and have consequently three basic types: (1) one-to-one, (2) one-to-many, and (3) many-to-many. Each of these cases is illustrated below.

A *one-to-one* (1-to-1) relationship specifies a correspondence between a pair of entities, one from each of the two connected entity sets. Suppose, for example, that the small retail enterprise had an operational rule that all purchases were to be paid for, in full, exactly five days after receipt. Each purchase event would correspond then to only one cash disbursement event as exhibited in Figure 3 (a). Chen's E-R diagram would depict this 1-to-1 relationship in the manner shown in Figure 3 (b).

A *one-to-many* (1-to-*n*) relationship specifies a correspondence between just a single entity in one entity set and many entities in another entity set. Using the example again, suppose that the enterprise billed its customers once a month for all sales during the preceding month and that the customers pay in full shortly thereafter. In this case, each cash receipt event would correspond to multiple sale events as seen in Figure 4 (a) and (b).

Finally, a *many-to-many* (*m*-to-*n*) relationship specifies not only a possible correspondence between one entity in a first set and many entities in a second set, but also a possible correspondence between one entity in the second set and many entities in the first set. To illustrate in the case of a relationship between the *SALE* and *INVENTORY* entity sets from the retail example, suppose not only that each sale consists of many products, but also that each product participates in many sales. This bidirectional mapping is shown in Figure 5 (a) and (b).

Extending this same kind of analysis, an E-R diagram can be specified for the entire retail enterprise as shown in Figure 6. In this particular example, the use of a limited list of entities and binary relationships has produced a relatively simple and well integrated E-R diagram; however, more realistic (and hence, more complicated) situations can be represented in a similar fashion. For instance, if the additional event of equipment disposal were included for the enterprise, it would be possible to model the acquisition of an asset for cash and a trade-in by showing

Figure 3.   A One-to-One Correspondence

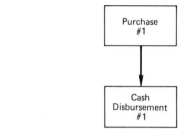

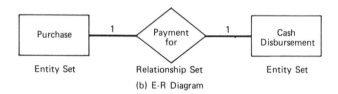

(a) Two Related Event Sets

(b) E-R Diagram

Figure 4.   A One-to-Many Correspondence

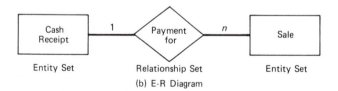

(a) Two Related Sets of Events

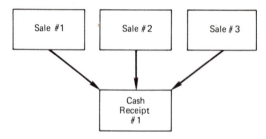

(b) E-R Diagram

a three-way association among the entities equipment acquisition, equipment disposal, and cash disbursement.

Identification of Characteristic Mappings

Once an E-R diagram has been constructed for the object system, the entity-relationship modeling process moves to a more detailed level of system design by starting to identify the relevant properties or characteristics of each entity/relationship set. Similar to the process of determining the entities and relationships themselves, this identification procedure can be described

Figure 5.   A Many-to-Many Correspondence

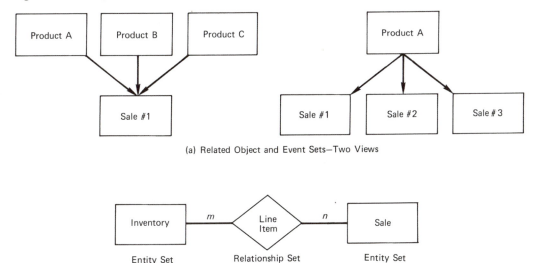

(a) Related Object and Event Sets—Two Views

(b) E-R Diagram

only in very general terms. The final listing of characteristics will be heavily dependent upon the designer's perception of the ultimate decision environment and information need. A framework proposed by Mock [1976, p. 88] addresses the needs of this design phase. His outline is based upon accepted principles of measurement theory and lists criteria certain to help in reducing the unstructured nature of this process.

Specifying all of the characteristics for each entity-relationship set given in Figure 6 would be a prohibitively long process. Therefore, this section will be limited to mappings for two entity sets — *SALE* and *INVENTORY* — and the relationship set that connects them — *SALE* line item. Additional mappings for the other sets, and possibly for these three sets as well, would have to be accomplished before the data model would be completely specified.

The characteristics of a particular member of an entity/relationship set can be expressed by a listing of *attribute/value* pairs. Examples of these pairs for a specified prod-

uct in the entity set *INVENTORY* might be "stock#/7432," "acquisition cost/$3.00," and "quantity-on-hand/269."

The first item in each of the pairs above — the *attribute* — is formally defined by Chen [1976, p. 12] "as a function which maps from an entity set or relationship set into a value set." This conceptualization of an attribute as a function is important because it allows the E-R model constructs to develop in a form free of certain unwanted properties such as addition, deletion, and update anomalies [Date, 1977, Ch. 9.].

The second item listed in each pair — the *value* — is taken from different *value sets* such as stock numbers, dollar-amounts, and number-of-units. These value sets are analogous to the relational database concept of "domain" described by Everest and Weber [1977] and, in a more limited sense, to the measurement concept of "numerical relational system" described by Mock [1976, Ch. 2]. Indeed, it can be seen that the entire characteristic identification process used in entity-relationship modeling fits in well with

Figure 6. E-R Diagram for the Entire Retail Enterprise

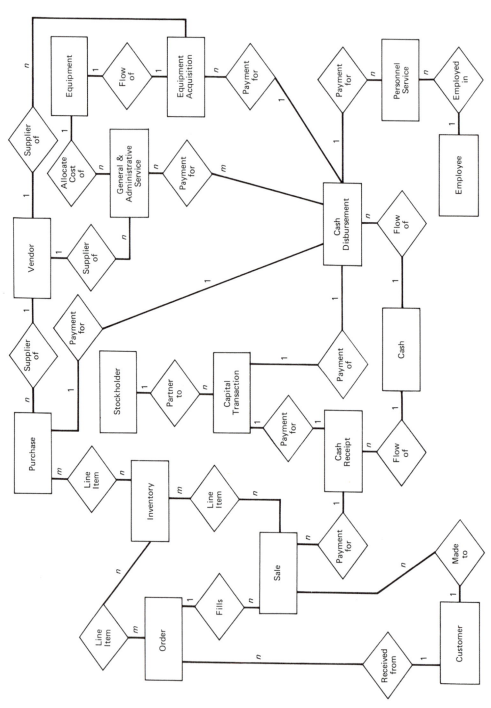

Mock's [1976, p. 107] call for emphasis on the measurement aspects of data to be used in accounting systems. For those characteristics whose values are numerical, Chen's attribute mappings and value sets correspond exactly to Mock's homomorphic mappings and numerical relational systems.

Figures 7 and 8 illustrate some of the characteristic mappings for the entity sets *INVENTORY* and *SALE*. The first function (F_1-STOCK#) in Figure 7 maps a particular element (e_J) in the set *INVENTORY* (that is, one particular product) to its stock number (7432). Likewise, the next four functions (F_2, F_3, F_4, F_5) all map that same element to

its various unit costs and unit price. F_6 simply couples a product to its value for quantity-on-hand.

In Figure 8, the first function maps a particular sale event (e_K) that happened on June 21 at 2:15 p.m. to a coded representation of its time occurrence, while F_2, F_3, and F_4 determine other relevant characteristics. The actual mappings for entities in a real enterprise would be obtained via observation or measurement.

The attribute mappings for the relationship set *SALE line item* are given in Figure 9. Although this particular example illustrates a case where the relationship itself possesses a

Figure 7.   Characteristic Mappings Defined on Entity Set *INVENTORY*

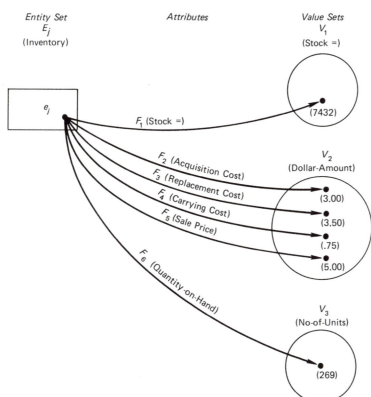

Figure 8.   Characteristic Mappings Defined on Entity Set *SALE*

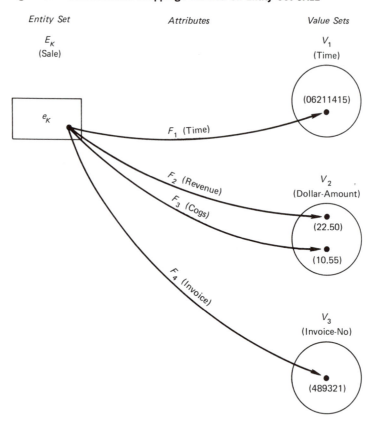

characteristic that cannot be fully identified with either of the participating entities, it is not necessary for all relationships to have properties of their own. In some cases (one of which will be seen later), the relationship simply specifies an association and possesses no further information content.

Before leaving this section, readers should note the close correspondence between the model as developed so far and the ideas of "events" accounting theorists such as Sorter [1969], Johnson [1970], and Colantoni, Manes, and Whinston [1971]. According to Sorter, "the purpose of accounting is to provide information about relevant economic events that might be useful in a variety of

possible decision models" [1969, p. 13]. Even with the limited presentation given to this point, it can be seen that an entity-relationship model accommodates well the things implied by Sorter's statement, such as multidimensional measures (dollars and time), different valuation bases (acquisition cost and replacement cost), and aspects of accounting entities useful in management science modeling (unit carrying cost for economic order quantity models).

Organization of Data Into Entity/Relationship Tables

The final step in the enterprise data modeling process involves (1) designation of

Figure 9. Characteristic Mappings Defined on Relationship Set *SALE line item*

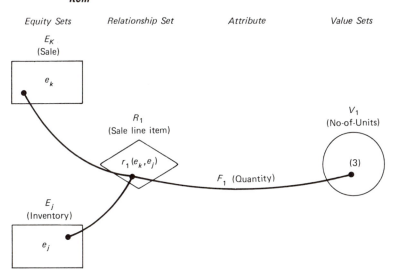

primary keys and (2) organization of the constructs identified above (entity sets, relationship sets, value sets, and attributes) into entity/relationship tables.

A primary key (PK) for an entity set (or a relationship set) is simply an identifying characteristic that maps one-to-one with the elements of that entity set, and thus is able to represent those elements in the data base. To do this, the identifying characteristic must be both universal—every entity must have it as an attribute—and unique—each entity's value for that characteristic must be different. An example of a PK would be the student number in a university data base or the Social Security number in the Internal Revenue Service data base. The primary key is not always a single characteristic; sometimes it is necessary to concatenate several attributes to identify something uniquely. Such is the case for all relationship sets in Chen's model, because he defines their PKs as the combined PKs of their involved entities.

The organization of data into *entity tables* is illustrated in Figure 10. As can be seen, the two tables correspond closely to the mappings shown in Figures 7 and 8. The only real difference is that now a primary key value is allowed to represent each element of the two entity sets, "STOCK#" for the *INVENTORY* entities and "TIME" for the *SALE* entities. This assumes that the company assigns each of its products a different stock number and that each sale event is mapped to a unique time identifier. (Methods for keying events in this manner are discussed in Lamport [1978].)

A relationship table for *SALE line item* is illustrated in Figure 11. Again, the table closely resembles the mappings derived earlier (Figure 9) except that a primary key value, the concatenated PKs of the involved entities, now represents an instance of the relationship. Chen's illustration of relationships in this manner resembles the use of case-grammar models by Roussopoulos and Mylopoulos [1975, p. 147], because it re-

Figure 10.

	Primary Key →			
Attribute	Time	Revenue	Cogs	Invoice
Value Set	Time	Dollar-Amount		Invoice-No.
Entities (one each row)	06211415 06211418 — —	22.50 150.00 — —	10.55 90.00 — —	489321 489322 — —

(a) *Sale* Entity Table

	Primary Key →					
Attribute	Stock =	Acquisition Cost	Replacement Cost	Carrying Cost	Sale Price	QOH
Value Set	Stock =	Dollar-Amount				No-of-Units
Entities (one each row)	7432 8519 6784 — — —	3.00 .30 .05 — — —	3.50 .32 .10 — — —	.75 .15 .06 — — —	5.00 1.00 .50 — — —	269 85 62 — — —

(b) *Inventory* Entity Table

Figure 11. Relationship Table for *SALE line item*

	← Primary Key →			
Entity Table Name	Sale	Inventory		
Role	Flow	Stock		
Entity Attribute	Time	Stock =	Quantity	Relationship Attribute
Value Set	Time	Stock =	No-of-Units	
Relationships (one each row)	06211415 06211415 06211415 06211418 — — —	7432 8519 6784 7432 — — —	3 4 — 30 — — —	

quires specification of "who plays the *roles* (or fills the *cases*)" associated with each relationship. In a complete data model, an entity could fill a number of widely varying roles depending upon the nature of the relationships it participated in.

Figure 12 illustrates two additional relationship tables to be used in later examples. The mappings for these two relationship sets were not shown previously, but the procedures involved would be identical to those used in obtaining the table for *SALE line item* (Figure 11). The table for the set *SALE payment* (Figure 12 (b)) illustrates two additional points. First, it portrays a relationship set which simply specifies a connection without any attributes of its own. Second, its role names are designated in accordance with the

Figure 12.

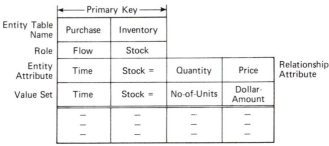

Entity Table Name	Purchase	Inventory			
		←——— Primary Key ———→			
Role	Flow	Stock			
Entity Attribute	Time	Stock =	Quantity	Price	Relationship Attribute
Value Set	Time	Stock =	No-of-Units	Dollar-Amount	
	—	—	—	—	
	—	—	—	—	

(a) Relationship Table for *Purchase Line Item*

Entity Table Name	Sale	Cash-Receipt
	←——— Primary Key ———→	
Role	Decrement	Increment
Entity Attribute	Time	Time
Value Set	Time	Time
	—	—
	—	—

(b) Relationship Table for *Sale Payment*

causal double-entry reasoning underlying the relationship itself. According to Ijiri [1975, Ch. 5], each occurrence of such a relationship requires specification of the increment and decrement involved. Additionally, the role names in this table would be used to qualify the attributes because the attribute names ("TIME" and "TIME") are not unique.

A total modeling effort for the retail enterprise would involve constructing a table for every set depicted in Figure 6. After these specifications were finished, the entity-relationship view of the enterprise's accounting system would be complete, and the data model would be ready for use with actual database systems. Discussion of the translation process involved in mapping E-R constructs into the specification language of a particular DBMS is beyond the scope of this paper. However, interested readers may consult Chen [1975, pp. 25–34] who describes such processing for relational and network systems.

RECONCILIATION OF TRADITIONAL ACCOUNTING WITH THE NEW DATA MODEL

The data model developed to this point for a small retail enterprise certainly differs radically from the traditional accounting paradigm generated by using a chart of accounts and double-entry bookkeeping. The question now arises, "Can such a model serve the everyday needs of accountants?" The new system is missing certain familiar and financially important items such as accounts-receivable, and its lack of a debit-credit framework might leave some with the uneasy feeling that all comings and goings are not being properly accounted for.

This section will demonstrate that an information system modeled on an entity-relationship basis can indeed accommodate the conventions of traditional accounting. To show this, part of the data model outlined in Figure 6 will be used, specifically two entity sets—*SALE* and *INVENTORY*—and three relationship sets—*SALE line item, PURCHASE line item,* and *SALE payment.* Tables representing each of these five sets were presented earlier in Figures 10, 11, and 12.

In the paragraphs below, two types of accounting procedures for the entity-relationship (E-R) model will be described: (1) the derivation of accounts-receivable and (2) the maintenance of perpetual inventory and cost of goods sold. These descriptions will concentrate primarily on the *set* aspects of the E-R constructs and will be very general in nature. In actual practice, the calculations discussed would be performed using the processing language of a particular database system. Readers interested in more specific explanations may consult McCarthy [1978] where a number of detailed accounting computations are done with the relational language SEQUEL [Chamberlin *et al.,* 1976].

At any time during its operations, the total of outstanding receivables for the example enterprise modeled in Figure 6 is equal to the revenue of sale events not yet paid for. This set of sale events is not present explicitly in the system, but it can be obtained easily by subtracting the set of paid-for sales (the elements in the relationship set *SALE payment*) from the set of all sales. After such a set difference operation is performed, accounts-receivable can be calculated by summing the revenue characteristic for all elements of the identified subset.

The relationships between object and event entities were characterized in the E-R modeling process as stock-flow interactions; that is, there existed a stock of some entity such as cash or equipment whose level was affected by flows of events such as cash receipts or equipment acquisitions. Yu [1976, p. 242] discusses the importance to financial reporting of properly accounting for these stock-flow interplays. In traditional

systems, their connection is directly accounted for by an entry to the asset (object) account upon the occurrence of a transaction (event), but in an entity-relationship model the interaction must be effected in another way—by defining certain updates to the stock entities that will be invoked upon the occurrence of flow entities. In the case of perpetually maintained inventory for the retail enterprise, these invoked procedures would take place in the following manner. When a purchase occurs in the object system (LEVEL 2 of Figure 1), the data model (LEVEL 3) would have new elements added to the sets *PURCHASE* and *PURCHASE line item.* These additions would then "trigger" the following updates to characteristics of the appropriate element in the set *INVENTORY:*

1. A new acquisition cost would be set (assuming that the cost scheme is one, such as the moving weighted average method, which can be updated on a perpetual basis);

2. A new replacement cost would be set (equal to the latest transaction price); and

3. A new quantity on hand would be calculated.

Mechanisms for implementing these triggered updates are described by Eswaran [1976]. The cost of goods sold characteristic of *SALE* elements would then be calculated at the time of sale using the perpetually maintained acquisition cost of the appropriate inventory entities.

The inventory and cost of goods sold figures calculated above are components of a perfectly consistent data base where all elements of the data model (LEVEL 3 in Figure 1) immediately and accurately mirror changes in the object system (LEVEL 2). There are times, however, when certain information is used only at specified intervals, in which case the characteristics involved can be produced by calculation and aggregation only when needed. In the retail accounting model, this stepwise production of information would apply to accounts-receivable and to periodic inventory and cost of goods sold. The process of choosing among the various temporal alternatives in database maintenance depends not so much upon the nature of the characteristic itself but upon its expected decision use. The bases for making such choices involve the issue of "conclusion materialization" and are discussed extensively by Bubenko [1976]. In all cases, the final choice of a consistency level should be "subject to the tradeoff between applications requirements (benefit) and economic feasibility (cost)" [ANSI/X3/SPARC, 1975, p. II-1].

This paper has now considered the fundamental features of Chen's entity-relationship methodology as it applies to the construction and maintenance of an accounting model. Before moving on to a summary, there remains one matter to be considered in the next section: comparison of the E-R accounting model with the relational accounting models of Everest and Weber.

COMPARISON WITH RELATIONAL MODEL

It was mentioned previously that an entity-relationship modeling process could be used as an initial step in actual implementation of many database systems, among them the relational model of Codd [1970]. In fact, the final products of an E-R design process — the entity/relationship tables — are nearly identical in both appearance and mathematical form to Codd relations, and one can see on inspection that the mapping of a Chen model to a relational model is relatively straightforward. There are, however, some

important features that differentiate the accounting system developed in this paper from the relational accounting systems developed by Everest and Weber [1977]. These differences stem from design considerations and are explained below.

The relational decomposition or transformation approach [Codd, 1972] to data modeling used by Everest and Weber starts with an arbitrary collection of relations (based upon a chart of accounts, for example) and proceeds, using the notion of functional dependencies, to recast them in a form free of certain undesirable properties such as addition, deletion, and update anomalies [Date, 1977]. In contrast, Chen's approach emphasizes the initial identification of entities and relationships and then proceeds by designating mappings that identify both relevant associations among entities and relevant characteristics of entities and relationships. Use in this paper of the second approach has led to an accounting model superior in two respects.

First, the E-R data model "fits" the object system better. This occurs because its design process begins with a priori identification of relevant aspects of the conceptual world rather than with use of a framework based on existing accounting methods. The effect on the Everest and Weber paradigm of using traditional accounting classification schemes is to introduce into the final (fully normalized) data model certain extraneous concepts such as "naming tree" relations and debit/credit account numbers while masking or omitting more essential features such as stock-flow interactions and causal double-entry. The two authors recognized that the use of accounting "artifacts" would cause such problems and suggested possible solutions. However, the use of entity-relationship modeling prevents the problems from occurring at all.

Second, the entity-relationship approach displays more clearly the organization of the object system. It concludes with a data model where each entity/relationship set is represented in a separate table (relation). Chen [1976, pp. 25–29] argues that such an arrangement leads to clearer semantic meaning and accommodates more easily changes in the nature of object system relationships. He also contends that his model clarifies better the nature of dependencies among data, because it differentiates between those mappings used to identify characteristics and those used to identify associations. Chen's modeling process also produces a convenient shorthand—the E-R diagram—that provides a clear overview of the object system and distinguishes explicitly to users the different 1-to-1, 1-to-n, and m-to-n asociations.

Finally in the matter of comparing the two approaches, the issue of multivalued dependencies and fourth normal form arises. Recent research (which postdated Everest and Weber's article) by Fagin [1977b] has identified deficiencies in the relational decomposition process and proposed an augmented approach to database design that uses a new semantic object called a "multivalued dependency" [1977b, p. 433]. The final product of this new design process is a "fourth normal form" [Fagin, 1977a] that eliminates from a data model further undesirable aspects of maintenance behavior. The question now is "How do Fagin's new concepts relate to entity-relationship modeling?," and the answer is, "They have already been accounted for." Multivalued dependencies (which are 1-to-n mappings) are identified clearly by Chen. More importantly, the storage problems caused by multivalued dependencies arise when a data model attempts to portray two independent relationships in one table [Fagin 1977a, p. 272]. As shown earlier, such a representation would not materialize in entity-relationship modeling.

In summary, the data model developed in this paper represents the accounting universe better than those developed by Everest and Weber. Its development is not encumbered with accounting artifacts, its concepts portray clearly the nature of the accounting object system, and its final form displays none of the undesirable anomalies identified in the normalization literature.

SUMMARY OF MODEL CONCEPTS AND ADVANTAGES

The presentation of an accounting information system based on entity and relationship sets is now complete. The steps necessary to model an object system have been outlined, and specific illustrations of each step for an example enterprise have been given. The paper will conclude by summarizing features of the entity-relationship approach relevant to accounting practice and research.

First, Chen's methodology represents one of the first attempts to construct an enterprise view of data [Chen, 1977], that is, a data model viewed from the perspective of the whole enterprise rather than from the perspective of individual users or particular database management systems. As such, it can be considered a "top-down" approach to system design and a definite aid to logical thought in a database environment. Accountants need a tool like this. With the use of database systems becoming more widespread, they need to be able to view many enterprise schemata in a clear, consistent, and somewhat standardized manner. In this sense E-R diagrams are analogous to flowcharts; they represent visual aids to be used in understanding the full significance of the data processing operations.

Second, the entity-relationship approach to accounting-database models provides a design framework that can be integrated into any of the database models previously proposed in the literature such as those of Colantoni, Manes, and Whinston [1971], Lieberman and Whinston [1975], and Haserman and Whinston [1976; 1977]. It is especially appropriate for Codd's [1970] relational model, because the transfer from Chen's entity-relationship tables to Codd relations is straightforward. Use of an E-R approach also avoids the drawbacks of decomposition.

Third, the entity-relationship model provides a specific vehicle for the incorporation of measurement concepts and causal double-entry into a single-entry database system. Proponents of these concepts [Mock, 1976 and Ijiri, 1975] have presented them for use in accounting systems, but their ideas do not fit well with journals and ledgers. As seen earlier in the paper, they do adapt well to an E-R model.

Fourth, entity-relationship modeling provides a sound theoretical basis for the expansion of the "events" approach to accounting [Sorter, 1969]. Consideration of a wide range of decision models using multidimensional measures, such as those advocated in two recent AAA reports [1969; 1971], is accomplished easily. Aggregation problems are reduced also because the information in an E-R based system can be stored in disaggregated form and summarized only according to the intent of a particular user.

On the whole, therefore, this paper has shown that the entity-relationship approach to accounting models represents a logical extension to work in the area of accounting information systems. It provides an overview of much of the work done in database systems, and it also offers practical aid to accountants who plan to do work in a database environment.

REFERENCES

1. American Accounting Association, "Report of Committee on Managerial Decision Models," THE ACCOUNTING REVIEW (Supplement 1969), pp. 43–76.

2. ———, "Report of the Committee on Non-Financial Measures of Effectiveness," THE ACCOUNTING REVIEW (Supplement 1971), pp. 164–211.

3. ANSI/X3/SPARC Study Group on Data Base Management Systems, "Interim Report," ACM-SIGMOD FDT (February 1975).

4. BUBENKO, J., "The Temporal Dimension in Information Modeling," Research Report RC 6187 (IBM Research Laboratories, Yorktown Heights, NY, November, 1976).

5. CHAMBERLIN, D. D., M. M. ASTRAHAN, K. P. ESWARAN, P. P. GRIFFITHS, R. A. LORIE, J. W. MEHL, P. REISNER, and B. W. WADE, "SEQUEL 2: A Unified Approach to Data Definition, Manipulation, and Control," IBM Journal of Research and Development (November 1976), pp. 560–75.

6. CHEN, P. P., "The Entity-Relationship Model — Toward a Unified View of Data," ACM Transactions on Database Systems (March 1976), pp. 9–36.

7. ———, "The Entity-Relationship Model: A Basis for the Enterprise View of Data," Proceedings of the National Computer

Conference, 1977 (AFIPS, 1977), pp. 77–84.

8. CODASYL Programming Language Committee, *Data Base Task Group Report* (Association for Computing Machinery, 1971).

9. CODD, E. F., "A Relational Model of Data for Large Shared Data Banks," *Communications of the ACM* (June 1970), pp. 377–87.

10. ———, "Further Normalization of the Data Base Relational Model," in R. Rustin, ed., *Data Base Systems* (Prentice-Hall, 1972), pp. 33–64.

11. Colantoni, C. S., R. P. Manes, and A. B. WHINSTON, "A Unified Approach to the Theory of Accounting and Information Systems," THE ACCOUNTING REVIEW (January 1971), pp. 90–102.

12. DATE, C. J., *An Introduction to Database Systems,* 2nd ed. (Addison-Wesley, 1977).

13. ESWARAN, K. P., "Specifications, Implementations and Interactions of a Trigger Subsystem in an Integrated Database System," Research Report RJ 1820 (IBM Research Laboratories, San Jose, CA, August, 1976).

14. EVEREST, G. C., and R. WEBER, "A Relational Approach to Accounting Models," THE ACCOUNTING REVIEW (April 1977), pp. 340–59.

15. FAGIN, R. (1977a), "Multivalued Dependencies and a New Normal Form for Relational Databases," *ACM Transactions of Database Systems* (September 1977), pp. 262–78.

16. ———, (1977b), "The Decomposition Versus the Synthetic Approach to Relational Database Design," *Proceedings of the Third International Conference on Very Large Data Bases,* 1977 (ACM, 1977), pp. 441–46.

17. HASEMAN, W. D., and A. B. WHINSTON, "Design of a Multidimensional Accounting System," THE ACCOUNTING REVIEW (January 1976), pp. 65–79.

18. ———, *Introduction to Data Management* (Richard D. Irwin, 1977).

19. IJIRI, Y., *Theory of Accounting Measurement* (American Accounting Association, 1975).

20. JOHNSON, O., "Toward an 'Events' Theory of Accounting," THE ACCOUNTING REVIEW (October 1970), pp. 641–53.

21. LAMPORT, L., "Time, Clocks, and the Ordering of Events in a Distributed System," *Communications of the ACM* (July 1 978), pp. 558–65.

22. LIEBERMAN, A. Z., and A. B. WHINSTON, "A Structuring of an Events-Accounting Information System," THE ACCOUNTING REVIEW (April 1975), pp. 246–58.

23. MATTESSICH, R., *Accounting and Analytical Methods* (Richard D. Irwin, 1964).

24. McCARTHY, W. E., "A Relational Model for Events-Based Accounting Systems," (doctoral dissertation, University of Massachusetts, 1978).

25. MOCK, T. J., *Measurement and Accounting Information Criteria* (American Accounting Association, 1976).

26. ROUSSOPOULOS, N., and J. MYLOPOULOS, "Using Sematic Networks for Data Base Management," *Proceedings of the First International Conference on Very Large Data Base,* 1975 (ACM, 1975), pp. 144–72.

27. SORTER, G. H., "An 'Events' Approach to Basic Accounting Theory," THE ACCOUNTING REVIEW (January 1969), pp. 12–19.

28. SUNDGREN, B., "Conceptual Foundation of the Infological Approach to Data

Bases," in J. W. Klimbie and K. L. Koffeman, eds., *Data Base Management* (North Holland Publishing Company, 1974), pp. 61–96.

29. TAGGART, W. M., and M. O. THARP, "A Survey of Information Requirements Analysis Techniques," *Computing Surveys* (December 1977), pp. 273–90.

30. WILL, H. J., "Auditing in Systems Perspective," THE ACCOUNTING REVIEW (October 1974), pp. 690–706.

31. YU, S. C., *The Structure of Accounting Theory* (The University Presses of Florida, 1976).

QUESTIONS

1. Several database concepts are mentioned in this article. Define the following:

    Entity
    Relationship
    Artifacts
    Primary Key
    Objects
    Agents
    Events
    Mapping

2. McCarthy provides a four-level view of the conceptual database design process, and Chen a four-step process for accounting data modeling. Has the other author in this database section offered design notions similar to either of these four-part ideas?

3. Early in the paper, the author mentions "mapping" and 1:1, 1:many, and many:many relationships. Does he imply specific DBMS selections early in the design process?

4. What is a "naming tree" and how is it utilized?

5. McCarthy mentions two major advantages of the E-R model as 1) differing valuation bases (historical and current cost), and 2) multiple units of measure (dollars, time quantities). Discuss the pros and cons of these two design options.

6. Does the E-R model serve accountant's needs?

7. How does the E-R model compare to a relational model? Is the concept of "normalization" an issue in the E-R approach?

TOPIC SIX

Decision Support Systems

Decision support systems (DSS) were first discussed in the early 1970s. Just a dozen or so years later they have become important tools for decision making in many organizations, and their future looks very bright. However, many misconceptions have arisen concerning their development and use within the framework of management information systems.

NATURE OF DSS'S

A DSS is a computer-based information system that assists managers in making many complex decisions, such as the decisions needed to solve poorly defined or semi-structured problems. Instead of replacing the manager in the decision process, the DSS supports the manager in his or her application of the decision process. In other words, it is an automated assistant that extends the mental capabilities of the manager. A nonbusiness application of a DSS would be a computer program that aided a chess player during a tournament (if the tournament rules allowed such assistance).

The DSS can be put into perspective by relating it to an organization's management

information system (MIS). Most authorities view the DSS as an integral part of the MIS, in that its primary purpose is to provide decision-making information to managerial decision makers. However, the DSS differs from the remaining portion of the MIS in at least two respects: (1) It is most suited to ad hoc, relatively unstructured decision situations, and (2) it supports the manager in a dynamic decision-making process. In most cases it is concerned with strategic or tactical planning, rather than operational control or operations. By contrast, the remaining portion of the MIS essentially provides information to aid in relatively structured decision situations, often at the operational level of an organization. In some cases the MIS even "replaces" the manager, in that it selects the alternative course of action and perhaps actually initiates the action. For instance, some MISs prepare purchase orders to be sent to vendors when the system detects that inventory items need replenishment.

The article by Neumann and Hadass clearly establishes the framework within which a DSS fits in a using organization. It contrasts the characteristics of the DSS with the more structured components of the information system. Furthermore, the article discusses approaches to the evolution of an organizational support unit that would aid in the development and use of a DSS.

The benefits that a DSS provides are in large part based on the capabilities of computers. One important benefit is promptness. A DSS can promptly provide the manager with desired information. A related benefit is responsiveness. A DSS can provide the information in exactly the desired format. For instance, a manager can specify that the information be presented in graphical form and projected for a specified number of years into the future. Still another benefit is experimentation. A DSS allows the manager to change assumptions concerning expected future conditions and to observe the effects on relevant criteria (e.g., net income). As a result of these direct benefits, a DSS enables the manager to gain a better understanding of the key factors affecting the decision. It enables the manager to evaluate a larger number of alternative courses of action within a reasonably short time frame. Consequently, the manager should be able to improve the quality of his or her decisions.

KEY ROLES IN DSS DEVELOPMENT AND USE

Several key roles are involved in the development and use of a DSS. In some cases two or more of these roles are filled by the same person.

The *user* of the DSS is the manager or managers who are faced with semi- or unstructured problems needing decision solutions.

The *system builder* or *designer* is the person who selects and assembles the suitable components to develop the DSS. Often this person is a member of the information system function, but he or she may be a staff assistant to the user-manager or even the manager.

The *intermediary* is the person who assists the user in making use of the developed DSS. Often this person is an administrative assistant who is facile with a terminal keyboard and/or who can interpret the information obtained.

The *technical specialist* is a person who develops various components that generally underlie more than one DSS within the organization. For instance, a specialist may expand the underlying data base or the dialog software.

KEY COMPONENTS OF DSS'S

While respective DSS's vary considerably in specific details and even in capabilities, they tend to consist of several key components. One component is the *model base,* the decision models that reflect relationships among the relevant factors in decision situations. Because of the complex and unstructured nature of most decisions being aided by a DSS, more than one model is often necessary for a single situation. The second component is the *data base,* the structured data needed for use in the models. Generally data for a DSS is largely drawn from external and non-transactional sources; however, some of the data may be based on summarized transaction data. The third major component is known as the *user interface.* This component consists of (1) the means of accessing the DSS, e.g., a terminal keyboard or joystick; (2) the means of providing the information, e.g., a graphical display or hard-copy printer; and (3) the means of communicating with the DSS, e.g., a dialog language or set of menus. In addition, of course, the user provides his or her knowledge base concerning the decision situation, and the DSS provides a knowledge base (e.g., "help" guides) concerning the use of the related hardware and software.

Required components and desirable attributes of a DSS are considered in both of the articles in this topic area; although neither of the treatments are thorough, a compilation from both articles provides a rather complete picture.

FINANCIAL PLANNING MODELS

Financial planning models represent a type of decision model commonly employed within a DSS. Thus, financial planning models are a component or a subset of the DSS universe. However, they are quite significant since they pertain to an important area of business activity and produce outputs whose formats are familiar to managers.

Financial planning models represent some aspect of the financial planning process of an organization. The financial planning process most often modeled is the annual budget process, although capital budgeting processes are also frequently modeled. The outputs of financial planning models tend to be such financial statements as forecasted income statements, balance sheets, and funds flow statements. Key data items involved in the models generally include forecasted sales, interest rates, growth trends, and cash flows.

A powerful feature of financial planning models is that they accommodate the use of a number of experimentation techniques, including "what-if" analyses, goal-seeking analyses, sensitivity analyses, and Monte Carlo simulation analyses. For instance, when various assumptions ("what-ifs") are made with respect to future sales levels, the impacts on net income levels can be quickly ascertained.

The article by El-Badawi describes the development of and experimentation with a corporate financial planning model. It illustrates the use of all of the above-mentioned techniques except goal-seeking. (To illustrate that technique, the author might have established a desired value for net income and determined, by working backwards, the level of sales needed to achieve the desired net income.) Also illustrated is the type of dialog that facilitates the interaction between the decision maker and the computer-based system containing the model.

DEVELOPMENT APPROACHES

Successful development of financial planning models and other types of DSS generally depends upon the presence of a sound planning process within the organization. Since a DSS is designed for the individual use of managers, it stands to reason that the active participation of these managers in the development process is also a requisite.

Assuming the presence of the above, should the DSS be (a) developed from the beginning in a full-blown state, or (b) developed in a more cautious evolutionary manner? While the former monolithic one-step approach appears to be more appealing, the latter iterative approach has proven to be more successful. Following this latter approach, the model builder works closely with the user to develop first a simplified model. After implementing and using this model, these same two parties redesign the model to include more of the desired dimensions; then they implement the expanded version. After repeating this cycle several times they should produce a relatively stable model (or set of models) that integrate(s) most if not all of the target dimensions.

DSS and financial planning models appear to have a very promising future. They are being introduced into many new firms, even some that are relatively small. This trend is facilitated by the increasing use of micro-computers and increasing development of modeling software packages designed for use with microcomputers. Furthermore, decision support systems are being developed for new applications and new situations. For in-stance, they are being developed (in con-junction with expert or "knowledge-based" systems) to aid in the solution of very com-plex and unstructured problems. They are beginning to be used within the frameworks of distributed networks and live data bases.

DSS and Strategic Decisions*

The high hopes and optimistic forecasts for computerized information systems in supporting decision-making processes have not been fulfilled. This is particularly true with regard to the top management levels.[1] The gap between expectation and realization has not been closed despite rapid progress in computer technology during the last decade, which has seen the arrival of cheaper hardware, new developments in hardware devices (minicomputers, terminals, storage and communication devices), and vastly improved computer software (communications, data base management systems, time sharing, and simple interactive languages). A better understanding of managerial decision making and problem solving has led to a demand for better decision support systems. However, studies carried out in various organizations have shown that the contribution of computerized information systems to strategic decisions has not been as great as might be expected.

REASONS FOR SLOW DEVELOPMENT

A survey of the literature shows that the causes of sluggish development can be broken down as follows:

- Lack of organizational policy. Lack of priorities and clearly articulated support of top management induces systems developers to be opportunistic, to get a system working quickly. Such systems are typically associated with the operational control level and not with the strategic planning and management control levels.

- The approach to and methods of management information systems (MIS) development. MIS support in decision making is given as a by-product of the computerized operational systems, not as an independent activity.[2] For example, in a supermarket chain, a decision to introduce a new product may be ad hoc, based on extra processing of routinely generated information used for reordering purposes, ignoring other relevant information not generated by the reordering system.

- The organizational function responsible for developing and maintaining the information systems supporting decision making. The desired structure, aims, and location within the organization — the very existence of the function and its relationships with the organizational levels it is supposed to serve — have not been examined from the standpoint of the products it is expected to provide. Where they exist, such organizational bodies have not been fitted to the task of building and maintaining top level decision support systems.[3]

*By Seev Neumann and Michael Hadass. Copyright © 1980 by the Regents of the University of California. Reprinted from *California Management Review*, Volume XXII, No. 3, pp. 77–84 by permission of the Regents.

For example, the data processing department in a bank that provides daily balances of checking accounts may be at a loss if asked to provide quick information to support a decision concerning the proposed opening of a new branch.

- Qualifications and characteristics of personnel. Because of the failure to define the function of management information systems in organizations, the personnel involved with the development and maintenance of MIS have not been chosen on the basis of a thorough understanding of the various aspects of the subject.[4] While the scope of a system designer developing a warehouse information system, for example, is narrow, the designer who develops an information system to support top level decision makers must understand the needs and problems of those concerned with more complex organizationwide functions.

Obviously the spectrum of causes is very broad and demands a radical and comprehensive solution. The next sections describe a proposal for solving one aspect of the problem: the organizational aspect. Before presenting this proposal two preliminary subjects that will be used later need to be examined. They are the framework for information systems in organizations and the characteristics of management information systems.

A FRAMEWORK FOR INFORMATION SYSTEMS IN ORGANIZATIONS

The framework and terminology of this discussion is based on classifying decisions into "structured," "unstructured," and "partially structured" (semistructured) decisions, and on conceptualizing the decision-making processes on the basis of concepts developed by H. A. Simon.[5]

Classification according to levels of management, as suggested by R. N. Anthony, was found irrelevant to the purposes of this paper since it is qualitative and cannot serve as a means of building the framework of a management information system.[6] Moreover, the ability of a computerized information system to support decision-making processes derives from the type of decision being supported.

In the context of this discussion, the concept of decision making includes both the recognition of a problem (short-range) and the identification and designing of opportunities (middle- and long-range). A decision maker is best described as "an entity, either an individual or a group, who is dissatisfied with some existing state or with the prospect of a future state, and who possesses the desire and authority to initiate actions designed to alter this state."[7]

Finally, it is assumed that the process of decision making, with respect to completely structured decisions, is rational. This process is subject to Simon's principle of bounded rationality with respect to unstructured or partially structured decisions. In this context, rationality means the examination of all alternatives in order to select the best among them according to decision criteria defined in advance. The principle of bounded rationality means that the number of alternatives examined is limited and the satisfying one is selected according to predefined criteria.

CLASSES OF DECISIONS

A distinction can be made between completely structured decisions and unstructured ones, although in reality there is a continuum with completely structured decisions at one extreme and completely unstructured ones at the other.

The process of making a completely structured decision is algorithmic (logical, quantitative, unequivocal, entirely defined). All of the alternatives and the consequences of their implementation are known and quantitatively defined. They may be compared to a quantitative criterion (the objective function) by which the optimal alternative can be selected.

The process of making an unstructured decision is heuristic. Not all variables can be identified and defined, and those that are cannot always be quantified. To make an unstructured decision, we must resort to hypotheses, intuition, evaluations, educated guesses, experience, and luck. It is a decision made under uncertainty that the alternative selected is optimal, so there is no predefined or best approach to making such a decision.

Decision making is not an activity performed at a specific time but a stepwise process. According to Simon, this process comprises three main phases: intelligence, analysis and design, and selection or choice. Scott Morton continued this line of thought and subdivided each of Simon's three phases into three subphases or steps: generation, manipulation, and selection.[8] These concepts are useful in defining the three classes of decisions:

- a structured decision, one in which all the steps in the decision-making process are structured,
- an unstructured decision, one in which all the steps in the decision-making process are unstructured, and
- a semistructured decision, one in which some of the steps in the decision-making process are structured and some are unstructured.

MANAGEMENT INFORMATION SYSTEMS

A management information system (MIS) can be defined in terms of its application to decision making. It is an information system that makes structured decisions. It supports the process of making unstructured or semistructured decisions by performing part of the process and providing relevant information. Table 1 describes MIS activities and contributions to the various classes of decisions.

The structure of MIS derives from its operational definition as seen above. Two types of logical components can be distinguished: structured decision systems (SDS), which make the structured decisions; and decision support systems (DSS), which support unstructured and semistructured decisions.

PHYSICAL STRUCTURE

SDS and DSS do not correspond to the actual physical structure of information systems in organizations. The physical structure consists of two information systems: decision support systems and administrative data processing systems (ADPS). The ADPS subdivides into a transactions processing system (TPS) and a structured decision system. Each of the components mentioned is not necessarily a single or distinct physical information system. There can be a confederation

Table 1. MIS Activities and Decision Classes

	MIS ACTIVITIES	
Decision Classes	Decision Making	Providing Supporting Information
Structured Decision	x	—
Semistructured Decision	x	x
Unstructured Decision	—	x

of information systems. This confederation of information systems may be called organizational information systems (OIS).

The term *confederation* is used to stress the fact that interrelations between the various information systems do exist but are not so tight as to impede independent development of each system at appropriate times. The adoption of a master plan for information systems will provide for efficient development under the right priorities but will keep sight of their vital interrelations. The chronological development of information systems usually goes from transactions processing systems to structured decision systems, and only then to decision support systems. According to the philosophy presented in this article, decision support systems should be developed immediately, using the technology available now (see Figure 1).

CHARACTERISTICS

The causes of the sluggish development of information systems to support top level decision making can be identified by analyzing the characteristics of the two logical components of MIS—structured decision systems and decision support systems. Table 2 shows the relevant characteristics as extremes in a continuum running from SDS to DSS. An analysis of these characteristics leads to the following conclusions:

- Since the characteristics of DSS are diametrically opposed to those of SDS, the development and maintenance of DSS must be entrusted to an independent body. This body should have aims, structure, location, staffing, status, methods, and resources entirely different from those of the organizational unit in charge of SDS. Because of the specialized nature of this independent body, its creation and its function must result from a clearly stated policy decision by management.

- The DSS may selectively utilize data from the common data base (developed by ADPS), but the structure and organization of the data base may be changed in order to conform to DSS activities.

- The structured decision systems develop in two directions: concurrently with the development of the transactions processing system, or as an expansion of the TPS; and by the transfer of decisions which become structured or pseudostructured in the course of time, from DSS to SDS.

Figure 1.   Information Systems in the Organization—A Physical Structure

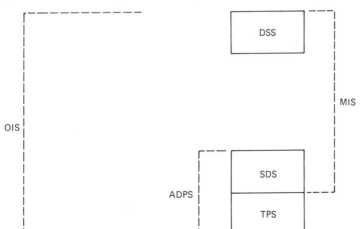

Table 2. Characteristics of SDS and DSS

SUBJECT	SDS	DSS
I. The Final User/Decision Maker		
Decision maker's environment (internal and external)	constant, simple	dynamic, complex
Decision maker's level	operational control	strategic planning
System development initiative	to decision maker	from decision maker
Decision maker's involvement in system development and use	passive	active
Decision-making style	predetermined	individual
II. The Decisions Supported by the System Structure	structured	unstructured
Time horizon	historical	future-oriented
Use	routine	ad hoc, unique
Decision-making process	defined, algorithmic, programmable	heuristic, iterative, exploratory, nonprogrammable
Importance to organization	local, operational	strategic, organizationwide
Decision phases supported	all phases	some phases
III. The Information System		
Data sources	largely internal	largely external
Design predetermination	structured	unstructured
Data base	well-defined, narrow, detailed	redundant, broad, integrated, aggregated
Model base	predetermined models, quantitative, universal O.R., explicit	tailor-made, qualitative model building blocks, heuristic, implicit
System design orientation	data orientation	decision oriented
Operating mode	batch	interactive
System success criteria	operational efficiency	flexibility
Frequency of use	predetermined	undefined frequency
IV. Information System Developers		
Organizational body	technicians, service unit	planners, staff unit
Involvement of developers in decision-making process	none	involved

A synopsis of these conclusions is exhibited in Figure 2.

AN ORGANIZATIONAL SOLUTION TO THE DSS PROBLEM

A distinct and independent organizational unit must be in charge of the decision support systems, since DSS characteristics are quite different from the structured decision systems. This section details the different aspects pertinent to the development and operation of the DSS unit.

Top Management Policy.   The DSS unit must be backed by positive and explicit high-level policy. Top management should realize that the development of computerized information systems to support unstructured decision making is a specialized technique requiring specialized means. This is why DSS must be kept separate from the administrative data processing unit. Top management itself must act as sponsor and advocate of the DSS unit. The importance of the decisions to be sponsored by DSS should guide management when allocating resources to it. The DSS unit must have the clout to implement as well; this is an important and necessary condition for success. Ability to communicate with and influence top management is essential for success.

Size and Scope of DSS.   Size and scope of the decision support systems will depend on the size, complexity, and specific requirements of the organization and its level of managerial and technological maturity. It can be staffed by one or dozens of professionals and can be centralized or decentralized. It is best to develop the unit by an evolutionary process, constantly monitoring its technological, economical and organizational feasibility.

Optimal Timing.   A DSS unit should not be established before an organization is mature enough to use it. Mistiming might be

Figure 2.   Organizational Information Systems (OIS), Together with Data and Model Bases

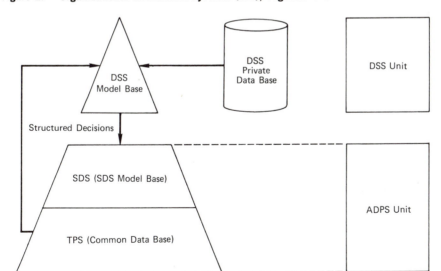

*Selective use of data from common data base, while changing their structure and organization.

fatal. One good indicator of organizational maturity is the size, scope, and level of the administrative data processing function. When the time seems ripe for starting a DSS unit, it is best to begin with a pilot project. This should be pinpointed to an area where there are good chances of making a successful contribution to the organization.

Location and Status. The DSS unit should be a staff function (in contrast to the administrative data processing function, which is usually a service unit). Its position in the organizational hierarchy will be defined by the level of its clients, to whom it should be subordinated.

Functions within the DSS Unit. Ultimately the organizational structure of the DSS unit will be determined by what it is expected to accomplish.

The DSS Staff. The complete process of decision support systems development and maintenance will require the following positions:

- Coordinators (liaison officers with the user managers). Ideally there should be a coordinator specializing in each manager's area with an acquaintance with the organization based on some actual line experience; the ability to structure processes; common language and confidence with users; ability to be integrated with the decision-making process; and training and knowledge of relevant

disciplines—computer technology, organizational, managerial and decision-making theory, operations research and statistics, behavioral sciences, economics of computers and information. The person with this function might be named a DSS administrator.

- Specialists in various disciplines required for DSS development and maintenance. They support the coordinators in complex cases requiring specialized knowledge. Their specialties might be operations research, decision making, management (finance, production), and behavioral science. These specialists might be named model base administrators.

- Operating personnel, including experts in computer technologies (especially data base, data communications), programmers, and computer operators.

Interrelations between User Managers and DSS. Interrelations may develop along different lines in different organizations at different periods. Four possible distributions of tasks between user managers and DSS are possible (see Table 3). Alternative A means that the user-manager performs all of the DSS functions himself and has no need for the DSS unit. Alternative B means that the user-manager uses only the operating facilities of the DSS unit and performs the other functions himself. Alternative C means that the user-manager performs the coordinative tasks himself but requires specialist and operating facilities from the DSS unit. Alternative D means that all the functions

Table 3.   Interrelations Between Managers and a DSS Unit

	DSS FUNCTIONS		
Alternative	**Coordinator**	**Specialist**	**Operator**
A	Manager	Manager	Manager
B	Manager	Manager	DSS
C	Manager	DSS	DSS
D	DSS	DSS	DSS

are performed by the DSS unit. Even so, the user-manager should be actively involved in the process of building the information system.

Organizational Structures of the DSS Unit. The coordinator has the most important function in the DSS unit because he is the direct liaison with the user-managers. He utilizes the specialist and operating pools according to need. What is proposed is, in effect, a matrix organization. A problem to be solved is analogous to a project, the coordinator like a project manager. The coordinator is usually subordinate to the user-manager but this is not mandatory. Different structures might work better in different situations. In addition, each user function in the organization might be assigned a dedicated group of coordinators, specialists, and operating personnel (decentralized structure of the DSS unit).

Adaptability and Learning Ability. No DSS unit can function effectively without the ability to adapt to dynamic and unstructured conditions. Besides the three functions already described, the DSS unit must include a function responsible for monitoring the unit's activities in the organizational environment. This monitoring should cover past requests for information, how they were answered, and how the managers used the information. This function may handle interrelations with the administrative data processing unit.(When the DSS unit is institutionalized, it may become a staff unit charged with the organization's long-range planning.)

Interrelations and Division of Tasks. Interrelations between the DSS unit and the administrative data processing unit exist in two main areas: sharing the common data base and handling decisions which have changed from unstructured to structured.

The Common Data Base. The DSS unit defines the model. The model determines the data required. The main available source of data is the transactions processing system data base, but this tends to be unsatisfactory from the DSS standpoint (too detailed, with historical data but no external data). The DSS unit is compelled to build and maintain private data bases and to collect ad hoc data. Even when decision support systems use data from the common data base, they may be restructured to fit DSS requirements.

On the other hand, since the ADP unit has a relative advantage in building and maintaining data bases, the DSS unit may use the ADP unit's experience and know-how (by using routines, modules and software developed by ADP). The DSS unit may also decide to incorporate its private data bases into the common base, placing them under the ADP unit's responsibility. All this underscores the need for close, systematic and formal relations between the two units.

Decisions That Become Structured. The functional division of tasks, as described above, entrusts the ADP unit with handling the structured and the DSS unit handling the other, not fully structured decisions. Unstructured or semistructured decisions may later become fully structured or pseudostructured and come into the ADP domain. Should a decision cease to be fully structured, it will return to the DSS domain.

Exceptional cases may come up where information originating in the common data base and aimed at supporting entirely unstructured decisions without models is produced by the ADP unit. This may happen when such information is produced periodically or triggered by the occurrence of predefined exceptions like summary financial reports. In such cases, the relative advantage in the processing ability of the ADP unit is utilized.

CONCLUSION

One of the main reasons for the slow development of computerized information systems designed to support unstructured and semistructured decisions has been the lack of an organizational unit specializing in the development and maintenance of such systems. Such a unit must be distinct from and independent of those responsible for developing and maintaining the transactions processing systems and the structured decision systems. Its creation and operation must be guided by deliberate and consistent top management policy.

It is suggested that the DSS unit be a staff function whose size, scope, and structure depends on the size, complexity, and specific requirements of the organization and its level of managerial and technological maturity.

Following the emergence of new specialized professionals among the information processing personnel, such as the data base administrator, the DSS unit may lead to the emergence of a DSS administrator and a model base administrator.

REFERENCES

1. R. L. ACKOFF, *A Concept of Corporate Planning* (Wiley, 1970), p. 113: P. G. W. KEEN, "Interactive Computer Systems for Managers: A Modest Proposal," *Sloan Management Review* (Fall 1976), p. 3; and G. A. GORRY, M. S. SCOTT MORTON, "A Framework for Management Information Systems," *Sloan Management Review* (Fall 1971), p. 55.

2. P. EIN-DOR, "Parallel Strategy for MIS," *Journal of Systems Management,* (March 1975), p. 30; GORRY and SCOTT MORTON, op. cit., pp. 59, 64, 66; G. A. GORRY, "The Development of Managerial Models," *Sloan Management Review* (Winter 1971), pp. 3–4; KEEN, op. cit., p. 4; T. P. GERRITY, "Design of Man-Machine Decision Systems: An Application to Portfolio Management," *Sloan Management Review* (Winter 1971), p. 59; S. L. ALTER, "How Effective Managers Use Information Systems," *Harvard Business Review* (November-December 1976), p. 104; C. L. MEADOR and D. N. NESS. "Decision Support Systems: An Application to Corporate Planning," *Sloan Management Review* (Winter 1974), p. 53.

3. GORRY and SCOTT MORTON, op. cit., p. 68; KEEN, op. cit., p. 16; MEADOR and NESS, op. cit., p. 68.

4. GORRY and SCOTT MORTON, op. cit., p. 64; MEADOR and NESS, op. cit., p. 52; J. C. EMERY, "Decision Models," *Datamation* (September 1970), p. 64.

5. H. A. SIMON, *The New Science of Management Decisions* (Harper and Row, 1960).

6. R. N. ANTHONY, *Planning and Control Systems: A Framework for Analysis* (Harvard University Press, 1965).

7. D. I. CLELAND and W. R. KING, *Systems Analysis and Project Management* (McGraw-Hill, 1975), p. 52.

8. M. S. SCOTT MORTON, *Management Decision Systems* (Harvard University Press, 1971).

QUESTIONS

1. Why have decision support systems (DSS) shown a slow pace of development in most organizations?
2. Describe the confederation of systems within the information system of an organization, with particular attention to the place of the DSS.
3. Contrast the characteristics of DSS's with those of structured decision systems and transaction processing systems.
4. The authors indicate that the classification of decisions suggested by Anthony (i.e., strategic planning, management control, operational control) is irrelevant to the framework of management information systems. However, other authors such as Sprague contend that decision support systems can be classified very logically in terms of these categories. Can these views be reconciled, i.e., can the categories of strategic planning, management control, and operational control be related to structured, partially structured, and unstructured decisions?
5. Identify the principal components of a DSS and their relationships to each other.
6. What steps should be taken by an organization to fit a DSS unit into its organizational structure?
7. What should be the relationships between a DSS organizational unit and:
   a. the information system director?
   b. the top management?
   c. the managers who will use DSS?
8. What attributes should an effective DSS possess, and how may the performance of the DSS be measured?
9. In what ways is a DSS for a large multidivisional corporation likely to differ from a DSS developed for a small local business?

A Computerized Corporate Financial Model*

Computerized corporate models are among decision aids available to management. Decision makers are able to evaluate the outcome of the alternative courses of action by simulating future changes.

The purpose of this paper is to develop a computerized interactive corporate financial model.[1] This model is designed to assist the manager charged with corporate planning in making the appropriate strategic decisions regarding the allocation of limited resources. The model, therefore, falls into the strategic planning category of the classification scheme for planning and control proposed by Anthony et al.[2] It is written in APL which is especially amenable to interface with the computer.

The model consists of three main sections. The first section represents a three-period forecast based upon five periods of prior data. Both the second and third sections are simulations. The second section, designed for sensitivity analysis, allows any 15 factors to be altered and also permits storage of the resulting relationships for use in later simulations. The third section uses a stochastic model (Monte Carlo simulation) to generate sales figures for variable performance projections. The user is able to switch easily from one mode to the other.

The model is, therefore, a combination of deterministic and probabilistic systems. A deterministic system operates in a perfectly predictable manner. The interaction among its parts is known with certainty. The probabilistic system may be described in terms of probable behavior, but a certain degree of error is always attached to the prediction.

If the stochastic mode is chosen, the projected financial statements (balance sheet, income statements, break-even point, and cash-flow statement) are produced three times for each period. These three projections include the pessimistic, most likely, and optimistic results.

Factors which may be simulated include external factors such as interest and income tax rates as well as internal factors including sales and the debt-to-capital ratio. The user may adjust the forecast, using these factors to account for various assumptions about future states of nature. The subsequent

*By Mohamed H. El-Badawi. The author wishes to acknowledge the contribution made by James Skorupski and John Warstler on an earlier version of this paper and the helpful reviews of Robert Strawser and Winston Shearon. Reprinted from an article appearing in *Cost and Management* by Mohamed H. El-Badawi, March-April 1984, by permission of The Society of Management Accountants of Canada.

actions of the user may be based upon the relative outcomes and payoffs perceived from the model output.

In terms of Simon's decision-making stages, the model may be described partly as an intelligence phase (aiding problem recognition) and partly as a decision-design phase (generation of alternatives). The final phase of the decision process, choice, is left to the decision maker.[3] Since the system answers "what if" types of questions and the user assigns his or her values and choices for the alternatives and takes actions, the system falls into the predictive category of Mason's five levels of management information systems.[4]

A case study model (heuristic) was chosen rather than an optimization model (linear programming). Since the case study approach allows the development of a hierarchy of objectives with emphasis on those objectives selected by the decision-maker, it promotes communication in the production of the financial statements, and it is easier to develop.[5]

An additional choice made in developing the model is the incorporation of an information generator type program versus an information compiler. The latter requires the data collected to be fed. The computer then performs the arithmetic manipulations which are necessary to consolidate the desired output. The former begins with only a few selected inputs but may generate new information based upon equations and mathematical logic.[6]

In summary, the model is designed to assist in the decision-making function through the use of "what if" types of questions. It may be used in either a deterministic or a probabilistic mode or in a selected combination of both modes. The interactive capabilities allow the user to project various states of future events and/or alternative courses of action. Output is in the form of a three-period forecast including balance sheet, income statement, break-even points, and cash-flow statements based upon past financial data and the user's projected state of future events.

The next section of this paper presents a detailed description of the system, while the conclusion outlines some problems, limitations and recommendations for further development of the system.[7] Finally, Appendix A consists of sample outputs from the model.

SYSTEM CAPABILITIES

As indicated previously, this financial model is designed to project three years of financial statements (balance sheet, income statement, break-even point and cash-flow statement) for the firm. It assumes that five years of prior financial data (balance sheet and income statements) are available and are stored as the data base within the computer (PRIOR DATA File).

Forecast. Upon initialization, the model considers each line item (factor) of the past financial statements and builds a relationship to allow projection into the future. The financial relationships vary depending upon these factors. Many factors relate to sales by a weighted average as suggested by Weston *et al.* while others are related to sales based upon a linear regression as suggested by Horngren.[8-10] All of the relationships are listed in Table 1. In summary, sales is established as the primary controlling variable for most accounts (factors). The only user input requested at this point is the corporate income tax rate, which is stored for later use in calculating net income.

These relationships are determined in the RELATION program, which is the initial

Table 1. Account Relationships

ACCOUNTS	RELATIONSHIPS
1. Cash	— Related to Sales by a Weighted Average
2. Receivables — net	— Related to Sales by a Weighted Average
3. Inventory	— Related to Sales by a Weighted Average
4. Fixed Assets	— Related to Sales by a Weighted Average
5. Allowance for Depreciation	= Last allowance for depreciation + depreciation expenses
6. Total Assets	= Sum of accounts 1–4 less account 5
7. Accounts Payable	— Related to Sales by a Weighted Average
8. Notes Payable	— Related to Sales by a Weighted Average
9. Long-Term Liabilities	= Total Assets — Accounts Payable — Notes Payable — Capital — Ret. Earnings
10. Capital	= (Total Assets) − (Accts. Pay. + Notes Pay. + L.T. Liab. + Retain. Earnings)
11. Retained Earnings	= Last Year's Ret. Earnings + Net Income
12. Total Liabilities and Equity	= Sum of Accounts 7–11
13. Sales	= Basic Variable
14. Mfg. Variable Cost	— Related to Sales by Linear Regression
15. General & Administrative Variable Cost	— Related to Sales by Linear Regression
16. Selling Variable Cost	— Related to Sales by Linear Regression
17. Contribution Margin	= Sales — All Variable Costs
18. Manufacturing Fixed Cost	= Last Year's Value
19. G. & A. Fixed Cost	= Last Year's Value
20. Selling Fixed Cost	= Last Year's Value
21. Mfg. Depreciation Expenses	— Related to Fixed Assets by Weighted Average
22. G. & A. Depreciation Expenses	— Related to Fixed Assets by Weighted Average
23. Selling Depreciation Expenses	— Related to Fixed Assets by Weighted Average
24. Interest Expenses	— Related to Notes Payable and Long-Term Debt by Weighted Average
25. Net Income	= Sales — All Costs

program executed in the model. The following Figures 1, 2, 3, and 4 show the flow of programs described in this paper. The RELATION program stores these relationships in a RELATIONSHIPS file for use by the TREND PROJECTION program and also stores fixed-cost data in several files. Finally, the RELATION program computes a sixth year of sales, based upon historical trendline projection, for use in computing an initial set of Financial Forecasts. RELATION then calls TREND PROJECTION.

Figure 1.   Overall Diagram

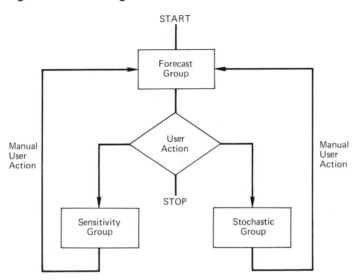

The TREND PROJECTION program initially computes a seventh and eighth year sales projection, based upon Trend Line projection of the five years of past historical sales data and a sixth year of sales, provided either by RELATION if historical (initial run only), by the SENSITIVITY group if deterministic, or by the STOCHASTIC group if probabilistic. (In the case of stochastic sales projections, explained later in this section, three sales amounts are actually provided for the sixth year; pessimistic, most likely, and optimistic, and three sets of three-year forecasts are computed). TREND PROJECTION then uses the sales figures for a given year and the RELATIONSHIPS file to compute the projections of each factor. The RELATIONSHIPS file may have been changed from the form built by RELATION if the SENSITIVITY group has been run. Also, the fixed-cost files are utilized in constructing the fixed-cost projections. All output projections are placed in a FINANCIAL STATEMENTS file

for use by OUTPUT in producing printed statements. TREND PROJECTION then calls OUTPUT. Upon conclusion, information statements are printed and TREND PROJECTION terminates.

The OUTPUT function is called by the TREND PROJECTION function to print the financial projections stored by TREND PROJECTION in the FINANCIAL STATEMENTS matrix. These data are separated into balance sheet and income statement formats. Because an information generation system is used, totals are not previously calculated and stored in the matrix. Consequently OUTPUT calculates and prints totals for assets, liabilities and equity, contribution margin, income before taxes, income taxes, net income, and the breakeven point for each of three years. In addition, the program performs calculations for cash flow, completes an internally-defined matrix, and then prints the data with appropriate headings and descriptions. Finally, the

Figure 2.   Forecast Group

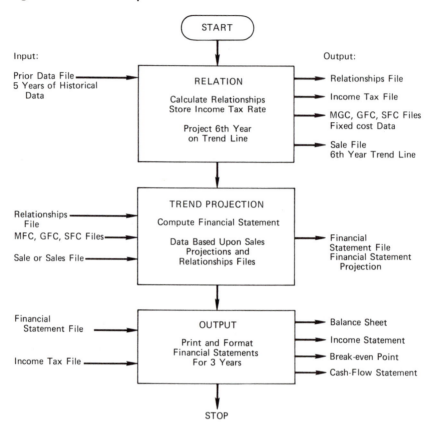

NOTE: At this point, the user may choose to do sensitivity adjustments to the relationships,
or to do stochastic analysis of sales probability.

program returns control to TREND PROJEC-
TION, which prints out information statements and ends.

Sensitivity. The sensitivity section permits the system user to alter 15 items of data
and relationships used in the projections for
the initial year of the three-year period. The
system then uses these changes to effect
changes in the two remaining years. The
CHANGES function controls other functions

in the group, calling them when the user
indicates by a number input from one to
eight the change or changes he wishes to
make. After the choice has been made and
the user has entered his other change, the
subprogram returns control to CHANGES.
The control program then permits the user
to indicate any additional changes desired
and proceeds as described above or allows
the user to exit the section to see projections based on the changes made. The user

Figure 3.   Sensitivity Group

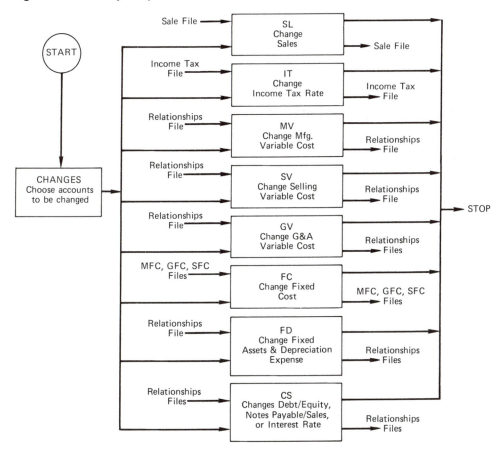

NOTE: Upon conclusion, the user calls TREND PROJECTION to obtain new financial statement
forecasts based upon these changes.

is then asked to call TREND PROJECTION (which in turn calls OUTPUT) to obtain new statements.

Stochastic. If the stochastic mode is chosen, STOCHASTIC is called by the user. This function instructs the user to input subjective probabilities for sales and determine the most likely, optimistic, and pessimistic sales amounts. These three amounts are then used as an input into the TREND PROJECTION functions as explained above.

The user inputs subjective probabilities for sales by means of intervals.[11] First, the user inputs the starting point of sales, the interval size, and the number of intervals. Then the probabilities for each interval are entered. Finally, the user inputs the number of desired iterations.

STOCHASTIC then calls a supporting

Figure 4.   Stochastic Group

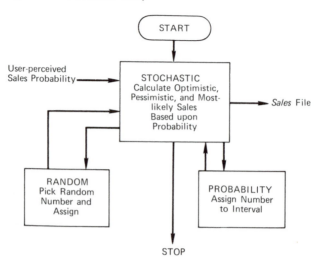

NOTE: Upon conclusion, the user calls TREND PROJECTION to
obtain new financial statements based upon these sales
projections.

function, PROBABILITY, to determine the cumulative probabilities for each interval and stores them in CUM PROBABILITY. STOCHASTIC then calls another supporting function, RANDOM, to generate random numbers and assign a value to them based upon the corresponding location of the cumulative probabilities of the intervals. The following example illustrates this process:

INTERVAL	PROB.	CUM. PROB.	RANDOM NUMBER
500–600	.05	.05	1–5
600–700	.50	.55	6–55
700–800	.45	1.00	56–100

Intervals and their probabilities are given. PROBABILITY determines the cumulative probabilities. RANDOM generates random

numbers between 1 and 100 and locates the interval which has the corresponding cumulative probability. That is, if the random number generated is between 1 and 5, it will be related to the first interval, if between 6 and 55 it will relate to the second interval, and so on. The random number is then converted into a sales value based upon the location of the random number. If the random number generated is 3, the sales value assigned (for this particular iteration) is the corresponding value in the interval as 3 in 1 to 5. That is, $500 + (\frac{3}{5} \times 100) = 560$ (the $\frac{3}{5}$ location of the first interval).

This process is repeated for the number of iterations requested by the user and stored in the vector DISTRIBUTION. STOCHASTIC then sorts and DISTRIBUTION assigns the first element, the mean, and the last element into the vector SALES which is used as an input for TREND PROJECTION. The program then instructs the user to call TREND PROJECTION (see TREND PROJECTION above).

Controls. Filtering is one of the control methods used in this model. Filtering is the process of reducing both the amounts and types of inputs allowed to enter a system. For example, in the sensitivity section, input controls limit the number of data input groups to one, sometimes two. Controls are also placed upon the ranges of permissible input data, in most cases requiring that input be greater than zero. (This restriction applies particularly to inputs affecting the income statement where a negative expense would be meaningless.) Also, in the sensitivity section, variable cost behavior is considered by means of a linear equation requiring user input of the equation's two variables. For such an equation, controls require both the input of two data groups and a slope restricted to a range of between zero and one. Finally, inputs requiring entry in percentage form have been restricted to a range between zero and one hundred.

For data inputs that are outside of allowable types and ranges, feedback control loops have been used to trigger error routines telling the system user what data are required. For example, in the stochastic section, user estimates of event probabilities are demanded. If the combined probability inputs do not sum to one, a response stating that the total of all probabilities must equal one is printed and the user is asked to make another entry. The principle is at work again in the forecast section where the user must input the average income tax rate as a percentage. If the entry is outside the allowable range, the control calls a response stating that the input is outside that range and requesting that the user make another attempt.

EVALUATION

The following is a summary of the system limitations and the related suggestions that may improve the model.

1. The relationships suggested by Horngren and Weston *et al.* are limited by their assumption of correlation to past trends. That is, an unusual year is "smoothed over" and not accurately reflected. A more sophisticated forecasting model that would compensate for these unusual past data and correlate external economic factors would be useful.

2. Since the model was tested using data from published financial statements, adjustments to convert the data from financial-oriented to managerial-oriented were required. Aggregation and disaggregation were arbitrarily made. Improving the data base by means of using the internal accounting records would better demonstrate the strengths and weaknesses of the model. This would facilitate improvement of the model.

3. Although the system utilizes a stochastic model to determine the range for sales, all other variables are determined based upon the sales range in a deterministic fashion. A more sophisticated model would determine each variable in a stochastic process based on the intrinsic probability distribution of each factor and the relationship to the other factors' probabilistic distribution. This is a very complex process and needs further development.

4. The model assumes unlimited ability to borrow and raise capital at no cost other

than the interest rate effect on the income statement. Constraints should be incorporated with the aid of linear programming to determine the optimal basis.

NOTES

1. This model is an extension of Lin, Sardinha, and El-Badawi, "An On-Line Interactive Corporate Financial Model," *Cost and Management,* July/August 1980, pp. 28–33.
2. R. N. Anthony, J. Dearden and R. F. Vancil, *Management Control Systems: Text, Cases, and Readings,* Revised Ed., 1972, Richard D. Irwin, Inc., p. 4.
3. H. A. Simon, *The New Science of Management Decisions,* Harper & Row Publishers, Inc., New York, 1980.
4. R. O. Mason, "Basic Concepts for Designing Management Information Systems," Reprinted in A. Rappaport, Editor, *Information for Decision Making: Quantitative and Behavior Dimensions,* 2nd ed., Prentice-Hall, 1975, pp. 2–16.
5. G. Gershefski, "Building a Corporate Financial Model," Harvard Business Review, July-August, 1969, p. 61.
6. *Ibid.*
7. System documentation such as APL Code, Hierarchical-Input-Process-Output (HIPO), and Data Base are available from the author upon request.
8. J. F. Weston and E. F. Brigham, *Managerial Finance,* 4th ed., Holt Rinehart and Winston, Inc., New York, 1972.
9. Files and program names have been changed to render them more descriptive to the reader.
10. C. T. Horngren, *Accounting for Management Control: An Introduction,* 3rd ed., Prentice Hall, Inc., Englewood Cliffs, New Jersey, 1974, see Chapter 10.
11. The author acknowledges that the idea used to determine the sales probability distribution was provided by Donna Driscoll.

APPENDIX A: SAMPLE MODEL OUTPUT

SAMPLE OUTPUT HISTORICAL PROJECTION

This model will first give you a three-year projection of our firm's financial data based upon historical trends of the last five years.

You will then have the option of changing some factors or of giving probabilistic projections to next year's sales. You may then request new projections of the financial statements based upon these changes.

Enter the firm's average income tax rate as 48 per cent.

The following financial forecast uses a projection of sales based upon historical data:

SAMPLE OUTPUT SENSITIVITY EXECUTION

Changes

You can do any **one** of the following:

1— Change the sales amount (SL)
2— Change the average income tax rate (IT)
3— Change the manufacturing variable cost equation (MV)
4— Change the selling variable cost equation (SV)
5— Change the general and administrative variable cost equation (GV)
6— Change the fixed cost amount (FC)
7— Change the fixed asset and depreciation expense amounts (FD)
8— Change the debt/equity ratio, and/or notes payable/sales ratio, and/or the average interest rate (CS)

You can then choose to change another variable or to exit the function in order to see financial projections based upon your change(s).

Type the letters shown between parentheses to indicate the change you wish to make.
SL
The present sales figure in thousands of dollars is:
638652.20
Enter the new sales figure.
690000
Do you wish to make any other changes— Yes or No?
No

(Projections are in thousands of dollars.)

BALANCE SHEET	1984	1985	1986
1—ASSETS			
Cash	18191	19983	21774
Receivable-Net	90852	99800	108749
Inventory	117051	128580	140109
Fixed Asset	419036	460311	501585
Allowance for Depreciation	87914	90643	93617
TOTAL ASSETS	557216	618031	678600
2—LIABILITIES AND EQUITY			
Accounts Payable	71757	78826	85892
Notes Payable	58817	64610	70404
Long-term Liabilities	225285	251262	277083
Capital	103238	103238	103238
Retained Earning	98119	120095	141983
TOTAL LIABILITIES AND EQUITY	557216	618031	678600
INCOME STATEMENT			
Sales	638652	701558	764464
Manufacturing Variable Cost	307180	338192	369204
General and Administrative Variable Cost	21495	24081	26667
Selling Variable Cost	32242	36121	39999
Contribution Margin	277735	303164	328594
Manufacturing Fixed Cost	171554	171554	171554
Manufacturing Depreciation Expenses	1242	1365	1487
General and Adm. Fixed Cost	13504	13504	13504
General and Adm. Depreciation Expenses	497	546	595
Selling Fixed Cost	20256	20256	20256
Selling Depreciation Expenses	745	819	892
Interest Expenses	36640	40737	44815
Income Before Taxes	33297	54383	75491
Income Taxes	15982	26104	36235
Net Income	17315	28279	39256
THE BREAK-EVEN POINTS ARE:	562088	575709	588837

SAMPLE OUTPUT STOCHASTIC EXECUTION

Stochastic

Enter the following for next year sales:
- (A) Sales Interval Indicating
  - (1) Starting Point,
  - (2) Interval Size, and
  - (3) No. of Intervals.
- (B) Your subjective probabilities for intervals in (A).

Do you need detailed description (Yes or No)?
Yes
Assuming the following is your sales intervals and their related probability distribution,

SALES INTERVAL	PROB.
500–549	.05
550–599	.25
600–649	.50
650–699	.20

Sales elements would be '500 50 4'.
Subjective probability elements would be '.05 .25 .50 .20'.
Enter three elements for sale.
630000 50 3
Enter elements for subjective probabilities,
.2 .4 .4

Enter desired no. of iterations for simulation (Up to 100)
250
You have chosen 250 iterations, which is out of the limit 0 to 100. Try again.
99

(Projections are in thousands of dollars.)

BALANCE SHEET	1984	1985	1986
1 — ASSETS			
Cash	19653	20958	22958
Receivable-Net	98156	104670	114662
Inventory	126462	134854	147729
Fixed Asset	452727	482771	528858
Allowance for Depreciation	88113	90976	94112
TOTAL ASSETS	608885	652277	720095
2 — LIABILITIES AND EQUITY			
Accounts Payable	77527	82672	90564
Notes Payable	63546	67763	74232
Long-term Liabilities	247784	266134	295084
Capital	113045	113045	113045
Retained Earning	106983	122663	147170
TOTAL LIABILITIES AND EQUITY	608885	652277	720095
INCOME STATEMENT			
Sales	690000	735790	806031
Manufacturing Variable Cost	332494	355068	389697
General and Administrative Variable Cost	23606	25488	28376
Selling Variable Cost	35408	38231	42562
Contribution Margin	298492	317003	345396
Manufacturing Fixed Cost	171554	171554	171554
Manufacturing Depreciation Expenses	1342	1431	1568
General and Adm. Fixed Cost	13504	13504	13504
General and Adm. Depreciation Expenses	537	537	627
Selling Fixed Cost	20256	20256	20256
Selling Depreciation Expenses	805	859	941
Interest Expenses	40152	43062	47630
Income Before Tax	50342	65764	89316
Income Taxes	24164	31567	42871
Net Income	26178	34197	46445
THE BREAK-EVEN POINTS ARE:	573629	583147	597598

MOST LIKELY PROJECTIONS
(Projections are in thousands of dollars.)

BALANCE SHEET	1984	1985	1986
1—ASSETS			
Cash	19192	20650	22585
Receivable-Net	95853	103134	112798
Inventory	123494	132876	145326
Fixed Asset	442103	475688	520258
Allowance for Depreciation	88050	90871	93956
TOTAL ASSETS	592592	641478	707010
2—LIABILITIES AND EQUITY			
Accounts Payable	75707	81459	89091
Notes Payable	62055	66769	73025
Long-term Liabilities	240690	261445	289408
Capital	109953	109953	109953
Retained Earning	104188	121853	145534
TOTAL LIABILITIES AND EQUITY	592592	641478	707010
INCOME STATEMENT			
Sales	673808	724995	792924
Manufacturing Variable Cost	324512	349747	383235
General and Administrative Variable Cost	22940	25044	27837
Selling Variable Cost	34410	37566	41754
Contribution Margin	291946	312638	340098
Manufacturing Fixed Cost	171554	171554	171554
Manufacturing Depreciation Expenses	1311	1410	1542
General and Adm. Fixed Cost	13504	13504	13504
General and Adm. Depreciation Expenses	524	564	617
Selling Fixed Cost	20256	20256	20256
Selling Depreciation Expenses	786	846	925
Interest Expenses	39044	42329	46742
Income Before Taxes	44967	62175	84957
Income Taxes	21584	29844	40779
Net Income	23383	32331	44178
THE BREAK-EVEN POINTS ARE:	570026	580815	594850

QUESTIONS

1. How does a corporate financial model (also called a financial planning model) differ from corporate simulation models and optimization models?
2. What technical options are available to a designer or planner or manager who decides to develop a corporate financial model?
3. Describe and contrast the following techniques of model experimentation:
   a. "What-if" analysis
   b. Goal-seeking analysis
   c. Sensitivity analysis
   d. Monte Carlo simulation analysis

4. How may models such as the one described be validated?

5. Evaluate the underlying assumptions upon which the described model is based, especially with respect to their validity.

6. Discuss reasons why certain financial planning models have failed in the past. What are likely to be the effects of these failures upon the organizations in which the failures occur?

7. Is the described model practical, i.e., likely to be accepted and used by managers of a real-world organization? If not, what features or limitations are likely to be most inhibiting to such managers?

8. If the model is not practical, does it have any value to anyone? What is its value, if any?

9. Describe ways in which the model may be rendered more useable and valid.

TOPIC SEVEN

Computer Control and Audit Concepts and Techniques

The notion of computer "hackers" breaking into a computer system makes for sensational reading and provides the basis for the popular movie *War Games.* Some people dismiss hackers as a trivial phenomenon while others call for the rethinking of national security. Are outsiders really a major threat to computer security, or are legitimate employees the critical area of exposure? What are the real costs of illegal access to an EDP system and which specific controls belong where? Finally, how does one audit "through" a computer? These questions, among others, will be addressed in Topic Seven.

NOTIONS REGARDING CONTROLS

Let us begin with the definition or purpose of a control.

> Control: The process of restraining or redirecting the activities of an organism.

The reader may find this definition a bit inappropriate. It is, however, the classic definition of control—in a medical context. An accounting system is quite similar to the human body in that both are composed of inputs, processes, and outputs, and both are concerned with achieving certain pre-

specified goals or objectives. Your body, like an accounting system, sends signals when activities are out of control! Think about it. Now that controls have been defined, it is relevant to address the location of controls and control types.

Consider the following three possible viewpoints of an EDP system:

Unintentional errors, intentional irregularities
(*Error Perspective*)
Inputs, processes, outputs
(*Processing Perspective*)
People, procedures, devices
(*Component Perspective*)

One way to categorize an EDP system is in the context of the errors which occur. Honest mistakes, such as classifying a transaction to a wrong account, are called "errors" while an illegal change to a payroll program for the purpose of perpetrating a crime is an "irregularity." The sensational irregularities appear in the *Wall Street Journal;* however, their occurrence is approximately $1/10,000$th as often as that of honest accounting errors. Thus, in terms of likelihood of occurrence, let us place a (1) over unintentional errors (for most likely) and a (3) over irregularities (for least likely).

If we view a system as being composed of inputs/processes/outputs, the outputs are only error-prone if the inputs or processes are deficient. Thus, outputs receive a (3). Well-written logic in processing applications should catch most errors of syntax and reasonableness. Processes receive a (2). The culprit is input. If an employee works "42" hours (with a limit check of 50 hours) and the busy key-puncher erroneously inputs "24" hours, you have an input error. Unfortunately, the input area is most vulnerable to systems mistakes. Place a (1) over the input category.

An EDP system may be viewed, from an error-proneness perspective, in regard to the components of the system. Any MIS system is composed of *people, procedures,* and *devices.* Most systems designers would argue that, given these three components, devices are almost infallible — so give this component a (3) as the one least likely to cause EDP errors. Well-written procedures should deter many systems errors, unless the procedures are disregarded or overwritten by people. Thus people are the crack in the armor which causes vulnerability — place a (1) above people and a (2) above procedures. The conclusion from this analysis of three EDP system viewpoints is obvious if you connect the (1)'s. Auditors and systems designers are concerned most with honest *people* causing *unintentional* errors at point of data *input* (capture).

We should hope to concentrate most upon EDP controls with the above findings in mind. It is not surprising to see the increasing number and variety of point-of-sale devices which facilitate data capture.

Controls may be categorized by their point of position and functional design characteristics. Most controls which occur *early* in the MIS are *preventive* in nature, designed to restrain an action from occurring. Let us assume two control violations: 1) the illegal access of a student file, and 2) a bank robbery. Two examples of preventive controls are 1) a computer password scheme, and 2) a 200-pound guard dog. The following drawing depicts a preventive control as one where the action (A) is completely frustrated as the control does not allow the action to proceed. In a detective control scenario, the action one wishes to perform is *completed!* The control is an after-the-fact review of completed events such as a console log review of people who accessed certain files and a ringing bank alarm. Obviously the detective control, in most situations, is far inferior to the preventive control. However all MIS events do not lend themselves to preventive control. The reconciliation of postings to account receivables and sales is a sound procedure for the detection of errors; no preventive control exists. *Statement on Auditing Standards No. 43* discusses both the concept of preventive and that of detective controls.

A third category of controls, *corrective,* has been added in recent years. Corrective controls are drawn similar to those in detective procedures. The difference is that corrective procedures not only detect an error, but they additionally take an *action* (depicted as A', i.e., A Prime) such as sending a signal to the internal auditors' terminal during an illegal file access, or notifying the police during a robbery. The reader is encouraged to categorize all further discussions of specific controls into preventive, detective, and corrective categories.

EDP AUDIT CONCERNS

The American Institute of CPA's (AICPA) enumerated their concerns regarding internal control exposures in *Statement on Auditing Standards No. 3.* The four major concerns listed are: lack of separation of duties, disap-

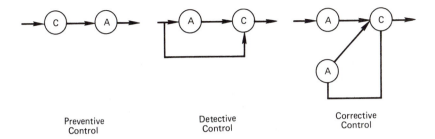

Preventive
Control

Detective
Control

Corrective
Control

pearance of the traditional audit trail, the shift in accounting data processing away from accountants and toward computer experts, and the speed of data processing (from a control perspective, slowness is good!). The AICPA also categorizes controls by the area that they cover (i.e. hardware, operations, people, data, programs, and documentation are *general controls*) or processing point (i.e. input, process, and output are *application controls*). *SAS 3* was written in 1973. As a follow-up, Lampe and Kneer (1984) in *The EDP Auditor* (Vol. III) surveyed EDP auditors regarding their EDP Concerns in distributed data processing systems (DDPS) and stand-alone micros. Exhibit 1

Exhibit 1. Mean Ranking of DDP/Micro System Exposures

RANK	EXPOSURE	MEAN SCORE
1	Unauthorized file access/processing	3.97
2	Inability of network software to restart/recover	3.77
3	Inability to separate duties within EDP depts.	3.76
4	Network software failure	3.71
5	Lack of transaction audit trail	3.64
6	Operator inability to restart/recover system	3.64
7	Lack of file integrity/correctness	3.62
8	Local data input errors (inadequate edit/validation)	3.60
9	Unauthorized program modification	3.57
10	Inadequate training and supervision of EDP personnel	3.55
11	Unauthorized transactions	3.50
12	Inability to recover lost input	3.43
13	File destruction	3.22
14	Message loss/destruction	3.19
15	Nonstandard line protocols	3.16
16	Unrestricted EDP facility access	3.12
17	DDP network hardware failure	3.10
18	Inadequate hardware maintenance	3.10

SCALE: 4 = profound disruptive effect upon internal control
3 = medium disruptive effect upon internal control
2 = strong disruptive effect upon internal control
1 = minimal disruptive effect upon internal control

reveals the top-rated exposures (sixteen of them) from a questionnaire containing over one hundred exposure items. Notice that very few *new* control concerns are introduced in the findings. Controls ranked one, eight, nine, eleven, and sixteen are all fundamental access issues, while three, six, and ten are people concerns. Items five, seven, and thirteen are of a file recovery nature. The only really new concerns highlighted in Exhibit 1 are networking or teleprocessing exposures (items two, four, twelve, and fourteen, fifteen, and seventeen). The reader is encouraged to develop a list of one preventive and one detective control for each exposure category in Exhibit 1.

COMPUTER CONTROLS FOR THE 1990s

Computer control and security form a constantly evolving scenario. Technological advances, often *not* designed with auditors in mind, offer new ways to implement controls into computer systems. Listed in Exhibit 2 are several new computer controls based upon clever applications of technology advancements in hardware or software.

Exhibit 2 is intended to provide a brief explanation of some advanced controls (although admittedly the two operations controls listed are not of a technological nature). Most of these advanced controls are discussed in the articles in this topic area, and also in Topic Four.

EDP AUDITING

Auditing in a computer environment does not change the basic objectives of the audit. That is, an auditor remains concerned with fundamental objectives such as validity, authorization, completeness, classification,

summarization, and valuation. Exhibit 3 indicates the procedures necessary to audit in a computer environment. Notice that even if general and application controls fail the compliance tests, or such controls are nonexistent, *user controls* may provide a reduction in the scope of the auditors' substantive tests. User controls consist of reconciliations and other kinds of review performed by the end-user as a check on the EDP department.

While the introduction of EDP does not alter audit objectives, the implementation of EDP hardware and software certainly modifies several audit processes. The major EDP audit techniques may be classified as auditing *around, through,* and *with* the computer.

Auditing "around": Vouching hardcopy inputs up to point of data processing, then comparing outputs to inputs. Appropriate if the computer performs no high-level accounting logic, such as automatically generated journal entries. If logic is in the machine, one must admit that logic.

Auditing "through": Using client hardware and software, coupled with auditor data. Examples are auditor dummy data (batch mode) or Integrated Test Facility (online mode). Appropriate to test logic of system for accepting invalid data and to trace data from file to file.

Auditing "with": Auditing via the combination of client data, auditor software, and client/auditor hardware. Examples of this approach are the usage of utilities or generalized audit software. Auditing "with" allows the auditor to query a file on a 100 percent basis to test for overdepreciation, or to simulate payroll program logic using live data.

The aforementioned EDP audit techniques are not mutually exclusive — more than one technique could be utilized on the same engagement. Professional judgement must be exercised in the determination of the proper EDP audit "mix."

Exhibit 2.   Advanced Computer Controls

AREA	CONTROL	REASON
I/O	Hardwiring of the edit routine in each local port	Puts edit close to user, prohibits edit override
	Hardwiring the port identification log on into each local port	Port cannot "act" or disguise itself as another port
	Hardwiring an audit routine into each local port (auditor-on-a-chip)	Allows auditor to scan each transaction as it occurs, for attributes of audit interest (postdated, related party)
Teleprocessing	Digital transmission	Reduces distortion in data transmission
	Encryption of data	2-key encryption codes are almost impossible to "crack"
	SNA network software	Provides a method of controlling the network via security "paths"
Operations	I/O control group	Acts as a buffer between user and data processing dept.
	End-user involvement	Users must scan output and compare to input
Programs	Code comparison software	Tests for illegal changes to source or object code
	Hardwiring of application programs via (PROM — not EPROM!)	Removes the concern of illegal program changes
	Lock up the compiler	Disallows anyone to change a program and recompile it

Exhibit 3. Flowchart of EDP Audit Procedures

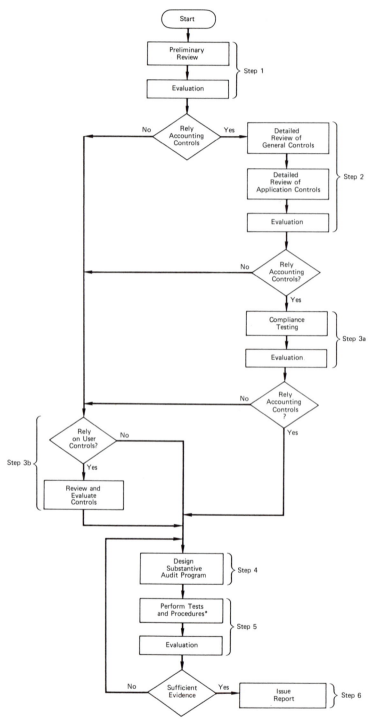

*Around, through or with computer.

ARTICLES

The two articles in Topic Seven range from an introductory discussion of audit complexities in an EDP environment to a sophisticated discussion of DBMS auditing.

The introductory article (Loebbecke, Mullarkey, and Zuber) crystalizes the complexities of an EDP system. The authors then offer a unique audit concept called "follow the flow" which breaks tradition with the premise of auditing from source document to financial statements. Two matrices of EDP errors/irregularities and EDP control techniques are presented to assist the reader in bridging from EDP exposure to control. Finally, the authors debate the advantages of EDP audit "specialists" versus "generalists."

The DBMS article (Summers, Fernandez, and Wood) discusses audit and control concepts in DBMSs. Computer frauds are categorized as input schemes, program modification schemes, and file alteration schemes. The authors depart from the classic general/application control designation to a three-tier grouping of "control practices." An *audit trail* is defined along with a "reliable" application system. Solutions are offered to network and DBMS control exposures with the reader being encouraged to ponder future technological exposures and controls. Finally, six features necessary to promote audit and control capabilities are presented for analysis.

It is hoped that the reader departs Topic Seven with a sound knowledge of the issues raised when auditing EDP systems. The area of EDP auditing should remain exciting as new computer technology constantly emerges.

Auditing in a Computer Environment*

In any society in which 10-year-old children interact with computers with the frequency and enthusiasm that many children of earlier generations played with dolls or toy soldiers, it can't be surprising that computers are an increasingly integral part of operating a business. As the computer becomes a more common tool in business, auditors will need to better understand the use of computers in the development of financial information.

This article discusses how auditors can audit in a computer environment. It describes what essential information an auditor should look for, how the auditor can efficiently obtain that information and how he or she can effectively evaluate those findings.

COMPUTER PROCESSING
IS DIFFERENT

Auditors who are unfamiliar with the workings of computers should be aware that some things change in a computer environment. The first is visibility. For example, the auditor may not be able to observe what initiated a transaction that was processed by a computer. To illustrate; a transaction may be initiated by making an entry directly into a computer terminal. Those entries may not produce any printed evidence of the transaction initiation. Also, even if a transaction is initiated by a written form, management is more likely to decide that a computer record of the transaction eliminates the need to retain the original written form supporting the transaction. As a result, written information may be available for only a limited period of time, or it may be stored in a manner that makes it difficult to observe.

An auditor also may find it difficult to observe what a computer did as it processed a transaction. Some transactions, such as interest calculations, may be initiated by a computer and performed with no visible evidence of the calculations made. Many internal accounting controls, such as edit checks and check digits, may reside within a computer program; therefore, no visible evidence that they were actually executed is available.

Furthermore, a computer has the ability to process transactions to simultaneously accomplish several purposes. For example, the production of a unit of finished goods inventory may be processed by a computer to simultaneously update perpetual inventory records, develop standard cost variances, reorder raw materials and develop production reports by location. Such reports may be produced by a computer without a visible audit trail that can be related to the individual transactions, and this problem may be further complicated by summarization of the related details.

The nature and extent of computer processing in a client's accounting system influences the auditor's examination of financial statements. The most significant way in which computer processing affects the audit is in regard to the study and evaluation of internal accounting control. This article examines that phase of the audit first. A discussion of the other principal aspect of the audit influenced by computer processing — the design of audit tests — follows.

The second difference in a computer environment is facilities. Although many small electronic data processing systems can be placed in a normal office environment and can operate practically without notice, large-scale computers require special facilities. These are generally described as separate "computer rooms," with environmental controls and security measures to prevent unauthorized access.

Staffing is the third difference. When a small EDP system is acquired, hardware and software may be included as a package, and the programs and equipment are operated by regular employees. These "turn-key" systems require training to be used but no programming or other special EDP skills. As a result with small systems, EDP technical people in large numbers don't have to be hired to manage and operate the EDP system. In large-scale systems, however, an entire department must be created to use the computer; this includes programmers, operators, a librarian, key-punch operators, data control clerks and managers.

The fourth difference is a computer's effect on segregation of duties. Data gathering and accumulating activities are centralized under EDP. This has the advantage of permitting a better application of centralized controls. However, it may adversely affect good segregation of duties because functions formerly performed separately by independent people are now performed by the computer, giving people within the EDP function access to many aspects of the record-keeping process.

The final difference brought about by the computer is uniformity of processing. Once information is placed into the computer system, it will be processed the same way as previous or subsequent information as long as some aspect of the system itself isn't changed. If data is being processed correctly, it will be processed correctly on a consistent basis. However, if it is being processed incorrectly because of program errors, it will be consistently incorrect as well.

IT'S A MATTER OF DEGREE

Simple computer applications are characterized by transaction trails that the auditor can easily trace through computer processing, with essentially all processing accomplished by one or a few simple programs. However, very complex applications can involve a number of sophisticated processing functions including updates of many different records and accounts. A significant loss of visible transaction trails often occurs, and controls over transactions before and after computer processing (user controls) are difficult or costly to establish in these cases. Often auditors examining financial statements prepared from accounting records that were generated by limited, simple computer processing were able to successfully "audit around the computer" by relying on user controls entirely. But as the complexity and pervasiveness of computer processing grows, it is increasingly difficult for an auditor to effectively audit around the computer, and the controls within the computer must be relied on.

Many auditors feel uncomfortable when faced with performing a study and evaluation of internal accounting control in a computer environment. Perhaps more than anything else, it is their emphasis on what is different in computer processing that creates that feeling. While the differences can't be overlooked, computer processing can be best understood if the auditor focuses his attention on the similarities, rather than the differences, between auditing in a computer environment and auditing in a traditional manual environment.

The primary focus of the audit is directed at assessing the likelihood of material errors or irregularities in the financial statements. Computer processing, like manual processing, can be visualized as a stream of processing from the source of a transaction to the inclusion of that transaction in the financial statements. That stream includes points at which errors or irregularities might occur. It is this stream of transaction processing and the related risks of errors and irregularities at processing points that should be the focus of the auditor's attention, regardless of the form of transaction processing. When viewed in these terms, the basic difference between a manual system and a computer system is that the computer system contains more points at which errors and irregularities can occur. The key to using that basic logic when auditing in a computer environment is knowing what and where these points are and to evaluate the related internal accounting controls. The following approach will help an auditor identify and evaluate the essential information he needs to perform a study and evaluation of internal accounting control in

any accounting system from simple, manual processing to the most complex computer environment.

FOLLOWING THE FLOW

First, the auditor should identify significant financial statement amounts. Significant financial statement amounts are amounts that can be expected to materially affect financial statement presentation. For example, customer receivables would ordinarily be expected to be significant financial statement amounts to a manufacturing company, while receivables from employees might not be significant to that company. The two forms of receivables are likely to be accounted for differently.

The auditor should trace the flow of transactions back from the financial statements to its source, regardless of whether the transactions flow through manual or computer processing. It is more efficient to follow individual transactions that make up significant financial statement amounts backwards to their sources because it reduces the likelihood that the auditor will spend time tracing the flow of financial information to points unrelated to the financial statements. For example, if the auditor is attempting to identify the flow of sales transactions from their origins to the financial statements, he generally would need to follow multiple copies of a sales invoice, some of which only generate internal information, such as sales reports by location. Because of the ability of a computer to simultaneously process data to produce numerous summarized reports, following the flow of multiple copies through a computer system is likely to result in a number of "false starts." Starting from the financial statements helps to assure that the auditor will follow only processing flows that relate directly to the significant financial statement amounts.

Once the auditor has identified the flow of transactions from financial statements back to the source, he needs to identify the processing points in that flow. Processing points are points at which transactions are initiated, recorded, changed, summarized, analyzed or reported. It is at these points that errors and irregularities can occur. Computer processing can include several or many identifiable processing points.

Because errors and irregularities can be introduced at every processing point, the auditor needs to consider what type of potential errors and irregularities might occur at each point and their possible effect on the financial statements. For example, a customer could place an order, and it could be incorrectly recorded. This might cause an error in sales revenue, cost of sales, accounts receivable and inventory. Exhibit 1 summarizes the most common types of errors and irregularities that occur in the EDP phases of processing. For each of these, the exhibit shows the most likely effect on the transactions being processed. This effect, along with the specific type of transactions, determines the effect on the financial statement accounts.

Auditors should note that the various effects on transactions processed shown in Exhibit 1 are directly related to the broad objectives of internal control cited in section 320 of Statement on Auditing Standards no. 1, *Codification of Auditing Standards and Procedures.* [1]

After the auditor has identified the risks at each processing point, he should identify the specific control procedures prescribed at each point. The control system should include controls over the processing points at which the transaction flow enters and leaves computer processing. Also, the computer programs should include controls over the processing of the transactions by the computer. Exhibit 2 illustrates some control techniques the auditor is likely to encounter for each of the EDP errors and irregularities listed in Exhibit 1.

Properly designed systems of internal accounting control include certain characteristics that help the auditor to assure that the specific control procedures are applied as prescribed. These "general controls" include, for example, hiring competent people who have integrity, assigning responsibility to employees in a manner that segregates incompatible duties and observing the overall operation of transaction processing. Although those general controls may not prevent or detect errors and irregularities without the application of specific control procedures, they help to assure that the prescribed specific control procedures function as designed. In computer processing, the general controls found in manual processing are generally absent or are less relevant. For example, duties that are traditionally considered to be incompatible may be concentrated in the computer processing department, providing little opportunity for personnel to observe improper transaction processing. However, computer processing uses different forms of general controls that help to assure that procedures designed to control the processing of transactions will function properly. General controls in computer processing include, for example, procedures designed to prevent or detect unauthorized changes to computer programs and procedures designed to prevent or detect unauthorized access to data stored on, or processed by, the computer or unauthorized access to the computer itself.

EVALUATING THE CONTROLS

Evaluating the effectiveness of general controls and specific control procedures designed to minimize the risk at each processing point may appear complex. One rea-

Exhibit 1. EDP Errors and Irregularities and Related Effects on Transactions Processed

IMPACT ON TRANSACTIONS PROCESSED

EDP ERRORS AND IRREGULARITIES	Transactions Are Improperly Authorized	Transactions Are Invalid	All Transactions Aren't Recorded	Amounts Are Incorrect	Transactions Are Improperly Classified	Cutoff Is Improper	Posting and Summarization Are Improper	Access to Assets Is Inappropriate	Recorded Accountability Isn't Properly Reconciled to Assets
Input errors									
Data lost			X						
Data duplicated		X						X	
Data inaccurate				X	X	X			
Data missing	X		X	X	X	X			
Blanket authorization of transaction	X	X							
Internal initiation of transaction	X	X	X					X	
Processing errors									
Wrong file	X		X						
Wrong record	X		X			X			
Incomplete			X				X		
Incorrect				X	X	X	X		
Untimely						X			
Inappropriate	X							X	
Lost files, programs			X						
Output errors									
Improper distribution	X							X	
Late or lost			X			X			
Erroneous but plausible	X	X		X	X	X	X		X
Excessive error correction	X		X	X	X		X		X
Other errors									
Unlimited access	X	X		X				X	X
Management override	X		X		X	X	X	X	X

Exhibit 2.   EDP Control Techniques

EDP CONTROL TECHNIQUES	Input Lost	Input Duplicated	Input Inaccurate	Missing Input Data	Blanket Authorization of Transaction	Internal Initiation of Transaction	Wrong File Processed	Wrong Record Processed	Incomplete Processing
Preprocessing authorization					X				
Preprocessing review	X		X	X					
Batching	X	X			X	X			X
Conversion verification			X	X					
Cutoff procedures									
Master file controls							X		
Balancing		X	X	X		X	X		X
Postprocessing review		X	X	X	X	X	X		X
Periodic internal audit			X	X	X	X			X
Input security controls						X			
Edits			X	X	X		X	X	
Error correction procedures	X	X	X						X
Correct file controls							X		
Programmed reasonableness tests		X	X	X	X				
System matching	X	X						X	
Processing security controls						X	X		
Scheduling							X		X
Recovery and backup procedures							X		

(Exhibit 2 continued on page 270)

son is that some specific control procedures and some general controls may be designed for several or all processing points. Also, an individual specific control procedure may only partially contribute to the control of one specific risk or, alternatively, the control may effectively reduce more than one risk.

To evaluate whether the controls have been adequately designed, the auditor needs to consider whether the potential errors and irregularities for each processing point will be adequately prevented or detected by the specified control procedures. One practical method of doing this is to design a table relating the controls to the risks. Exhibit 2, in effect, constitutes one such table in normative terms. The vertical columns list the potential risks that the auditor has identified for each processing point. The horizontal rows identify the related controls, including both specific control procedures and general controls.

To use such a table in an actual situation, an auditor first would list the risks he has identified at each of the processing points in the transaction stream for the significant financial statement amount. Next, he would describe the internal accounting controls prescribed for that transaction stream. The auditor then would consider each control and

Exhibit 2.   (continued)

EDP CONTROL TECHNIQUES	Incorrect Processing	Untimely Processing	Inappropriate Processing	Lost Files, Programs	Improper Distribution of Output	Late or Lost Output	Erroneous but Plausible Output	Excessive Error Correction	Unlimited Access	Management Override
Preprocessing authorization			X						X	X
Preprocessing review		X								
Batching		X	X						X	
Conversion verification										
Cutoff procedures		X								
Master file controls				X					X	
Balancing	X						X	X	X	
Postprocessing review	X		X		X	X	X	X		X
Periodic internal audit	X		X				X	X	X	X
Input security controls			X						X	X
Edits										
Error correction procedures	X						X	X		
Correct file controls									X	
Programmed reasonableness tests							X			
System matching										
Processing security controls			X	X	X	X			X	X
Scheduling		X	X	X	X	X			X	X
Recovery and backup procedures				X				X		

decide which of the risks are partially or fully controlled by that procedure. If the control is essential to adequately reducing the risk, a symbol would be marked in the box corresponding to the specific control procedure and the related risk. If the procedure is essentially redundant, a different symbol would be marked in the appropriate box. No mark would be made if the control doesn't contribute to reducing the risk. After considering all the controls, the auditor would review the entries in the column for each risk and evaluate whether the prescribed controls are adequate to reduce that risk. The auditor could also add a final column to his table and mark in the appropriate boxes his evaluations of the degree to which the risk has been limited. These, in turn, would be interpreted in terms of transactions and would affect the accounts, as illustrated in Exhibit 1.

SKILLS AND SPECIALISTS

Many auditors using this approach will find that they can perform the review without the assistance of a computer specialist. The transaction flow and the related controls for many simple forms of computer processing can generally be obtained from client procedures manuals or from discussion with client personnel. These should be understandable to an auditor with basic computer skills. Such skills ordinarily include a general understanding of basic computer controls and the basic capabilities of computer software.

If reliance on controls over systems that involve very complex computer processing technology is either desirable or essential for performing an audit, the auditor may need the assistance of a computer specialist to identify some or all of the essential information described in this article. If the auditor doesn't have a computer specialist on his staff, he should consider obtaining the assistance of a specialist from an asssociation of CPA firms, the staff of another CPA firm, a university professor or a computer consulting firm. The approach in this article is especially helpful to an auditor using the assistance of a computer specialist because it allows the auditor to

- efficiently communicate what essential information is required from the computer specialist
- review the sufficiency of the work of the computer specialist, and
- integrate information provided by the computer specialist into his overall understanding and evaluation of the accounting and control systems.

DESIGNING AUDIT TESTS

An auditor considers the computer in several ways when he designs audit tests.

- The auditor needs to test internal accounting controls over computer processing on which he plans to rely. As pointed out, some controls, such as edit checks and check digits, may not provide visible evidence of performance. The auditor will need to design procedures using the computer to test those controls.
- It may be more efficient to use the assistance of a computer in performing substantive tests of accounting data that is recorded on a computer file even though it is possible to test that data without using a computer. For example, it may be faster and less expensive to use a computer to recalculate depreciation expense for all fixed assets maintained on computer records than to recompute depreciation manually for a selection of fixed assets.
- The accounting system may include transactions that can't be properly tested without the assistance of a computer. For example, if transaction processing doesn't provide visible evidence of what was performed or if accounting records are maintained only in computer-readable form, the auditor may need to design substantive tests using the assistance of a computer.

Although a discussion on the design of specific procedures for the circumstances described above is beyond the scope of this article, the explicit approach described in this article will be especially helpful to the auditor in accomplishing this task. The auditor should first identify the assertions the client is making in the financial statements. For example, one assertion may be that sales are for a certain amount. The auditor should then formulate an audit objective directed toward each assertion and decide what information is essential to achieving that objective. For example, the objective may be to assess the likelihood of error in the amount of a sale or the classification of sales in the financial statements. Once the auditor has identified the essential information, he should design an appropriate procedure to gather the information.

Sometimes even an auditor who possesses basic computer skills may find it necessary to seek assistance from a computer specialist to design complex technical procedures. However, the auditor who first identifies the essential information required to meet the related audit objective will be able to specify the role of the computer specialist, review the sufficiency of that work and evaluate the results of his findings.

SUMMARY

The approach to understanding transaction processing and the related controls described in this article can be applied to either manual or computer processing. It is especially useful in evaluating controls over computer processing because it allows the auditor to deal with more complexity and a greater level of detail when assessing the likelihood of errors and irregularities.

NOTES

1. Statement on Auditing Standards no. 1, *Codification of Auditing Standards and Procedures* (New York: AICPA, 1973). See also *AICPA Professional Standards,* vol. 1 (Chicago: Commerce Clearing House), AU section 320. For a discussion of the objectives of internal control, see James K. Loebbecke and George R. Zuber, "Evaluating Internal Control," JofA, Feb. 80, pp. 49–56.

QUESTIONS

1. The shift from a manual accounting system to a computer system introduces several new control risks, such as lack of a traditional audit trail and potential loss of separation of duties. List ten exposures that occur because of a shift to EDP.

2. The authors briefly mention auditing "around" versus auditing "through" the computer. Briefly describe the differences in these audit techniques from the standpoint of audit procedures and objectives.

3. The suggested audit philosophy in this paper is to "follow the flow" from financial statements to source documents, and not vice versa. Is this concept defensible, or should tests occur in both directions?

4. Exhibit 2 offers a matrix approach for control evaluation. Can you improve this matrix through quantification of control strength or other means?

5. Differentiate between application and general controls. Give three examples of each type.

6. How would you go about testing the reliability of a control embedded in software, such as an internal edit check?

7. The issue of utilizing computer audit specialists was raised in this paper. Do you agree that firms should have audit "generalists" and "specialists," or do you believe that all auditors should have EDP expertise?

8. Some people offer the viewpoint that it is easier to teach audit savvy to a computer information systems graduate than it is to train an auditor in complex computer topics. Defend one of these positions as superior to the other.

Auditing and Controls in a Database Environment*

INTRODUCTION

Many of the principles developed by auditors over the years for traditional accounting systems remain highly relevant for today's database systems. These principles have important implications for the design and use of database systems, but they are too often neglected by system designers. In practice there is a good amount of overlap in the *objectives* of auditors and system designers, but their points of view are different. In this chapter we describe the principles and practices of audit and control from a database security viewpoint. The chapter should also provide some insight into the auditor's view of security and integrity.

BASIC CONCEPTS

The Objectives of Auditing and Controls

Auditing is the examination of information by someone other than the persons who produced it or who use it. The goal is to establish the reliability of the information and thus to make it more useful. The best-known use of auditing is by certified public accountants, who conduct an audit so that they can *attest* to financial statements (that is, assume responsibility for the fairness of the statements). This *independent* or *external* audit, conducted by objective outside persons, examines not only the financial statements but also accounting records and other relevant information. The auditors write a report based on the audit, expressing their opinion of the financial statement.

Internal audit is carried out *within* an enterprise, usually by an internal audit group that reports to a high level in the enterprise or to an audit committee of the board of directors. Internal auditors are therefore independent of the audited function or department. One of the main purposes of internal audit is to monitor and evaluate the system of *internal control,* which includes a wide variety of measures taken to promote effective operation of the enterprise. It is the goal of internal control to ensure that management policy is carried out, that various kinds of exposures are prevented, and that the enterprise operates efficiently. An adequate system of internal control is required by U.S. law for all companies that report to the Securities and Exchange Commission [5]. The Foreign Cor-

*By Rita C. Summers, Eduardo B. Fernandez, and Christopher Wood. R. Summers, E. Fernandez, and C. Wood, *Database Security and Integrity,* © 1981, Addison-Wesley, Reading, Massachusetts. Excerpted material from Chapter 9. Reprinted with permission.

rupt Practices Act of 1977 requires such a company to maintain an internal control system to ensure that:

- Transactions are executed in accordance with management authorization.[1]
- Transactions are recorded in order to prepare an accurate financial statement and to account for assets.
- Access to assets is permitted only in accordance with management's authorization.

When the enterprise relies on a computerized information system, the objectives of internal control encompass those of database security and integrity.

Effect of the Database Environment

Although the goals remain the same, some dramatic differences are apparent when we consider auditing and controls in a computer environment.

- Because the more technical steps are now automated, the remaining manual procedures are often performed by people who are unfamiliar with the data and with accounting practices and are therefore less able to review or check.
- The elimination of manual steps has also eliminated both visual checking and traditional paper audit trails. As EFT systems grow in usage, visible audit trails will become even more rare.
- Perpetrators of fraud can copy information or destroy evidence extremely rapidly and less visibly. (Compare erasing a tape with burning a bushel of documents.)
- Human beings cannot directly see the data. This means that error or fraud is less likely to be detected by chance. It also means that the auditor either must use independent programs to examine data, or must rely on the audited system's programs.

A database environment implies further differences:

- Functions and data previously separated (operating data and financial data, for exam-

ple) are being integrated. While this is a positive step in most respects, one result is that redundancy and independent sources for comparison are lost. A single program may perform a combination of tasks that would be considered incompatible (for control purposes) if performed by a human being.
- Today's database and application systems span many different functional areas of the enterprise. The complexity of these integrated systems makes it difficult for the auditor to understand them.
- The sheer size of many databases makes it difficult to scan them for irregularities.

When the database system also processes online transactions still other differences appear:

- Often the user who initiates a transaction also enters the data, so there is less opportunity for checking.
- Transactions are initiated from remote terminals, which may be outside the administrative control of the computer installation or even the enterprise.
- The sequence of processing is less repeatable, because transactions arrive randomly.
- Transactions are processed singly rather than in batches, so various batch controls cannot be used.
- Continuous operation makes auditing more difficult, since activity on the database cannot be stopped while auditing is done.
- Update in place eliminates the automatic creation of generations of files that formerly served as useful controls. It also means that a complete file is rarely processed at one time, so there is no occasion to check control information.

On the other hand, the database environment makes it possible to *improve* audit and control. The computer itself is a valuable tool. For example, the auditor can perform sophisticated statistical sampling of records to be examined, scan complete databases, or calculate relationships among different records. A number of the traditional controls can be supported by the DBMS, and new types of control are possible using DBMS features. Online inquiry restores the visibility of data, making it easier to detect errors. The increased use of distributed processing is making it possible to reintroduce some traditional controls. A node in a distributed system can collect a batch of transactions and compute control information before passing the batch to another node for processing. In an EFT system, for example, both the terminal device and the central system can maintain control totals and transaction logs.

Control Principles

A thorough survey [41] turned up numerous control practices, but nearly all of them reflect a very few basic principles or policies:

1. **Establish separation of responsibility.** This is always good practice. For example, one person authorizes paychecks, and another person prepares them. One person changes a program, a committee approves the change, and someone else installs it. Responsibility should also be rotated. The data processing department should be independent of users.

2. **Prevent errors and violations.** Errors are prevented by various types of "passive" controls, such as the careful design of display screens and input forms to reduce input errors. A more "active" measure is to restrict the portion of the database a program can access.

3. **Check validity of processing and data.** Checking of validity while a process is being performed (sometimes called *in-process audit*) is exemplified by the checking of semantic integrity constraints. Redundant information may be entered or kept in the database to support this checking, which is done at *control points*. When a problem is found, it is important to *follow up* to determine the cause and to correct both the cause and its effects. *Editing* of input data

detects errors that passive controls did not prevent.

4. **Produce an audit trail.** An audit trail is a history of the activities of a system. It is produced during processing and used for *post-process audit*. This audit can be more global than in-process audit, reviewing transactions and their results over a long period of time. More complex analysis is possible.

The Audit Process

In this section we first summarize the major steps in *independent* audits. These steps are followed whether or not computers are involved, but computer-based systems require new methodology in each step.

1. **Review internal control.** In this step the auditor obtains an understanding of the system of internal control (through interviews, observation, and studying documentation) and writes a description that is used in other steps of the audit.

2. **Test the system.** The auditor determines, through *tests of compliance,* whether the internal control system actually behaves according to its description. One type of compliance test, called a *transaction test,* follows specific transactions through the system. For example, the auditor might follow a sample of sales orders through all of their processing. In *functional tests* the auditor concentrates on whether a single procedure has been performed consistently and effectively on all transactions. Other tests trace actions back to the transactions that caused them.

3. **Evaluate the system.** The results of the first two steps determine (a) whether the auditors recommend improvements to the internal control system, and (b) how much the remainder of the audit can rely on data produced by the system.

4. **Conduct substantive tests.** Substantive tests are directed at the values of specific items of the financial statement. Such a test might check, for example,

that the accounts receivable amount is correct.

Audit of Computer-based Systems

Because of the technical knowledge required for auditing computerized systems, there is now an auditing specialty known as *EDP audit,* and the American Institute of Certified Public Accountants has published a statement on standards for the independent audit of these systems [18, 38], as well as guidelines for study and evaluation of the internal controls [4]. The auditor's responsibilities have been interpreted for a computer environment as:

- understanding the system,
- verifying the phases of processing, and
- verifying the results of processing.

Techniques to help the auditor carry out each of these responsibilities are described in the section on Computer Auditing Techniques.

Types of Audits

Audits — outside or internal — of computer-based systems can have varying objectives [17, 25]. Some examples are:

- *Installation security audit.* The focus here is on computer assets, including hardware, software, and data. Examples of the items covered are: access to the media library, casualty insurance, and disaster recovery plans.
- *Operation audit.* This is an audit of the operation of a computer installation.
- *Application system audit.* The term *application system* refers to an integrated set of programs, such as those that make up a billing system. This type of audit (also called the *"postinstallation audit"*) reviews the entire application system, including controls, program logic, and data.
- *Fraud audit.* An audit to determine whether fraudulent manipulation has occurred will tend to be more complete (and more costly) than an audit with more general goals.

COMMON FORMS OF COMPUTER FRAUD

It is useful to consider which types of computer fraud occur most frequently. Most of the cases fall into three general categories [1, 20], where the fraud is perpetrated either by manipulating input transactions, by modifying programs, or by altering files. We briefly describe each of these techniques in turn.

Input Manipulation Schemes. These schemes, which showed up most frequently in a study of 150 fraud cases, may be categorized further as follows:

- An extra transaction is entered that benefits the perpetrator in some way. This might be, for example, a phony purchase order.
- A valid transaction is not entered. An example is the failure to record the death of a pensioner, thus allowing payments to continue.
- An authorized transaction is modified so that incorrect information is placed in the database.
- Error-correction procedures are misused. These procedures are often vulnerable to fraudulent use, especially if they bypass the normal security measures.

Program Modification Schemes. Programs can be modified to perform or aid many different types of fraudulent action. For example, undocumented transactions can be included in the code, control totals can be incorrectly maintained, and files incorrectly modified. These modifications can be made when the program is initially written, when authorized changes are made, or at any other time, if access to the program library can be obtained.

File Alteration Schemes. While many file alteration schemes are really variants of the two previous types of schemes, there are some specific techniques, such as:

• use of a utility or special-purpose program to modify a master file, or
• substitution of an alternative file for the real file.

We will discuss in the following sections controls that can be used to prevent these types of fraud.

CONTROL PRACTICES

In auditing standards, controls are classified as "general" or "application." Figures 1 and 2 list the controls according to this classification, and Fig. 3 lists some additional database considerations used by auditors in reviewing general controls. Since the distinction between general and application controls is less relevant in a database environment, we group control practices here as they pertain to:

• transaction initiation and data entry,
• database content, processing, and access, and
• database storage.

Although we concentrate on controls *within* the automated system, *external* controls and procedures are equally important, as is the relationship between the two kinds of controls.

Figure 1.   Categories of General Controls

GENERAL CONTROLS

Organization and Operation Controls
1. Segregation of functions between EDP department and users.
2. Authorization over execution of transactions.
3. Segregation of functions within EDP.

Systems Development and Documentation Controls
4. Active participation by users, accounting department, and internal auditors in system design and software acquisition.
5. Written specifications, reviewed by management and user departments.
6. Testing a joint effort of users and EDP, including manual and computerized parts of system.
7. Final approval from management, users, and EDP before placing system in operation.
8. Control of the file conversion to prevent unauthorized changes.
9. Approval of all changes to the operational system.
10. Formal documentation procedures.

Hardware and Systems Software Controls
11. Maximal utilization of control features of hardware, operating system, and other software.
12. Change control for systems software.

Access Controls
13. Need-to-know access to program documentation.
14. Need-to-know access to data files and programs.
15. Control of access to hardware.

Data and Procedural Controls
16. Controls on data receipt and recording, error followup, and distribution of output.
17. Written manual for computer operations.
18. Review and evaluation of systems by internal auditors at critical stages of development.
19. Continuing review and test by internal auditors.

Figure 2.   Categories of Application Controls

APPLICATION CONTROLS

Input Controls
1. Only authorized and approved input accepted by EDP.
2. Verification of all codes used to represent data.
3. Control of conversion of data into machine-sensible form.
4. Control of movement of data between processing steps, or between departments.
5. Control of error correction and resubmission of corrected transactions.

Processing Controls
6. Control totals produced during processing reconciled with input control totals.
7. Controls to prevent processing the wrong file, detect file manipulation errors, and highlight operator-caused errors.
8. Limit and reasonableness checks.
9. Verification of control totals at appropriate points in the processing cycle.

Output Controls
10. Output control totals reconciled with input and processing controls.
11. Output tested by comparison to original source documents.
12. Output distributed only to authorized users.

Figure 3.   Database Considerations in Review of General Controls

AUDITORS' CRITERIA

Adequacy of database administration
Control functions performed by DBA
Separation of data control from application
  development
DBMS used
Number of databases and their usage
Adequacy of database documentation
Access control for database documentation

Controls on Transaction Initiation and Data Entry

It is important to limit (if possible through access rules) who can initiate each type of transaction. This type of control supports a least-privilege "need-to-do" policy. Controls on transaction initiation also enforce separation of responsibility. An organization may draw up a "transaction-conflicts matrix,"

specifying which combinations of transactions should not be available to the same person. For example, a cash refund transaction may conflict with a transaction that alters customers records. In the matrix of Fig. 4, transactions T_1 and T_2 conflict.

Additional control is achieved by authorizing only certain terminals for a transaction, and by restricting the people who can use a terminal. This can be done by access rules, by keeping the terminal in a controlled area, or through a lock on the terminal. It is also important to log *unsuccessful attempts* to initiate a transaction.

Figure 4.   Transaction-Conflicts Matrix

	T_1	T_2	T_3
T_1		X	
T_2	X		
T_3			

When a transaction is started, it can be assigned a unique identifier, such as a sequence number, which is displayed to the user. The user and the system use this identifier to ensure that no transaction is lost and that no transaction is processed more than once. It is often desirable, for both efficiency and control, to collect a *batch* of transactions, which are then processed as a group. The collection is done either manually, by a central processor, or by a cluster controller or distributed processor. Certain *control totals* are computed for the batch and checked against the results. For example, suppose a branch office authorizes payroll checks for its staff and specifies their amounts, and a central office prepares the checks. The branch can compute the number of checks and the dollar total, for comparison against the returned checks.

Some application systems automatically generate transactions. For example, when the quantity of an item in stock reaches the order level, a replenishment transaction may be generated. It is essential to produce a visible log or report of such system-generated transactions.

A number of control techniques are aimed at accurate data entry [30, 41]. Since error is always possible in any manual data entry, the amount of data to be entered should be kept to a minimum. Techniques to reduce data entry include preformatted display screens and menus, default responses, and *turnaround documents,* such as a utility bill, which is returned with the payment and which contains a machine-readable account number. Appropriate design of identifiers allows the system to detect data entry errors.

Account numbers usually include one or more check digits, which are a function of all the other digits. (This is just one example of redundancy as a control technique.) Applications can be programmed to expect certain

data (such as a time card for each employee) and to produce exception reports about missing data.

Input can be edited for appropriate formats: alphabetic or numeric, proper number of fields and characters. Input editing also uses criteria that play the same role as database semantic integrity constraints. *Reasonableness checks* compare the input value against preestablished criteria. A value for a person can be tested for extreme deviation from a group average, or from that person's own past history. (Did the customer's electricity utilization for March differ greatly from that of the previous March?) One user response can be tested for consistency with others. For example, the answers to "How many persons in your family?" and "Name the persons." More complex checks use statistical properties of the database to determine what is reasonable [21].

The *database* integrity constraints potentially could be used for input editing. What is needed is a specification to the input-editing program of what database item corresponds to an input item, and a way for the editor to invoke the DBMS constraint-checking mechanism.

Interactive data entry has the advantage that the system can detect errors immediately. If the system uses display screens the erroneous information can be highlighted and the correct information protected from change until the user corrects the error. If a batch transaction is rejected because of invalid data, there must be logging and follow-up to ensure that the corrected transaction eventually is performed. Otherwise the execution of transactions could be prevented simply by creating errors. Error-correction transactions are often quite complicated and may introduce additional errors. An error should be corrected by the group that introduced it, and not by the data processing department. Corrections need the same editing checks as the original transaction, as well as additional controls, including authorization by someone other than the person who made the original error.

Controls on Data Content and Access

Control Information in the Database. Special information can be kept in the database specifically for control purposes. Since an application system may involve checking at various stages and by a number of different programs, an item sometimes carries a *data quality flag* indicating what checks it has passed. It may have an *expiration date,* which can be used to periodically purge obsolete data.

Redundancy that exists in the database for efficiency reasons may also be used for control. *Item counts,* for example, should be maintained whenever random updating occurs and checked whenever the set of items is processed sequentially. (This checking should always be done when the set of items is copied.) Periodic scanning of a database to check controls of this type is useful. Unfortunately, it is difficult for designers to select a good time in the processing cycle for checking. For one thing, the database may rarely be free of update activity and therefore available for checking control information. This problem can be alleviated somewhat by partitioning a file or database into sections, each of which has its own control data. Then only one section at a time has to be locked for auditing. Control totals can also reduce the level of concurrency in the system if many different update transactions have to increment the same controls.

Cross-footing balance checks (Figure 5) involve categorizing items in different ways, computing totals for each category, and comparing the grand totals for the different categorizations. *Hash totals* are meaning-

Figure 5.   Cross-Footing Balance Controls

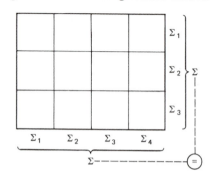

less totals used to verify that all items are correctly transmitted, processed, or stored. A hash total might be computed, for example, by summing all the customer numbers in a batch of sales orders. A *control total* is some meaningful total, such as the dollar total of a batch of paychecks.

Labels on storage volumes should be checked by the operating system to ensure that the right data is processed, and any bypass of this checking should be logged.

Semantic integrity constraints (whether implemented by application programs or by the DBMS) also depend on special control information.

Controls on Database Access. Need-to-know access control supports the principle of separation of responsibility, and flexible authorization facilities make it possible to rotate responsibility frequently.

Coadministration, which spreads the data control and authorization function among several administrators, is a useful control because it makes collusion necessary to grant access improperly. Different types of coadministration policies can be specified [9], such as:

- all the coadministrators must agree,
- the majority of the coadministrators must agree, or

• at least a specified number of coadministrators must agree.

In another possible approach to separation of responsibility [13, 26], sometimes called "cooperative authorization," the actual access of some object by a subject requires the approval or cooperation of other subjects. Subjects receive rights that are conditional or incomplete; they must be complemented with other subjects' rights to perform some action. This contrasts with co-administration, where only the *granting* of a right by an administrator requires approval from other administrators.

Authorizing programs to access specific data, as in IMS, is a good control practice, as is control of program-to-program linkage.

Most systems exhibit regular patterns of usage of programs and data. Deviations from these patterns, such as great increases or decreases in activity on particular parts of the database, can be detected by operators or by analysis of logs, and should result in exception reports. Periodic reports on dormant data may reveal irregularities. If the dormant data is obsolete it should be purged, both to comply with privacy standards and to conserve resources.

Program Library. As a particularly critical component of the database, the program library needs special controls. The system's production load modules should be kept in separate libraries, to which access is strictly limited. Strict control of access to source programs and documentation is equally important. A change to a production program normally must be approved by several independent groups or individuals. It is good practice to maintain a log of these changes and approvals. Changes that are not emergency fixes are best saved in batches for "block cut-in" (analogous to a software vendor's release), rather than being applied one at a time. Versions should be clearly identified, and old versions retained. Vendor-supplied software sometimes includes control features to identify modules that have been changed from the shipped version. (This is part of a more general need to verify the authenticity of software.) Other useful controls include hash totals and comparing modules for differences.

Controls on Database Storage

The online access control of a DBMS must be supplemented by control over the storage media such as disks, tapes, diskettes, and hard-copy documents. The media library should be a separate function, with its own authorized personnel in organizations that are large enough, and with a separate space to which access can be controlled. The library maintains inventory records and media-use records, and controls the retention and release of media. Encryption can be used to protect storage media against unauthorized reading and to reduce the gain from theft. Storage of copies off-site is also valuable. (A practical set of guidelines for control of the media library is given in [20].)

THE AUDIT TRAIL

The audit trail serves as a bridge between controls (which produce the audit trail) and auditing (which uses it). It provides the information that allows auditors to verify the system of controls and the results of processing. The audit trail must be complete, or at least must select what to record in a way that cannot be predicted and that covers all actions that may later have to be audited. The audit trail then becomes a significant deterrent to fraud. The audit trail allows post-process auditing to reconstruct a sequence of actions: who initiated them, the time, and the results.

Bjork [6] has provided an excellent summary of audit trail requirements for transaction-oriented database applications. The audit-trail function has three main aspects:

- detection of the actions to be recorded,
- the actual recording, and
- support for auditing.

Some desirable features in a generalized audit-trail function are:

- It is transparent to the process being audited.
- It is a generalized facility supporting *all* applications.
- It allows the real sequence of events to be reconstructed.
- Recording can be selectively and dynamically started and stopped.
- Events to be recorded can be specified in terms of: the process (or application) to be audited, time, data objects and their values, database operations, transaction type, or combinations of these criteria.
- What to record for each event can be specified.

We mentioned earlier that database systems, with their destructive updating, lose certain advantages of older systems, which retained generations of files. A generalized audit trail would allow these advantages to be regained by adding a time dimension to the database. An earlier version of a data item could be accessed; an earlier version could even be *corrected,* in the sense that all its uses would be recorded and could be "undone." Suppose, for example, that an error were found in the records about an individual. All uses of the erroneous data could be traced. If erroneous reports had been sent, corrections could be mailed. The propagation of the error through the database could also be traced.

Some of the items to be included in the audit-trail entry are:

- operation or event that caused the entry to be made,

- time of the event,
- application program,
- transaction sequence number,
- user,
- terminal (or line or port),
- name of the data object (if one is involved),
- some means of identifying the *occurrence* [2] of the object,
- new value and old value.

(Some of these can be factored out so that they need not appear in each entry.) An audit-trail entry describes a specific execution of a request. However, the audit trail need not be limited to *database* requests; it can also include user and operator commands.

Although it is common practice to combine the audit trail and the recovery log, they are conceptually distinct. Each needs data not needed for the other, one major difference being that a recovery log does not usually record *read* operations. (See Figure 6.) There is therefore some argument for physically separating the recovery log and the audit trail. Processing of the recovery log should not be slowed by the need to pass over audit data. The recovery procedure itself must appear in the audit trail. A separate audit trail is more secure, since access can be restricted to the auditor. However, maintaining separate logs is undoubtedly more expensive.

A number of issues remain to be resolved for a generalized audit trail. For example, we would like it to be valid "forever." But will the entries remain meaningful after the structure of the database changes? What *level* of event or operation is recorded? If higher-level events are recorded the audit must "trust" the system's mapping of these to lower-level events. Is there one audit trail or several? Some ways to distribute the audit trail would be: by data class, by user class, by type of database operation, by application

Figure 6.   Relationship Between Recovery Log and Audit Trail

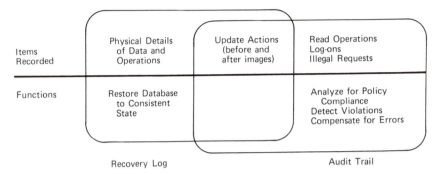

Items Recorded	Physical Details of Data and Operations	Update Actions (before and after images)	Read Operations Log-ons Illegal Requests
Functions	Restore Database to Consistent State		Analyze for Policy Compliance Detect Violations Compensate for Errors

Recovery Log   Audit Trail

system, or by transaction type. Another issue is the privacy question raised by auditors' examination of the audit trail.

COMPUTER AUDITING TECHNIQUES

In this section we turn to the topic of auditing techniques. The literature on EDP auditing, including a comprehensive survey of the practices of many organizations [41], reveals that auditing practices lag far behind advances in database art. Auditing tends to be file-oriented and to take little account of continuous online operation. Fortunately, the cultural gap between auditors and database practitioners is rapidly narrowing. There is increasing agreement that the DBMS can be used as an audit tool.

Descriptions of auditing techniques and tools can be found in many textbooks, reports, and articles. A number of Generalized Audit software packages are available, but they are designed primarily for use with sequential file structures. Their value has therefore declined with the growing use of DBMSs, and there is no comprehensive tool to replace them. However, many of the techniques used with these packages also apply in a database environment. Our purpose here is to convey some flavor of the techniques, which in many cases are the same ones used

by software developers, but with different names. As shown in Figure 7 we organize the techniques into three major categories, corresponding to the auditor's responsibilities of "understanding the system," "verifying phases of processing," and "verifying results of processing."

Techniques for Understanding the System

Gaining understanding is an organizational and behavioral problem as well as a technical one. The tools are much the same as those used for understanding any complex system. The auditor reviews documentation, such as program listings, flowcharts or HIPO charts [39], and narrative descriptions. System designers and programmers are interviewed, and questionnaires can supplement these interviews. Auditors have also developed a set of analytical auditing symbols for flowcharting the controls of a system. An example control flowchart is shown in Figure 8. Although the symbols and method are file-oriented, the concepts apply to database systems. Automated system-description tools are also becoming available.

Techniques for Verifying Processing

Techniques in this category have the objective of ensuring that all processing is

Figure 7.   Auditing Techniques

UNDERSTANDING THE SYSTEM	VERIFYING PHASES OF PROCESSING	VERIFYING RESULTS OF PROCESSING
Documents:	Test data	*Data selection and extraction:*
Program listings	Base-case system evaluation	Embedded audit-data collection
Flowcharts	Integrated test facility	Extended records
HIPO charts	Tagging	Backup dumps
Narrative	Tracing	Audit package record extraction
Interviews	Mapping	DBMS facilities
Questionnaires	Transaction selection	
Control flowcharting	Parallel simulation	*Data examination:*
System description tools		Control verification
		Semantic integrity
		Independent source comparison

being carried out properly and that controls are working correctly. The techniques apply to both substantive tests and tests of compliance.

1. **Transaction selection.** A sample of transactions can be selected for detailed analysis, according to criteria established by the auditor. The sample can be random or can include, for example, all payment transactions involving over $1,000. The selection software either scans a batch of input transactions, or is invoked by the system's transaction-management component.

2. **Test data.** This technique is an extension of program testing. The auditor prepares transactions to be processed by the system being audited. The correct results are predicted by some independent method and are compared with the actual results. When the test-data method is extended to provide a comprehensive and continually maintained set of test transactions, plus efficient ways of comparing the expected and actual results, it is sometimes called *base case system evaluation.*

   The major problem with this technique is the difficulty of preparing sufficently comprehensive inputs. Test-data generators can help. The test transactions also need a database to run against, so that the real database is not affected; copies or backup versions can sometimes be used. With this and other techniques the auditor must determine that the test data is processed by the programs normally used on real data. This is particularly a problem for outside auditors who audit a company only once or twice a year.

3. **Integrated test facility.** This technique extends the test-data approach by embedding in the database some dummy entities against which to run tests. These entities are there all the time and sometimes form a "mini-company" whose data is processed along with the real company's data. This technique is more realistic, since it uses the normal procedures for system operation.

   Tests can be made all through the year, thus increasing confidence that the audited programs are indeed the ones regularly used. The test data must be removed from the system, however, or its effects undone, so that real results are not affected. (The real company does not want to issue paychecks to employees of the minicompany.) Removing the test data may endanger real data. Care must be taken to guard against this.

Figure 8.   Control Flowcharting

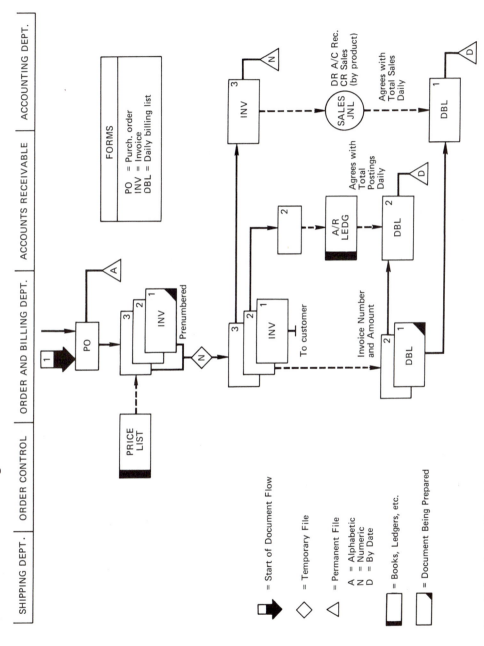

From *Systems Auditability and Control Study.* Copyright © 1977 by the Institute of Internal Auditors, Inc., 249 Maitland Ave., Altamonte Springs, Florida 32701. Reprinted with permission.

4. **Transaction tagging (snapshot), tracing, and mapping.** Special logic is sometimes added to programs at key points to display or record relevant information when processing "tagged" test data (Figure 9). (This auditor manipulation of application code is itself an exposure, however.) Detailed tracing of program execution is occasionally used by internal auditors on complex and critical programs. "Mapping" techniques determine how often sections of code are executed, or which sections are never executed.

5. **Parallel simulation.** With this technique the auditor creates application programs that simulate key functions of the operational system. When the real and simulated systems are given the same data, their results can be compared. The input to the simulation can be taken from the audit trail of the real system (see Figure 10). The simulation is costly to prepare, but special high-level languages can help reduce this cost. Also, the simulation is typically simpler than the real application. For example, simulating the interest computation for a savings account is much simpler than doing the complete account update. Parallel simulation is a promising tool, especially for substantive tests [41], and it remains applicable in a database environment.

Techniques for Verifying Results of Processing

In these techniques, the auditor focuses on the data rather than on the processes. We discuss two problems here:

- how to select and extract the data, and
- what to look for in the data.

Selecting and Extracting Data

1. *The embedded audit data collection* technique inserts into application programs audit modules that collect data according to criteria specified by the auditor. Exception conditions can thus be monitored. This technique could be replaced by a generalized audit trail function.

2. *The extended records* technique establishes a complete audit trail for a transaction, including application-oriented items. The technique requires a substantial amount of application programming, which could be reduced if a generalized audit-trail function allowed the application to augment the general items with its own information.

3. *Backup dumps* that are taken for recovery purposes are also useful for auditing. For example, where an audit trail is available, two successive dumps can be compared

Figure 9.   Transaction Tagging

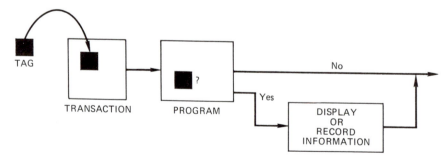

TAG

TRANSACTION   PROGRAM

?

Yes

No

DISPLAY
OR
RECORD
INFORMATION

Figure 10. Parallel Simulation

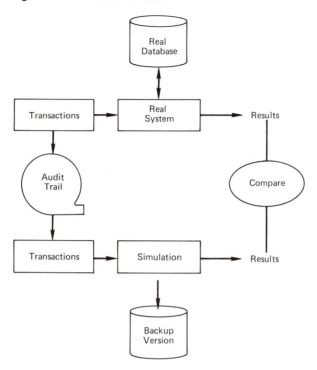

to determine whether all differences are accounted for by transactions. As database storage structures grow more complex, however, the use of dumps becomes more difficult, since the software required to analyze them becomes more complex.

4. The *record extraction* facilities of generalized audit packages have been used widely. They allow records of files to be selected on the basis of combinations of attribute values, or randomly, and placed in work files for further analysis.

5. The *query facilities of the DBMS* can be used to extract the data. These facilities can be used on the database and also on the audit trail if it can be accessed as a normal object of the DBMS. The data-selection capabilities of the query language can then be used to find information such as "Who modified field x at a given time of day?" Although questions have been raised about the auditor's ability to retain independence while relying so heavily on vendor and client software, use of the DBMS may provide the only practical way to extract data.

What to Look For

Once the data has been extracted, the auditor can:

- *Check control information.* Control totals, hash totals, and any other control information can be verified.
- *Check semantic-integrity constraints.*
- *Check the data with an independent source.* The data can be checked against the real-

world object it represents (inventory, for example). It can be checked against related data kept by a different department or even by another company. Another node in a distributed system may also keep redundant data that can be used for checking.

DEVELOPING RELIABLE APPLICATION SYSTEMS

Even with the best of DBMS support, a great deal of responsibility rests with the application system for ensuring that the application meets its specifications, follows enterprise policy, and does not provide openings for fraud on the part of either system developers or end users. In this section we discuss the development of reliable application systems, considering:

- characteristics of reliable systems, and
- the system development process.

Our emphasis is on technical rather than administrative techniques and on software rather than user interfaces or hardware. It should be stressed, however, that people who have analyzed system development from an audit viewpoint feel that *programming* is often overemphasized. It is only one part of the process. Although the principles of reliable software also apply to system software (such as the DBMS or operating system), problems specific to systems software are not discussed here.

Reliable and Secure Systems

Reliability has been defined in [10] in terms of two properties: *correctness* and *robustness.* A correct system properly performs its intended functions and does nothing else. A robust system continues to operate reasonably even in the face of irregular conditions, such as hardware failure or bad input data. A reliable system thus has high *system integrity.* We can see that re-

liability is a necessary condition for most kinds of security and for data integrity.

Principles of Reliable Software

Modularity. Modularity has been defined [33] as *purposeful structuring.* That is, the structure of a modular system makes it easier to attain goals such as modifiability or reliability. The components of such a structure are called *modules.* The idea is to decompose an extremely complex system into parts that are small enough to be understood. Some of the issues that arise in this context are:

- the nature of the structural relationship of modules, such as hierarchical;
- the best method of decomposing into modules, taking into account *module strength* (relationships within the module), *module coupling* (relationships between modules), and optimum module size;
- defining the interfaces between modules.

Figure 11 shows a hierarchical structure of modules for an accounts payable application. In a hierarchical structure, a lower-level module cannot use a higher-level one. Some approaches to modularity start with *processes* and then consider data; others reverse that emphasis.

Modular approaches may eventually make it possible to design systems out of an inventory of standard "replaceable parts" analogous to the parts used by hardware designers. This would have many advantages for reliability, since these standard parts could be more thoroughly tested and understood.

Abstraction. Abstraction is a good way to achieve modularity. Abstraction means extracting the essential properties of some component of a system, omitting nonessential detail. This principle is most often applied to the description of a component as

Figure 11.   Hierarchical modular structure

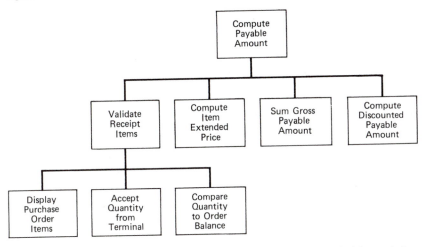

seen by other components that use it. The module that computes item extended price (in Fig. 11) is seen by the module that uses it only in terms of its function. When that module changes internally, no change is needed in the modules that use it, as long as it continues to support the same abstraction. This is an example of *procedural* abstraction [36]. A *data abstraction* also would be seen by components that use it only in terms of its behavior.

Least Privilege.   The policy of least privilege applies to software components as well as to users. In this context it has two aspects: *information hiding* and *access rights*. Each module hides its inner workings from other modules, revealing only those properties used by the other modules. These other modules have no "need to know" the inner workings. Information hiding is a way of enforcing abstraction. A module may consist of certain data structures and also the procedures that have access rights to those structures. Other procedures cannot access that data. Pro-

gramming language features can support this least-privilege principle.

Confirmability.   It is important to design software from the beginning in ways that will help us to determine whether it is correct. This principle is discussed further in connection with program testing.

The System Development Process

The System Development Life Cycle. Most disciplined approaches to application system development assume some kind of *life cycle*. A typical set of stages for the life cycle is:

- Analysis of needs,
- Specification,
- Architectural design,
- Detailed design,
- Implementation and component testing,
- System test,
- Operation,
- Maintenance and modification.

At control points in the cycle auditors can check on the security and integrity of the system being developed, as well as on the progress of development. There is also a trend toward including auditors in the design team, but there is a question whether this can be done in a way that does not compromise later audits of the system.

Various techniques have been introduced to improve the quality (and efficiency) of system development. Some of these are organizational or procedural (such as the chief-programmer team, or design and code inspection). Others are automated tools. We mention here three major topics: system-description tools, programming languages, and program-testing techniques.

System Description.   The specification and design stages of the life cycle are too often carried out without any systematic computer aid. Even where documentation is computer-maintained, this is often done in a nonuniform way. A better approach is to use a computer-aided design system, which allows designers to describe the system and to analyze the description. One such system is PSL/PSA [42]. PSL (Problem Statement Language) is based on an entity-relationship information model. Systems are described in terms of *objects* (entities), *properties* of objects (attributes), and *relationships* between objects. Figure 12 shows the major aspects of a PSL description. PSA (Problem State-

Figure 12.   Aspects of PSL System Description

PSL DESCRIPTION
System input/output flow
System structure
Data structure
Data derivation
System size and volume
System dynamics
System properties
Project management

ment Analyzer) analyzes the description, detecting errors, omissions, and inconsistency. PSA produces reports that give considerable insight, showing, for example, which processes use which data, or showing the hierarchies of objects. System-description tools contribute to reliability by detecting errors in the logic of the design and by preventing mechanical errors.

Programming-Language Support for Reliability.   Appropriate design and use of programming languages can significantly enhance reliability. The use of high-level languages reduces error by reducing the amount of detail that must be managed. Well-designed languages prevent errors by being simple and uniform in structure. Languages provide varying degrees of support for *static analysis,* thus allowing errors to be found without executing the program.

One very helpful feature is the *typing* of variables, which allows the compiler to catch many programming errors. Some languages (Pascal, for example) provide a set of built-in types (such as INTEGER or CHAR) and also allow the programmer to define new types. The compiler can then detect an illegal operation on a type or an attempt to assign a variable of one type to a variable of another type.

Languages can also support modularity, abstraction, and access rights. It should, of course, be possbile to compile modules independently. Languages such as Modula [44] and ADA [32] enforce information hiding by allowing modules to declare which of their variables are visible outside the module, and which outside variables they use. It is interesting that the languages with the most reliability support were not designed for database applications but rather for highly reliable real-time systems. There is certainly a need to apply the same concepts to the typical database environment.

Abstract Data Types. An *abstract data type* (ADT) [14] is a class of objects characterized by a set of operations that provides the only means for creating and manipulating those objects. For example, the ADT named Queue might be manipulated by the operations ADD (which adds an item to a queue) and REMOVE (which removes an item.) Users of the ADTs have no way of knowing how the data objects are represented or how the operations are implemented. That information is hidden. ADTs support the principles of modularity, abstraction, and information hiding. Abstract types are defined in a representation-free way — algebraically, for example. Since this kind of definition removes nonessential detail, it is easier to understand; since it is formal, it helps in verifying correctness of a design. The specifications can also aid in achieving and verifying correctness of the representation.

Abstract types can be used without any support from the programming language. With such support, however, it is possible to *encapsulate* the representation of both the data structures and operations. Some programming languages (for example, Simula) allow users to define new ADTs, which can then be used along with the built-in types.

Building on such languages, Jones and Liskov [19] have proposed language extensions to control the kinds of access allowed to data objects. With this scheme, access-control restrictions are stated explicitly in programs and enforced by the compiler. The programs thus become both more reliable and more understandable (since their rights are explicitly stated.) An ADT has a set of *rights,* which is equivalent to the set of allowed operations. Each program variable corresponds to an ADT and also has a set of rights, which are declared in the program. These rights must be included in the rights of the ADT. All uses of the variable can be checked by the compiler for both type compatibility and access correctness.

Program Testing. Program testing is a crucial part of several phases of the life cycle. The goal of testing is to arrive at correct programs; that is, programs that do not contain errors. In large part, therefore, testing is directed at uncovering errors [27, 28]. There are two main classes of errors. First, the program may not behave as its specifiers intended, because they did not understand the application, or because they specified the program incorrectly, or because the specifications were misunderstood. That is, the program does not meet its *functional specifications.* Secondly, the program may fail to meet its *design specifications.* It may implement the right functions, but inefficiently, or with incorrect algorithms, or with coding errors.

Most software testing effort goes into maintenance rather than the initial testing. Maintenance is necessary to correct the two types of error and also to make improvements in both function and design. Changing programs tends to introduce new errors. It is therefore necessary to do *regression testing;* that is, to repeat the tests performed at initial testing and subsequently. This means that test cases and testing procedures must be very systematically maintained. The techniques we discuss are beginning to provide some help with this very difficult problem.

Many errors can be detected without any execution of the program. This static analysis can be done by people (as in structured walkthroughs), by compilers, and by more sophisticated tools not currently available in compilers. The errors or possible errors that a static analysis can detect include variables not initialized, code segments that can never be reached, variables set but not used, the use of undefined variables, and mismatched types. Static analysis uses the concept of a *control-flow graph,* which represents all possible control paths through a program. The nodes of the graph are statements or groups of statements, and the edges represent control flow.

Static analysis fails to detect many errors, but it takes very little tester time [12]. Static analysis and the flow graph are also useful in planning dynamic testing. Commonly used dynamic methods are to traverse every edge at least once, or to traverse each path from the setting of a variable to its use. These techniques are timeconsuming, however, and do not catch all errors. The most effective test cases are constructed using knowledge of the program and the application and intuition about which kinds of errors are likely. These cases usually test at least all boundary conditions. Once a good set of test cases has been constructed, they and the procedures for running them must be maintained and used for regression testing.

A promising technique still in the research stage is *symbolic execution,* which combines aspects of both static analysis and dynamic testing. The program is executed (interpretively), but *symbols* are used as values in place of the usual data values. A program tester can derive quite a bit of information from symbolic execution without having to develop any test data. Symbolic execution can also help in the preparation of efficient test data and can serve as a tool in another program-validation technique, formal proof of correctness.

The tracing and mapping techniques used by auditors are examples of *program instrumentation* [15], where the program is manipulated in some way to produce information beyond its normal outputs. Such information might be, for example, counts of the number of times each node or edge of the control-flow graph is encountered. Program instrumentation can also support the monitoring of program variables or the testing of assertions about them [40], directed by statements such as:

MONITOR NUMERIC RANGE (X)
or
ASSERT (X > I).

DBMS SUPPORT OF AUDIT AND CONTROL

In this section we consider what characteristics the DBMS needs in order to support audit and control. First, the system must be credible; it must have high reliability or integrity, so that auditors can trust both its controls and its modes of accessing the data for auditing. There must be some way to *authenticate* the DBMS: to determine whether the system that is running really is the system described in the specifications. Another requirement is for people who are not primarily database experts to understand the operation of the DBMS, as well as the application systems that are produced on it. To this end, the DBMS needs clean design and clear documentation.

DBMS features needed for audit and control include:

- *Semantic integrity support.* This support can be used to implement controls on the "results of processing." As indicated earlier it may also assist in verifying data input.
- *Flexible access control.* Access rules allow responsibility to be separated and ensure that the areas of responsibility are well defined in terms of the transactions and data objects that a person can use.
- *A generalized audit trail.* The events to be recorded can be specified in access or integrity rules, and the contents of the audit trail can be controlled by auxiliary procedures specified in those rules.
- *Protection for the production program library.*

• *An integrated data dictionary.* A repository for descriptions of all system objects — their structure, their relationships, and their use as well as any access and integrity constraints — is valuable for understanding the system and for establishing and verifying controls.

• *Scheduling facilities.* The DBMS could support follow-up on errors by rescheduling a controls check at intervals until the error is corrected.

SUMMARY

We have introduced the vitally important topic of auditing and controls as they relate to principles of database security and integrity. We have given a brief survey of the many approaches to developing reliable software. Finally, we have drawn conclusions about what DBMSs must provide to support auditing and controls.

REFERENCES

1. B. ALLEN, "The biggest computer frauds: Lessons for CPAs." *Journal of Accountancy 143*, 5 (May 1977), 52–62.

2. "An Analysis of Computer Security Safeguards for Detecting and Preventing Intentional Computer Misuse." Nat. Bureau of Standards Special Publication 500–25 (January 1978). Nat. Bureau of Standards, Washington D.C.

3. "Audit Considerations in Electronic Funds Transfer Systems." American Institute of Certified Public Accountants, New York, 1978. Reviews the regulatory and legislative environment of EFT systems and suggests changes implied by EFT for the controls described in [4].

4. "The Auditor's Study and Evaluation of Internal Control in EDP Systems." American Institute of Certified Public Accountants, New York, 1977.

5. H. BARUCH, "The Foreign Corrupt Practices Act." *Harvard Business Review 57*. 1 (Jan-Feb 1979), 32–50.

6. L. A. BJORK, JR., "Generalized audit-trail requirements and concepts for data base applications." *IBM Systems J.* 14, 3 (1975), 229–245. Presents a model of an audit trail, including the concept of time addressing, which adds the time dimension to the values stored in the database, allowing reference to past versions of data. The contents of an audit trail are defined in detail, and some possible architectures are considered.

7. J. I. CASH, A. D. BAILEY, and A. B. WHINSTON, "A survey of techniques for auditing EDP-based accounting information systems." *The Accounting Review* LII, 4 (October 1977), 813–832.

8. R. E. FAIRLEY, "Tutorial: Static analysis and dynamic testing of computer software." *Computer* 11, 4 (April 1978), 14–23. A very readable introduction to modern methods of testing, covering both static and dynamic techniques.

9. E. B. FERNANDEZ and H. KASUGA, "Data Control in a Distributed Database System." IBM Los Angeles Scientific Center Report G320–2693, Sept. 1977.

10. P. FREEMAN, "Software reliability and design: A survey." Reprinted in [43], 75–85.

11. R. FRIED, "Monitoring data integrity." *Datamation* 24, 6 (June 1978), 176–181. Describes how one organization uses periodic scans of databases or files to determine how well they meet integrity criteria. Different user-oriented reports on the condition of data are

produced for the different users of a database.

12. C. GANNON, "Error detection using path testing and static analysis." *Computer* 12, 8 (August 1979), 26–31.

13. H. M. GLADNEY, "Administrative control of computing service." *IBM Systems J.* 17, 2 (1978), 151–178. Describes general principles for the administration of computing resources. The need for accountability of actions and the importance of auditing are emphasized. Several of these principles were incorporated in the design of RACF.

14. J. GUTTAG, "Abstract data types and the development of data structures." *Comm. ACM* 20, 6 (June 1977), 396–404.

15. J. C. HUANG, "Program instrumentation and software testing." *Computer* 11, 4 (April 1978), 25–32.

16. IBM Corporation, "Data Security Controls and Procedures — A Philosophy for DP Installations." IBM Form No. G320–5649–01. White Plains, N.Y., March 1977. A management-oriented overview of tools and procedures to promote security. Among the chapters are Interface Controls (e.g., journaling); Traditional Classes of Control (Organizational, Personnel, Operational, Development); Functional Duties; Plans and Programs.

17. E. G. JANCURA, *Audit and Control of Computer Systems.* Petrocelli/Charter, New York, 1974.

18. E. G. JANCURA and F. L. LILLY, "SAS No. 3 and the evaluation of internal control." *Journal of Accountancy* 143, 3 (March 1977), 69–74.

19. A. K. JONES and B. H. LISKOV, "A language extension for expressing constraints on data access." *Comm. ACM* 21, 5 (May 1978), 358–367.

20. L. I. KRAUSS and A. MACGAHAN, *Computer Fraud and Countermeasures.* Prentice-Hall, Englewood Cliffs, N.J., 1979. A practical management-oriented guide to protection against computer fraud.

21. R. C. T. LEE, J. R. SLAGLE, and C. T. MONG, "Towards automatic auditing of records." *IEEE Trans. Software Eng.* SE-4, 5 (Sept. 1978), 441–448.

22. W. C. MAIR, D. R. WOOD, and K. W. DAVIS, *Computer Control and Audit.* Institute of Internal Auditors, distributed by Q.E.D. Information Sciences, Inc., Wellesley, Mass., 1978. A standard text on EDP auditing.

23. E. C. MAXSON and N. R. LYONS, "Designing the next generation of auditing software." *The Internal Auditor* 35, 6 (Dec. 1978), 73–83. Proposes an audit command language, which could be translated to a programming language such as COBOL and then compiled to run on various DBMSs.

24. W. B. MEIGS, E. J. LARSEN, and R. F. MEIGS, *Principles of Auditing.* R. D. Irwin, Inc., Homewood, Illinois, 1977. A standard textbook on auditing.

25. T. L. MILLER, "EDP . . . A matter of definition." *The Internal Auditor* 32, 4 (July/August, 1975), 31–38.

26. N. MINSKY, "Cooperative authorization in computer systems." *Proc. IEEE COMPSAC 77 Conf.,* 729–733; available from IEEE.

27. G. J. MYERS, *Software Reliability: Principles and Practices.* Wiley, New York, 1976.

28. G. J. MYERS, *The Art of Software Testing.* New York, 1979.

29. A. J. Neumann, "Features of Seven Audit Software Packages — Principles and Capabilities." Special Publication 500–13, Nat. Bureau of Standards, Washington, D.C., July 1977. A survey, oriented to the computer professional, of features of some generalized audit packages. A summary of the U.S. General Accounting Office Auditing Standards is also provided.

30. R. L. Patrick, "Performance Assurance and Data Integrity Practices." Report PB–276 400, Nat. Bureau of Standards, Washington, D.C., January 1978.

31. W. T. Porter and W. E. Perry, *EDP Controls and Auditing.* Wadsworth Publishing Co., Belmont, Calif., 1977.

32. "Preliminary ADA Reference Manual." *SIGPLAN Notices* 14, 6 (June 1979), Part A.

33. D. A. Ross, J. B. Goodenough, and C. A. Irvine, "Software engineering: Process, principles, and goals." Reprinted in [43], 62–72.

34. Z. G. Ruthberg and R. G. McKenzie (Eds.), "Audit and Evaluation of Computer Security." Nat. Bureau of Standards Publication SP 500–19, Washington, D.C., October 1977. Report of a 1977 workshop that brought together experts in auditing and computing.

35. G. M. Scott, "Auditing the data base." *Canadian Chartered Accountant* III, 10 (October 1978), 52–59. Suggests two possible solutions to the "crisis" in audit software:

    1. For packages to directly access the database storage, bypassing the DBMS. This could be done, for example, by accessing backup dumps of the database.

    2. For the packages to retrieve data through the DBMS and for audit functions to be built into the DBMS.

36. K. S. Shankar, "Tutorial: Data structures, types, and abstractions." *Computer* 13, 4 (April 1980), 67–77.

37. "Special Collection from Workshop on Software Testing and Test Documentation, 1978." *IEEE Trans. Software Eng.* SE-6, 3 (May 1980), 236–290. A collection of six papers on program testing.

38. Statement on Auditing Standards No. 3, "The Effects of EDP on the Auditor's Study and Evaluation of Internal Control." American Institute of Certified Public Accountants, New York, 1974. The auditing standard for computerized systems. Divides accounting controls into *general controls,* which apply to the overall operation, and *application controls,* which apply to specific tasks. General controls apply either to the "computer service center" (or "information processing facility") or to the system-development process [41].

39. J. F. Stay, "HIPO and integrated program design." *IBM Systems J.* 15, 2 (1976), 143–154.

40. L. G. Stucki and G. L. Foshee, "New assertion concepts for self-metric software validation." *Proc. 1975 Int. Conf. on Reliable Software,* 1975, 59–71.

41. "Systems Auditability and Control Study." Institute of Internal Auditors, Altamonte Springs, Florida, 1977. This comprehensive survey of auditing and control practices was prepared by SRI, administered by the Institute of Internal Auditors, and supported by a grant from IBM. Intensive interviews were conducted at 45 selected enterprises in the U.S., Canada, Europe, and Japan, and several hundred organizations were surveyed by questionnaire. The practices

surveyed do not reflect a database orientation. The conclusions include:

- Top management is responsible for overall internal control, and users should have operational responsibilities. (Currently, control is often entrusted to the data processing organization.)
- Internal auditors must participate in the development of new information systems to ensure that audit and control features are included.
- Current EDP audit tools and techniques are inadequate.

42. D. TEICHROEW and E. A. HERSHEY, "PSL/PSA: A Computer-Aided Technique for Structured Documentation and Analysis of Information Processing Systems." Reprinted in [43], 195–202.

43. *Tutorial on Software Design Techniques* (Second ed.), IEEE Computer Society, Long Beach, Calif., 1977.

44. N. WIRTH, "Modula: A language for modular multiprogramming." *Software-Practice and Experience 7,* 1 (1977), 3–35.

NOTES

1. The term "transaction," as used in auditing standards (and in this chapter), refers to an *enterprise* transaction, such as an exchange with another enterprise, or a transfer of assets within the enterprise.

2. This is by no means trivial, since in a complex database it may be necessary to record the object's relationship to other objects.

QUESTIONS

1. Describe the several effects, on auditing and systems control, of converting to a DBMS environment. Are there any audit or control advantages of this conversion?

2. Do you agree with the three "common forms of computer fraud" delineated by the authors? Name a recent occurrence of each form which has made local or national newspaper headlines.

3. The authors move away from the general/application classification of controls to a three-group designation of "control practices." Are you more comfortable with their classification scheme?

4. Does Figure 3 really raise new auditor concerns, or are these issues common to any file protection scheme?

5. Define, in your own words, an audit trail. Compare your definition to that of Bjork.

6. What should be the ideal content of a DBMS audit trail?

7. Define a "before/after" image.

8. Do the explanations of EDP audit techniques in this paper clarify or confuse the discussions in the Boockholdt and Weiss paper?

9. Define a "reliable" application system.

10. The authors list six features necessary in a DBMS to promote audit and control capabilities. Do you concur with this list?

TOPIC EIGHT

Emerging Technology

Writing a topic outline on emerging technology is a humbling experience as such a task requires one to look far into the future of computer innovations. Surely voice recognition and natural languages will soon reach maturity, and artificial intelligence will become commonplace in business and home applications. Both the Japanese and American computer industries are rushing toward the development of fifth-generation machines built upon an architecture different from what now exists. These supercomputers will change computing technology forever.

However, to journey into the future we must first be well educated in the present. A logical building block for a discussion of the future is the microcomputer — the manifestation of an end-user desire for computing power. Subsequent to a discussion of micros this section journeys into the exciting world of office automation (OA). OA combines current hardware (micros) and software (DBMS, DSS, graphics) into local area networks (LANs) which encourage improved firmwide computing literacy.

The third area of discussion is the natural man/machine interface known as artificial intelligence (AI) which represents the modeling of expert human judgment into a set of decision rules. This final paper serves as a capstone for various MIS and technology issues while also thrusting you into a consideration of the future marriage of MIS and technology.

MICROCOMPUTERS

The emergence of mini- and microcomputers (herein all referred to as microcomputers) was founded in technology and fanned by the desires of end-users. It is a mind-boggling fact that one can place on a desk top a small hunk of iron with the equivalence of an IBM 370–158. Turbocharged micros come equipped with 640–1024K in internal RAM! Besides their impact on technology, end-users have become a driving force in the development and acquisition of micro-computers in an MIS. End-users have become purchasers of machines for their children and as such have been "bitten by the bug" of exploring personal computing. User-friendly small system magazines like *PC World* and *Personal Computing* further improve the computing intellect of the population.

The most positive aspect of the proliferation of microcomputers has been that end-users overcome the computer "phobia" associated with being an unfamiliar user of the corporate mainframe. This overcoming of computer phobia, coupled with an immense increase in friendly software (both application and operating systems), positions the computer-user quite nicely for the 1990s. However, even the wonderful world of computing has its "dark side." How does the corporate MIS react to satisfy this end-user awareness of computing? Is distributed data processing the solution? The large corporations must find ways to satisfy end-users while maintaining their desired integrity in regard to the MIS.

Yet the placement of a microcomputer in a small business environment is quite different from implementing DDP in a large MIS. Consider that the microcomputer, in a small firm, is a replacement for a *manual system!* Do the procedures for the acquisition of a microcomputer mirror the traditional systems development life cycle of a large facility? How well prepared is a small business to deal with requests for proposals (RFPs) and systems implementation? What happens to basic internal controls like an audit trail and the separation of duties? Clearly the small business could be flirting with a disaster if the systems life cycle process is not considered.

ROLE AND GROWTH OF MICROCOMPUTERS

The evolution of hardware and software, and the overcoming of personnel computer phobias have been reflected in the *role* and *growth* of microcomputers. In many instances the first application of small computers has been *word processing*. This application, although not terribly sophisticated from a computer science or accounting application, at least got the machine out of the box

and into the job stream. Initial accounting applications were *financial* in nature, usually being payroll or general ledger systems.

One of the more interesting phenomena associated with small computers has been the tremendous growth in *managerial* applications vis-à-vis spreadsheet software. Cost-volume-profit analysis, direct costing and variance analysis have become common topics of discussion among all levels of management. End-users now understand the building of templates and the advantages of "what if" break-even analysis on the minicomputer. Such pent-up demand for managerial data analysis likely would not have surfaced in a pencil and paper world.

Other causes for the growth of the microcomputer are its portability, expansion capabilities, and software support. The notion of a user taking the computer home was unheard of in the recent past. Some users had acoustical couplers with which to "dial in" to the mainframe. Yet the ability to have a monitor in one's home was a farfetched idea, unless one had the wiring for an IBM 360-158. Portability has led to home use of the computer, which reduces computer phobia even more. The expansion capability of the micro has introduced such design as DDP and *local area networks* (LANs). Both minis and micros are capable of supporting multiple workstations and functions. Advances in software have provided end-users with tools for exploration unheard of until recent years. Microcomputer-based programs exist in such exotic areas as artificial intelligence, four-dimensional graphics, and full-scale relational database management. Firms may now perform key work searches in the legal area (LEXIS) and the accounting area (NAARS) from their microcomputers.

Several advantages of microcomputers have been presented. What are the organizational implications of these small and powerful boxes which merit consideration *prior* to their acquisition?

ISSUES REGARDING SMALL COMPUTERS

Think back in time to your first notions about computers. What attributes of the computer made it more attractive than a manual system? Surely the *speed* of a computer is a major benefit, along with the fact that machines do not fatigue, and therefore they are highly *accurate* regarding mathematical computations. Computers provide *flexibility,* as many different applications will run on the same system; and, finally, computers provide *analytic capabilities* because of their ability to perform high level mathematics.

Given these computer advantages, why are many firms unhappy with their new EDP systems? One reason is that computers encourage less documentation of basic business events, thereby destroying the traditional *audit trail.* Furthermore, computers make judgment errors unless told otherwise. That is, a computer will accept the notion of a "pregnant man" without question. The *time to process* a transaction in an EDP system is much quicker than in manual systems, thereby eliminating the possibility of several individuals performing a "sniff test" on the source document. *Separation of duties* in a small MIS becomes another control concern, and system *back-up and recovery* procedures usually are quite lax. The single biggest concern regarding exposures in a microcomputer environment remains the issue of *illegal access.* More sophisticated access control mechanisms, such as dynamic passwords and voice recognition, must become commercially cost-feasible to eliminate the major exposure to access.

We previously asked the question, does microcomputer acquisition and implementation follow the traditional systems development life cycle? The SDLC for a large MIS may span five years while the SDLC in a minicomputer environment could be as brief as five days! Should the small business person be concerned with system specifications or merely walk into a store, buy a Banana 9000, and learn by trial-and-error? Truly the growth of the computer is in the hands-on learning stage, while the propriety of system selection is in the planning stage. Could an argument be made that "any computer is better than no computer"?

What options are available to the firm regarding the system's growth and its movement toward increased end-user computing? One thing is sure: If the firm does not grant end-users more *authorized computing power,* a lot of illegal file copies are going to be generated. The larger MISs could maintain a centralized format, and risk the odds of end-user disenchantment. A more likely scenario would be a movement toward some form of DDP. What about the options in a very small firm? If management fears control problems, a backlash movement toward an outside service bureau could be justified. Service bureaus seem the only middle ground between the bipolar extremes of "manual system" and "minicomputer." Is the service bureau a viable solution, or is it merely sticking one's head in the sand to avoid the computing issue? Only time will tell. It is an indisputable fact, however, that small computers are here to stay.

OFFICE *AUTOMATION* AND LOCAL AREA NETWORKS

Office automation (OA) is the concept of utilizing the computer to replace the technology behind several business tasks. Word processing, electronic mail, and spreadsheets are intended not to decrease the quantity of work, but rather to improve the quality of efforts. OA is a business support notion, not based upon esoteric ideas but founded in the interface of a diverse set of technologies. *Local area networks* (LANs) carry OA one step further toward the concept that no user needs a dedicated machine and no system a single-purpose machine. LANs project a system concept of "shared logic." OA and LANs are confronted with further behavioral and design issues as users are coming forward and admitting "phobias" regarding computer comfort and literacy. Again, only the future will decide the success of OA and LANs.

ARTIFICIAL INTELLIGENCE

Artificial intelligence requires the ability of a query language to traverse through an expert *knowledge base* via an *inference engine*. The knowledge base is a set of data gathered from experts in a particular field, while an inference engine describes the logical premises (if-thens) loaded into the system. A foundation of AI is the ability of the machine to "reason" based upon experts' heuristics, or rules-of-thumb. One of the most sophisticated and most often referenced AI models

(MYCIN) is in the area of medical diagnosis. Over a decade of effort has been spent on this international system. The knowledge base consists of basic facts known to doctors regarding specific diseases and related symptoms. The inference engine locates causes and effects, with the problem-solving component using basic patient facts to query the knowledge base. The result is the system offering suggestions to the doctor regarding additional tests.

Artificial intelligence is closely related to expert systems and decision support systems (the latter two items are subsets of AI). The growth in AI will come as inexperienced users gain familiarity with models, and as hardware is developed to facilitate large knowledge bases. Business applications of AI are already in the prototype stages in such areas as:

  Computer Auditing
  Income Tax Planning
  Income Tax Allocations
  MFG Plant Location
  Law Suit Damages Determination
  Cost Allocation Decisions

Another boon to AI is the development of "shells" or programs which facilitate design of the knowledge base. AI shells like AL/X provide the means for easy expert system construction via a structured process of

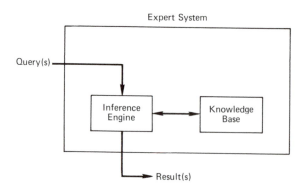

decision "rule" design and linkage. Future AI applications are limited only by one's imagination.

ARTICLES

The microcomputer article (Romney and Stocks) does an excellent job of promoting an awareness of the many problems in small computer selection and implementation. The authors examine the SDLC and pose a series of "Error" notions for your consideration. As you read this work, try and rank-order the "Errors" and test your rankings with those of other students. The article should be considered as introductory material providing a sound framework, or list of questions, for more in-depth consideration and analysis when contemplating a small MIS.

The OA paper (Meyer) calls for an improvement in computer literacy and the elimination of barriers such as departmental "territorialism." An entire range of OA applications is offered from simple word processing to full LANs with the elimination of "dedicated machines." The OA of the future is to operate in an environment of "shared logic" for all end-users.

The article on AI (Luconi, Malone, and Morton) introduces concepts such as *expert system, inference engine,* and *frames of information.* This very readable paper serves as a starting point for a consideration of the systems of the future. The mechanics of the design of a knowledge engine are explained in detail. Then the author points out that expert systems, a subset of AI, have surfaced even in accounting applications (tax) in recent years, and that the future looks bright for MIS users of knowledge engineering. "Problems and risks" of expert systems are then discussed in the closing section.

Upon completion of Topic Eight you should be more aware of the design and control issues introduced by small computers. Microcomputer applications will increase in *both* the small and the large MIS. Consequently, you should constantly consider the impact of small computer technology and related software development on both small and large systems. Much of the technology in this section exists in a developmental stage. Where graphics, AI, OA, and LANs are headed is anyone's guess. However, computer impact upon MIS is evolutionary, and the process cannot be reversed.

You should now be aware of emerging technology and should be better equipped to face the MIS challenges ahead. It is certain that the students of the 1980s will launch the world onto a new technological level of MIS design and application. The future looks exciting; the future is now.

How to Buy a Small Computer System*

CPAs don't just use small computer systems — more and more, they're helping managements and clients select them.

Technological advances and the interplay of market forces have made the cost and size of mini and microcomputers attractive to small and medium-sized companies. Even divisions of large corporations are increasingly drawn to small computer systems.

Now that the price tag is feasible and a computer's potential benefits are becoming clearer, are business managers having an easy time selecting and implementing a system?

The answer is no — especially when a new computer system must interface with other operations already in place.

To help CPAs who want to provide guidance in this complex process we offer a sequential approach of eight steps (see Exhibit 1). As with most difficult processes, it's always useful to have some caveats in advance of taking the plunge. Accordingly, as the step-by-step approach is described, some common errors will also be highlighted.

STEP 1: ANALYZING COMPANY NEEDS

The first step in selecting a small computer system is to analyze the company's needs. A business manager often asks, "Which computer should we buy?" But a better first question is, "Do we really need a computer?"

A thorough analysis includes the following:

- Reviewing business priorities: What are the general business plans and management's priorities? Are there areas that could or should be computerized? Can the company afford a computer now?

- Gathering pertinent data: current budgets, organization charts, job descriptions, business plans, financial reports and projections, marketplace information, a description of any current systems and their weaknesses.

- Determining the potential benefits of a system: competitive edge, better information, cost savings, growth, improved customer service.

- Identifying specific applications: accounting applications, such as general ledger and re-

Exhibit 1:   Eight Steps to a Small Computer System

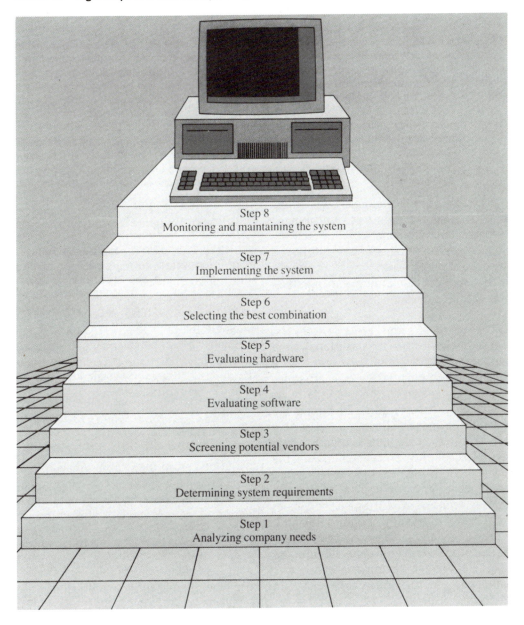

ceivables, and general applications, such as word processing, integrated spreadsheets, graphics and telecommunications.

- Assessing the business environment and the organizational structure.
- Estimating costs.

After the analysis a decision must be made to abandon the process or to proceed. Several common errors are associated with this step.

Error: the Bandwagon Purchase. Many companies have purchased small computer systems simply because competitors have done so — a business version of "keeping up with the Joneses." In effect, the computer is seen as a status symbol, not as a productive asset. Clearly, a close examination of motives is in order before deciding to make the purchase.

Error: the "Free" Needs Analysis. Many vendors offer a "free" needs analysis to determine if a system would be useful for a company. Such an offer can be attractive to a business manager who has little or no experience with computers. By having the vendor do the analysis, the buyer will be able to benefit from the vendor's expertise and avoid the time, effort and cost of making the analysis from within the company.

But the danger in this approach lies in the vendor's incentive to sell. Since the vendor earns money by selling computers — not by providing free needs analyses — these studies often exaggerate the benefits of computers. Hidden costs frequently aren't mentioned, and the anticipated costs are amortized over unrealistically long asset-life periods to reduce expenses. All to often the analysis results in the conclusion that what the company needs is a system just like the one the vendor is selling.

Error: Overstating Benefits. It's not uncommon for a vendor to exaggerate the benefits of a system while underestimating the costs. The potential benefits can be significant, but it's also true that many, when analyzed in terms of a specific company, realistically can't be achieved.

In fact, it has been estimated that only half of all the computer installations in the United States are paying for themselves.

Identifying what a computer system won't do for a company is, then, as important as identifying what it will do.

A computer won't, for example, replace staff immediately. In the beginning, probably more staff or overtime hours will be required. Nor will a computer replace the accountant. More information will be available for decision making, but the CPA's training and judgment will still be needed. A computer can't save a sick business — it will simply automate the problems.

Finally, a computer can't help a person accomplish what he or she doesn't understand — the computer will merely make the same or more mistakes faster.

Error: Ignoring Nonquantifiable Aspects. There are many aspects of using computers that aren't easily quantified but should be part of the decision-making process. Examples include increased timeliness and accuracy of information, increased or decreased employee job satisfaction, increased service to customers and expanded market capabilities.

Error: Ignoring Hidden Costs. The base price quoted for a small business system typically is the cost of the hardware. But the additional costs required to bring the system to a useful state are also significant. Some of these hidden costs are shown in Exhibit 2. All costs associated with the ac-

Exhibit 2.   Hidden Costs

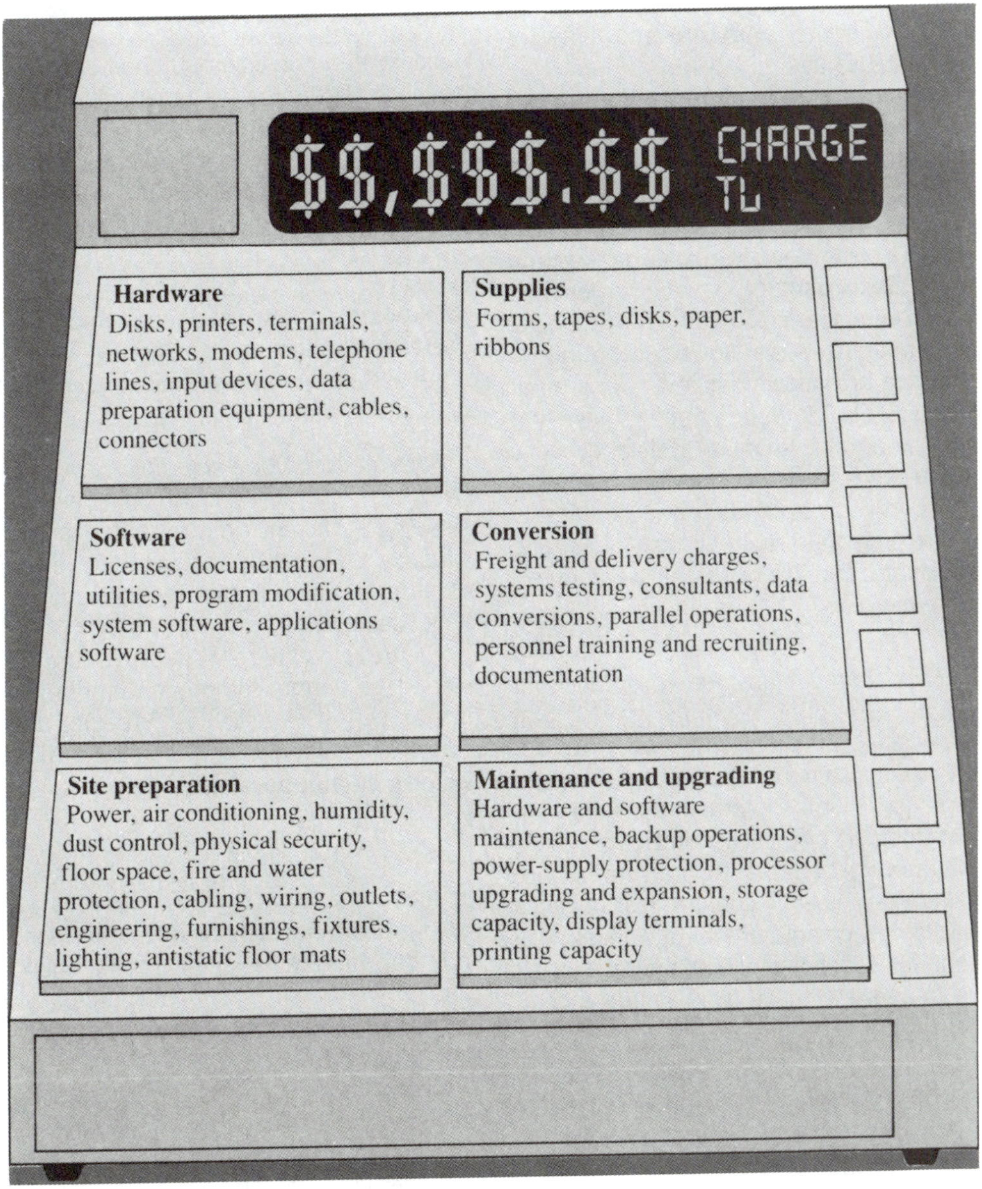

Hardware
Disks, printers, terminals, networks, modems, telephone lines, input devices, data preparation equipment, cables, connectors

Supplies
Forms, tapes, disks, paper, ribbons

Software
Licenses, documentation, utilities, program modification, system software, applications software

Conversion
Freight and delivery charges, systems testing, consultants, data conversions, parallel operations, personnel training and recruiting, documentation

Site preparation
Power, air conditioning, humidity, dust control, physical security, floor space, fire and water protection, cabling, wiring, outlets, engineering, furnishings, fixtures, lighting, antistatic floor mats

Maintenance and upgrading
Hardware and software maintenance, backup operations, power-supply protection, processor upgrading and expansion, storage capacity, display terminals, printing capacity

quisition, implementation and operation of the computer system under consideration should be identified.

Error: Lack of Security. Like manual systems, computer systems require physical security. Unlike manual systems, great amounts of information can be copied rapidly and removed on concealable disks. In addition, computer hardware and software have market value.

Of perhaps more importance than physical security is the possibility of sabotage or system breakdown. White-collar crime involving computers is escalating. An untrained or a disgruntled employee with access to a computer can quickly damage the system. Such damage can be expensive, time-consuming and difficult to repair.

A computerized system is susceptible to many more breakdown dangers than a manual system. For example, power outages that may slow down a manual system cause a computerized system to stop. Such outages often result in loss of data and damage to software programs. Dust, sunlight, heat and cold can also damage or destroy a computerized system.

Error: Taking Employee Acceptance for Granted.   It is often taken for granted that all company personnel will readily accept and adapt to using a computer. But universal acceptance is unlikely without significant effort on the part of management.

Negative reactions to computers are based on fear: fear of change, fear of being replaced by a computer, fear of working with unfamiliar technology. Management must work to alleviate these fears before a computer system is introduced.

Error: Believing a Computer Can Solve All Problems.   It's a mistake to think that a computerized system will, by itself, solve problems. Computers don't solve problems — only people do. The realistic attitude is that management can use computers as tools to help solve problems.

STEP 2: DETERMINING COMPUTER SYSTEM REQUIREMENTS

The next step in the computer-selection process is to determine the organization's specific computer requirements. Determining requirements is essential because it provides a checklist of what the system will need to do. This checklist, moreover, will serve as the basis for selecting the vendor, software and hardware.

The better defined the requirements, the greater the probability of selecting an appropriate system. A faulty or inadequate checklist leads to problems.

Error: Not Understanding Current Operations.   The most common mistake is not spending sufficient time to understand the company's current operations. Most managers, after all, believe that they already know their business.

To identify all the specifics that are needed to define computer requirements, time and effort are essential. Studying a past review of operations may not be sufficient because of later developments.

Error: Automating the Existing System.   Many companies automate an existing function without trying to improve it. But automating an existing function without an in-depth examination of that function results in inefficient use of resources — like purchasing a sophisticated calculator to do simple addition.

When designing a new system, management should eliminate known weaknesses in the existing system's procedures and try not to perpetuate problems. The most efficient uses of the system should be identified.

Error: Buying Unnecessary Bells and Whistles.   Computer systems often include many optional features or capabilities. Management must differentiate between necessary features and features that would be "neat" or "fun" but aren't essential. Each optional feature or capability, remember, adds to the total cost.

Error: Lack of Program Controls. A common error is the belief that internally developed computer programs don't need the controls and documentation required for larger systems. But neither the size of a system nor the place of development has a relationship to the necessity for controls and documentation.

What does affect this need is the fact that in smaller businesses separation of duties among a number of people often isn't possible. And without that separation, control and documentation become increasingly important.

STEP 3: SCREENING POTENTIAL VENDORS

The third step in the selection process is screening potential vendors. A good vendor is a valuable asset and can assist in selecting the appropriate computer system, providing training and implementation, and offering ongoing maintenance and software support.

Vendors differ in their knowledge, professionalism and level of commitment. Ideally, a purchaser engages a vendor who is qualified in computer technology and in business. It is also important that the vendor has had previous experience in installing systems similar to the one being considered.

An examination of three major characteristics of the contemplated system can help determine the level of vendor sophistication needed:

1. Application system characteristics. The more industry-specific and complicated the application systems, the more sophisticated the vendor needed.
2. Work-station characteristics. The more work stations needed, the higher the volume of transactions and the more coordinated the access and processing requirements, the more sophisticated the vendor needed.
3. Cost and assistance required. The higher the expenditure and the higher the level of involvement expected of the vendor, the higher the level of sophistication needed.

Poor screening of potential vendors — or no evaluation at all — may be an invitation to future headaches.

Error: Buying Future Promises. Many computer systems are sold on the basis of future promises: "The component will be available shortly" or "These programs should be on the market very soon." But what does the vendor mean by "shortly" or "very soon"? Next week? Next month? Two years from now?

Most computer companies announce forthcoming products. But unforeseen conditions or technical problems often delay their availability for months or even years. Even major companies have announced products in advance and then made customers wait 6 to 18 months for delivery.

Moreover, there is also the risk that the product won't perform as anticipated or won't be compatible with the current system. And new products may still have some "bugs."

Error: Lowballing. Some vendors anxious to make a sale bid very low, or lowball, to attract customers. Other vendors may be operating under a quota and sell systems at reduced prices in order to meet the specified volume. Since these vendors are in business to make a profit, they often try to renegotiate the price once the company is well into implementing the system.

Another tactic is to sell a system with insufficient capacity. Once this lack of capacity is evident, the vendor attempts to sell a larger, more expensive system.

Error: Accepting Oral Promises. Don't rely on spoken promises; have the vendor put all arrangements in writing. Vendors often make many promises about delivery date, training, program modifications, system upgrading and maintenance. But if arrangements are in writing, the vendor is less likely to "offer the moon."

Error: Hardware Smoke Screen. Some vendors will use the technical specifications of their equipment as a smoke screen to hide the flaws of the total system. But software, peripherals and service are almost always more important than the hardware specifications. There is a long list of failed computer companies that produced machines with excellent specifications and lots of hardware horsepower but without the other necessary elements for a successful system.

Error: Being a Showcase. Some vendors offer substantial price discounts to companies that showcase their products. The showcase company will serve as a guinea pig for the vendor in the attempt to develop, test and market products for a selected new market.

For the company the reduced purchase price is quickly offset by the burden of financing the vendor's research and development, to say nothing of the time wasted in showing others the system. The net result is a higher financial outlay than for an established, field-tested system.

Error: Accepting Free Trials. Many vendors offer free, no-obligation use of their packaged software. But these alluring offers frequently entail charges for such services as installation, delivery and training. Also, these offers often are accompanied by secrecy agreements, the violation of which may involve serious risks to the purchaser.

Error: Lack of Adequate Service. Always select a vendor who is willing and able to provide timely, cost-effective service. System problems can result in downtime, slowdowns, erroneous reports and statements or system failure. In these situations the willingness and competence of the vendor to provide prompt and quality repair service are invaluable.

STEP 4: EVALUATING SOFTWARE

The fourth step in the selection process is evaluating software, the programs that operate the computer. Identifying the appropriate software is essential to establishing a system that will provide the output and the operating functions desired. Software programs range from the simple to the highly sophisticated. The required level and type of software will serve as a basis for selecting the hardware components.

This is a tricky stage.

Error: Overemphasizing Hardware. Users of small computer systems generally purchase packaged, or "canned," software. And most software programs are limited to certain hardware makers and configurations.

Thus, the primary emphasis must be on the software desired, for it will indicate, to a great extent, the needed hardware configuration. Hardware without the appropriate software is virtually useless.

Error: Buying Unproven Products.   New software is continuously appearing on the market. Each product is promoted as an improvement or enhancement of prior or competitor products. But remember that almost every new program will have a number of errors or bugs. It's usually wisest, then, to buy programs from dependable companies that have proven performance records. Programs are successful in the marketplace over time because they perform as designed with few or no problems.

Error: Believing Packaged Software Can Be Easily Modified.   Since finding a software program that exactly meets the needs of a company isn't always possible, many managers buy a program with the intention of modifying the software. But this attempt is risky, difficult and time-consuming at best. Many programs weren't designed in a way that encourages modification. In addition, such modification often is illegal and usually voids any warranty or support supplied by the original developer.

STEP 5: EVALUATING HARDWARE

The next step in the process is evaluating hardware components. Although the selection of hardware isn't as important as the right software or vendor, it remains a vital part of the process. Hardware components include the central processing unit, input devices (tape drives and disk drives), output devices (disk drives, printers and display terminals) and communication devices (modems). Errors are also common at this stage.

Error: Buying a Dead-end Machine.   A common mistake made in evaluating hard-

ware is not examining growth needs before purchase. All computer hardware has power and expansion limitations, and it's important that present and future speed and capacity needs are identified beforehand.

Speed refers to the time required to process programs or print reports. Capacity refers to the memory size, the number of expansion slots and the number of peripherals that may be attached. As needs grow, slow or unexpandable hardware eventually will block progress.

Error: Thinking Bigger Is Better.   In the case of computer hardware, too, bigger isn't always better. Focus on computing power, not on the price of a computer or the size of the hardware. Refer to independently run tests of performance. Publishers of these tests run standardized programs on different systems and identify which systems offer the best performance for the price.

Error: Lack of Adequate Backup.   When a part is faulty or worn out, processing is slowed down or stopped. Because most companies can't operate efficiently without adequate data processing, backup is essential. Make arrangements with another company that has a similar system to use its system in off hours, or arrange for a "loaner" that will be available if needed.

STEP 6: SELECTING THE BEST COMBINATION

When computer needs are sophisticated, requests for proposals should be sent to specific people at several vendor companies in order to gather information about the alternatives they can provide. The relative merits of each component (software and hardware) and vendor are then evaluated.

In the course of this evaluation the following questions should be considered:

- How well does each alternative satisfy the system requirements?
- What support is available from the vendor?
- What is the system's capacity and flexibility?
- How good are the alternative contract and product warranties?
- What are the costs and financing arrangements of each alternative?te?

Error: Poor Proposal Format.   The purpose of sending requests for proposals is to gather information from several vendors, so the requests must be tailored to the specific situation. But the proposals have value only if they can be evaluated in comparison with one another. If no specific response format is requested, the task of making valid comparisons among proposed systems is difficult, if not impossible.

Error: Inadequate or No "Test Drive." Don't buy a system without sufficient hands-on experience with the same model and configuration. And remember, if it doesn't work in the vendor's showroom, it won't work in the office. The test drive should resolve questions on the speed of the system as well as on the amount of training and effort that will be required.

Impatience at this stage can cause grief later on. Take the time to make a detailed evaluation of the system being demonstrated. And be sure to try to make the system fail. Testing limits will provide a good idea of how well the system works.

Error: Not Talking to Users of Similar Systems.   Many purchasing errors can be avoided by talking to other users of similar systems recently installed by the vendor. This information will provide a reliable indication of system performance and the service that can be expected from that vendor.

But don't let the vendor select the other users to contact. To get a balanced view, find a user group, an industry association or some other reliable source.

Error: Poor Contract Negotiations. Sometimes buying a system requires contract negotiations, especially if the system involves a minicomputer or if the software has been custom written. Make sure that all the key points are in the contract, including the attachment of all system requirements. This means that signing a standard industry contract usually isn't advantageous to the buyer; it's designed to protect the vendor. In negotiating the contract, it's advisable to have legal counsel.

STEP 7: IMPLEMENTING THE SYSTEM

The next step is implementing the purchased system. This stage is time-consuming and will affect people throughout the company. A step-by-step plan must be established so that as many problems and difficulties as possible can be eliminated or reduced.

The implementation plan should address, at a minimum, each of the following:

- The tasks to be performed, including the interrelationships and interdependence of the tasks.
- The time frame for completing the tasks.
- The sequence in which the tasks must be performed.
- An estimate of the amount of time and effort required to complete each task.
- The person responsible for each task and the role of other personnel during the implementation process.
- The end products desired from implementation.

It's essential to have a competent project manager who will be responsible for coordinating and supervising the implementation process.

Implementation is the stage at which if anything can go wrong, it will — even with good planning and preparation.

Error: Implementing Too Much Too Fast. Companies and staff can absorb only so much change in a certain amount of time. Implementing at too fast a rate can cause personnel difficulties, errors in files and data, and errors in systems use. Implementation should be careful and orderly. There must be time to assimilate each implementation step. And extra time should be scheduled for unexpected delays.

Error: No Attention to Interfaces. An interface is the point of interaction between components of a system. For example, a word processing package frequently interfaces with a data base package containing name and address lists to create and print a series of letters.

Good interfacing allows the hardware and software components to communicate and interact effectively. If information can't be readily transferred among the various parts of the system, the system will be of limited use.

Error: Assuming the System Is Operational. A common error made at this stage is assuming that the system will arrive ready to plug in and operate. This assumption reveals a lack of understanding of what is required to make a system operational.

Before this can happen, time and money must be spent on equipment installation, hardware and software testing, staff training, conversion from the old system to the new, and verification that the new system is operating correctly. And remember not to make the time estimates unrealistically short.

Error: Lack of Management Participation. Because implementation affects the entire organization, it's vital that top management play an active role in the process. Only management has the authority to resolve problems that cross department or division boundaries. And only management can ensure the necessary resources.

Error: No Attention to Problems. During implementation, expect the unexpected. Don't defer dealing with each unanticipated problem. Try to resolve each problem as it surfaces.

Error: Not Freezing the System Design. During the implementation phase it's important to freeze the design. Changes to the system at this stage can seriously affect the schedule and the number of difficulties experienced. All nonessential changes should be avoided so that efforts are concentrated on implementation. Once the system is operational, then modifications can be incorporated.

Error: No Recognition of New Procedures. Implementing a new computer system usually means modifying procedures. It's naive to assume that all former procedures will now operate the new system properly and efficiently. Similarly, management shouldn't assume that all personnel will immediately understand how the new system works and what each person is now supposed to do.

Error: Lack of Training. Some managers feel that training programs are a waste of time and money. This attitude may have been appropriate when the damage that could result from the mistakes of inexperienced employees was limited.

But with a computerized system, untrained personnel can cause tremendous damage or delay through relatively simple mistakes — for example, pulling the plug, spilling coffee, mixing codes, entering erroneous data. As the cost of potential errors increases, so does the need for a good training program.

STEP 8: MONITORING AND MAINTAINING THE SYSTEM

The final step of the process is monitoring and maintaining the new computer system. Several interrelated procedures are involved:

- Establishing and implementing a mechanism to address system problems.
- Establishing and implementing backup schedules.
- Updating documentation on a regular basis.
- Comparing system performance with the plans and objectives established earlier.
- Performing an annual data processing review to highlight problem areas and possible areas for improvement.
- Developing ongoing hardware maintenance and service guidelines — "preventive medicine" usually is less costly.

If an operational system is, as it were, left to fend for itself for too long, problems are sure to develop.

Error: Only One Trained Employee. To save money, sometimes a company trains only one person to operate a system. This approach can result in a major dislocation when that employee is ill or on vacation, is promoted or leaves the company.

Although additional costs are incurred, it's advisable to system-train more than one person. This additional expertise also allows duties to be rotated, thereby improving internal control.

Error: Keeping Outdated Documentation. As a computer system is used the system itself and its operating procedures change as enhancements and modifications are made. As these changes occur it's important to modify documentation appropri-

ately. Failure to do so continuously will, in a short time, result in documentation that has little relationship to the existing system.

And the last thing management wants in a computer system is irrelevance.

CPAS AS GUIDES

Accountants, of course, were among the earliest users of small computer systems, and they would now seem well positioned to play the helpful role of guide to others. From this overview of an important, complicated process it should be apparent that CPA guidance can save managements and clients not just time and money — but perhaps a grueling experience as well.

QUESTIONS

1. Does the authors' eight-step approach to SCS selection mirror the traditional systems development life cycle? Should it?

2. Step 1 contains the error "overstating the benefits" of an SCS. What do you believe are the five major benefits for an SCS?

3. Would you rather have management over- or underinvolved in computer selection?

4. Which of the Step #2 "errors" concerns you the most?

5. Offer arguments for purchased-off-the-shelf software and for in-house program development.

6. Are small businesses more guilty of buying computers that are too small or too large?

7. Is the concept of an RFP relevant for small firms, or shouldn't the systems

vendor take over the process of documenting systems specifications?

8. Are firms really guilty of the first "error" in Step #7, or do they traditionally drag their feet?

9. How many people would comprise the EDP staff of a small business? What are the behavioral, organizational, and audit implications of this staff size?

Office Automation: A Progress Report*

SUMMARY

Many articles in this first issue deal primarily with people issues and a knowledge of the technology is assumed. Meyer's article takes the reader on a quick tour of office information tools. As a foundation for discussion, it defines the scope, history, and current status of office automation. The office technology of today rests on a basis laid over decades by a number of management disciplines. Although there is a plenty of proof that office automation can quantitatively increase office output, it is the combination of qualitative and quantitative improvements that distinguishes today's office automation. The means to achieving this balance is a good office automation manager, able to coordinate various technologies and equally able to manage the people issues.

INTRODUCTION

Office automation is a broadly used term, often unclear in its definition. Yet it represents a new profession, a new integration of technologies, a new perception of the potential of information tools and a boom industry in the 1980s.

The variety of views of office automation is in part a product of the backgrounds of those involved in the field. Today there is interest and active involvement on the part of a number of professional groups and academic disciplines: data processing, word processing, administration, telecommunications, management sciences and library sciences, to mention but a few. Each is making a unique contribution but represents only a portion of the requisite technologies and skills.

Differences in perspective are also partly due to the stage of growth and experience level of practitioners and authors. While those new to the field often view office automation as simply an extension of their previous work (e.g. word or data processing), those with more experience see it as an entirely new phenomenon, based on a number of earlier disciplines but with a significantly different set of issues and challenges.

This article defines office automation in the broadest sense, melding the many contributing perspectives. It offers a historic perspective on the evolution of office automation, tracing the contribution of a variety of disciplines. With this broad view of the field, it then describes what is different about office automation today. It gauges progress in North America to date, and describes the issues facing senior managers of office automation. It is intended to provide common definitions as an anchoring point for the coming discussions in this new journal, *OFFICE: Technology and People*.

THE SCOPE OF OFFICE AUTOMATION

The search for a definition of office automation (OA) might begin by describing its intent. I think most practitioners will agree that the purpose of OA is to support those who work with information by applying computer- and communications-based tools, making the users both more efficient and more effective. This statement, while hinting of motherhood and apple pie, at least narrows the field to a focus on:

- work,
- information processes,
- computer- and communications-based tools.

To be more specific, however, brings difficulties. For example, to place too much emphasis on the word "office" excludes a growing interest in (at least part-time) work at home, enabled by home terminals and micro-computers. However, I think it would be presumptuous to suggest that factory automation is a subset of OA. At a minimum, OA may be defined as addressing the types of information work that are typically done in offices.

Similarly, a literal interpretation of the term "automation" narrows the field to a focus on the routine, well-structured tasks which can be delegated to a computer. This ignores the more lucrative and relevant area of unstructured managerial/professional support. OA may deliver a variety of business benefits, including a mix of:

- Efficiency: reducing the unit cost of routine business transactions through mechanization or automation.
- Effectiveness: allowing people to do better work, or to do things they could not do before.
- Quality of work life: improving the quality of job content and organizational environment, e.g. by relieving people of mundane information tasks and allowing more time to collaborate and be creative.

Any attempt to define the field in terms of technologies becomes obsolete as fast as the technologies change. And to do so may focus the practitioner on means rather than ends. For example, OA certainly cannot be equated with word processing, a limited application of text-editing tools to reduce the cost of clerical tasks. Indeed, the primary emphasis of the field today is on the application of systems that integrate a variety of information tools. Thus, OA should be defined to include *all* tools which support information work, including text, numbers and graphics handling, internal and external data bases and telecommunications tools. (These tools will be described in more detail below.)

Furthermore, OA must extend beyond the rational analysis of information processes and the application of systems. New tools bring significant changes to the way people work; and these changes do not come easily or quickly. Even in cases where users are anxious for new toys, the desired benefits (particularly effectiveness and quality of work life) do not seem to happen without careful management of the process of social as well as technical change. The OA professional must understand the users' psychological, social and political environment to effectively integrate new tools with business practice. Thus the study of office automation must balance business, technical and behavioral perspectives.

Such a broad definition encroaches on the territory of virtually every existing staff group! But there is a reason for defining OA so broadly. Business practice is inherently integrated, moving information and ideas through a wide variety of tools and processes in many locations to get the job done. Yet the information environment that we have built to date is not nearly so well integrated. This necessitates transcription between media and replication of information and processes. It also precludes the kinds of synergy that result from a well-integrated information environment, limiting the depth to which these tools can support management work.

We are experiencing diminishing returns on the margin as individual stand-alone tools become increasingly sophisticated. Only by drawing the many relevant fields together can we expect to explore the next frontier in information support. Without intending to be technical experts in all of these areas, the OA professional can provide a focal point—an integrated umbrella—bringing together on each project all of those with the common goal of supporting office information work.

THE HISTORY OF OFFICE AUTOMATION

This potential for the integration of technologies and disciplines is a recent event, the product of the evolution of a variety of fields relating to information and office practices. Each might be described as a wave of innovation, following an S-curve as it spreads through an organization and through the society. Consider some recent waves of innovation and the decade in which they grew most quickly, each of which is relevant to OA today:

- Telephones in the 1920s: the foundation of the telecommunications infrastructure.
- Industrial engineering in the 1940s: a ratio-nal look at business practice, providing the essential techniques for systems analysis; now being applied to the identification and measurement of structured business transactions and the evaluation of resulting efficiency benefits.
- Operations research in the 1950s: the application of mathematics to decision making; today it provides a theoretic base for systems and network design, and the foundation for a variety of today's structured analytic tools.
- Data processing in the 1950s: the delegation to a computer of routine well-structured business transactions (accounting, inventory, payroll, order processing, etc.), fueling a shift in job-mix away from the routine and towards jobs that manage information and change; today it provides a foundation of structured-transactions processing and the basis of programming techniques.
- Telecommunications management in the 1960s: designated responsibility for managing investments in telecommunications, a profession with skills in traffic analysis and interconnection; provides the basic telecommunications networks, tools for synchronous teleconferencing and techniques for traffic analysis and network design.
- Management information systems in the 1960s: gathering and structuring large transaction-oriented data bases and providing reports to support management decision-making; a primary source of data for today's offices and the basis for public-information provider services.
- Digital networks in the 1970s: tying large computers together nationwide; provides a basic infrastructure for multi-computer information environments, geographic independence for terminal access and a variety of asynchronous communications tools (such as computer-based message systems).
- Distributed processing in the 1970s: mini-computers serving local needs with local computers and data bases; providing the foundation technology for application- and

user-tailored local systems and design techniques for local networks.

- Word processing in the 1970s: the application of minicomputers to text editing, a major revolution in office practices; today it provides a foundation of machine-readable office files and a transcription capability, as well as many local office data bases.
- Organizational development in the 1970s: the application of the behavioral sciences to the management of organizational change; a critical skill in the implementation of the far-reaching changes that come with today's OA tools.
- Decision support systems in the 1980s: the integration of data-base and numeric-analysis tools to provide ad hoc model building capabilities; a shift in focus from the OR/MS provision of solutions to a process-oriented provision for tools.
- Management workstations in the 1980s: coming into commercial use after two decades of research and development, management work-stations provide a variety of document-oriented information tools for managers and professionals.

Each of the above disciplines is important in and of itself. Each has a research base, a unique technical expertise, defined staff groups in many organizations and its own professional societies and curricula. Each will continue as a profession, as it is a full-time job to keep up with developments in any one of these fields.

OA is emerging, not as a competing technology or profession, but as a synthesis of these areas. The OA professional implements a mix of tools and techniques to address business objectives. The OA team generally includes a combination of the above skills, serving as an intermediary between the user and each of the more specialized disciplines — as a smart buyer, if you will — blending skills on project teams to match user needs. It is this integration of disciplines that gives OA the potential for dramatic improvements in office information handling.

OFFICE AUTOMATION TOOLS TODAY

The OA implementor today has a choice of a wide variety of systems and services, all commercially available, relatively easy to use and cost-effective. This myriad of offerings, as seen in trade shows and the press, may seem confusing. However, the variety offers flexibility and helps the implementor to adapt the technologies to the local business needs. The confusion can be reduced and systems can be compared through a framework of information tools in the office. Office information tools fall into four basic categories:

- Text and graphics handling: tools which manipulate documents, for both clerical and managerial/professional use.
- Number handling: decision support systems and other analytic tools which manipulate structured data.
- Information sources: storage and retrieval including information held within the local office, broader organizational information bases such as MIS, and the public data bases available through commercial and government information-providing organizations.
- Communications: synchronous and asynchronous transmission — of text, graphics, numbers and voice — between information workers.

Text and Graphics Handling

Text-editing tools that focus on clerical and secretarial support are termed "word processing". Word processors are simply mini- or micro-computers devoted to text editing. They are distinguished from electronic typewriters by their permanent memory, allowing one to maintain documents in machine-readable form indefinitely for future reference and editing. (This memory also provides a local office data base capability which may be applied to a variety of office files.) Word processors based on mini-computers may support a number of terminals with one computer (shared-logic). Micro-computer word processors may be "stand-alone", or may be hooked together to share printers and storage devices (shared-resource). Those with displays provide much faster editing than those with printers only ("blind").

The most basic word-processing capabilities allow entry and editing of a document. Advanced capabilities include moving blocks of text, editing across files, merging address lists with form letters, scanning for content, and a variety of formatting capabilities. Word processors are often combined with optical-character readers and phototypesetters. They also may be connected to telephone lines or local area networks for transmission of documents to other word processors or for exchanging files with data-processing systems.

Word processors are in common use throughout many businesses, bringing savings in typing efficiency of both everyday correspondence and production typing. In support of professionals, they reduce proofreading time and permit more and better tailored drafts. They make feasible original-document mailings to more people and faster authorship of those documents.

In the early days word processors were very expensive, and the typing function was centralized to warrant this large investment in office technology. This process of tearing the organization to shreds for the sake of machine efficiency did a great deal of damage to administrative careers and professional work patterns, and is rarely recommended today. The newer, less expensive equipment allows putting the computer power where the need is by providing local office machines (often shared by a number of secretaries). In a well-managed change effort, office administrative staff can be very creative in their application of text-handling tools.

The realm of document production tools includes more than word processors. Professionals who author text and graphics can benefit from direct use of terminals. In the most advanced system, paragraphs (and graphics) exist within a hierarchical structure, e.g. chapters, sections, paragraphs and bullets. The structure makes a qualitative difference in the use of the text-editing tools, permitting the author to sketch concepts and edit the flow of thoughts as easily as the words themselves. This more powerful kind of text-handling tool is applied from the very start of the thinking process, not just to capture text after the writing is initially done. It permits new perspectives on one's writing, easy understanding of other people's work and powerful group thinking support. Writing productivity typically doubles, and the results are better organized and communicate more clearly. Since a great deal of business communications take place through written words, these professional text-handling tools provide the foundation of future integrated management-workstations.

Number Handling

Analytic tools focus on the manipulation of structured numeric data. There are a range of tools available as software packages on either micro-computers, local office mini-computers or large timesharing systems. In many organizations, the first professional use of computer terminals was for access to numeric data bases and analytic packages.

Analytic tools may be as simple as custom ("exception") report generators which filter and sort data bases for business analyses. Many organizations use statistical analysis packages for understanding data (such as market research, sales trends, forecasting). Some organizations have developed models of their business which assist in forecasting and analyzing alternatives. Others may use large models (e.g. of the economy) developed by others, available on a subscription basis.

Of particular interest today are Decision Support Systems which are designed to permit ad hoc modeling. These are typically English-like languages which allow a decision maker to sketch out equations that represent one's intuition about the way the world works (e.g. revenue is a function of GNP, interest rates, pricing, etc.) A very good example of a simple DSS is VisiCalc[1] for microcomputers. The more powerful DSS are often combined with numeric data bases (e.g., with economic or accounting data). The benefits of a DSS are both in explicating and improving intuitions through the model development process, and in the use of the model to analyze "what if" alternatives. The intent is to shift planning away from forecasting into a proactive analysis of future options.

Information Sources

Businesses work with information from a variety of sources, both internal and external to the company. When hearing the term "data base", many people think of their internal Management Information System (MIS). MIS usually refers to large internal data bases that result from the transactions-data processing which is central to the business (e.g. accounting, order processing, inventories, personnel and payroll, etc.). In addition to periodic reports ("piles of dingy green printouts"), the MIS often provides custom reports and, in some cases, an alert service ("show me only those items which are more then 10% over budget"). With regard to

MIS, the primary concern of OA is to extract the right data and bring it into an environment where people can work with it.

Many organizations are now organizing their large data bases (either from their MIS or from the outside) in ways that provide safer maintenance and better access by a wider group of people. Efforts to organize documents and data bases on an organization-wide basis are termed Records Management (often utilizing microforms) or Information Resource Management. These provide another source of internal information relevant in the office.

Also internal to the organization are a variety of local office data bases, such as calendars, ticklers, correspondence, forms, reports, etc. These are often very heavily used but with little attention to their maintenance. Word processors, for example, may play a role in providing better access to these critical local office documents and data bases.

In addition to internal data, there is a wide variety of data bases for sale which are maintained by government and commercial organizations. They may be delivered on paper, microforms or on-line. These public data bases address virtually every imaginable discipline, including general business, finance, law, engineering, medicine, current events, travel, etc. They may be bibliographies of the published literature in a field, or may include the full text (or numeric tables) as reference data bases. Getting the right information for a decision can have dramatic impacts on the quality and timeliness of decisions. Hundreds of dollars spent on data base searches can have a significant impact on million-dollar decisions.

Communications

Since managers spend a majority of their time in activities related to communications, telecommunications tools are particularly relevant to their concerns. There are essentially two types of telecommunications tool: synchronous and asynchronous.

Synchronous telecommunications tools allow people to talk interactively when both parties are available at the same time. The most widespread example is the telephone. Electronic meetings, using teleconferencing, allow more than two people to participate, either through speaker-phones and/or by bridging more than two telephone terminals together.

Audio teleconferences are much more effective when participants can exchange notes and documents; one can do so with facsimile, electronic blackboards or writing pads, synchronized projectors, etc. This is termed audiographic teleconferencing. While these devices are inexpensive and readily available, they are often very slow and do not permit both preparation of materials in advance and interactive modifications during the meeting. A relatively new and very powerful form of teleconferencing is "slow-scan" video, where a standard video camera may be focused on documents, slide screens, people or physical objects. By freezing each frame and transmitting it slowly (30–40 seconds), slow-scan teleconferencing provides tremendous flexibility at the low cost of standard telephone lines.

The most powerful form of teleconferencing is full-motion video, similar to broadcast television. This requires high bandwidth telecommunications lines, typically via satellite. It may be done internally with devoted rooms and private satellite channels. Alternatively, public services may provide one-way video with two-way audio (like Holiday Inn's HI-Net[2], most appropriate for conference-like applications) or full two-way interactive video (ATT's Picturephone Meeting Service[3]). While extremely expensive, there are a few applications that could not be done with slow-scan which can be effective with full-motion.

Teleconferencing may reduce travel by as much as 40%, or may be used to cope with a reduced travel budget for economic reasons. The primary impact of travel reduction is on those who travel very frequently, as they tend to travel to meetings which are more susceptible to substitution. Teleconferencing can also permit better collaboration by allowing meetings that would not have warranted travel, meetings at extremely short notice (e.g. during a crisis), and attendees (local experts) that might not have traveled to a remote meeting.

Synchronous tools require that all parties be available at the same time. However, many people experience frustration with so-called "telephone tag," with only 20–30% of calls reaching the intended party on each try. This is particularly a problem with very busy people and with communications across time zones. Asynchronous telecommunications tools ("electronic mail") permit the sender and receiver to communicate regardless of schedule mismatches. Telex/TWX and private terminal-based message systems provide a common example, although they tend to be remote from the office and used for administrative messages that are not private in nature. Facsimile and communicating word processors serve to put the local office administrative systems in contact and may be used for sending urgent documents in lieu of the postal system.

The most common starting point for managerial use of office automation is the computer-based message system (CBMS). A CBMS provides an on-line message system, permitting people to type in messages on local terminals and send them to one or more distant colleagues. The messages are delivered instantly to an on-line file that is the recipient's in-basket. Then, when the recipient next checks into the computer, he or she is notified of new mail. The recipient may scan the in-basket, read messages, file or delete them and respond with another message. Messages are typically brief (4-8 lines) and informal.

CBMS's replace telephones more than memoranda. They provide a person-to-person telecommunications environment that can widen one's communications circles and pick up the metabolism of project teams. They are easy to use, relatively inexpensive and tend to spread rapidly through an organization. While some users ask their secretaries to handle the system for them, CMBS's have generated many case studies that demonstrate that managers do indeed type — not documents, but quick and rough messages — when the tools address a real perceived need in business and when they can be easily learned and operated.

WHAT MAKES OFFICE AUTOMATION DIFFERENT

The concept of "value added" is the key to differentiating OA from past waves of innovation. Value added applications address the function for which an office was designed. Information tools may enable new ways of thinking and collaborating, and enable better (not just faster) work. The target user is the manager or professional, as well as administrative staff. The intent is to improve effectiveness rather than simply to reduce the cost of support functions.

These benefits, termed "value added", make a qualitative difference in the impact OA has on the user. The leverage on the bottom line is most significant when information tools address the central business purpose of the user group, rather than the support functions which surround their work [1]. For example:

- Computer-based message systems can help a geographically dispersed project team deliver more timely and better results, permitting collaboration daily rather than at monthly meetings in one city or another.
- Teleconferencing can not only replace some travel costs but also permits more frequent meetings and the inclusion of a larger number of relevant people.
- Interactive retrieval of information from public data bases gives managers more comprehensive, current and relevant information pertaining to a particular question, with much less effort than it would take to scan even a portion of those publications on a regular basis.
- Structured text-handling tools, like the one with which this paper was written, do more than support the capture and editing of text; they are used from the very start of the thinking process, capturing ideas and allowing the author to interactively structure his or her thoughts.
- Decision support systems permit planners to consider alternative scenarios and business strategies, rather than generate a forecast that represents a single guess at the future.

The integration of the variety of tools and techniques in OA produces synergy — benefits beyond the sum of the parts [2]. The tools not only support a broader variety of tasks, but permit new ways of working that could not have happened before. The potential impacts on working patterns and effectiveness are dramatic, often with a return on investment counted in the thousands. One's information world expands, allowing wider circles of close collaboration, new kinds of interactions with concepts and analyses, more time and support for creative thinking and more professional outputs. An increasing portion of each business transaction — or thought process — is done on-line. Both the process and the tools are applicable to increasingly higher levels of management.

Value-added benefits are more difficult to measure than cost-displacement. There is no single right way to measure it, just as there is no one way to evaluate what your day yesterday was worth to your employer. However value-added benefits are far from "soft". They are typically far more significant (in both size and relevance) than administrative efficiency. Metrics can be generated which convert value-added to real dollars, but only after business objectives have been clearly defined.

This focus on managerial/professional effectiveness, over and above efficiency, is the current frontier in the application of information tools. This wave of innovation, still in its early stages, refers specifically to applications which focus on the value added by the integration of information tools in the office.

WHERE WE STAND

Progress in this wave of innovation termed "value added" can be gauged by stages of growth. Based on patterns in previous diffusions of innovation, we can see current issues in perspective and anticipate some managerial issues in advance. There are a number of stage hypotheses that describe various types of growth pattern. Larry Day, while Director of the Diebold Automated Office Program, developed a Stages of Growth in Office Automation terminology that is useful [3]:

1. Conception: first understanding of the concept of value added, and willingness to invest in it.
2. Initiation: the first few managerial/professional information systems pilots.

3. Contagion: the rapid expansion of value-added information tools throughout the organization
4. Consolidation: the integration and consolidation necessary to make an operationally efficient system; provides the basis for the next wave of innovation.

One may speculate as to the next wave of innovation — perhaps cybernetics, a whole-organization information perspective. But in the early 1980s it is more useful to focus on the first three stages of growth: conception, initiation and contagion.

In 1978, a very small number of organizations in the United States were actively experimenting with value added OA. But by 1980, fully one out of three of the Fortune 1000 were experimenting with managerial/professional tools, and over 20% were applying them in user applications [4]. One year later, those proportions grew to two-thirds with value-added pilots and one-third with users directly using terminals [5].

In other words, a majority of corporations have value-added pilots in process. One can expect this number to approach 100% by the mid-1980s, with an ever-growing number of organizations experiencing widespread use. And at the same time, pilots will spread downward to smaller businesses. By the latter half of the decade, advanced management workstations might well be common in most business offices.

Thus, OA managers today range from just getting started to managing the rapid growth of the contagion stage. The issues about which they express concern vary with the stage:

1. In the conception stage, the OA manager must convince executive management that the concept of value added is worth experimentation. This may involve organizational plans, small-scale demonstrations and various forms of manage-

ment education. At the same time, the OA manager (to be) is rapidly educating him/herself in the available tools and techniques of the trade. In many organizations, interest in OA arises out of successes in word processing or interactive MIS. Formalized staff groups are the exception. The manager is generally concerned with getting seed money, building a charter and beginning a staff. Graduation to Stage 2 most frequently occurs with the implementation of an advanced pilot within the OA group itself.

2. In the initiation stage, the first value-added pilot is built. A majority of organizations start within the OA team itself, to learn, evaluate and to build the credibility of the implementors. The choice of the first user and application is critical, as this opinion leader must work closely with the team to ensure success. Managerial concerns include identification of an influential opinion leader, selection of technologies with consideration for future integration, effective management of change and developing an acceptable cost-justification. Once it has clearly been demonstrated that managers do indeed type (when it solves their problem), Stage 3 occurs before you know it.

3. In the contagion stage, responsibility for cost justification is placed with the user and standard approaches to justification are routinely accepted. The OA staff must grow rapidly and must formalize design and implementation methodologies to ensure widespread successes. Customer service must be professional and dependable. Many functions begin to be moved off to operational management. Primary management concerns are hiring and training OA staff, getting enough hardware, maintaining the user's patience and managing the overall diffusion process rather than individual projects.

While the nature of the challenge changes dramatically through the stages of growth, some issues never change. Those who are most successful play a proactive role in managing change. Most are quick to point out that they always focus on the business problem to be solved, not a technology to be sold. Successful OA managers seem to focus at least as much of their attention on the process as they do on the content — on the people issues rather than chiefly on the new technologies. The most successful OA managers recognize their role in business growth and develop the OA function as a key strategic resource.

CONCLUSIONS

Many OA managers have found it useful to view their challenge as one of developing and implementing a strategy for diffusion of innovation — i.e., a plan for setting up a new staff function and driving change. Developing such a strategy can be significantly aided by learning from the experience of others, both more advanced OA organizations and prior waves of innovation. While there are many significant issues that are technical in nature, the primary concerns of OA managers at all stages of growth are organizational. They may be summarized in three broad areas:

1. Building an organization to support office automation.
2. Implementing pilots of advanced information tools in key areas to initiate change.
3. Planning for the eventual integration of all of the information tools in the office.

There are many open issues in all of these areas facing the OA community of practitioners, consultants and researchers. An OA manager would be considered very successful indeed if an inevitable revolution looks anything like well-managed evolution, as captured in an evolving strategy for the implementation of OA. This new journal provides us with a forum for the exchange of ideas and experiences, so that we can all contribute to a more gentle and effective wave of innovation.

REFERENCES

1. N. DEAN MEYER, A day in the office of the future, Telecommunications Policy, December 1979.
2. N. DEAN MEYER, Planning for integration in office automation, Systems Objectives Solutions, Vol. 1, No. 4.
3. LARRY DAY, Stages of growth in office automation, Fourth Plenary Meeting, The Diebold Automated Office Program, October 1979.
4. N. DEAN MEYER, Strategies for getting started in office automation, Fifth Plenary Meeting, The Diebold Automated Office Program, February 1980.
5. N. DEAN MEYER, Research report: Human resource impacts of office automation, Seventh Plenary Meeting, The Diebold Automated Office Program, March 1981.

NOTES

1. Trademark: Personal Software, Inc.
2. Trademark: Holiday Inns, Inc.
3. Trademark: American Telephone and Telegraph, Inc.

QUESTIONS

1. Define office automation (OA) in your own terms. How does your definition compare with that of Meyer?
2. Is it possible that OA may not be at all efficient, at least in the short run?
3. The author offers a decade-by-decade description of the history of OA. Project OA into the years 1990 and 2000. What do you see?
4. Which OA "tool" do you perceive as most beneficial to task reduction: text handlers, number handlers, information sources, or communication devices?
5. Which OA tool most encourages creativity?
6. The author calls MISs "piles of dingy green printouts." How can you offset such a misconception via OA?
7. Is there a real future for teleconferencing as a management decision tool?
8. Larry Day is quoted as presenting a four-stage OA growth process. Do you perceive other steps in such an evolution? How about contamination (uncontrolled OA growth), control (designing security into OA), and conclusion (new technology replaces the current OA)?
9. Is it conceivable to link OA with DBMS, DDP, DBMS, or AI? Which pairings are most naturally attractive?

Expert Systems: The Next Challenge for Managers*

INTRODUCTION

In this age of the "microchip revolution," effective managers are finding ways to learn and profitably use the myriad applications of the silicon chip. These applications include personal computers, office automation, robotics, computer graphics, and the various forms of broad-band and narrow-band communication. One of the most intriguing of these new applications to emerge from the research labs and move into the practical world of business is Expert Systems (ES). Most literature about Expert Systems describes the technical concepts upon which they are based and the small number of systems already in use.

In this article we shift this focus and discuss how these systems can be used in a broad range of business applications. We will argue that in many business applications, the knowledge that can be feasibly encoded in an Expert System is not in itself sufficient to make satisfactory decisions. Therefore we believe that our focus should increasingly be on designing Expert *Support* Systems (ESS) that will aid, rather than replace, human decision makers.

After briefly defining a few Expert Systems concepts, we offer an expansion of a classical framework for understanding managerial problem-solving. We then use this framework to identify the limits of current expert systems and decision support systems technology, and show how expert support systems can be seen as the next logical step in both fields.

BASIC CONCEPTS

Broadly defined, Artificial Intelligence (AI) is the area which involves the design and construction of computer systems that can perform at the level of intelligent human behavior. The prospect of machines that *reason intelligently* has fueled the current publicity of AI in the popular press (3, 6). There is no doubt the AI has been grossly oversold, particularly with respect to the claims about natural language understanding, and progress in machine vision. Despite this business journal "hype" and the inevitable

*By Fred L. Luconi, Thomas W. Malone, and Michael S. Scott Morton. Reprinted from "Expert Systems: The Next Challenge for Managers," by Fred L. Luconi, Thomas W. Malone, and Michael S. Scott Morton, *Sloan Management Review,* Summer 1986, by permission of the publisher. Copyright © 1986 by the Sloan Management Review Association. All rights reserved.

backlash that is just beginning, it is an indisputable fact that there are an increasing number of practical business applications of Expert Systems in use today.

When one stops to look at reality it turns out that AI technology has been used to develop two types of systems of particular interest to management: Expert Systems and a variation of Expert Systems that we will call Expert Support Systems.

Expert Systems

Expert Systems can be used to increase a human's ability to exploit available knowledge that is in limited supply. They do this by building on the captured and encoded relevant experience of an expert in the field. This experience is then available as a resource to the less expert. For example, the Schlumberger Corporation uses its "Dipmeter Advisor" to access the interpretive abilities of a handful of their most productive geological experts and make it available to their field geologists all over the world (16). The program takes oil well log data about the geological characteristics of a well and makes inferences about the probable location of oil in that region.

Another example of an early system in practical use is known as XCON. Developed at Digital Equipment Corporation in a joint effort with Carnegie-Mellon University, XCON uses some 3300 rules and 5500 product descriptions to configure the specific detailed components of VAX and other computer systems in response to the customers' overall orders. The system first determines what, if any, substitutions and additions have to be made to the order so that it is complete and consistent, and then this system produces a number of diagrams showing the electrical connections and room layout for the 50 to 150 components in a typical system (4).

This application was attempted unsuccessfully several times using traditional programming techniques before the AI effort was initiated. The system has been in daily use now for over four years and the savings have been substantial, not only in terms of the technical editor's scarce time, but also in ensuring that no component is missing at installation time, an occurrence that delays the customer's acceptance of the system (12).

Expert Support Systems

ESS (Expert Support Systems) take ES techniques and apply them to a much wider class of problems than is possible with pure expert systems. They do this by pairing the human with the expert system, thus creating a joint decision process in which the human is the dominant partner, providing overall problem-solving direction as well as specific knowledge not incorporated in the system. Some of this knowledge can be thought of beforehand and made explicit, thus becoming embedded in the expert system. However, much of the knowledge may be imprecise and will remain below the level of consciousness, to be recalled to the conscious level of the decision-maker only when triggered by the evolving problem context. Such systems represent the next generation of Decision Support Systems (DSS).

Expert Systems are also called *knowledge-based systems.* They incorporate not only data but the expert knowledge that represents how that data is to be interpreted and used. Recent progress in the field of Expert Systems has been greatly aided by two factors. One has been the enormous increase in the computer power available per dollar. The so-called "LISP" machines are on the market at low prices and are well-suited for dealing with heuristics which involve much probing and reprobing of the relevant knowledge base as the system weaves together an alternative worthy of suggestion (1).

A second factor making AI applications, such as Expert Systems, feasible today is the development of programming tools for non-specialists that are capable of supporting symbol manipulation and incremental development. These facilities permit one to prototype, experiment and modify as required and have resulted in "Power Tools for Programmers" (14)—environments of significantly greater potential than those usually provided by traditional data processing resources.

Definitions

With these examples in mind we can now define Expert Systems as follows:

> Expert Systems—computer programs that use specialized symbolic reasoning to solve difficult problems well.

In other words Expert Systems: (1) use specialized knowledge about a particular problem area (such as geological analysis or computer configuration) rather than just general purpose knowledge that would apply to all problems, (2) use symbolic (and often qualitative) reasoning rather than just numerical calculations, and (3) perform at a level of competence that is better than that of non-expert humans.

Expert Support Systems use all these same techniques but focus on helping people solve the problems:

> Expert Support Systems—computer programs that use specialized symbolic reasoning to help people solve difficult problems well.

Heuristic Reasoning

One of the most important ways in which expert systems differ from traditional computer applications is in their use of heuristic reasoning. Traditional applications are completely understood and therefore can employ algorithms, that is, precise rules that, when followed, lead to the correct conclusion. For example, the amount of a payroll check for an employee is calculated according to a precise set of rules. Expert Systems use heuristic techniques. An heuristic system involves judgemental reasoning, trial and error, and therefore is appropriate for more complex problems. The heuristic decision rules or inference procedures generally provide a good—but not necessarily optimum—answer.

Problems appropriate for AI techniques are those that cannot be solved algorithmically; that is, by precise rules. The problems are either too large, such as the possibilities encountered in the game of chess, or too imprecise, such as the diagnosis of a particular person's medical condition.

Components of Expert Systems

To begin to see how expert systems (and expert support systems) are different from traditional computer applications, it is important to understand what the components of a typical expert system are (See Figure 1). In addition to the *user interface* for commu-

Figure 1.   Expert Systems Architecture

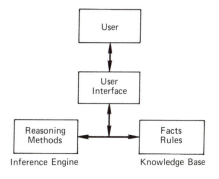

nicating with a human user, a typical expert system also has (1) a *knowledge base* of facts and rules related to the problem and (2) an *inference engine* or reasoning methods for using the information in the knowledge base to solve problems. Separating these two components makes it much easier to change the system as the problem changes or becomes better understood. For example, new rules can be added to the knowledge base, one by one, in such a way that all the old facts and reasoning methods can still be used.

Knowledge Base

In order to flexibly use specialized knowledge about many different kinds of problems, AI researchers have developed a number of new "knowledge representation" techniques. Using these techniques to provide structure for a body of knowledge is still very much an art, and is practiced by an emerging group of professionals known as "knowledge engineers". Knowledge engineers in this field are akin to the systems analysts of Data Processing (DP) applications. They work with the "experts" and draw out the relevant expertise in a form that can be encoded in a computer program. Three of the most important techniques for encoding this knowledge are: (1) production rules, (2) semantic nets, and (3) frames.

Production Rules. Production rules are particularly useful in building systems based on heuristic methods (17). These are simple "if-then" rules that are often used to represent the empirical consequences of a given condition: or the action that should be taken in a given situation. For example, a medical diagnosis system might have a rule like

If: 1. The patient has fever, and 2. The patient has a runny nose

Then: It is very likely (.9) that the patient has a cold.

A computer configuration system might have a rule like

If: 1. There is an unassigned single port disk drive, and 2. There is a free controller,

Then: Assign the disk drive to the controller port.

Semantic Nets.   Another formalism that is often more convenient than production rules for representing certain kinds of relational knowledge is called "semantic networks" or "semantic nets." For example, in order to apply the rule about assigning disk drives that was shown above, a system would need to know what part numbers corresponded to single port disk drives, controllers, and so forth. Figure 2 shows how this knowledge might be represented in a network of "nodes" connected by "links" that signify which classes of components are subsets of other classes.

Frames.   In many cases, it is convenient to gather into one place a number of different kinds of information about an object. For example, Figure 3 shows how several dimensions (such as length, width, and power requirements) that describe electrical components might be represented as different "slots" in a "frame" about electrical components. Unlike traditional records in a data base, frames often contain additional features such as "default values" and "attached procedures." For example, if the default value for voltage requirement of an electrical component is 110 volts then the system would infer that a new electrical component required 110 volts unless explicit information to the contrary was provided. An attached procedure might automatically update the "volume" slot, whenever "length," "height," or "width" are changed.

Figure 2.   Semantic Networks

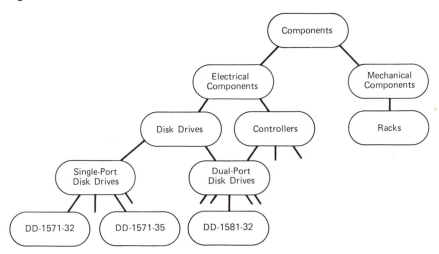

These three knowledge representation techniques, production rules, semantic nets, and frames, have considerable power as they permit us to capture knowledge in a way that can be exploited by the "inference engine" to produce good, workable answers to the questions at hand.

Figure 3.   Frames

Electrical Component	
Part No.	
Length	
Width	
Height	
Volume	
Voltage	

Inference Engine

The inference engine contains the reasoning methods that might be used by human problem solvers when attacking problems. As these are separate from the knowledge base it permits either to be changed relatively independent of the other. Two reasoning methods often employed with production rules are *forward chaining* and *backward chaining*. Imagine, for instance, that we have a set of production rules like those shown in Figure 4 for a personal financial planning expert system. Imagine also that we know the current client's tax bracket is 50%, his liquidity is greater than $100,000, and he has a high tolerance for risk. By forward chaining through the rules, one at a time, the system could infer that exploratory oil and gas investments should be recommended for this client. With a larger rule base, many other investment recommendations might be deduced as well.

Now imagine that we only want to know that whether exploratory oil and gas investments are appropriate for a particular client and we are not interested in any other investments at the moment. The system can use exactly the same rule base to answer this specific question more efficiently by

Figure 4.

Forward Chaining

If	Tax bracket = 50% and
	liquidity is greater than $100,000
Then	A tax shelter is indicated.
If	A tax shelter is indicated
	and risk tolerance is low
Then	Recommend developmental oil
	and gas investments.
If	A tax shelter is indicated
	and risk tolerance is high
Then	Recommend exploratory oil
	and gas investments.

Backward Chaining (Subgoaling)

What about exploratory oil and gas?

If	Tax bracket = 50% and
	liquidity is greater than $100,000
Then	A tax shelter is indicated.
If	A tax shelter is indicated
	and risk tolerance is low
Then	Recommend developmental oil
	and gas investments.
If	A tax shelter is indicated
	and risk tolerance is high
Then	Recommend exploratory oil
	and gas investments.

"backward chaining" through the rules. When backward chaining the system starts with a goal (e.g., "show that this client needs exploratory oil and gas investments") and asks at each stage what subgoals it would need to reach to achieve this goal. For instance, in this example, to conclude that the client needs exploratory oil and gas investments, we can use the third rule if we know that risk tolerance is high (which we already do know) and that a tax shelter is indicated. To conclude that a tax shelter is indicated we

have to find another rule (in this case, the first one) and then check whether its conditions are satisfied. In this case, they are, so our goal is achieved: we know we can recommend exploratory oil and gas investments to this client.

With these basic concepts in mind we turn now to a framework that puts Expert Systems and Expert Support Systems into a management context.

FRAMEWORK FOR EXPERT SUPPORT SYSTEMS

The framework developed in this section begins to allow us to identify those classes of business problems that are appropriate for Data Processing (DP), Decision Support Systems (DSS), Expert Systems (ES), and Expert Support Systems (ESS). We can, in addition, clarify the relative contributions of humans and computers in the various classes of applications.

This framework extends the earlier work of Gorry and Scott Morton, "Framework of Management Information Systems," (8) in which they relate Herbert Simon's seminal work on structured vs. unstructured decision making (15) to Robert Anthony's strategic planning, management control, and operational control (2). Figure 5 presents this original framework. Gorry and Scott Morton argued that to improve the quality of decisions, the manager must seek not only to match the type and quality of information and its presentation to the category of decision, but also to choose a system that reflects the degree of the problem's structure.

With the benefit of experience in building and using Decision Support Systems, and in light of the insights garnered from the field of Artificial Intelligence, it is useful to expand and rethink the structured/unstructured dimension of the original framework. Simon

Figure 5.

	STRATEGIC PLANNING	MANAGEMENT CONTROL	OPERATIONAL CONTROL
Structured			
Semi-Structured			
Unstructured			

had broken down decision making into three phases; Intelligence, Design, and Choice (I,D,C). It was argued in the original article that a structured decision was one where all three phases (I,D,C) were fully understood and "computable" by the human decision maker. As a result they could be programmed. In unstructured decisions, one or more of these three phases was not fully understood.

We can extend this distinction by replacing Simon's, Intelligence, Design and Choice with Alan Newell's insightful categorization of problem solving (13), as consisting of the following components:

Goals; Constraints; State Space; Search Control Knowledge; and Operators.

In a business context, it seems helpful to relabel these problem characteristics and group them into four categories:

1. *Data* — the dimensions and values necessary to represent the state of the world that is relevant to the problem (i.e., the "state space")
2. *Procedures* — the sequences of steps (or "operators") used in solving the problem
3. *Goals and Constraints* — the desired results of problem solving and the constraints on what can and cannot be done
4. *Strategies* — the flexible strategies used in deciding which procedures to apply to achieve goals (i.e. the "search control knowledge")

Thus we argue that the structured-unstructured continuum of the original framework can be thought of using these four elements. A problem is fully structured when all four elements are well understood and fully unstructured when the four remain vague. Such a categorization helps us to match classes of system with types of problem, as illustrated in Figure 6.

For some problems we can apply a standard procedure (i.e., an algorithm or formula) and proceed directly to a conclusion with no need for flexible problem-solving strategies. For example, we can use standard procedures to compute withholding taxes and prepare employee paychecks and we can use the classical economic order quantity formula to solve straightforward inventory control problems. In other cases a solution can be found only by identifying alternative approaches, and thinking through (in some cases via simulation) the effects of these alternative courses of action. One then chooses the approach that appears to create the best result. For example, to determine which of three sales strategies to use for a new product, a manager might want to explore the consequences of each for advertising expenses, sales force utilization, revenue, and so forth. In the remainder of this section we will discuss the range of these different types of problems and the appropriate kinds of systems for each.

Figure 6.   Problem Types

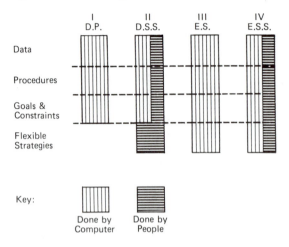

Key: Done by Computer   Done by People

Type I Problems — Data Processing

A fully structured problem is one in which all four of the elements of the problem are structured. That is, we have well stated goals, and we can specify the input data needed, and there are standard procedures by which a solution may be calculated. No complex strategies for generating and evaluating alternatives are needed. Fully structured problems are computable and one can decide if such computation is justifiable given the amounts of time and computing resource involved.

These problems are well suited to the use of conventional programming techniques. In conventional programming, virtually everything about the problem is well defined. In effect, the expert (i.e., the analyst/programmer) has already solved the problem. He or she must only sequence the data through the particular program. Figure 6 represents pictorially the class of decision problems that can be solved economically using conventional programming techniques. We will refer to this class as Type I problems, prob-

lems historically thought of as ones suited for Data Processing.

It is interesting to note that the economics of conventional programming are being fundamentally altered with the provision of new tools such as an "analyst's workbench." (14) These are professional work stations used by the systems analyst to develop flow chart representations of the problem and then move automatically to testable, running code. The more advanced of these stations happen to use AI techniques, thus turning these new techniques into tools to make our old approaches more effective in classical DP application areas.

Type II Problems — Decision Support Systems

As we leave problems which are fully structured we begin to deal with many of the problems organizations have to grapple with each day. These are cases where standard procedures are helpful but not sufficient by themselves, where the data may be incompletely represented, and where the goals and constraints are only partially understood. Traditional data processing systems cannot solve these problems. Fortunately, we have the possibility in these cases, of letting the computer perform the well-understood parts of the problem solving while relying on humans to use their goals, intuition, and general knowledge to formulate problems, modify and control the problem solving and interpret the results. As Figure 6 shows, the human users may provide or modify data, procedures or goals, and they may use their knowledge of all these factors to decide on problem-solving strategies.

In many of the best known Decision Support Systems (11) for example, the computer applies standard procedures to certain highly structured data but relies on the human users to decide which procedures are appropriate in a given situation and whether a given result is satisfactory or not. For example, the investment managers who used the portfolio management system (11) did not rely on the computer for either making final decisions about portfolio composition or for deciding on which procedures to use for analysis. They used the computer to execute the procedures they felt were appropriate, for example calculating portfolio diversity and expected returns, but the managers themselves proposed alternative portfolios and decided whether a given diversification or return was acceptable. Many people who use spreadsheet programs today for "what if" analyses follow a similar flexible strategy of proposing an action, letting the computer predict its consequences and then deciding what action to propose next.

Type III — Expert Systems

Using AI programming techniques like production rules and frames, expert systems are able to encode some of the same kinds of goals, heuristics, and strategies that people use in solving problems but that have previously been very difficult to use in computer programs. These techniques make it possible to design systems that don't just follow standard procedures, but instead use flexible problem-solving strategies to explore a number of possible alternatives before picking a solution.

For some cases, like the XCON system, these techniques can capture almost all the relevant knowledge about the problem. As of 1983, fewer than one out of every 1000 orders configured by XCON was misconfigured because of missing or incorrect rules. (Only about 10% of the orders had to be corrected for any reason at all and almost all of these errors were due to missing descriptions of rarely used parts (4).)

We call the problems where essentially all the relevant knowledge for flexible problem solving can be encoded Type III Problems. The systems that solve them are Expert Systems.

It is instructive to note, however, that even with XCON, which is probably the most extensively tested system in commercial use today, new knowledge is continually being added and humans still check every order the system configures. As the developers of XCON remark (4, p. 27):

> "There is no more reason to believe now than there was [in 1979] that [XCON] has all the knowledge relevant to its configuration task. This, coupled with the fact that [XCON] deals with an ever-changing domain implies its development will never be finished."

If XCON, which operates in the fairly restricted domain of computer order configuration, never contains all the knowledge relevant to its problem, it appears much less likely that we will ever be able to codify all the knowledge needed for less clearly bounded problems like financial analysis, strategic planning, and project management. Even in what might appear to be the fairly simple case of job shop scheduling, there are often very many continually changing and possibly implicit constraints on what people, machines, and parts are needed and available for different steps in a manufacturing process (7).

What this suggests is that for very many of the problems of practical importance in business we should focus our attention on designing systems that *support* expert users rather than replacing them.

Type IV — Expert Support Systems

Even in situations where important kinds of problem-solving knowledge in all four areas of the problem cannot feasibly be encoded, it is still possible to use expert systems techniques. This dramatically extends the capabilities of computers beyond previous technologies such as DP and DSS.

What is important, in these cases, is to design Expert Support Systems (See Figure 6) with very good and deeply embedded "user interfaces" that enable their human users to easily inspect and control the problem-solving process. In other words, a good expert support system should be both *accessible* and *malleable*. Many expert support systems make their problem-solving process accessible to users by providing explanation capabilities. For example, the MYCIN medical diagnosis program can explain to a doctor at any time why it is asking for a given piece of information or what rules it used to arrive at a given conclusion. For a system to be malleable, users should be able to easily change data, procedures, goals, or strategies at any important point in the

problem-solving process. Systems with this capability are still rare, but an early version of the Dipmeter Advisor suggests how it might be provided (5). In this version there was no satisfactory way to automatically detect certain kinds of geological patterns, so human experts used a graphical display of the data to mark and annotate these patterns. The system then continued its analysis using this information.

An even more vivid example of how a system can be made accessible and malleable is provided by the Steamer Program (10) for teaching people to reason about operating a steam plant. This system has colorful graphic displays of the schematic flows in the simulated plant, the status of different valves and gauges, and the pressures in different places. Users of the system can manipulate these displays (using a "mouse" pointing device) to control the valves, temperatures, and so forth. The system continually updates its simulation results and expert diagnostics based on these user actions.

Summary of Framework

This framework helps clarify a number of issues. First, it highlights, as did the original Gorry and Scott Morton framework, the importance of matching system type to problem type. In the original 1971 article, however, the primary practical points to be made were that traditional DP technologies should not be used for semi-structured and unstructured problems where new DSS technologies were more appropriate; secondly that interactive human/computer use opened up an extended class of problems where computers could be usefully exploited. The most important practical point to be made today is again two-fold: first, that "pure" expert systems should not be used for partially understood problems where expert support systems are more appropriate, and second that expert systems techniques can be used to dramatically extend the capabilities of traditional decision support systems.

Figure 7 shows, in an admittedly simplified way, how we can view expert support systems as the next logical step in each of two somewhat separate progressions. On the left side of the figure, we see that DSS developed out of a practical recognition of the limits of DP for helping real human beings solve complex problems in actual organizations. The right side of the figure reflects a largely independent evolution that took place in computer science research laboratories and that developed from a recognition of the limits of traditional computer science techniques for solving the kinds of complex problems that people are able to solve. We are now at the point where these two separate progressions can be united to help solve a broad range of important practical problems.

THE IMPORTANCE OF EXPERT SUPPORT SYSTEMS FOR MANAGEMENT

The real importance of ESS lies in the ability of these systems to harness and make full use of our scarcest resource: the talent and experience of key members of the organization. There can be considerable benefits in capturing the expert's experience and making it available to those in an organization who are less expert in the subject in question.

As organizations and their problems become more complex, management can benefit from initiating prototype ES and ESSs. The question now facing managers is when to start, and in which areas.

The "when" to start is relatively easy to answer. It is "now" for exploratory work. For some organizations this will be a program of education and active monitoring of the field. For others the initial investment may take the form of an experimental low budget prototype. For a few, once the exploration is over, it will make good economic sense to go forward with a full-fledged working prototype. Conceptual and technological developments have made it possible to begin an active prototype development phase. These developments have taken place in several areas, for example:

- Hardware is getting smaller, cheaper, and more powerful. Programming languages such as LISP enable us to deal with AI concepts (18). In addition, the concepts, tools, and techniques for knowledge engineering—the work involved in capturing and codifying the knowledge of an expert—are beginning to be understood. AI research has always been characterized by its need for large amounts of computing resources. As the cost of hardware becomes irrelevant to the economics of problem solution, the techniques of AI are becoming more economically viable.
- As companies begin to install global communications networks of either the broad or narrow band varieties, possibilities abound for the collection and interpretation of data. In some organizations, this development will provide the potential for enhanced decision

Figure 7.   Progressions in Computer System Development

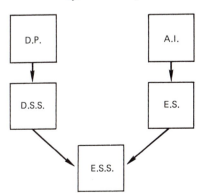

making and the opportunity for effective use of AI techniques.

- The recent proliferation of firms offering specialized AI services has resulted in the creation of new software and an increasingly large group of knowledge engineers. Some have started companies and are hiring and training people who are focussing on business applications (3).

The second question facing managers is the one of where to start. One possible area for initial experimentation is the productive use of an organization's assets. In what looks to be a decade of low growth, it will be essential to acquire and use assets astutely. Digital Equipment Corporation's use of an Expert System for "equipment configuration control" is one example. A second sensible place in which to begin using AI is in those areas in which the organization stands to gain a distinct competitive advantage. Schlumberger would seem to feel that their ES used as a drilling advisor is one such example.

It is interesting that of the more than 20 organizations personally known to the authors to be investing in work in ES and ESS almost none would allow themselves to be quoted. The reasons given basically boiled down to the fact that they were experimenting with prototypes that they were expecting to give them a competitive advantage in making or delivering their product or service. Examples of this where we can quote without attribution are cases such as an ESS for supporting the cross-selling of financial services products, such as an insurance salesman selling a tax shelter. In another case it is the desire of a financial services organization to evaluate the credit worthiness of a loan applicant.

It is clear that there are a great many problem areas where even our somewhat primitive ability to deal with ES can permit the building of useful first generation systems. With ESS the situation is even brighter, as any help we can provide the beleaguered "expert" will provide leverage for the organization.

The Problems, Risks, and Issues

It would be irresponsible to conclude this article without commenting on the fact that Expert Systems and Expert Support Systems are in their infancy, and researchers and users alike must be realistic about the capabilities of these new systems. One risk, already apparent, is that the expert systems will be poorly defined and oversold, and the resulting backlash will hinder progress. It can be argued that the Western economies lost the most recent round on the economic battlefield to Japan, due in part to their failure to manage productivity and quality as well as their inability to select the markets in which they wished to excel. We face a similar risk with Expert Systems and their applications, and if we are careless we will lose out in exploiting this particular potential of the information era.

There is a danger of proceeding too quickly, too recklessly, without paying careful attention to what we are doing. One example is that we may well embed our knowledge (necessarily incomplete at any moment in time) into a system that is effective when used by the person who created it. When this same system is used by others, however, there is a risk of misapplication; holes in another user's knowledge could represent a pivotal element in the logic leading to a solution. While these holes are implicitly recognized by the creator of the knowledge base, they may be quite invisible to a new user of the knowledge base.

The challenge of proceeding at an appropriate pace can be met if managers treat the subjects of Artificial Intelligence, Expert Systems, Expert Support Systems, and Decision Support Systems as serious topics which will require management attention if they are to be exploited properly. Managers must recognize the differences between Type I and II problems, for which the older techniques are appropriate, and the new methods available for Types III and IV.

CONCLUSIONS

There are, then, some basic risks and constraints which will be with us for some time. However, the potential of AI techniques are obvious, and if we proceed cautiously, acknowledging the problems, we can begin to achieve worthwhile results.

The illustrations used here are merely two of some fifteen or twenty that have been described in some detail (see References) and have been built in a relatively brief period of time with primitive tools. This is a start-up phase for Expert Systems and Expert Support Systems, Phase Zero. Business has attempted to develop expert systems applications since 1980 and, despite the enormity of some of the problems, has succeeded in developing a number of simple and powerful prototypes.

The state of the art is such that everyone building an expert system must endure this primitive start-up phase in order to learn what is involved in this fascinating new field. We expect that it will take until about 1990 for ES and ESS to be fully recognized as having achieved worthwhile business results.

However Expert Systems and Expert Support Systems are with us now, albeit in a primitive form. The challenge for management is to harness these tools to increase the effectiveness of the organization and thus add value for its stakeholders. The pioneering firms are leading the way; once a section of territory has been staked out, the experience gained by these leaders will be hard to equal. The time to examine the options carefully is now.

REFERENCES

1. ALEXANDER, T., "The Next Revolution in Computer Programming," *Fortune,* October 29, 1984, pp. 81–86.

2. ANTHONY, R. N., "Planning and Control Systems: A Framework for Analysis," Boston: Harvard University Graduate School of Business Administration, 1965.

3. *Business Week,* "Artificial Intelligence: The Second Computer Age Begins," March 3, 1982.

4. BACHANT, J., and McDERMOTT, J., "R1 Revisited: Four Years in the Trenches," AI Magazine, Fall, 1984. pp. 21–32.

5. DAVIS, R., AUSTIN, H., CARLBORN, I., FRAWLEY, B., PRUCHNIK, P., SNEIDERMAN, R., GILREATH, J. A., "The Dipmeter Advisor: Interpretation of Geological Signals," *Proceedings of the Seventh International Joint Conference on Artificial Intelligence,* Vancouver, Canada: 1981, pp. 846–849.

6. *Fortune,* "Teaching Computers the Art of Reason," May 17, 1982, and "Computers on the Road to Self-Improvement," June 14, 1982.

7. FOX, M. S., "Constraint-Directed Search: A Case Study of Job-Shop Scheduling," Carnegie-Mellon University Robotics Institute, Technical Report No CMU-RI-TR-83-22, Pittsburgh, Pennsylvania: 1983.

8. GORRY, ANTHONY, AND MICHAEL S. SCOTT MORTON, "A Framework for Management Information Systems," Sloan Manage-

ment Review, Massachusetts Institute of Technology, Vol. 13, No. 1, Fall 1971.

9. HAYES-ROTH, FREDERICK, DONALD A. WATERMAN, DOUGLAS B. LENAT, Editors, *Building Expert Systems,* Addison-Wesley, 1983.

10. HOLLAN, J. D., HUTCHINS, E. L. & WEITZMAN, L., "Steamer: An Interactive, Inspectable Simulation-Based Training System," AI Magazine, Summer, 1984, pp. 15–28.

11. KEEN, PETER, AND MICHAEL S. SCOTT Morton, *Decision Support Systems: An Organizational Perspective,* Reading, Massachusetts: Addison-Wesley Publishing Company, Inc., 1978.

12. MCDERMOTT, JOHN, "R1: A Rule-Based Configurer of Computer Systems," *Artificial Intelligence,* Vol. 19, No. 1, 1982.

13. NEWELL, A., "Reasoning: Problem Solving, and Decision Processes: The Problem Space as a Fundamental Category," In R. Nickerson (Ed.) *Attention and Performance VIII,* Hillsdale, N.J.: Erlbaum, 1980.

14. B. SHEIL, "Power Tools for Programmers," *Datamation,* February, 1983, pp. 131–144.

15. SIMON, HERBERT A., *The New Science of Management Decision,* N.Y. Harper & Row, 1960.

16. WINSTON, PATRICK HENRY, *Artificial Intelligence,* 2nd Ed., Addison-Wesley Publ. Co., Inc., 1984, 1977.

17. WINSTON, *supra,* p. 88, 132–134.
18. HAYES-ROTH, *supra,* Chs. 5, 6, 9.

QUESTIONS

1. What are the definitional differences between expert systems and expert support systems?

2. Define heuristics. Give five examples of heuristics in a context familiar to you (maybe sports or diet). Now provide five business examples of heuristics.

3. Expert systems are founded upon a knowledge base generated by experts in that particular field. Let's test for a consensus of experts. Who would be included in your list of five experts for: base stealing in baseball; painting of artwork; real estate investment; database management systems. Compare your answers with those of fellow students.

4. Describe, in your own words, an inference engine.

5. Do you agree with the statement being made in Figure 6?

6. What areas of business would lend themselves to an expert support system? Are tax decisions possible? How about financial statement analysis or analytic review by auditors?

7. A few "problems, risks, and issues" relating to expert systems are offered in the last section of the paper. Do you agree with the authors' conclusions? Expand this list and discuss your answers in class.